Model Stock Purchase Agreement

with Commentary

Committee on Negotiated Acquisitions

Section of Business Law

ABA Section of Business Law

ABA Defending Liberty Pursuing Justice

AF796641

The materials contained herein represent the opinions of the authors and editors and should not be construed to be the action of either the American Bar Association or the Section of Business Law unless adopted pursuant to the bylaws of the Association.

Nothing contained in this book is to be considered as the rendering of legal advice for specific cases, and readers are responsible for obtaining such advice from their own legal counsel. This book and any forms and agreements herein are intended for educational and informational purposes only.

© 1995 by the American Bar Association. All rights reserved.
Printed in the United States of America.

The Prefaces, Preliminary Notes, Appendices, and Commentary to the Model Stock Purchase Agreement, Exhibits, and Ancillary Documents are protected under the United States copyright law and may not be reproduced in any manner without express permission. The Model Stock Purchase Agreement, Exhibits, and Ancillary Documents may be freely reproduced by the reader.

No part of the publication may be reproduced, stored in a retrieval system, or transmitted in any form or by any means, electronic, mechanical, photocopying, recording, or otherwise, without the prior written permission of the publisher. Permission requests should be sent to the American Bar Association Copyrights & Contracts Department via e-mail at copyright@abanet.org or via fax at (312) 988-6030.

Library of Congress Catalog Card Number 94-73555
ISBN 1-57073-105-5 (paperback)
ISBN 1-57073-409-7 (loose-leaf)

Cover design by Laura Jacobson for Seven Rays, Inc.

Discounts are available for books ordered in bulk. Special consideration is given to state and local bars, CLE programs, and other bar-related organizations. Inquire at ABA Publishing, American Bar Association, 321 North Clark Street, Chicago, Illinois 60610.

07 7 6

Summary Table of Contents

Editor's Preface

The Model Stock Purchase Agreement, Exhibits, Appendices and accompanying Commentary are the products of a nine-year collaborative effort of the members of the Committee on Negotiated Acquisitions of the Section of Business Law of the American Bar Association. The members of the Committee on Negotiated Acquisitions are senior lawyers practicing throughout the United States and Canada who specialize in general corporate law and mergers and acquisitions, in particular. The Model Stock Purchase Agreement and accompanying Commentary were edited by the Editorial Subcommittee of the Committee on Negotiated Acquisitions. The members of the Editorial Subcommittee who rendered substantial assistance in the editing of the documents are listed below:

David A. Bronner, Co-Chair	Chicago, IL
Richard E. Climan	San Francisco/Palo Alto, CA
Jonathan I. Cope	Chicago, IL
Karl J. Ege	Tacoma, WA
Joel I. Greenberg, Co-Chair	New York, NY
Robert T. Harper	Pittsburgh, PA
Peter L. Koerber	New Orleans, LA
Thomas R. McGuisan	Miami, FL
Arthur H. Miller	Philadelphia, PA
Samuel W. Oliver, Jr.	Birmingham, AL
Eric M. Reifschneider	Chicago, IL
W. Scott Seeley	Cleveland, OH
Robert E. Shields	Philadelphia, PA
H. Lawrence Tafe III	Boston, MA
Robert M. Walmsley, Jr.	New Orleans, LA
Leigh Walton	Nashville, TN

Dale A. Oesterle, Montfort Professor of Commercial Law, University of Colorado, served as the Reporter to the Committee.

The following members of the Subcommittee on Preliminary and Ancillary Documents wrote the Exhibits, Ancillary Documents, and related Commentary which are included as part of the Model Stock Purchase Agreement:

David A. Bronner	Chicago, IL
Richard E. Climan	San Francisco/Palo Alto, CA
Nathaniel L. Doliner, Chairman	Tampa, FL
Byron F. Egan	Dallas, TX
Joel I. Greenberg	New York, NY
Tom B. Hyman, Jr.	Atlanta, GA
Stephen H. Knee	Newark, NJ
Theodore W. Lenz	Nashville, TN
John W. Leopold	Montreal, Canada
Karen W. McDonie	Philadelphia, PA
Donald I.N. McKenzie	Nashville, TN
Arthur H. Miller	Philadelphia, PA
Martin C. Oetting	Detroit, MI
Eric M. Reifschneider	Chicago, IL
Frank B. Reilly, Jr.	Newark, NJ
Steven R. Suleski	Madison, WI
Arnold F. Williams	Los Angeles, CA

Past and present Committee Chairs to the Committee on Negotiated Acquisitions include:

Karl J. Ege	Tacoma, WA
J. Patrick Garrett	Houston, TX

Chair's Preface

Legal representation of a party to the acquisition of a business enterprise is a common role undertaken by the business lawyer. Although there is no requirement that parties to an acquisition be represented by counsel, because of the significant legal consequences of both buyers and sellers of business interests occasioned by such transactions, it is common practice today for lawyers to be involved in all but the most modest business acquisitions. This involvement is preferably from the time of initial discussions, but most often during the formal negotiations and documentation of the transaction through the closing of the acquisition.

It has been nearly a decade since a group of acquisition lawyers observed that no existing committee of the Section of Business Law dealt directly with the legal issues involved in a non-hostile, privately negotiated acquisition transaction. From the time of its formation, the Committee on Negotiated Acquisitions has focused on the development of a series of annotated "model" agreements that reflect generally accepted acquisition practices in the business and legal communities in the United States. The Model Stock Purchase Agreement set forth in this publication represents the first fruit of the Committee's deliberations and labors. It manifests the cumulative effort of more than 120 merger and acquisition practitioners, from law firms and corporations, large and small, practicing in financial centers as well as in smaller communities in 34 states and two provinces of Canada. Participation and comment were also sought from specialists in substantive areas such as taxation, labor, employee benefits, environmental, intellectual property and antitrust law, as well as from leading academics.

The hypothetical fact pattern around which the Model Stock Purchase Agreement was created—the acquisition of all of the capital stock of a private company—is one commonly encountered by acquisition counsel. This fact pattern also provided the Committee with the best opportunity to discuss in detail in the accompanying Commentary the intent and purpose of the terms and conditions contained in the Model Stock Purchase Agreement. In providing sample language for the provisions that customarily appear in an acquisition agreement, the Committee has selected provisions that are comprehensive in scope. It recognized that in less complex and relatively straightforward transactions, many of the operative provisions contained in the Model Stock Purchase Agreement will either not apply or may be scaled back substantially. The result is a model document that is intended to serve buyer's counsel as a starting point from which to fashion a fully-negotiated acquisition agreement. It should also serve as an effective educational tool for four distinct groups—lawyers who deal with acquisitions on an occasional basis, and who wish to sharpen their negotiation and representation skills; less experienced lawyers seeking to gain greater insight into the acquisition process and the documentation of business transactions; law professors desiring a more comprehensive vehicle for introducing law students to the subject of business transactions; and experienced acquisition counsel seeking to reflect on the intent and purpose of provisions that have become commonplace and familiar.

This publication is the first of what the Committee hopes will be a series of acquisition and transaction related documents that reflect the collective input from experienced private practitioners, corporate counsel and academicians. Future publications are expected to address asset acquisitions, mergers, joint venture agreements and other similar transactions. Since the documents produced by the Committee are intended to reflect a broad spectrum of current acquisition practice, your comments, suggestions and recommendations are welcome.

Karl J. Ege
Chair

Preliminary Note

ASSUMPTIONS

The Model Stock Purchase Agreement and its attachments are based on the hypothetical acquisition by a single corporate buyer (the "Buyer") of all of the outstanding stock of a privately-held United States company (the "Company"). The Company has two individual stockholders (the "Sellers"), engages in a full range of business activity, and has several subsidiaries (along with the Company, the "Acquired Companies"). The Buyer is offering a combination of cash and promissory notes in payment.

PERSPECTIVE

The Model Stock Purchase Agreement is a Buyer's reasonable first draft. The Buyer's counsel will usually prepare the first draft of an acquisition agreement unless the Sellers are conducting an auction with more than one potential buyer. As the Buyer's first draft, the provisions generally favor the Buyer and may not be typical of the final language in a fully negotiated and consummated transaction. The Sellers usually will not agree to all of the provisions, and the Sellers' counsel can be expected to negotiate for language less burdensome to the Sellers. The Commentary notes some sections that are likely to prompt objections by the Sellers. If the Buyer anticipates delicate negotiations with the Sellers—perhaps because competitive offers for the Company weaken the Buyer's negotiating position—the Buyer's counsel may not want to use all of the more aggressive provisions, or may want to temper them with qualifying language favorable to the Sellers, even in a first draft.

The Buyer obtains two benefits from submitting a first draft with provisions that may not survive detailed negotiations. First, the negotiations may force the Sellers to disclose significant information about the Acquired Companies, which aids the Buyer in assessing the benefits and risks of the acquisition and in pricing the transaction. In this respect, the Buyer's first draft serves as a request for information and a disclosure device. The Sellers' counsel should view it as such and respond accordingly.

Second, the first draft establishes the Buyer's position in negotiating the allocation of risk from contingencies such as future environmental or tort liability. A Buyer's reasonable first draft asks the Sellers to bear most of the risk associated with future events or discoveries that directly or indirectly relate to the period prior to the Buyer's acquisition of the Company—issues that may be material to the price of the acquisition. The Sellers may counter that unknown contingencies are risks inherent in operating any business and should be borne by the owner of the business at the time they arise. With the lines drawn in this manner, the negotiations begin.

There is no standard acquisition agreement applicable to all transactions. The Model Stock Purchase Agreement does not substitute for a lawyer's careful exercise of judgment in a specific transaction. Every provision in the Model Stock Purchase Agreement is subject to variation reflecting the facts and circumstances of a particular acquisition. Some of the provisions in the Model Stock Purchase Agreement may be unnecessary if the Company has a simple structure. The magnitude of the purchase price also will influence the time and effort spent on negotiating and drafting the acquisition agreement. If the Company is organized under the laws of, or has significant assets or operations in, a foreign jurisdiction, many of the provisions in the Model Stock Purchase Agreement will require modification to suit the laws of that jurisdiction.

ORGANIZATION

The structure of the Model Stock Purchase Agreement follows current practice. Section 1 is a glossary of defined terms. This section enhances ease of usage and organization of the acquisition agreement and includes cross-references to definitions in various places in the agreement. Section 2 contains the economic and operative terms of the acquisition, including the stock to be acquired, the consideration to be paid, and the basic mechanics of the closing.

Sections 3 and 4 are the representations and warranties of the Sellers and the Buyer, respectively. The representations and warranties are statements of fact that exist or will exist at the time of the closing. The Sellers' representation and warranties, which contain detailed statements about the Acquired Companies' businesses, are much more comprehensive than the Buyer's and include extensive provisions regarding matters such as environmental problems, employee benefits, and intellectual property that could result in significant liabilities for the Buyer after the closing if not covered by adequate representations and warranties (and the corresponding indemnification obligations) by the Sellers. The Buyer's representations and warranties deal mainly with the Buyer's ability to enter into the acquisition agreement and to consummate the acquisition.

Sections 5 and 6 contain covenants in which the parties commit to perform (affirmative covenants) or not to perform (negative covenants) certain acts in the period between signing the acquisition agreement and closing the acquisition. The main burden of the covenants falls on the Sellers, who must take organizational steps toward consummating the acquisition and operate the Acquired Companies in the manner provided in the agreement after signing the agreement and before the closing.

Sections 7 and 8 contain conditions precedent to the obligations of the Buyer and the Sellers, respectively, to consummate the acquisition. These sections specify what each party is entitled to expect from the other at the closing. If a condition is not satisfied by one party, the other party may be able to elect not to complete the acquisition.

Section 9 outlines the circumstances in which each party may terminate the acquisition agreement and the effects of such termination. Section 10 contains indemnification provisions giving each party specific remedies for the other's breach of certain obligations under the acquisition agreement. These provisions cover matters such as the measure of damages, recovery of expenses and costs (including legal fees) in addition to damages (a right that may not exist absent an indemnification provision), and procedures for claiming damages. Section 11 contains general provisions such as notice, severability, and choice of law.

COMMENTARY

The Commentary to the various provisions of the Model Stock Purchase Agreement serves three main purposes. First, the Commentary explains the meaning and function of a provision and its relationship to other provisions. In some instances, the Commentary also provides a brief discussion of the law relevant to a provision, although such discussions are not comprehensive, do not identify variations from state to state, and will not reflect changes in the law that occur after the preparation of the Model Stock Purchase Agreement. Finally, the Commentary highlights provisions that are likely to be the subject of negotiation and the positions that the Buyer and the Sellers may take during these negotiations. In a few instances, the Commentary contains alternative language that the Buyer may want to include in the initial draft or that the Sellers may propose as a replacement to the provisions of the Model Stock Purchase Agreement. The Commentary reflects the years of collective experience in drafting and negotiating acquisition agreements of the members of Editorial Subcommittee of the Committee on Negotiated Acquisitions of the Section of Business Law of the American Bar Association.

EXHIBITS AND ANCILLARY DOCUMENTS

The Exhibits to the Model Stock Purchase Agreement are forms of the disclosure letter and various ancillary documents to be delivered at the closing of the acquisition (including the Promissory Note, the Release, the Employment Agreement, the Noncompetition Agreement, and the legal opinions). The Ancillary Documents include certain agreements (such as the Confidentiality Agreement and the Letter of Intent) which are executed prior to signing the Model Stock Purchase Agreement.

APPENDICES

Appendix A to the Model Stock Purchase Agreement presents nine hypothetical scenarios that illustrate the operation and interaction of certain of the Sellers' representations and warranties in Section 3, the Sellers' pre-closing covenants in Section 5, the closing conditions in Section 7, and the indemnification provisions in Section 10. A tabular summary of these hypothetical scenarios appears at the end of the Appendix.

Appendix B is the Reporter's Note to the Model Stock Purchase Agreement. Written by the law professor who served on the committee that prepared the Model Stock Purchase Agreement, the Reporter's Note discusses the significance of precise legal drafting of acquisition agreements in the light of cases construing and interpreting such agreements.

ACQUISITION REVIEW MANUAL

Attorneys engaged in acquisitions may also want to consult the *Manual on Acquisition Review*, which has also been published by the Section of Business Law of the American Bar Association. The *Manual on Acquisition Review* identifies factual inquiries and legal analyses regularly used in the Buyer's pre-closing review of the Acquired Companies. Each chapter of the *Manual on Acquisition Review* treats a substantive area of law that may be implicated by the Sellers' representations and warranties in the Model Stock Purchase Agreement. It describes the documents and other information that the Buyer should request from the Sellers, as well as the legal issues relevant in reviewing such information, to understand properly the legal consequences of the Acquired Companies' affairs. The inquiries described in the *Manual on Acquisition Review* include not only matters on which the Buyer generally relies upon its legal counsel, but also factual issues that usually are assigned to the Buyer's other professional advisors such as accountants and environmental consultants or, in some instances, to the Buyer's corporate staff. The *Manual on Acquisition Review* is designed to aid all of the Buyer's employees and advisors participating in the acquisition.

STOCK PURCHASE AGREEMENT

between

____

and

____

Dated _____________, 199_

Table of Contents

ANCILLARY DOCUMENTS

APPENDICES

Stock Purchase Agreement

This Stock Purchase Agreement ("Agreement") is made as of _________, 199__, by ___________, a ___________ corporation ("Buyer"), ___________, an individual resident in ___________ ("A"), and __________, an individual resident in ___________ ("B" and, collectively with A, "Sellers").

COMMENT

Parties. The Buyer should ensure that the persons or entities that are the record owners of the shares are parties to the acquisition agreement. If the record owners of the shares are not the beneficial owners, the Buyer may want to include the beneficial owners as parties to the acquisition agreement.

The Model Stock Purchase Agreement does not include the Company as a party to the agreement. However, the Buyer often wants to include the Company as a party so that the Buyer will have an additional party against which to pursue its indemnification rights if the acquisition is not consummated because of a breach of any of the representations and pre-closing covenants provided for the Buyer's benefit.

Making the Company a party to the acquisition agreement will not benefit the Buyer if the acquisition is ultimately consummated, because the Company will become a wholly-owned subsidiary of the Buyer upon completion of the acquisition. Indeed, if the Company is a party to the acquisition agreement, the Sellers could have a right of indemnification or contribution against the Company in an action brought by the Buyer after the closing based on a breach of representations that presumably were made, jointly and severally, by the Company and the Sellers.

Therefore, when the Company is made a party to the acquisition agreement, the Buyer should be careful to protect the Company from any claims by the Sellers after consummation of the acquisition by providing that the Company's representations terminate at the closing and that the Sellers release the Company from all claims arising out of the acquisition based on indemnification or contribution.

The Buyer should be aware that if the Company is a party to the acquisition agreement, the acquisition agreement will not be enforceable against the Company unless there is adequate consideration. The Buyer may be able to demonstrate adequate consideration by showing that the acquisition would benefit the Company. For example, if the Buyer proposes to invest funds in the Company after the acquisition, the Buyer's proposed investment may be adequate consideration.

Finally, the Buyer may also want to consider adding the Sellers' spouses as parties to the acquisition agreement or, alternatively, obtaining spousal consents or waivers from the Sellers' spouses, even if the spouses do not own the shares. By having the Sellers' spouses acknowledge the sale of the shares to the Buyer and agree to look to the Sellers' other assets to satisfy any claims the spouses may have against the Sellers, the Buyer will be protected from claims by the Sellers' spouses against the shares in the event of a divorce.

Choice of Structure. The parties to an acquisition typically have a choice of several methods by which to accomplish the same goal—the Buyer's acquisition of the Company's business. Common forms of an acquisition include (i) a sale of stock by the shareholders of the Company to the Buyer, (ii) a sale of substantially all of the Company's assets to the Buyer or a subsidiary of the Buyer, (iii) a merger of the Company into the Buyer or a subsidiary of the Buyer (a "forward merger") or a merger of the Buyer or a subsidiary of the Buyer into the Company (a "reverse merger"), and (iv) if permitted by the laws of the state in which the Company is incorporated, a binding share exchange in which the stock of the Company's shareholders is exchanged for the consideration the Buyer has agreed to pay. The Model Stock Purchase Agreement presupposes that the parties have determined that a stock acquisition is the best structure for the Buyer to acquire the businesses of the Acquired Companies.

The choice of structure of an acquisition is a function of the parties' analysis of a variety of tax, accounting, and other considerations, including risks of unknown liabilities, the ability of the Company to assign contract rights to third parties, and the availability of appraisal rights for dissenting shareholders. *See generally* Bangser & Sinanian, *Legal Considerations Relating to the Structuring, Planning and Negotiation of the Various Types of Acquisitions and Mergers*, in Herz & Baller, *Business Acquisitions* 3-36 (2d ed. Supp. 1986); Freund, *Anatomy of a Merger* ch. 4 (1975); Kling & Nugent Simon, *Negotiated Acquisitions of Companies, Subsidiaries and Divisions* chs. 1-3 (1992); Guth, Tufts, Copeland, Hoffman, Shea & Binke, *Drafting Agreements for the Sale of Businesses* § 2.44 (2d ed. 1988). For a discussion of the tax considerations that may affect the choice of structure, see Ginsburg & Levin, *Mergers, Acquisitions and Leveraged Buyouts* (1993). ■

RECITALS

Sellers desire to sell, and Buyer desires to purchase, all of the issued and outstanding shares (the "Shares") of capital stock of ____, a _____ corporation (the "Company"), for the consideration and on the terms set forth in this Agreement.

COMMENT

While there is no legal requirement that an acquisition agreement contain recitals, recitals can help the reader understand the basic context and structure of the acquisition. Recitals are typically declarative statements of fact, but these statements normally do not serve as separate representations or warranties of the parties. The parties and their counsel should, however, be aware of the possible legal effect of recitals. *See, e.g.,* Cal. Evidence Code § 622 ("The facts recited in a written instrument are conclusively presumed to be true as between the parties thereto . . . ."). ■

Agreement

The parties, intending to be legally bound, agree as follows:

1. DEFINITIONS

COMMENT

It is useful, both to reduce the length of other sections and to facilitate changes during negotiations, to have a section of the acquisition agreement that lists all defined terms appearing in more than one section of the agreement. A common dilemma in drafting definitions is whether to include long lists of terms with similar but slightly different meanings. If the goal is to draft a comprehensive, all-inclusive definition, the tendency is to list every term that comes to mind. However, if too many terms are listed, the absence of a particular term may be accorded more significance than intended, even if a phrase such as "without limitation" or a catchall term beginning with "any other" is used. (The Model Stock Purchase Agreement avoids repetitive use of such a phrase and contains a general disclaimer in Section 11.12 instead.) Also, long lists of terms with similar meanings perpetuate a cumbersome and arcane style of drafting that many lawyers and clients find annoying at best and confusing at worst. The Model Stock Purchase Agreement resolves this dilemma in favor of short lists of terms that are intended to have their broadest possible meaning. ■

For purposes of this Agreement, the following terms have the meanings specified or referred to in this Section 1:

"Acquired Companies"—the Company and its Subsidiaries, collectively.

COMMENT

The Buyer may want to expand this definition to include predecessors of the Company (such as a corporation that was merged into the Company) so that the Sellers' representations apply to predecessors as well. This is especially important for the representations concerning environmental matters and product liability because of the potentially large liability of the Company's predecessors that may be imposed on the Company. ■

"Adjustment Amount"—as defined in Section 2.5.

COMMENT

The term "Adjustment Amount" appears in Sections 2.2, 2.5, and 2.6. ■

"Applicable Contract"—any Contract (a) under which any Acquired Company has or may acquire any rights, (b) under which any Acquired Company has or may become subject to any obligation or liability, or (c) by which any Acquired Company or any of the assets owned or used by it is or may become bound.

COMMENT

The term "Applicable Contract" appears in Sections 3.1, 3.2, and 3.17. For a discussion of the scope of this definition and examples of the types of contracts that could be included within this term, see the second-to-last and third-to-last paragraphs of the Commentary to Section 3.2. ■

"Balance Sheet"—as defined in Section 3.4.

COMMENT

The term "Balance Sheet" appears in Sections 2.6, 3.4, 3.6, 3.8, 3.9, 3.10, 3.11, 3.12, and 3.16. ■

"Best Efforts"—the efforts that a prudent Person desirous of achieving a result would use in similar circumstances to ensure that such result is achieved as expeditiously as possible [; *provided, however,* that an obligation to use Best Efforts under this Agreement does not require the Person subject to that obligation to take actions that would result in a materially adverse change in the benefits to such Person of this Agreement and the Contemplated Transactions].

COMMENT

The term "Best Efforts" appears in Sections 5.2, 5.8, and 6.2. Case law provides little guidance for interpreting a commitment to use "best efforts." *See generally* Farnsworth, *On Trying to Keep One's Promises: The Duty of Best Efforts in Contract Law*, 46 U. Pitt. L. Rev. 1 (1984). Some courts have held that "best efforts" is equivalent to "good faith" or a type of "good faith." *See, e.g., Gestetner Corp. v. Case Equip. Co.*, 815 F.2d 806, 811 (1st Cir. 1987); *Western Geophysical Co. of Am. v. Bolt Assocs., Inc.*, 584 F.2d 1164, 1171 (2d Cir. 1978); *Kubik v. J. & R. Foods of Or., Inc.*, 577 P.2d 518, 520 (Or. 1978). Other courts view "best efforts" as a more exacting standard than "good faith." *See, e.g., Bloor v. Falstaff Brewing Corp.*, 601 F.2d 609, 615 (2d Cir. 1979); *Grossman v. Lowell*, 703 F. Supp. 282, 284 (S.D.N.Y. 1989); *In re Heard*, 6 B.R. 876, 884 (Bankr. W.D. Ky. 1980). The standard is not definable by a fixed formula but takes its meaning from the circumstances. *See, e.g., Triple-A Baseball Club Ass'n v. Northeastern Baseball, Inc.*, 832 F.2d 214, 225 (1st Cir. 1987), *cert. denied*, 485 U.S. 935 (1988); *Joyce Beverages of N.Y., Inc. v. Royal Crown Cola Co.*, 555 F. Supp. 271, 275 (S.D.N.Y. 1983); *Polyglycoat Corp. v. C.P.C. Distribs., Inc.*, 534 F. Supp. 200, 203 (S.D.N.Y. 1982).

The Model Stock Purchase Agreement definition requires more than good faith but stops short of requiring a party to subject itself to economic hardship. The bracketed language, which states that a party subject to a "best efforts" duty is not required to take action that would cause that party significant loss or disadvantage relative to that party's expected benefits from the acquisition, is often embodied in the duty to use "reasonable commercial efforts." Because "best efforts" duties apply most often to the Sellers, a high standard of what constitutes "best efforts" generally favors the Buyer. ■

"Breach"—a "Breach" of a representation, warranty, covenant, obligation, or other provision of this Agreement or any instrument delivered pursuant to this Agreement will be deemed to have occurred if there is or has been (a) any inaccuracy in or breach of, or any failure to perform or comply with, such representation, warranty, covenant, obligation, or other provision, or (b) any claim (by any Person) or other occurrence or circumstance that is or was inconsistent with such representation, warranty, covenant, obligation, or other provision, and the term "Breach" means any such inaccuracy, breach, failure, claim, occurrence, or circumstance.

COMMENT

The term "Breach" appears in Sections 5.5, 9.1, 9.2, 10.2, 10.4, 10.6, and 10.7. ■

"Buyer"—as defined in the first paragraph of this Agreement.

"Closing"—as defined in Section 2.3.

"Closing Date"—the date and time as of which the Closing actually takes place.

"Company"—as defined in the Recitals of this Agreement.

"Consent"—any approval, consent, ratification, waiver, or other authorization (including any Governmental Authorization).

COMMENT

The term "Consent" appears in Sections 3.2, 4.2, 7.3, and 8.3. ■

"Contemplated Transactions"—all of the transactions contemplated by this Agreement, including:

(a) the sale of the Shares by Sellers to Buyer;

(b) the execution, delivery, and performance of the Promissory Note, the Employment Agreements, the Noncompetition Agreements, the Sellers' Releases, and the Escrow Agreement;

(c) the performance by Buyer and Sellers of their respective covenants and obligations under this Agreement; and

(d) Buyer's acquisition and ownership of the Shares and exercise of control over the Acquired Companies.

"Contract"—any agreement, contract, obligation, promise, or undertaking (whether written or oral and whether express or implied) that is legally binding.

COMMENT

The term "Contract" appears in Sections 3.2, 3.3, 3.16, 3.17, 3.18, 3.21, 3.25, and 4.2. This definition includes all legally binding obligations, however characterized, but excludes documents and statements that are not legally binding obligations. In certain circumstances, it may be appropriate to broaden the definition to include statements that are not legally binding. The Buyer may, for example, want to know about statements by an Acquired Company to its distributors that the Acquired Company will look favorably on a request for a return for credit of unsold products when the Acquired Company introduces a replacement product. The Buyer may also want to encompass established practices of the Acquired Companies within this definition. Similarly, the Buyer may want the definition to encompass "comfort letters" confirming an Acquired Company's intention to provide financial support to a subsidiary or other related person and assurances to employees regarding compensation, benefits, and tenure, whether or not such letters or assurances are legally binding. The Buyer may accomplish these objectives either by expanding the definition or by adding specific representations and warranties. ■

"Damages"—as defined in Section 10.2.

COMMENT

The term "Damages" appears in Sections 10.2, 10.4, 10.6, and 10.7. ■

"Disclosure Letter"—the disclosure letter delivered by Sellers to Buyer concurrently with the execution and delivery of this Agreement.

COMMENT

The form and content of the Disclosure Letter should be negotiated and drafted concurrently with the negotiation and drafting of the acquisition agreement. The Disclosure Letter is an integral component of the acquisition documentation and should be prepared and reviewed as carefully as the acquisition agreement itself. Exhibit 1 to the Model Stock Purchase Agreement contains a sample format for the Disclosure Letter. The Buyer or the Sellers may prefer to attach multiple schedules or exhibits to the acquisition agreement instead of using a disclosure letter. ■

"Employment Agreements"—as defined in Section 2.4(a)(iii).

COMMENT

The term "Employment Agreements" appears in Sections 2.4, 3.2, and 4.2. ■

"Encumbrance"—any charge, claim, community property interest, condition, equitable interest, lien, option, pledge, security interest, right of first refusal, or restriction of any kind, including any restriction on use, voting, transfer, receipt of income, or exercise of any other attribute of ownership.

COMMENT

The term "Encumbrance" appears in Sections 3.2, 3.3, and 3.6. Although this definition includes all types of restrictions and limitations on owned property, the terms used in this definition apply most often to personal property. If the term "Encumbrance" will be used with respect to real property, the definition could also include other appropriate terms such as mortgage, easement, servitude, and right of way. ■

"Environment"—soil, land surface or subsurface strata, surface waters (including navigable waters, ocean waters, streams, ponds, drainage basins, and wetlands), groundwaters, drinking water supply, stream sediments, ambient air (including indoor air), plant and animal life, and any other environmental medium or natural resource.

COMMENT

The term "Environment" appears in Section 3.19. This definition comes primarily from the Comprehensive Environmental Response, Compensation, and Liability Act ("CERCLA"), 42 U.S.C. § 9601 et seq. (1988). It has been modified to include a reference to indoor air, which is not covered under CERCLA but may be subject to regulation under other environmental statutes. ■

"Environmental, Health, and Safety Liabilities"—any cost, damages, expense, liability, obligation, or other responsibility arising from or under Environmental Law or Occupational Safety and Health Law and consisting of or relating to:

(a) any environmental, health, or safety matters or conditions (including on-site or off-site contamination, occupational safety and health, and regulation of chemical substances or products);

(b) fines, penalties, judgments, awards, settlements, legal or administrative proceedings, damages, losses, claims, demands and response, investigative, remedial, or inspection costs and expenses arising under Environmental Law or Occupational Safety and Health Law;

(c) financial responsibility under Environmental Law or Occupational Safety and Health Law for cleanup costs or corrective action, including any investigation, cleanup, removal, containment, or other remediation or response actions ("Cleanup") required by applicable Environmental Law or Occupational Safety and Health Law (whether or not such Cleanup has been required or requested by any Governmental Body or any other Person) and for any natural resource damages; or

(d) any other compliance, corrective, investigative, or remedial measures required under Environmental Law or Occupational Safety and Health Law.

The terms "removal," "remedial," and "response action," include the types of activities covered by the United States Comprehensive Environmental Response, Compensation, and Liability Act, 42 U.S.C. § 9601 et seq., as amended ("CERCLA").

COMMENT

The term "Environmental, Health, and Safety Liabilities" appears in Sections 3.19 and 10.3. This definition is quite broad in scope and incorporates other broadly defined terms. The Sellers will likely want to limit their responsibilities under the representations and warranties and indemnification provisions that use these definitions, and the logical first step is by narrowing the definition. The Sellers may want to add a materiality qualification either to the entire definition (for example, by limiting the definition to "material" damages, as that term would be further defined, or to damages in excess of a specified amount) or to each clause ((a) through (d)) separately. Because the latter requires a case-by-case analysis of whether a specific paragraph should be qualified, the Buyer will usually prefer that option to a general qualification of the entire definition. ■

"Environmental Law"—any Legal Requirement that requires or relates to:

(a) advising appropriate authorities, employees, and the public of intended or actual releases of pollutants or hazardous substances or materials, violations of discharge limits, or other prohibitions and of the commencements of activities, such as resource extraction or construction, that could have significant impact on the Environment;

(b) preventing or reducing to acceptable levels the release of pollutants or hazardous substances or materials into the Environment;

(c) reducing the quantities, preventing the release, or minimizing the hazardous characteristics of wastes that are generated;

(d) assuring that products are designed, formulated, packaged, and used so that they do not present unreasonable risks to human health or the Environment when used or disposed of;

(e) protecting resources, species, or ecological amenities;

(f) reducing to acceptable levels the risks inherent in the transportation of hazardous substances, pollutants, oil, or other potentially harmful substances;

(g) cleaning up pollutants that have been released, preventing the threat of release, or paying the costs of such clean up or prevention; or

(h) making responsible parties pay private parties, or groups of them, for damages done to their health or the Environment, or permitting self-appointed representatives of the public interest to recover for injuries done to public assets.

COMMENT

The term "Environmental Law" appears in Section 3.19. A short form of this definition is: "Legal Requirements designed to minimize, prevent, punish, or remedy the consequences of actions that damage or threaten the Environment or public health and safety." Using other environmental terms such as "Hazardous Materials" in the definition of "Environmental Law" would make the definitions circular and should be avoided.

The Sellers may seek to limit these definitions to exclude areas such as occupational health and safety and materials not considered hazardous under CERCLA. Such limitations may be acceptable to the Buyer depending upon the nature of the Acquired Companies' businesses.

A broad definition of "Environmental Law" is important to the Buyer for several reasons. For example, the Buyer may be a public company or may in the future want to become a public company. SEC disclosure rules relating to environmental issues use a broad definition that includes federal, state, and local laws regulating the discharge of materials into the environment or otherwise enacted primarily to protect the environment. *See*

SEC Regulation S-K, Item 103, Instruction 5. Therefore, comprehensive disclosures from the Sellers will help the Buyer meet its disclosure requirements under federal securities law.

Although the definitions of "Legal Requirements" and "Order" encompass most of what is included in the definition of "Environmental Law," the latter term includes additional elements such as common law and governmental permits, compliance with which is important to the Buyer. In addition, a separate "Environmental Law" definition is necessary when there are separate environmental representations and indemnifications. If the Buyer relies upon the representations in Sections 3.14 and 3.15 and the general indemnification provisions of Section 11.3, the Buyer's counsel should review those provisions carefully to ensure that the additional elements addressed here are adequately covered.

The Buyer may want the definition to list specific federal or state laws that apply to the Acquired Companies' businesses. Some states, such as Connecticut and New Jersey, require that certain filings be made, and possibly environmental investigation and remedial measures be taken, prior to the transfer of property in the state from one "owner" or "operator" to another. *See, e.g.*, Connecticut Transfer Act, Conn. Gen. Stat. Ann. § 22a-134(d) (West 1989); Industrial Site Recovery Act, N.J. Stat. Ann. § 13.1k-6 et seq. (P.L. 1993, Ch. 139), formerly known as the Environmental Cleanup Responsibility Act or "ECRA." The requirements are generally triggered by a "change of control" of the owner or operator, including the purchase of its stock. Some states have regulations that require the filing of a "cleanup plan" to be implemented by the owner or operator. Generally, the Sellers will be responsible for implementing the cleanup plan, although that responsibility may be assumed by the Buyer. Because in some states the state environmental agency has the ability to void a sale if no cleanup plan or "negative declaration" has been filed, and because there are significant fines for failure to comply with these regulations, the Buyer should identify such regulations and require that their compliance be a condition to the closing. If the Buyer assumes the cleanup responsibility, it should negotiate for an adjustment to the purchase price or a right to terminate the acquisition agreement if its due diligence reveals the plan to be too costly. ■

"ERISA"—the Employee Retirement Income Security Act of 1974 or any successor law, and regulations and rules issued pursuant to that Act or any successor law.

COMMENT

The term "ERISA" appears in Section 3.13. ■

"Escrow Agreement"—as defined in Section 2.4.

"Facilities"—any real property, leaseholds, or other interests currently or formerly owned or operated by any Acquired Company and any buildings, plants, structures, or equipment (including motor vehicles, tank cars, and rolling stock) currently or formerly owned or operated by any Acquired Company.

COMMENT

The term "Facilities" appears in Sections 3.19 and 10.3. The Sellers will likely want to limit their responsibilities to existing facilities or even to those for which the Buyer can demonstrate a real basis for concern based on their character and use or that of the adjoining property. At the least, the Sellers may want to include only facilities in existence during their ownership of the Acquired Companies and insist that representations concerning other facilities be limited by a knowledge qualification.

The Buyer may view such limitations as more appropriate in representations and warranties than in indemnification provisions. However, CERCLA liability may extend to prior owners of a facility who owned the facility at the time of the disposal of a hazardous substance. Therefore, if a problem with a facility formerly owned by an Acquired Company is discovered before the closing and is not covered by the representations and warranties, the Buyer may not have the right to terminate the acquisition agreement because of this problem. The Buyer should consider conducting extensive environmental investigation of facilities not included in this definition, although this may be impossible for facilities no longer owned by an Acquired Company. ■

"GAAP"—generally accepted United States accounting principles, applied on a basis consistent with the basis on which the Balance Sheet and the other financial statements referred to in Section 3.4(b) were prepared.

COMMENT

The term "GAAP" appears in Sections 2.5, 3.4, 3.11, and 3.13. The American Institute of Certified Public Accountants defines GAAP as:

> a technical accounting term that encompasses the conventions, rules, and procedures necessary to define accepted accounting practice at a particular time. It includes not only broad guidelines of general application, but also detailed practices and procedures. . . . Those conventions, rules, and procedures provide a standard by which to measure financial presentations.

American Inst. of Certified Pub. Accountants, *Statement on Auditing Standards No. 69*, § 2 (1992).

The use of this term in an acquisition agreement is customary. Although the requirement that financial statements be prepared in accordance with GAAP provides some comfort to the Buyer, the Buyer should understand the wide latitude of accepted accounting practices within GAAP. GAAP describes a broad group of concepts and methods for preparing financial statements. GAAP thus represents a boundary of accepted practice but does not necessarily characterize a "good" financial statement.

GAAP is not a static concept—a financial statement will change as GAAP changes. The principal authority determining the "conventions, rules, and procedures" that constitute GAAP is the Financial Accounting Standards Board (FASB), although custom and usage also play a role. The FASB often issues Financial Accounting Standards (FAS) bulletins that present guidelines for financial accounting in special circumstances or changes in accepted practices. The adoption of FAS 106, for example, changed the presentation of retiree health costs by requiring such costs to be recorded as a liability rather than charged to expenses as incurred.

GAAP permits the exercise of professional judgement in deciding how to present financial results fairly. GAAP permits different methods of accounting for items such as inventory valuation ("FIFO," "LIFO," or average cost), depreciation (straight line or accelerated methods), and accounting for repairs and small tools. Changes in these alternative methods can substantially affect reported results even though there has been no change in the underlying economic position of the Company. The Buyer should examine the Company's financial statements from previous years to ensure their consistency from year to year. The Buyer should also determine whether there are any pending FAS bulletins that would require a change in the Company's accounting practices, and the Buyer may want the Sellers to represent and covenant that there have been (within the past five years, for example) and will be (prior to the closing) no voluntary changes in the Company's accounting practices. For a further discussion of these issues, see the Commentary to Section 3.16.

Although GAAP is the standard used in the preparation of nearly all financial statements, the SEC reserves the right to mandate specific accounting methods for public companies. When dealing with financial statements of public companies, the Buyer may want to amend the definition of GAAP to include compliance with SEC accounting standards.

In international transactions, the parties should be aware that there are important differences between the GAAP standards of different nations. The Buyer should consider whether to require that foreign financial statements be restated to conform to United States GAAP or accompanied by a reconciliation to United States GAAP. ■

"Governmental Authorization"—any approval, consent, license, permit, waiver, or other authorization issued, granted, given, or otherwise made available by or under the authority of any Governmental Body or pursuant to any Legal Requirement.

COMMENT

The term "Governmental Authorization" appears in Sections 3.2 and 3.14. ■

"Governmental Body"—any:

(a) nation, state, county, city, town, village, district, or other jurisdiction of any nature;

(b) federal, state, local, municipal, foreign, or other government;

(c) governmental or quasi-governmental authority of any nature (including any governmental agency, branch, department, official, or entity and any court or other tribunal);

(d) multi-national organization or body; or

(e) body exercising, or entitled to exercise, any administrative, executive, judicial, legislative, police, regulatory, or taxing authority or power of any nature.

COMMENT

The term "Governmental Body" appears in the definitions of Order, Person, Proceeding, Tax, and Tax Return and in Sections 3.2, 3.11, 3.14, 3.15, 3.21, and 6.1. The Buyer may want to make specific reference to the political or governmental entities that exist in the jurisdictions in which the Acquired Companies are located or do business (such as commonwealths, provinces, and parishes). ■

"Hazardous Activity"—the distribution, generation, handling, importing, management, manufacturing, processing, production, refinement, Release, storage, transfer, transportation, treatment, or use (including any withdrawal or other use of groundwater) of Hazardous Materials in, on, under, about, or from the Facilities or any part thereof into the Environment, and any other act, business, operation, or thing that increases the danger, or risk of danger, or poses an unreasonable risk of harm to persons or property on or off the Facilities, or that may affect the value of the Facilities or the Acquired Companies.

COMMENT

The term "Hazardous Activity" appears in Sections 3.19 and 10.3. The latter portion of this definition, beginning with "and any other act," is quite expansive, and the Sellers may seek to limit the definition to activities that pose only environmental risks. ■

"Hazardous Materials"—any waste or other substance that is listed, defined, designated, or classified as, or otherwise determined to be, hazardous, radioactive, or toxic or a pollutant or a contaminant under or pursuant to any Environmental Law, including any admixture or solution thereof, and specifically including petroleum and all derivatives thereof or synthetic substitutes therefor and asbestos or asbestos-containing materials.

COMMENT

The term "Hazardous Materials" appears in Sections 3.19 and 10.3. The definition includes petroleum because many state and federal laws exclude it even though it can cause environmental problems. The definition includes asbestos for states with little or no environmental law. In certain circumstances, carefully defined exceptions may be made for materials governed by environmental law. In California, for example, the Safe Drinking Water and Toxic Enforcement Act (Proposition 65) designates substances with extremely small tolerances for quantity, which include alcoholic beverages, aspirin, chewing tobacco, engine exhaust, gasoline, nicotine, oral contraceptives, saccharin, and tobacco smoke. Exceptions may be granted for such materials with clauses such as "not more than usually present in dwellings for routine consumer and household use."

The Sellers will likely object to the definition's inclusion of substances that in the future could be determined to be hazardous, and attempt to limit their responsibilities to substances that are considered hazardous at the date of signing the acquisition agreement or the date of the closing. If the Sellers' representations are so limited, the Buyer should be sure that the representations, and the definition, are updated through the closing.

An alternate definition that favors the approach of referring to specific laws is as follows:

"Hazardous Materials"—includes any (i) "hazardous substance," "pollutants," or "contaminant" (as defined in Sections 101(14) and (33) of CERCLA or the regulations issued pursuant to Section 102 of CERCLA and found at 40 C.F.R. § 302), including any element, compound, mixture, solution, or substance that is or may be designated pursuant to Section 102 of CERCLA; (ii) substance that is or may be designated pursuant to Section 311(b)(2)(A) of the Federal Water Pollution Control Act, as amended (33 U.S.C. §§ 1251, 1321(b)(2)(A)) ("FWPCA"); (iii) hazardous waste having the characteristics identified under or listed pursuant to Section 3001 of the Resource Conservation and Recovery Act, as amended (42 U.S.C. §§ 6901, 6921) ("RCRA") or having characteristics that may subsequently be considered under RCRA to constitute a hazardous waste; (iv) substance containing petroleum, as that term is defined in Section 9001(8) of RCRA; (v) toxic pollutant that is or may be listed under Section 307(a) of FWPCA; (vi) hazardous air pollutant that is or may be listed under Section 112 of the Clean Air Act, as amended (42 U.S.C. §§ 7401, 7412); (vii) imminently hazardous chemical substance or mixture with respect to which action has been or may be taken pursuant to Section 7 of the Toxic Substances Control Act, as amended (15 U.S.C. §§ 2601, 2606); (viii) source, special nuclear, or by-product material as defined by the Atomic Energy Act of 1954, as amended (42 U.S.C. § 2011 et seq.); (ix) asbestos, asbestos-containing material, or urea formaldehyde or material that contains it; (x) waste oil and other petroleum products; and (xii) any other toxic materials, contaminants, or hazardous substances or wastes pursuant to any Environmental Law.

Listing CERCLA and the substances designated pursuant to CERCLA (*see* 42 U.S.C. §§ 9601(14) & (33)) includes all substances designated by RCRA, the Clean Air Act, the Clean Water Act, and the Toxic Substance Control Act (43 U.S.C. § 9602(14)). ■

"HSR Act"—the Hart-Scott-Rodino Antitrust Improvements Act of 1976 or any successor law, and regulations and rules issued pursuant to that Act or any successor law.

COMMENT

The term "HSR Act" appears in Sections 2.3, 5.4, 6.1, and 11.1. The HSR Act requires the parties to a proposed acquisition within the scope of the Act to give prior notice of the transaction to the Federal Trade Commission and the Assistant Attorney General in charge of the Antitrust Division of the Department of Justice and to delay consummation of the acquisition until expiration of a specified waiting period. The purpose of the HSR Act is to allow the government an opportunity to evaluate the anticompetitive aspects of a proposed acquisition and to seek to enjoin its consummation in appropriate circumstances. Subject to certain statutory exemptions, the HSR Act's premerger notification filings and waiting period requirements apply to acquisitions in which (i) a party is engaged in commerce or in any activity affecting commerce, (ii) the parties satisfy certain size requirements, and (iii) the acquisition itself satisfies certain size requirements. Even acquisitions with small purchase prices may fall within these requirements.

Notification filings are made on the Notification and Report Form set forth in the appendix to 16 C.F.R. § 803; copies of the form may be obtained by writing to the Premerger Notification Office, Room 303, Federal Trade Commission, Washington,

D.C. 20580. All information filed pursuant to the HSR Act is confidential and exempt from disclosure under the Freedom of Information Act except as may be relevant to any administrative or judicial action or proceeding. *See* 15 U.S.C. § 18a(h) (1988).

Failure to comply with any provisions of the HSR Act may cause the imposition of a civil penalty of up to $10,000 per day. *See* 15 U.S.C. § 18a(g) (1988). Any device used to avoid the requirements of the HSR Act will be disregarded, and the HSR Act will be applied to the substance of the acquisition. *See* 16 C.F.R. § 801.90 (1993).

The Buyer must pay a filing fee of $25,000 at the time of the filing. The parties may agree to reallocate responsibility for the cost of the filing fee (see Section 11.1). ■

"Indemnified Persons"—as defined in Section 10.2.

"Intellectual Property Assets" —as defined in Section 3.22.

COMMENT

The term "Intellectual Property Assets" appears in Sections 3.16, 3.17, and 3.22. ■

"Interim Balance Sheet"—as defined in Section 3.4.

COMMENT

The term "Interim Balance Sheet" appears in Sections 3.4, 3.6, 3.8, 3.9, 3.10, and 3.11. ■

"IRC"—the Internal Revenue Code of 1986 or any successor law, and regulations issued by the IRS pursuant to the Internal Revenue Code or any successor law.

COMMENT

The term "IRC" appears in Sections 3.11 and 3.13. ■

"IRS"—the United States Internal Revenue Service or any successor agency, and, to the extent relevant, the United States Department of the Treasury.

COMMENT

The term "IRS" appears in the definition of "IRC" and in Sections 3.11 and 3.13. ■

"Knowledge"—an individual will be deemed to have "Knowledge" of a particular fact or other matter if:

(a) such individual is actually aware of such fact or other matter; or

(b) a prudent individual could be expected to discover or otherwise become aware of such fact or other matter in the course of conducting a reasonably comprehensive investigation concerning the existence of such fact or other matter.

A Person (other than an individual) will be deemed to have "Knowledge" of a particular fact or other matter if any individual who is serving, or who has at any time served, as a director, officer, partner, executor, or trustee of such Person (or in any similar capacity) has, or at any time had, Knowledge of such fact or other matter.

COMMENT

The term "Knowledge" appears in Sections 3.13, 3.15, 3.17, 3.19, 3.20, 3.21, 3.22, 3.23, 4.4, 10.1, and 10.6. The Sellers will attempt to use knowledge qualifications to limit many of their representations and warranties. The inclusion of a knowledge qualification in the representation concerning threatened litigation has become accepted practice. Otherwise, there is no standard practice for determining which representations, if any, should contain such qualifications. Ultimately, the issue is allocation of risk—should the Buyer or the Sellers bear the risk of the unknown? The Buyer will often argue that the Sellers have more knowledge of and are in a better position to investigate the Acquired Companies' businesses and therefore should bear the risk of unknown matters. The Sellers' frequent response is that they have made all information they have about the Acquired Companies available to the Buyer and that the Buyer is acquiring the Acquired Companies as an on-going enterprise with the possibility of either unexpected gains or unexpected losses. Resolution of this issue usually involves much negotiation.

The addition of a knowledge qualification to a representation made by the Sellers should not limit the Buyer's "walk rights." See the Commentary to Section 3 under the caption "The Effect of Knowledge Qualifications in Representations."

If the Buyer agrees to a knowledge qualification, the next issue is *whose* knowledge is relevant. The Buyer will seek to have the group of people be as broad as possible and to ensure that this group includes the people who are the most knowledgeable about the specific representation being qualified. The broader the group and the greater the knowledge of the people in the group, the greater will be the risk retained by the Sellers.

The knowledge qualifications in Section 3 of the Model Stock Purchase Agreement refer not only to the knowledge of the individual Sellers, but also to the knowledge of the Acquired Companies. Because of the final sentence of the definition of "Knowledge," each reference to the knowledge of the Acquired Companies encompasses the knowledge of all of their current and former directors and officers. The Sellers may seek to narrow the definition of "Knowledge" by eliminating the reference to former directors and officers. The Buyer, however, may want to expand the scope of this definition to include the knowledge of *all* employees of the Acquired Companies (including non-officer employees).

The parties must also determine the scope of the investigation to be built into the definition of "Knowledge." Some acquisition agreements define knowledge as actual knowledge without any investigation requirement, while others (like the Model Stock Purchase Agreement) define it to require some level of investigation by the party making the representation. ■

"Legal Requirement"—any federal, state, local, municipal, foreign, international, multinational, or other administrative order, constitution, law, ordinance, principle of common law, regulation, statute, or treaty.

COMMENT

The term "Legal Requirement" appears in Sections 3.2, 3.3, 3.11, 3.14, 3.17, 3.18, 3.21, 4.2, 5.4, 6.1, 7.7, 8.5, 10.9, and 11.2. This definition is not limited to laws in effect on the date of the acquisition agreement. As a result, when this definition is used in representations that contemplate future events or circumstances (such as the "compliance with laws" representations in Section 3.14), it includes laws (and amendments to existing laws) passed after the acquisition agreement is signed. The Sellers may object to this on the grounds that they have no ability to take corrective action prior to signing the agreement to comply with laws passed after the agreement is signed. ■

"Noncompetition Agreements"—as defined in Section 2.4(a)(iv).

COMMENT

The term "Noncompetition Agreements" appears in Sections 2.4, 3.2, and 7.4. ■

"Occupational Safety and Health Law"—any Legal Requirement designed to provide safe and healthful working conditions and to reduce occupational safety and health hazards, and any program, whether governmental or private (including those promulgated or sponsored by industry associations and insurance companies), designed to provide safe and healthful working conditions.

COMMENT

The definition includes private programs because some industries have been more extensively regulated in this area by their insurers than by the government. Such requirements may be introduced into any legal proceeding to establish a known hazard and negligence by management, and hence are an independent source of liability for the Acquired Companies. ■

"Order"—any award, decision, injunction, judgment, order, ruling, subpoena, or verdict entered, issued, made, or rendered by any court, administrative agency, or other Governmental Body or by any arbitrator.

COMMENT

The term "Order" appears in Sections 3.2, 3.15, 3.19, 4.2, 7.7, and 8.5. ■

"Ordinary Course of Business"—an action taken by a Person will be deemed to have been taken in the "Ordinary Course of Business" only if:

(a) such action is consistent with the past practices of such Person and is taken in the ordinary course of the normal day-to-day operations of such Person;

(b) such action is not required to be authorized by the board of directors of such Person (or by any Person or group of Persons exercising similar authority) [and is not required to be specifically authorized by the parent company (if any) of such Person]; and

(c) such action is similar in nature and magnitude to actions customarily taken, without any authorization by the board of directors (or by any Person or group of Persons exercising similar authority), in the ordinary course of the normal day-to-day operations of other Persons that are in the same line of business as such Person.

COMMENT

The term "Ordinary Course of Business" appears in Sections 3.6, 3.8, 3.9, 3.10, 3.16, 3.17, 3.25, 5.2, and 5.7. When the acquisition agreement is signed, the Buyer obtains an interest in being consulted about matters affecting the Acquired Companies. However, the Sellers need to be able to operate the Acquired Companies' daily business without obtaining countless approvals, which can significantly delay ordinary business operations. This tension is analogous to that found in other areas of the law that use the concept of "in the ordinary course of business":

1. Under bankruptcy law, certain transactions undertaken by the debtor "other than in the ordinary course of business" require approval of the Bankruptcy Court. *See* 11 U.S.C. § 363(b)(1) (1988).
2. The Revised Model Business Corporation Act, Section 12.02, requires shareholder approval for a sale of all or substantially all of a corporation's assets other than in the regular course of business, and most states' general corporations laws contain similar provisions.
3. A regulation under the Securities Exchange Act allows management to omit a shareholder proposal from a proxy statement "[i]f the proposal deals with a matter relating to the conduct of the ordinary business operations of the [company]." *See* 17 C.F.R. § 14a-8(c)(7) (1993).

An important consideration in drafting this definition is the relevant standard for distinguishing between major and routine matters: the past practices of the Acquired Companies, common practice in the Acquired Companies' industries, or both. In one of the few cases that have interpreted the term "ordinary course of business" in the context of an acquisition, the jury was allowed to decide whether fees paid in connection with obtaining a construction loan, which were not reflected on the company's last balance sheet, were incurred in the ordinary course of business. *See Medigroup, Inc. v. Schildknecht*, 463 F.2d 525 (7th Cir. 1972). The trial judge defined "ordinary course of business" as "that course of conduct that reasonably prudent men would use in conducting business affairs as they may occur from day to day," and instructed the jury that the past practices of the company being sold, not "the general conduct of business throughout the community," was the relevant standard. *Id.* at 529; *cf. In re Fulghum Constr. Corp.*, 872 F.2d 739, 743 & n.5 (6th Cir. 1989) (stating that, in the bankruptcy context, the relevant standard is "the business practices which were unique to the particular parties under consideration and not to the practices which generally prevailed in the industry," but acknowledging that "industry practice may be relevant" in arriving at a definition of "ordinary business terms"). *But see In re Yurika Foods Corp.*, 888 F.2d 42, 44 (6th Cir. 1989) (noting that it might be necessary to examine industry standards as well as the parties' prior dealings to define "ordinary course of business"); *In re Dant & Russell, Inc.*, 853 F.2d 700, 704 (9th Cir. 1988) (applying, in the bankruptcy context, a "horizontal dimension test" based on industry practices); *In re Hills Oil & Transfer, Inc.*, 143 B.R. 207, 209 (Bankr. C.D. Ill. 1992) (relying on industry practices and standards to define "ordinary course of business" in a bankruptcy context).

The Model Stock Purchase Agreement definition distinguishes between major and routine matters based on the historic practices of both the Acquired Companies and others in the same industry and on the need for board or shareholder approval. The definition is derived primarily from the analysis of "ordinary course of business" in bankruptcy, which examines both the past practice of the debtor and the ordinary practice of the industry. *See, e.g., In re Roth American, Inc.*, 975 F.2d 949, 952-53 (3d Cir. 1992); *In re Johns-Manville Corp.*, 60 B.R. 612, 616-18 (Bankr. S.D.N.Y. 1986). No standard can eliminate all ambiguity regarding the need for consultation between the Buyer and the Sellers. In doubtful cases, the Sellers may want to consult with the Buyer and obtain its approval.

The Buyer should be aware that its knowledge of transactions the Acquired Companies plan to enter into before the closing may expand the scope of this definition. One court has stated:

> If a buyer did not know the selling corporation had made arrangements to construct a large addition to its plant, "the ordinary course of business" might refer to such transac-

> tions as billing customers and purchasing supplies. But a buyer aware of expansion plans would intend "the ordinary course of business" to include whatever transactions are normally incurred in effectuating such plans.

Medigroup, 463 F.2d at 529. Thus, the Buyer should monitor its knowledge of the Sellers' plans for operating the Acquired Companies before the closing, and if the Buyer knows about any plans to undertake projects or enter into transactions different from those occurring in the past practice of the Acquired Companies and other companies in the same industries, the Buyer may want specifically to exclude such projects or transactions, and all related transactions, from the definition of "ordinary course of business."

Clause (b) of the definition has special significance in a parent-subsidiary relationship. State law does not normally require parent company authorization for actions taken by subsidiaries. Unless the certificate or articles of incorporation provide otherwise, most state laws require shareholder approval only for amendments to the charter, mergers, sales of all or substantially all of the assets, dissolutions, and other major events. Therefore, the Model Stock Purchase Agreement definition excludes any action requiring authorization by the parent company not only for subsidiary actions requiring shareholder authorization under state law, but also for subsidiary actions requiring parent authorization under the operating procedures in effect between the parent and the subsidiary. ■

"Organizational Documents"—(a) the articles or certificate of incorporation and the bylaws of a corporation; (b) the partnership agreement and any statement of partnership of a general partnership; (c) the limited partnership agreement and the certificate of limited partnership of a limited partnership; (d) any charter or similar document adopted or filed in connection with the creation, formation, or organization of a Person; and (e) any amendment to any of the foregoing.

COMMENT

The term "Organizational Documents" appears in Sections 3.1, 3.2, and 3.16. ■

"Person"—any individual, corporation (including any non-profit corporation), general or limited partnership, limited liability company, joint venture, estate, trust, association, organization, labor union, or other entity or Governmental Body.

"Plan"—as defined in Section 3.13.

COMMENT

The term "Plan" appears in Section 3.13. ■

"Proceeding"—any action, arbitration, audit, hearing, investigation, litigation, or suit (whether civil, criminal, administrative, investigative, or informal) commenced, brought, conducted, or heard by or before, or otherwise involving, any Governmental Body or arbitrator.

COMMENT

The term "Proceeding" appears in Sections 3.15, 4.4, 7.5, and 10.9. ■

"Promissory Notes"—as defined in Section 2.4(b)(ii).

COMMENT

The term "Promissory Notes" appears in Sections 2.4, 2.6, and 3.2. ■

"Related Person"—with respect to a particular individual:

(a) each other member of such individual's Family;

(b) any Person that is directly or indirectly controlled by such individual or one or more members of such individual's Family;

(c) any Person in which such individual or members of such individual's Family hold (individually or in the aggregate) a Material Interest; and

(d) any Person with respect to which such individual or one or more members of such individual's Family serves as a director, officer, partner, executor, or trustee (or in a similar capacity).

With respect to a specified Person other than an individual:

(a) any Person that directly or indirectly controls, is directly or indirectly controlled by, or is directly or indirectly under common control with such specified Person;

(b) any Person that holds a Material Interest in such specified Person;

(c) each Person that serves as a director, officer, partner, executor, or trustee of such specified Person (or in a similar capacity);

(d) any Person in which such specified Person holds a Material Interest;

(e) any Person with respect to which such specified Person serves as a general partner or a trustee (or in a similar capacity); and

(f) any Related Person of any individual described in clause (b) or (c).

For purposes of this definition, (a) the "Family" of an individual includes (i) the individual, (ii) the individual's spouse [and former spouses], (iii) any other natural person who is related to the individual or the individual's spouse within the second degree, and (iv) any other natural person who resides with such individual, and (b) "Material Interest" means direct or indirect beneficial ownership (as defined in Rule 13d-3 under the Securities Exchange Act of 1934) of voting securities or other voting interests representing at least __% of the outstanding voting power of a Person or equity securities or other equity interests representing at least __% of the outstanding equity securities or equity interests in a Person.

COMMENT

The term "Related Persons" appears in Sections 3.25, 5.6, and 6.1. The main purpose of the representations concerning relationships with related persons (see Section 3.25) is to identify "sweetheart" deals benefitting the Acquired Companies (which may disappear after the closing), transactions with related persons on terms unfavorable to the Acquired Companies (which the Buyer may not be able to terminate after the closing), and possibly diverted corporate opportunities. Thus, the Buyer will want a broad definition of "related persons." For individuals, the Model Stock Purchase Agreement definition focuses on relationships with and arising from members of an individual's family; depending on the circumstances, a broader definition may be necessary to capture other relationships such as important business or social relationships and college friendships. ■

"Release"—any spilling, leaking, emitting, discharging, depositing, escaping, leaching, dumping, or other releasing into the Environment, whether intentional or unintentional.

COMMENT

The term "Release" appears in Sections 2.4 and 3.2. This definition is a short version of the CERCLA definition found at 42 U.S.C. § 9601(22) (1988). The Sellers may object to the inclusion of escaping, leaching, and dumping because the Acquired Companies may not be able to observe or control such events. However, because federal law may impose liability for such activities on the Acquired Companies and because such matters are hard to evaluate, the Buyer may resist modifications to this definition. ■

"Representative"—with respect to a particular Person, any director, officer, employee, agent, consultant, advisor, or other representative of such Person, including legal counsel, accountants, and financial advisors.

COMMENT

The term "Representative" appears in Sections 5.1 and 5.7. ■

"Securities Act"—the Securities Act of 1933 or any successor law, and regulations and rules issued pursuant to that Act or any successor law.

COMMENT

The term "Securities Act" appears in Sections 2.3, 3.2, 3.3, 3.24, and 4.3. Section 5 of the Securities Act of 1933, 15 U.S.C. § 77e(c) (1988), prohibits the sale of a security unless a registration statement with respect to that security has become effective or a statutory exemption is available. The sale of the Company's stock to the Buyer and the issuance of the Buyer's promissory note are potentially sales of securities subject to this registration requirement. *See Landreth Timber Co. v. Landreth*, 471 U.S. 681 (1985) (holding that the sale of all of the stock of a family business was a sale of securities within the meaning of the Securities Act). Preparation and filing of a registration statement is a costly and time-consuming process. The Securities Act provides various exemptions from registration. The Model Stock Purchase Agreement seeks to take advantage of the § 4(2) (non-public) exemption for the issuance of the Buyer's notes (see Section 3.2) and the so-called § 4(1½) (private resale) exemption for the transfer of the stock of the Company to the Buyer (see Section 4.3). ■

"Sellers"—as defined in the first paragraph of this Agreement.

"Sellers' Releases"—as defined in Section 2.4.

COMMENT

The term "Sellers' Releases" appears in Sections 2.4, 3.2, and 7.4. ■

"Shares"—as defined in the Recitals of this Agreement.

"Subsidiary"—with respect to any Person (the "Owner"), any corporation or other Person of which securities or other interests having the power to elect a majority of that corporation's or other Person's board of directors or similar governing body, or otherwise having the power to direct the business and policies of that corporation or other Person (other than securities or other interests having such power only upon the happening of a contingency that has not occurred) are held by the Owner or one or more of its Subsidiaries; when used without reference to a particular Person, "Subsidiary" means a Subsidiary of the Company.

COMMENT

The term "Subsidiary" appears in the definition of "Acquired Company" and in Section 11.9. ■

"Tax"—any tax (including any income tax, capital gains tax, value-added tax, sales tax, property tax, gift tax, or estate tax), levy, assessment, tariff, duty (including any customs duty), deficiency, or other fee, and any related charge or amount (including any fine, penalty, interest, or addition to tax), imposed, assessed, or collected by or under the authority of any Governmental Body or payable pursuant to any tax-sharing agreement or any other Contract relating to the sharing or payment of any such tax, levy, assessment, tariff, duty, deficiency, or fee.

COMMENT

The term "Tax" appears in Sections 3.2, 3.11, and 10.9. ■

"Tax Return"—any return (including any information return), report, statement, schedule, notice, form, or other document or information filed with or submitted to, or required to be filed with or submitted to, any Governmental Body in connection with the determination, assessment, collection, or payment of any Tax or in connection with the administration, implementation, or enforcement of or compliance with any Legal Requirement relating to any Tax.

COMMENT

The term "Tax Return" appears in Section 3.11. ■

"Threat of Release"—a substantial likelihood of a Release that may require action in order to prevent or mitigate damage to the Environment that may result from such Release.

COMMENT

The term "Threat of Release" appears in Section 3.19. The Sellers will often seek to exclude this phrase from the representations in Section 3.19 because they want to make representations only with respect to actual releases. A possible compromise is to add a knowledge qualification to representations concerning future releases, or for somewhat broader protection, the Buyer can use the defined term "Threatened," which uses a "prudent person" standard and is not qualified by reference to possible mitigation. ■

"Threatened"—a claim, Proceeding, dispute, action, or other matter will be deemed to have been "Threatened" if any demand or statement has been made (orally or in writing) or any notice has been given (orally or in writing), or if any other event has occurred or any other circumstances exist, that would lead a prudent Person to conclude that such a claim, Proceeding, dispute, action, or other matter is likely to be asserted, commenced, taken, or otherwise pursued in the future.

COMMENT

The term "Threatened" appears in Sections 3.13, 3.15, 3.19, 3.21, 3.22, 4.4, 7.5, and 7.6. A typical representation concerning litigation, for example, will require the Sellers to represent that "To the knowledge of Sellers and the Acquired Companies, no proceeding [involving an Acquired Company] has been Threatened." The word "Threatened" connotes action that a prudent person would expect to be taken based either upon receipt of a written demand, letter threatening litigation, or notice of an impending investigation or audit or upon facts that a prudent person would believe indicate that action likely will be taken by another person (for example, a recent, well-publicized industrial accident likely to give rise to claims even though no claims have yet been filed). When the term "Threatened" is used in conjunction with a knowledge qualification, the Buyer will normally insist that the Sellers' knowledge be based upon some inquiry or process of investigation, while the Sellers may attempt to limit their knowledge of threatened action to the actual knowledge of the Sellers and perhaps the Acquired Companies' senior management (or a limited number of designated officers) without any independent investigation.

By comparison, the ABA Statement of Policy Regarding Lawyers' Responses to Auditors' Requests for Information (December 1975) (the "Policy Statement") also contains standards for determining when threatened litigation must be disclosed. The Policy Statement examines the appropriateness of responses by lawyers to auditors' requests for information concerning loss contingencies of their clients. The Policy Statement is the result of a carefully negotiated compromise between the ABA and the American Institute of Certified Public Accountants. The compromise involved the balancing of the public interest in protecting the confidentiality of lawyer-client communications, as well as the attorney-client privilege, with the need for public confidence in published financial statements. Under the terms of the Policy Statement, only "overtly threatened" litigation need be disclosed. The customary threshold for disclosure in a business acquisition is lower, and the Policy Statement is not considered an appropriate benchmark for the allocation of risk between the sellers and the buyers in business acquisitions.

In addition to the representations concerning pending or threatened litigation (see Section 3.15), other provisions of the acquisition agreement may require disclosure of items that the Sellers are aware of and may affect the Acquired Companies. For example, the expected effect of a possible catastrophe may be covered by representations concerning the financial statements (see Section 3.4) or the absence of certain changes and events (see Section 3.16) or provisions regarding disclosure (see Section 3.24). Even if such a matter does not warrant disclosure by means of a reserve, a provision, or a footnote in the Company's financial statements, and even if its significance cannot yet be fully assessed, the Sellers' failure to disclose it in the Disclosure Letter may give the Buyer the right to elect not to close or to seek indemnity. ■

2. SALE AND TRANSFER OF SHARES; CLOSING

2.1 Shares

Subject to the terms and conditions of this Agreement, at the Closing, Sellers will sell and transfer the Shares to Buyer, and Buyer will purchase the Shares from Sellers.

COMMENT

The Buyer is the beneficiary of certain warranties under the Uniform Commercial Code ("UCC") in addition to the representations and warranties that the Buyer receives under the acquisition agreement. Section 8.301(1) of the UCC provides that the Buyer acquires from the Sellers all of the rights of the Sellers in the transferred shares, except to the extent that the Buyer is a party to a fraud or has notice of an adverse claim. In addition, under § 8.302(3) of the UCC, if the Buyer is a "bona fide purchaser," the Buyer acquires the Sellers' interest in the transferred shares free of any adverse claim. Under § 8.306(2), the Sellers warrant to the Buyer that their transfer is effective and rightful, that the transferred shares are genuine and have not been materially altered, and that they know of no fact that may impair the validity of the transferred shares. ■

2.2 Purchase Price

The purchase price (the "Purchase Price") for the Shares will be $_________________ plus the Adjustment Amount.

COMMENT

The purchase price and the method of its payment can take a wide variety of forms, an in-depth discussion of which is beyond the scope of this Commentary. The amount the Buyer is willing to pay for the Company depends on several factors, including the Company's industry and stage of development, and can be based on some measure of historical or future revenues, earnings, cash flow, or book value (or some combination of revenues, earnings, cash flow, and book value), as well as the risks inherent in the Acquired Companies' businesses.

The method of payment also depends on a variety of factors, including the Buyer's ability to pay, the parties' views on the value of the Company, the parties' tolerance (or lack thereof) for risk, and the tax and accounting consequences to the parties (especially if the Buyer is a public company). The method of payment may include some combination of cash, debt, and stock and may also have a contingent component based on future performance. For example, if the Buyer does not have sufficient cash or wants to reduce its initial cash outlay, the Buyer could require that a portion of the purchase price be paid by a note. The Sellers may then seek to structure the transaction, if possible, so that it qualifies for treatment as an installment sale under the Internal Revenue Code, which allows the Sellers to defer payment of their tax liability over the period during which the installments are paid (with in some cases the current payment of interest on the deferred tax). If the method of payment includes a debt component, issues such as security, subordination, and covenants will have to be resolved. Similarly, if the method of payment includes a stock component, issues such as valuation and registration rights will have to be resolved.

If the Buyer and the Sellers cannot agree on the value of the Company, they may make a portion of the purchase price contingent on the performance of the Company after the acquisition. The contingent portion of the purchase price (often called an "earnout") is commonly based on the Company's earnings (or other agreed-upon criterion such as sales) over a specified period of time after the acquisition. Although an earnout may bridge a gap between the Buyer's and the Sellers' views of the value of the Company, constructing an earnout raises many issues, including how earnings will be determined, the formula for calculating the payment amount and how that amount will be paid (cash or stock), how the Acquired Companies' businesses will be operated and who will have the authority to make major decisions, and the effect of a sale of the Buyer during the earnout period. Resolving these issues may be more difficult than agreeing on a purchase price.

The Model Stock Purchase Agreement assumes that the parties have agreed to a fixed price, subject only to an adjustment based on changes in the Company's consolidated stockholders' equity between the date of the balance sheet and the date of closing (see Sections 2.5 and 2.6). ■

2.3 CLOSING

The purchase and sale (the "Closing") provided for in this Agreement will take place at the offices of Buyer's counsel at ______________, at 10:00 a.m. (local time) on the later of (i) __________, 199__ or (ii) the date that is two business days following the termination of the applicable waiting period under the HSR Act, or at such other time and place as the parties may agree. Subject to the provisions of Section 9, failure to consummate the purchase and sale provided for in this Agreement on the date and time and at the place determined pursuant to this Section 2.3 will not result in the termination of this Agreement and will not relieve any party of any obligation under this Agreement.

COMMENT

Depending on the nature of the acquisition and the interest of the parties in completing the acquisition within a certain time frame, there are many ways to set the date of the closing. *See* Freund, *Anatomy of a Merger* 321-23 (1975). The acquisition agreement generally provides that the closing will occur within a relatively short period following the satisfaction of the conditions that will take the most amount of time to satisfy. Conditions that typically take a long time to satisfy include shareholder approval (in the case of a public company), effectiveness of a registration statement under the Securities Act (when securities will be issued as part of the consideration and an exemption from registration is not available), termination of the waiting period under the HSR Act (if applicable), and receipt of all regulatory approvals (when an Acquired Company is in a regulated industry). The Model Stock Purchase Agreement provides that the closing will occur within a short period of time after termination of the waiting period under the HSR Act. The Model Stock Purchase Agreement also provides in Section 9.1(d) that either party may terminate the agreement if the closing has not taken place by a specified "drop dead" date. The inclusion of a drop dead date assures both parties that they will not be bound by the acquisition agreement (and, in particular, by pre-closing covenants concerning exclusivity) for an unreasonably long period of time.

In certain circumstances, such as when the Buyer needs to obtain financing, the parties may want to provide that the closing will not take place prior to a certain date. Clause (i) of Section 2.3 provides the mechanism for the parties to specify the earliest date that the closing may occur. In addition, one or both of the parties may want to have the right to postpone the closing for a specified period of time if it is unable to satisfy a condition.

There are also tax, accounting, and other practical considerations in scheduling the closing. For example, if the Buyer is paying the purchase price in funds that are not immediately available (see the Commentary to Section 2.4), the Sellers will not want to close on a Friday (especially the Friday before a three-day weekend) because the Sellers would not have use of the funds over the weekend. If the Buyer is paying the purchase price by a wire transfer of immediately available funds, the Sellers should know the time by which their bank must receive the funds in order to invest the funds overnight. The amount the Sellers could lose through not having use of the funds for a few days depends on the purchase price, but may be substantial in large transactions. In some cases, accounting issues may require that the closing occur on the last business day of a month or other fiscal period.

The last sentence of Section 2.3 establishes that failure to consummate the acquisition on the date and time and at the place specified does not give either party an independent right to terminate the acquisition agreement unless the party has the right to do so under Section 9. It also establishes that such a failure does not relieve a party from its obligations under the acquisition agreement. Thus, if a party fails to satisfy a condition and that failure also is a breach of one of that party's covenants, the party is not relieved of any liability arising from its breach of covenant. ■

2.4 Closing Obligations

At the Closing:

(a) Sellers will deliver to Buyer:

(i) certificates representing the Shares, duly endorsed (or accompanied by duly executed stock powers), with signatures guaranteed by a commercial bank or by a member firm of the New York Stock Exchange, for transfer to Buyer;

(ii) releases in the form of Exhibit 2.4(a)(ii) executed by Sellers (collectively, "Sellers' Releases");

(iii) employment agreements in the form of Exhibit 2.4(a)(iii), executed by Sellers (collectively, "Employment Agreements");

(iv) noncompetition agreements in the form of Exhibit 2.4(a)(iv), executed by Sellers (collectively, the "Noncompetition Agreements"); and

(v) a certificate executed by Sellers representing and warranting to Buyer that each of Sellers' representations and warranties in this Agreement was accurate in all respects as of the date of this Agreement and is accurate in all respects as of the Closing Date as if made on the Closing Date (giving full effect to any supplements to the Disclosure Letter that were delivered by Sellers to Buyer prior to the Closing Date in accordance with Section 5.5); and

(b) Buyer will deliver to Sellers:

(i) the following amounts by bank cashier's or certified check payable to the order of [or by wire transfer to accounts specified by] A and B, respectively: $________ to A and $_________ to B;

(ii) promissory notes payable to A and B in the respective principal amounts of $_______ and $______ in the form of Exhibit 2.4(b) (the "Promissory Notes");

(iii) the sum of $________ to the escrow agent referred to in Section 2.4(c) by bank cashier's or certified check;

(iv) a certificate executed by Buyer to the effect that, except as otherwise stated in such certificate, each of Buyer's representations and warranties in this Agreement was accurate in all respects as of the date of this Agreement and is accurate in all respects as of the Closing Date as if made on the Closing Date; and

(v) the Employment Agreements, executed by Buyer.

(c) Buyer and Sellers will enter into an escrow agreement in the form of Exhibit 2.4(c) (the "Escrow Agreement") with __________.

COMMENT

Many acquisition agreements list the documents that will be exchanged at the closing so that the parties have a checklist. In the interests of simplicity, the Model Stock Purchase Agreement does not independently list those documents because the principal documents to be delivered at the closing are identified in Sections 2, 7, and 8.

The parties should be aware of the distinction between deliveries to be treated as covenants, the breach of which will give the non-breaching party a right to damages, and deliveries to be treated as conditions, the breach of which will give the non-breaching party the right to terminate the acquisition (that is, a "walk right") but not a right to damages. In Section 2.4, the parties covenant to make certain deliveries. Therefore, if the Sellers fail to deliver the certificates for the shares or the Buyer fails to make the specified payments, for example, the non-breaching party can pursue its damage remedy. In contrast, if the Sellers fail to deliver the legal opinion or consents (or other documents reasonably requested by the Buyer) contemplated by Section 7, the Buyer would have the right to terminate the acquisition, but it would not have the right to damages unless the Sellers breached their covenant in Section 5.8 to use their best efforts to obtain such documents. If, however, the Sellers covenanted to deliver a particular consent (because, for example, the Sellers or a party related to the Sellers was the lessor under a lease with one of the Acquired Companies that required a consent), the Sellers' failure to deliver that consent (regardless of the efforts used) would give the Buyer a right to damages as well as the right to terminate the acquisition (see the second and third paragraphs of the Commentary to Section 7).

Guaranty of Endorsement of Stock Certificates. The guaranty of the Sellers' signatures on the certificates representing the shares provides the Buyer with additional protection. Under Section 8.312(1) of the UCC, a person guaranteeing the signature of an endorser warrants that the signature is genuine, that the signer is an appropriate person to endorse, and that the signer has the legal capacity to sign. Under Section 8.312(8) of the UCC, these warranties extend to any person taking the security (in this case, the stock certificate) in reliance on the guaranty, and the guarantor is liable to such a person for any loss resulting from a breach of these warranties.

Sellers' Closing Certificate. Section 2.4(a)(v) requires the Sellers to deliver a "bring down" certificate to the Buyer at the closing. In many acquisition agreements, the "bring down" certificate provides the basis for the Buyer's assertion of post-closing indemnification claims relating to representations that are inaccurate as "brought down" to the closing date. The Model Stock Purchase Agreement, however, contains a separate "bring down" provision in the indemnity section (see Section 10.2(b)) which enables the Buyer to assert such indemnification claims. Thus, the "bring down" certificate contemplated by Section 2.4(a)(v) is arguably superfluous. The Model Stock Purchase Agreement nonetheless requires the delivery of a "bring down" certificate so that the Sellers are required to reconsider whether their representations remain accurate at the closing and to confirm to the Buyer that this is the case.

Section 2.4(a)(v) provides that supplements to the Sellers' disclosure letter are always taken into account for purposes of determining the accuracy of the representations in the "bring down" certificate. The Sellers thus will not be required to sign a certificate that they know is false. In contrast, supplements to the Disclosure Letter are not always given effect in the context of other provisions of the Model Stock Purchase Agreement (see Sections 7.1 and 10.2 and the related Commentary).

In some circumstances, it may be desirable for the Sellers to include in their "bring down" certificate an express statement to the effect that the Buyer has a "walk right" as a result of a particular event disclosed in a disclosure letter supplement. See Section 10.2(b) and the related Commentary; see also Appendix A, scenario 5, and the Commentary to Sections 5.5 and 7.1.

For a further discussion of the use of "bring down" certificates in acquisition agreements, see Kling & Nugent Simon, *Negotiated Acquisitions of Companies, Subsidiaries and Divisions* § 14.02[5] (1992).

Manner of Payment. The Model Stock Purchase Agreement provides for payment by bank cashier's or certified check, although it recognizes that the parties may agree that payment will be made by wire transfer. While all three forms of payment are commonly used and should be acceptable to the Sellers, the parties should be aware of certain differences in the Buyer's ability to stop payment and in the availability of the funds for use by the Sellers.

A certified check is a check of the drawer that contains the drawee bank's certification on its face. As a result of the bank's certification, the drawee bank's liability is substituted for that of the drawer. A cashier's check is a check drawn by a bank on itself. Thus, a cashier's check is the primary promissory obligation of the drawee bank. Once a certified check has been certified and delivered, and once a cashier's check has been delivered to the payee, the customer who procured the check has no right to stop payment. Although there have been a few cases involving banks that stopped payment on certified and cashier's checks at the request of customers, courts generally have held that the customer has no right to stop payment. *See* Clark, *The Law of Bank Deposits, Collections and Credit Cards* ¶¶ 1.01[1], 2.06[3], 3.02 (3d ed. 1990) (citing cases).

Unlike checks, which are instructions by a customer to its bank to debit an account in the amount of the check, wire transfers are transfers of credit through a series of contractual obligations, usually from one bank to another. As a result, in the case of a check, the drawer's ability to pay is not determined until the check is presented for payment, while in the case of a wire transfer, the customer's ability to pay is determined when the customer gives the payment order to its bank. Although the customer's ability to pay is determined earlier for wire transfers, Article 4A of the UCC (which governs wire transfers) and relevant case law recognize that wire transfers can be cancelled if the beneficiary's bank has not accepted the payment order (and even when the beneficiary's bank has accepted the payment order in the case of an unauthorized transfer or a mistake). Although cancellation of a wire transfer is analogous to a stop payment order for a check and may present some risks to the beneficiary, the risk to the Sellers is limited if receipt of the wire transfer in the correct amount to the correct account is confirmed at the closing. *See* Clark, *The Law of Bank Deposits, Collections and Credit Cards* ¶¶ 13.01-13.03 (3d ed. 1990) (citing cases).

The form of payment may also affect the time when funds become available to the Sellers. For example, a wire transfer over the Fedwire operated by the Federal Reserve Board is commonly referred to as "immediately available" because it is immediately credited to the payee bank when received by that bank, while a wire transfer over the Clearing House Interbank Payments System (CHIPS) is commonly referred to as "same day availability" because it is not credited until the end of the business day during which the wire was received. In the case of cashier's checks and certified checks, a bank into which such checks are deposited is required to make the funds available to the payee or beneficiary no later than the business day following the deposit. Therefore, if the Sellers want immediate use of the funds, the acquisition agreement should specify that payment will be made by a wire transfer of immediately available funds or delivery of a check drawn on a federal reserve bank. *See generally* Clark, *The Law of Bank Deposits, Collections and Credit Cards* ¶¶ 6.01-6.24 (3d ed. 1990). If there is any possibility of ambiguity, the agreement should specify the currency in which amounts are stated and payments are to be made.

Promissory Notes. Exhibit 2.4(b) of the Model Stock Purchase Agreement contains a form of the Buyer's Promissory Notes to be delivered to the Sellers. The Promissory Notes are subject to rights of set-off in favor of the Buyer, which provide some security to the Buyer for the enforcement of the Sellers' post-closing indemnification obligations. The Promissory Notes bear interest, are subject to prepayment without penalty, and may be accelerated following the occurrence of an event of default.

The Promissory Notes are neither subordinated to the rights of other creditors of the Buyer nor secured by a security interest in favor of the Sellers. Whether such features are included depends on the amount of cash funds being raised, who is providing cash funds, and the bargaining position of the parties. When the Promissory Notes are subordinated with regard to payment, the parties must determine the degree of subordination. A full subordination of payments prohibits any payment of interest or principal under the notes until completion of payment of all senior debt. Alternatively, the parties may agree to prohibit subordinated payments only when an event of default has occurred or in the event of a bankruptcy or reorganization proceeding involving the Buyer.

Sellers in a strong bargaining position may demand collateral for the Buyer's Promissory Notes, especially if the Buyer is weak financially. Such collateral could be a pledge of all or a portion of the shares of the Company. The collateral could be perfected as a pledge by depositing the stock certificates representing the shares acquired by the Buyer, along with stock powers endorsed in blank by the Buyer, with the Sellers or an escrow agent. To prevent the value of the collateral from being unduly diminished, the Sellers may also seek certain covenants from the Buyer regarding the operation of the Acquired Companies after the closing.

The security agreement can provide for the Sellers to have all of the remedies of a secured party under the provisions of the UCC upon the occurrence of an event of default. Alternatively, the enforcement rights of the Sellers as secured parties can be subordinated to those of other secured creditors and require the Sellers to take no action until those creditors exercise their rights or for a specified period of time. If the stock certificates representing the transferred shares being acquired are pledged to the Sellers and held by an escrow agent, the Escrow Agreement should provide for delivery of the stock certificates to the Sellers following an event of default (although the escrow agent is likely to "freeze" and retain the collateral in the event of a dispute) and for the Sellers, rather than the escrow agent, to exercise the remedies. The pledge agreement should also contain provisions regarding voting rights with respect to regular and extraordinary matters, receipt of dividends and distributions, and adjustments for stock splits, recapitalizations, and mergers.

The Promissory Notes are non-negotiable to protect the Buyer's set-off rights. Under the *D'Oench, Duhme* doctrine, which arose from a 1942 Supreme Court decision and has since been expanded by various statutes and judicial decisions, defenses such as set-off rights under an acquisition agreement generally are not effective against the Federal Deposit Insurance Corporation (FDIC), the Resolution Trust Corporation (RTC), and subsequent assignees or holders in due course of notes that once were in the possession of the FDIC or the RTC. *See D'Oench, Duhme & Co. v. FDIC*, 315 U.S. 447 (1942); *see also* 12 U.S.C. § 1823(e); *Porras v. Petroplex Sav. Ass'n*, 903 F.2d 379 (5th Cir. 1990); *Bell & Murphy Assoc. v. InterFirst Bank Gateway, N.A.*, 894 F.2d 750 (5th Cir.), *cert. denied*, 498 U.S. 895 (1990); *FSLIC v. Murray*, 853 F.2d 1251 (5th Cir. 1988). An exception to the *D'Oench, Duhme* doctrine exists when the asserted defense arises from an agreement reflected in the failed bank's records. *See FDIC v. Plato*, 981 F.2d 852 (5th Cir. 1993); *RTC v. Oaks Apartments Joint Venture*, 966 F.2d 995 (5th Cir. 1992). Therefore, if the Buyer gives the Sellers non-negotiable Promissory Notes and those notes ever come into the possession of a bank that later fails, the Buyer could lose its set-off rights under the acquisition agreement unless the failed bank had reflected in its records the acquisition agreement and the Buyer's set-off rights. The Buyer could issue notes that can be transferred only to persons who agree in writing to recognize in their official records both the acquisition agreement and the Buyer's set-off rights.

Escrow Agreement. The Escrow Agreement provides for an escrow to assist the Buyer in realizing on any successful indemnification claims that it may have under the acquisition agreement for matters such as breaches of the Sellers' representations (see Section 10). ■

2.5 Adjustment Amount

The Adjustment Amount (which may be a positive or negative number) will be equal to (a) the consolidated stockholders' equity of the Acquired Companies as of the Closing Date determined in accordance with GAAP, minus (b) $_____________.

COMMENT

The adjustment amount used in the Model Stock Purchase Agreement is based on the net worth or stockholders' equity of the Company on a consolidated basis as reflected in the closing financial statements. Stockholders' equity is the difference between assets and liabilities, for this purpose as reflected on the audited balance sheet included in the closing financial statements.

In most acquisitions, the purchase price is determined, at least in part, on the basis of the last audited consolidated financial statements and any interim financial statements of the Company delivered to the Buyer. The purchase price adjustment protects the Buyer against a diminution in the value of the Company during the period between the date of signing the acquisition agreement and the closing. If the closing financial statements differ substantially and adversely from the last audited financial statements and interim statements delivered to the Buyer, the Buyer should consider, as an alternative to the purchase price adjustment, remedies available to it under the Sellers' representations concerning the financial statements and possibly under theories of fraud.

Purchase price adjustment provisions can include a *de minimis* "window" — a range of closing date stockholders' equity values within which neither party pays a purchase price adjustment amount. Other alternative provisions include "caps," "collars," and “floors.” A “cap” is the upper limit on the adjustment amount to be paid by the Buyer; a “floor” is the upper limit on the adjustment amount to be refunded by the Sellers. A “collar” refers to the use of both a “cap” and a “floor.”

Parties applying “caps,” “collars,” and “floors” to purchase price adjustment provisions should consider the financial and contractual consequences of reaching the limits of the “cap” or “floor.” Is the “cap” or “floor” a risk-allocation feature under which one party benefits and one party suffers with no further contractual remedies? Does the “cap” or “floor” instead require the parties to turn to other contractual provisions such as an “unwind” provision, a deferred payment provision, or the indemnity provisions? If the acquisition agreement is silent on the rights, for example, of the Buyer if a “floor” is reached, the Sellers may then take the risk that the Buyer will seek a remedy under the indemnity provisions for a breach of a representation such as the financial statements, accounts receivable, or no material adverse change representation.

The parties can also place a portion of the purchase price paid, or funds in excess of the purchase price, in escrow to facilitate payment of the adjustment amount.

The Model Stock Purchase Agreement defines the adjustment amount as “the consolidated stockholders’ equity of the Acquired Companies as of the Closing Date determined in accordance with GAAP” (less the portion of the purchase price paid in cash and notes at the closing). Both the Buyer and the Sellers should be aware of the flexibility permitted by GAAP (see the fourth paragraph of the Commentary to the definition of GAAP in Section 1). The parties may want to negotiate, or confirm in writing at the time the acquisition agreement is signed, the method of valuation of significant line items on the closing financial statements. The parties should also consider describing “past practice” in writing as a schedule to the acquisition agreement. Accountants for both parties should be involved in these discussions. If the parties agree on specific guidelines concerning the determination of stockholders’ equity for purposes of the adjustment amount, the acquisition agreement should specify that, in the event of a conflict between GAAP and the guidelines, the guidelines control. ■

2.6 Adjustment Procedure

(a) Sellers will prepare and will cause ____________________, the Company's certified public accountants, to audit consolidated financial statements ("Closing Financial Statements") of the Company as of the Closing Date and for the period from the date of the Balance Sheet through the Closing Date, including a computation of consolidated stockholders' equity as of the Closing Date. Sellers will deliver the Closing Financial Statements to Buyer within sixty days after the Closing Date. If within thirty days following delivery of the Closing Financial Statements, Buyer has not given Sellers notice of its objection to the Closing Financial Statements (such notice must contain a statement of the basis of Buyer's objection), then the consolidated stockholders' equity reflected in the Closing Financial Statements will be used in computing the Adjustment Amount. If Buyer gives such notice of objection, then the issues in dispute will be submitted to ________________, certified public accountants (the "Accountants"), for resolution. If issues in dispute are submitted to the Accountants for resolution, (i) each party will furnish to the Accountants such workpapers and other documents and information relating to the disputed issues as the Accountants may request and are available to that party or its Subsidiaries (or its independent public accountants), and will be afforded the opportunity to present to the Accountants any material relating to the determination and to discuss the determination with the Accountants; (ii) the determination by the Accountants, as set forth in a notice delivered to both parties by the Accountants, will be binding and conclusive on the parties; and (iii) Buyer and Sellers will each bear 50% of the fees of the Accountants for such determination.

(b) On the tenth business day following the final determination of the Adjustment Amount, if the Purchase Price is greater than the aggregate of the payments made pursuant to Sections 2.4(b)(i) and 2.4(b)(iii) and the aggregate principal amount of the Promissory Notes, Buyer will pay the difference to Sellers, and if the Purchase Price is less than such aggregate amount, Sellers will pay the difference to Buyer. All payments will be made together with interest at _____% compounded daily beginning on the Closing Date and ending on the date of payment. Payments must be made in immediately available funds. Payments to Sellers must be made in the manner and will be allocated in the proportions set forth in Section 2.4(b)(i). Payments to Buyer must be made by wire transfer to such bank account as Buyer will specify.

COMMENT

Section 2.6 provides that the Sellers will prepare and cause the Company's accountants to audit the closing financial statements. If the Sellers will no longer be affiliated with the Company (as employees, consultants, or otherwise) after the closing, the Buyer may be in a better position to do this. Because determination of stockholders' equity under GAAP is not a science, parties frequently seek to have their own accountants make this determination. The initial determination will then be subject to objection, accompanied by an explanation of the objection, by the party not controlling the initial determination. Provisions establishing dispute resolution procedures should follow the provision for the initial determination and objection.

The Model Stock Purchase Agreement provides for dispute resolution by independent accountants previously agreed to by the parties; if the acquisition agreement does not specify who will serve as these independent accountants, it should contain provisions establishing the procedure for their selection. Often the acquisition agreement instructs these accountants to act as arbitrators and not as auditors. The phrase "issues in dispute" in the third sentence of paragraph (a) limits the inquiry of the independent accountants to the specific line items to which the objecting party has objected. The parties should consider setting parameters on the submission of issues in dispute to the independent accountants. For example, the parties could agree that if the amount in dispute is less than a specified amount, they will split the difference and avoid the cost of the accountants' fees and the time and effort involved in resolving the dispute. The parties may want to add an exception for manifest error to the statement that the accountants' decision will be binding and conclusive.

Under the Model Stock Purchase Agreement, the Buyer has the right to object to the initial determination of stockholders' equity as of the closing date. Because the Sellers usually have a relationship with the Company's accountants, the Buyer should assume that the accountants will resolve items involving the accountants' judgment in favor of the Sellers. The Company's accountants may seek to continue to represent the Company, however, and not the Sellers. Thus, the Sellers may, upon evaluating their relationship with the Company's accountants, seek an objection right similar to that of the Buyer.

Section 2.6(b) provides that any payments of the adjustment amount are to be made in immediately available funds. The parties may want to provide that a portion or all of the adjustment amount will be paid by adjusting the amount of the promissory notes. The Buyer should negotiate for a set-off right under the promissory notes if the Sellers fail to pay the adjustment amount.

The Sellers may want to include in these provisions a statement to the effect that any liabilities included in the calculation of the adjustment amount will not constitute a breach of any of the Sellers' representations in the acquisition agreement and will not give the Buyer any right to indemnification. The rationale for such a clause is that the Buyer is protected from damages associated with such liabilities by the purchase price adjustment. ■

3. REPRESENTATIONS AND WARRANTIES OF SELLERS

Sellers represent and warrant to Buyer as follows:

COMMENT

The Sellers' representations and warranties are the Sellers' formal description of the Acquired Companies and their businesses. The technical difference between representations and warranties—representations are statements of past or existing facts and warranties are promises that existing or future facts are or will be true—has proven unimportant in acquisition practice. *See* Freund, *Anatomy of a Merger* 153 (1975). Separating them explicitly in an acquisition agreement is a drafting nuisance, and the legal import of the separation has been all but eliminated. *See Reliance Finance Corp. v. Miller*, 557 F.2d 674, 682 (9th Cir. 1977) (the distinction between representations and warranties is inappropriate when interpreting a stock acquisition agreement). The Commentary to the Model Stock Purchase Agreement generally refers only to representations, although the Model Stock Purchase Agreement follows common practice and refers to both representations and warranties.

Bare representations, if false, may support claims in tort and for federal securities act violations and also claims for breach of an implied warranty, breach of an implied promise that a representation is true, or breach of an express warranty if the description is basic to the bargain. *Cf.* U.C.C. § 2-313. *See generally Business Acquisitions* ch. 31 (Herz & Baller eds., 2d ed. 1981). The Model Stock Purchase Agreement, following common practice, stipulates remedies for breaches of representations that are equivalent to those provided for breaches of warranties (see Sections 1 (definition of "Breach"), 7.1 (conditions to the Buyer's obligations to complete the acquisition), and 10.2(a) and (b) (the Sellers' indemnification obligations)).

Purposes of the Sellers' Representations: The Sellers' representations serve three overlapping purposes. First, they are a device for obtaining disclosure about the Acquired Companies before the signing of the acquisition agreement. A thorough Buyer's draft elicits information about the Acquired Companies and their businesses relevant to the Buyer's decision to buy the Company.

The Sellers' representations also provide a foundation for the Buyer's right to terminate the acquisition before or at the closing. After the signing of the acquisition agreement and before the closing, the Buyer usually undertakes a due diligence investigation of the Acquired Companies. Detailed Sellers' representations give the Buyer, on its subsequent discovery of adverse facts, the right not to proceed with the acquisition, even if the adverse facts do not rise to the level of common law "materiality" defined by judges in fraud and contract cases (see Section 7.1 and the related Commentary).

Finally, the Sellers' representations provide a basis for the Buyer's right to indemnification (and other remedies) if the Buyer discovers after the closing that the Sellers have breached one or more of the representations (see Section 10.2 and the related Commentary). In this regard, the Sellers' representations serve as a mechanism for allocating economic risks between the Buyer and the Sellers.

Considerations When Drafting "Adverse Effect" Language in Representations: The importance of the content and detail of the Sellers' representations cannot be understated. As noted above, the Sellers' representations provide the foundation for both the Buyer's "walk rights" in Section 7.1 and the Buyer's indemnification rights in Section 10.2. The specific wording of the representations can be quite important because of this dual purpose.

Consider, for example, the following simplified version of the Sellers' litigation representation: "There is no lawsuit pending against the Company that will have an adverse effect on the Company." The phrase "that will have an adverse effect on the Company" clearly provides adequate protection to the Buyer in the context of a post-closing indemnification claim against the Sellers—if there is a previously undisclosed lawsuit against the Company that has an adverse effect on the Company (because, for example, a judgment is ultimately rendered against the Company in the lawsuit), the Buyer will be able to recover damages from the Sellers because of the Sellers' breach of the litigation representation (see Section 10.2(a)). However, the quoted phrase may not adequately protect the Buyer if the Buyer is seeking to terminate the acquisition because of the lawsuit. To terminate the acquisition (without incurring any liability to the Sellers), the Buyer will have to demonstrate, on the scheduled closing date, that the lawsuit "will have an adverse effect on the Company" (see Section 7.1). The Buyer may find it difficult to make this showing, especially if there is doubt about the ultimate outcome of the lawsuit.

To address this problem, the Buyer might be tempted to reword the litigation representation so that it covers lawsuits that "could reasonably be expected to have" an adverse effect on the Company (as distinguished from lawsuits that definitely "will" have such an effect). However, while this change in wording clearly expands the scope of the Buyer's "walk rights," it may actually limit the Buyer's indemnification rights—even if the lawsuit ultimately has an adverse effect on the Company, the Sellers may be able to avoid liability to the Buyer by showing that, as of the closing date, it was unreasonable to expect that the lawsuit would have such an effect.

To protect both its indemnification rights and its "walk rights" in the context of undisclosed litigation, the Buyer may propose that the litigation representation be reworded to cover any lawsuit "that *may* have an adverse effect" on the Company (see Section 3.15(a)). If the Sellers object to the breadth of this language, the Buyer may propose, as a compromise, that the litigation representation be reworded to cover lawsuits "that will, or that could reasonably be expected to," have an adverse effect on the Company.

Considerations When Drafting Representations Incorporating Specific Time Periods: Representations that focus on specific time periods require careful drafting due to the expectations of the "bring down" clause in Sections 7.1 and 10.2(b) (the clauses focusing on the accuracy of the Sellers' representations as of the closing date). For example, consider the representation in Section 3.14(a)(iii), which states that no Acquired Company has received notice of any alleged legal violation "since" a specified date. In some acquisition agreements, this representation is worded differently, stating that no notice of an alleged violation has been received at any time during a specified time period (such as a five-year period) "prior to the date of this agreement." If the representation were drafted in this manner, the Buyer would not have a "walk right" or an indemnification right if an Acquired Company received notice of a significant alleged violation between the signing date and the closing date—the representation would remain accurate as "brought down" to the scheduled closing date pursuant to Section 7.1(a) and Section 10.2(b), because the notice would not have been received "prior to" the date of the agreement. In contrast, if the representation were drafted as in Section 3.14(a)(iii), the representation would be materially inaccurate as "brought down" to the scheduled closing date (because the notice of the alleged violation would have been received "since" the date specified in Section 3.14(a)(iii)), and the Buyer therefore would have a "walk right" pursuant to Section 7.1(a) and a basis for claiming indemnification pursuant to Section 10.2(b).

The Effect of "Knowledge" Qualifications in Representations: Sections 3.13, 3.15, 3.17, 3.19, 3.20, 3.21, 3.22, and 3.23 contain knowledge qualifications. The addition of knowledge qualifications to the Sellers' representations in Section 3 can significantly limit the Buyer's post-closing indemnification rights (by shifting to the Buyer the economic risks of unknown facts). However, such qualifications should not affect the Buyer's "walk rights" under Section 7.1. If, prior to the closing, the Buyer learns of a fact (not already known to the Sellers) that is inconsistent with a representation containing a knowledge qualification, the Buyer should simply disclose this fact to the Sellers. The Sellers will thus acquire knowledge of the fact, and the representation will be inaccurate despite the knowledge qualification. For further discussion of knowledge qualifications, see the Commentary to the definition of "Knowledge" in Section 1 and to the sections listed above.

The Absence of "Materiality" Qualifications: The Sellers' representations in the Model Stock Purchase Agreement generally do not contain materiality qualifications. Rather, the issue of materiality is addressed in the remedies sections. Section 7.1(a) specifies that only material breaches of representations give the Buyer a "walk right." Section 7.1(b) covers the few representations that contain their own materiality qualification (see the Commentary to Section 7.1 under the caption "Absence of Materiality Qualification in Section 7.1(b)"). The indemnification provisions replace a general and open-ended materiality qualification with a quantified "basket" in Section 10.6 that exonerates the Sellers from liability for breaches resulting in damages below a specified amount.

The Sellers may object to the absence of materiality qualifications in their representations by arguing that, in light of the comprehensive and detailed nature of the representations, it is unrealistic to expect that every representation will be accurate in all respects. They might point out, for example, that the Company undoubtedly will have been a few days late in making a payment due under one of the routine contracts to which it is a party, and that this insignificant delay in making a contractual payment will place the Sellers in breach of the "no default" representation in Section 3.17(b)(i). The Sellers may be reluctant to sign a document containing representations that are not completely accurate.

The Buyer may respond by pointing out that, because of the limited purposes served by the Sellers' representations, the Sellers should not be concerned about the presence of immaterial inaccuracies in these representations. Under the Model Stock Purchase Agreement, the only remedies available to the Buyer for a breach of the Sellers' representations are the Buyer's "walk rights" and indemnification rights, neither of which may be exercised if the breach is not material (see above). Also, to exercise its indemnification rights on the basis of a breach by the Sellers, the Buyer must be able to demonstrate that it was actually damaged by the breach (see Section 10.2). If the Buyer accedes to the Sellers' request that specific materiality qualifications be added to each representation, the Buyer could be left without any remedies if a series of individually insignificant inaccuracies in the Sellers' representations causes damages that are material when measured on a cumulative basis. See the Commentary to Section 7.1 under the captions "Materiality Qualification in Section 7.1(a)" and "Absence of Materiality Qualification in Section 7.1(b)"; see also the second paragraph of the Commentary to Section 10.6 (relating to the indemnification "basket").

The Absence of a "Bring Down" Representation: For a discussion of the absence of a "bring down" representation in the Model Stock Purchase Agreement, see the Commentary to Section 7.1. ■

3.1 Organization and Good Standing

(a) Part 3.1 of the Disclosure Letter contains a complete and accurate list for each Acquired Company of its name, its jurisdiction of incorporation, other jurisdictions in which it is authorized to do business, and its capitalization (including the identity of each stockholder and the number of shares held by each). Each Acquired Company is a corporation duly organized, validly existing, and in good standing under the laws of its jurisdiction of incorporation, with full corporate power and authority to conduct its business as it is now being conducted, to own or use the properties and assets that it purports to own or use, and to perform all its obligations under Applicable Contracts. Each Acquired Company is duly qualified to do business as a foreign corporation and is in good standing under the laws of each state or other jurisdiction in which either the ownership or use of the properties owned or used by it, or the nature of the activities conducted by it, requires such qualification.

(b) Sellers have delivered to Buyer copies of the Organizational Documents of each Acquired Company, as currently in effect.

COMMENT

The representation concerning the Acquired Companies' power and authority is generally qualified by a reference to "corporate" power and authority. Use of the word "corporate" limits the representation to mean that the Acquired Company is authorized to conduct its business (as it is currently conducted) under applicable business corporation laws and its charter and by-laws—that is, such action is not "ultra vires." If the word "corporate" is omitted, the term "power and authority" could be interpreted to mean "full power and authority" under all applicable laws and regulations; that the Acquired Companies have such authority is a much broader representation covered by other sections of the acquisition agreement.

The representation concerning qualification of each Acquired Company as a foreign corporation in other jurisdictions occasionally contains an exception for jurisdictions in which "the failure to be so qualified would have a material adverse effect on the business or properties of the Acquired Company." Because most states provide for qualification only of foreign corporations and limited partnerships, the representation in the last sentence applies only to those entities. Requiring a list of foreign jurisdictions does not limit or expand the breadth of the previous sentence but does help force the Sellers to give proper attention to this matter.

If the Buyer has concern that an Acquired Company might be an inadvertent "investment company" (for example, if an Acquired Company's assets include significant investment assets and ownership is widespread), the Buyer should seek a representation such as: "None of the Acquired Companies is an 'investment company' within the meaning of the Investment Company Act of 1940."

See Chapter II, "Basic Corporate Documents," of the *Manual on Acquisition Review.* ■

3.2 Authority; No Conflict

(a) This Agreement constitutes the legal, valid, and binding obligation of Sellers, enforceable against Sellers in accordance with its terms. Upon the execution and delivery by Sellers of the Escrow Agreement, the Employment Agreements, the Sellers' Releases, and the Noncompetition Agreements (collectively, the "Sellers' Closing Documents"), the Sellers' Closing Documents will constitute the legal, valid, and binding obligations of Sellers, enforceable against Sellers in accordance with their respective terms. Sellers have the absolute and unrestricted right, power, authority, and capacity to execute and deliver this Agreement and the Sellers' Closing Documents and to perform their obligations under this Agreement and the Sellers' Closing Documents.

(b) Except as set forth in Part 3.2 of the Disclosure Letter, neither the execution and delivery of this Agreement nor the consummation or performance of any of the Contemplated Transactions will, directly or indirectly (with or without notice or lapse of time):

(i) contravene, conflict with, or result in a violation of (A) any provision of the Organizational Documents of the Acquired Companies, or (B) any resolution adopted by the board of directors or the stockholders of any Acquired Company;

(ii) contravene, conflict with, or result in a violation of, or give any Governmental Body or other Person the right to challenge any of the Contemplated Transactions or to exercise any remedy or obtain any relief under, any Legal Requirement or any Order to which any Acquired Company or either Seller, or any of the assets owned or used by any Acquired Company, may be subject;

(iii) contravene, conflict with, or result in a violation of any of the terms or requirements of, or give any Governmental Body the right to revoke, withdraw, suspend, cancel, terminate, or modify, any Governmental Authorization that is held by any Acquired Company or that otherwise relates to the business of, or any of the assets owned or used by, any Acquired Company;

(iv) cause Buyer or any Acquired Company to become subject to, or to become liable for the payment of, any Tax;

(v) cause any of the assets owned by any Acquired Company to be reassessed or revalued by any taxing authority or other Governmental Body;

(vi) contravene, conflict with, or result in a violation or breach of any provision of, or give any Person the right to declare a default or exercise any remedy under, or to accelerate the maturity or performance of, or to cancel, terminate, or modify, any Applicable Contract; or

(vii) result in the imposition or creation of any Encumbrance upon or with respect to any of the assets owned or used by any Acquired Company.

Except as set forth in Part 3.2 of the Disclosure Letter, no Seller or Acquired Company is or will be required to give any notice to or obtain any Consent from any Person in connection with the execution and delivery of this Agreement or the consummation or performance of any of the Contemplated Transactions.

(c) Sellers are acquiring the Promissory Notes for their own account and not with a view to their distribution within the meaning of Section 2(11) of the Securities Act. Each Seller is an "accredited investor" as such term is defined in Rule 501(a) under the Securities Act.

COMMENT

Section 3.2(b) contains the Sellers' "no conflict" representation. The purpose of this representation is to assure the Buyer that, except as disclosed by the Sellers in the Disclosure Letter, the acquisition will not violate (or otherwise trigger adverse consequences under) any legal or contractual requirement applicable to the Sellers or the Acquired Companies.

The purpose served by the no conflict representation differs from that served by the more general representations concerning legal requirements, governmental authorizations, orders, and contracts (see Sections 3.14, 3.15, and 3.17), which alert the Buyer to violations and other potential problems not connected with the acquisition. The no conflict representation focuses specifically on violations and other potential problems that would be triggered by the consummation of the acquisition and related transactions.

The term "Contemplated Transactions" is defined broadly in Section 1 to include not only the sale of the shares to the Buyer at the closing, but also the performance of the Employment Agreement, the Buyer's exercise of control over the Acquired Companies, and various other actions that may be taken *after* the closing date. The use of an expansive definition of the term "Contemplated Transactions" makes the scope of the no conflict representation very broad. The Sellers may argue for a narrower definition of the term "Contemplated Transactions" and may also seek to clarify that the no conflict representation does not extend to laws, contracts, or other requirements that are adopted or otherwise take effect after the closing date. In addition, the Sellers may seek to clarify that the no conflict representation applies only to violations arising from the *Sellers'* consummation of the acquisition and related transactions (and not to violations arising from actions taken by the Buyer).

The no conflict representation relates both to requirements binding upon the Acquired Companies and to requirements binding upon the Sellers. (Requirements binding upon the Buyer are separately covered by the Buyer's "no conflict" representation in Section 4.2 and the closing condition in Section 7.7.) The Sellers may seek to eliminate the references to laws, regulations, orders, and contracts binding upon the Sellers, arguing that violations of requirements applicable only to the Sellers (and not also applicable to the Acquired Companies) should be of no concern to the Buyer because the Buyer is not making an investment in the Sellers. The Buyer may respond to such an argument by pointing out that a violation of a law, regulation, order, or contract binding upon the Sellers can be of substantial concern to the Buyer if such a violation would provide a governmental body or a third party with grounds to set aside or challenge the acquisition. The Buyer may also point out that, if the Sellers were to incur a significant financial liability as a result of such a violation, the Sellers' ability to satisfy their indemnification obligations and other post-closing obligations to the Buyer could be impaired.

The phrase "with or without notice or lapse of time," which appears in the introduction to the "no conflict" representation, requires the Sellers to advise the Buyer of any "potential" or "unmatured" violations or defaults (circumstances that, while not technically constituting a violation or default, could become an actual violation or default when a specified grace period elapses or when a formal notice of violation or default is delivered) that may be caused by the acquisition or related transactions.

Clause (ii) of the "no conflict" representation focuses specifically on laws, regulations, and orders that might be contravened by the acquisition or related transactions. The broad language of this provision requires disclosure not only of legal violations, but also of other types of adverse legal consequences that may be triggered by the Contemplated Transactions. For example, the "Exon-Florio" regulations, 31 C.F.R. § 800.01 et seq., provide for the submission of notices to the Committee on Foreign Investment in the United States in connection with acquisitions of U.S. companies by "foreign persons." Because the filing of an "Exon-Florio" notice is voluntary, the failure to file such a notice is not a regulatory violation. However, the filing of such a notice shortens the time period within which the President can exercise divestment authority and certain other legal remedies with respect to the acquisition described in the notice. Thus, the failure to file such a notice can have an adverse effect on an Acquired Company. Clause (ii) alerts the Buyer to the existence of regulatory provisions of this type.

The parties may face a troublesome dilemma if both the Buyer and the Sellers are aware of a possible violation of law that might occur as a consequence of the acquisition or related transactions. If the possible violation is not disclosed by the Sellers in the Disclosure Letter, the Sellers will bear the risks associated with any violation (see Section 10.2(a)). But if the Sellers elect to disclose the possible violation in their disclosure letter, they may be providing a discoverable "road map for a lawsuit by the government or a third party." Kling & Nugent Simon, *Negotiated Acquisitions of Companies, Subsidiaries and Divisions* § 11.04(7) (1992).

Although clause (iii) (which addresses the possible revocation of governmental authorizations) overlaps to some extent with clause (ii), clause (iii) is included because a governmental authorization may become subject to revocation without any statutory or regulatory "violation" actually having occurred.

Clauses (iv) and (v) are important because, under some laws and regulations regarding transfer taxes and property tax assessments, a change in the control or stock ownership of a corporation that owns property may be treated like a sale of the property by the corporation. *See, e.g.*, California Revenue & Taxation Code § 64(c) (1993). For other examples of statutory provisions that may be violated (or that may provide for the revocation of governmental authorizations) as a consequence of a change in control or a change in the stock ownership of a corporation, see Blumberg & Strasser, *The Law of Corporate Groups — Problems of Parent and Subsidiary Corporations under Statutory Law Specifically Applying Enterprise Principles* (1992).

Clause (vi) deals with contractual defaults and other contractual consequences that may be triggered by the acquisition or related transactions. Normally, the sale of a corporation's outstanding stock by its shareholders to a third party does not constitute a violation of a standard anti-assignment clause in a lease or other contract to which the corporation is a party. *See, e.g., Alabama Vermiculite Corp. v. Patterson*, 124 F. Supp. 441 (W.D.S.C. 1954); *Rubenstein Bros. v. Ole of 34th Street, Inc.*, 421 N.Y.S.2d 534 (N.Y. Cir. Ct. 1979); *Richardson v. La Rancherita La Jolla*, 98 Cal. App. 3d 73 (1979); *Branmar Theatre Co. v. Branmar, Inc.*, 264 A.2d 526 (Del. Ch. 1970); *Posner v. Air Brakes & Equip. Corp.*, 62 A.2d 711 (N.J. Ch. 1948). In some contracts, however, the anti-assignment provision is broad enough to encompass a change in control or a transfer of the stock of a contracting party. *See, e.g.*, *Associated Cotton Shops, Inc. v. Evergreen Park Shopping Plaza of Delaware, Inc.*, 170 N.E.2d 35 (Ill. App. 1960). Clause (vi) alerts the Buyer to the existence of any such contracts.

Even if a contract does not expressly characterize a change in control of a party as a "breach," "default," or "violation" by that party, the contract may nonetheless require a party undergoing a change in control to make a substantial cash payment (as in the case of a "golden parachute" employment agreement) or may otherwise provide for the exercise of various remedies by the other party. Clause (vi) thus covers not only events constituting a breach, default, or violation of a contract, but also events that would allow a party to the contract to exercise certain other rights under the contract.

Clause (vi) applies to "Applicable Contracts," the definition of which extends both to contracts to which an Acquired Company is a party and to contracts under which an Acquired Company has any rights or by which an Acquired Company may be bound. The inclusion of the latter type of contracts may be important to the Buyer. For example, the Buyer will want to know if an Acquired Company's rights under a promissory note or a guaranty given by a third party and held by the Acquired Company would be terminated or otherwise impaired as a result of the acquisition. Because such a promissory note or guaranty would presumably be signed only by the third party maker or guarantor (and would not be executed on behalf of the Acquired Company in its capacity as payee or beneficiary), the Acquired Company might not be considered a party to the note or guaranty.

Other examples of contracts that may be covered by the expansive definition of "Applicable Contract" include the following:

1. contracts under which an Acquired Company is a third party beneficiary;
2. contracts under which a party's rights or obligations have been assigned to or assumed by an Acquired Company;
3. contracts containing obligations that have been guaranteed by an Acquired Company;
4. recorded agreements or declarations that relate to real property owned by an Acquired Company and that con-

tain covenants or restrictions "running with the land"; and

5. contracts entered into by a partnership in which an Acquired Company is a general partner.

The Sellers are required to provide (in part 3.2 of the Disclosure Letter) a list of governmental and third-party consents needed to consummate the acquisition. Some of these consents may be sufficiently important to justify giving the Buyer (and, in some cases, the Sellers) a "walk right" if they are not ultimately obtained (see Sections 7.3 and 8.3 and the related Commentary). ■

3.3 Capitalization

The authorized equity securities of the Company consist of _______ shares of common stock, par value $_____ per share, of which __________ shares are issued and outstanding and constitute the Shares. Sellers are and will be on the Closing Date the record and beneficial owners and holders of the Shares, free and clear of all Encumbrances. A owns _____ of the Shares and B owns _____ of the Shares. With the exception of the Shares (which are owned by Sellers), all of the outstanding equity securities and other securities of each Acquired Company are owned of record and beneficially by one or more of the Acquired Companies, free and clear of all Encumbrances. No legend or other reference to any purported Encumbrance appears upon any certificate representing equity securities of any Acquired Company. All of the outstanding equity securities of each Acquired Company have been duly authorized and validly issued and are fully paid and nonassessable. There are no Contracts relating to the issuance, sale, or transfer of any equity securities or other securities of any Acquired Company. None of the outstanding equity securities or other securities of any Acquired Company was issued in violation of the Securities Act or any other Legal Requirement. No Acquired Company owns, or has any Contract to acquire, any equity securities or other securities of any Person (other than Acquired Companies) or any direct or indirect equity or ownership interest in any other business.

COMMENT

This representation elicits information about the number of outstanding shares of the Company so that the Buyer can verify that it is acquiring all of the outstanding shares. The Buyer will also want to know the number of authorized shares to ensure that the outstanding shares were validly issued and that there are sufficient shares authorized to cover outstanding warrants, options, and convertible securities. The Sellers may want to specify that this information is as of a given date, such as the date of the acquisition agreement. This is acceptable if, as in Section 5.2(a), the issuance of any additional shares between the date of the acquisition agreement and the closing is prohibited, thus rendering this representation correct at all relevant times.

References to "marketable" title should be avoided since this term applies primarily to real estate, not to securities. The Buyer also should obtain assurance that no other party has any right to shares of the Company, either from the Sellers or from the Company itself.

Section 3.3 should be read in conjunction with Section 7.6, which provides as a closing condition that no person claims to own or has the right to acquire shares in any of the Acquired Companies.

See Chapter II, "Basic Corporate Documents," of the *Manual on Acquisition Review.* ■

3.4 Financial Statements

Sellers have delivered to Buyer: (a) [unaudited] consolidated balance sheets of the Acquired Companies as at ____________ in each of the years ___ through ___, and the related [unaudited] consolidated statements of income, changes in stockholders' equity, and cash flow for each of the fiscal years then ended, [together with the report thereon of ___________, independent certified public accountants,] (b) a consolidated balance sheet of the Acquired Companies as at __________ (including the notes thereto, the "Balance Sheet"), and the related consolidated statements of income, changes in stockholders' equity, and cash flow for the fiscal year then ended, together with the report thereon of ____________, independent certified public accountants, and (c) an unaudited consolidated balance sheet of the Acquired Companies as at ____________ (the "Interim Balance Sheet") and the related unaudited consolidated statements of income, changes in stockholders' equity, and cash flow for the ___ months then ended, including in each case the notes thereto. Such financial statements and notes fairly present the financial condition and the results of operations, changes in stockholders' equity, and cash flow of the Acquired Companies as at the respective dates of and for the periods referred to in such financial statements, all in accordance with GAAP [, subject, in the case of interim financial statements, to normal recurring year-end adjustments (the effect of which will not, individually or in the aggregate, be materially adverse) and the absence of notes (that, if presented, would not differ materially from those included in the Balance Sheet)]; the financial statements referred to in this Section 3.4 reflect the consistent application of such accounting principles throughout the periods involved [, except as disclosed in the notes to such financial statements]. No financial statements of any Person other than the Acquired Companies are required by GAAP to be included in the consolidated financial statements of the Company.

COMMENT

This representation, which requires the delivery of specified financial statements of the Acquired Companies and provides assurances regarding the quality of those financial statements, is almost universally present in an acquisition agreement. Financial statements are key items in the evaluation of nearly all potential business acquisitions. The Model Stock Purchase Agreement representation requires financial statements to be delivered and provides a basis for contractual remedies if they prove to be inaccurate. Other provisions of the typical acquisition agreement also relate to the financial statements, including representations that deal with specific parts of the financial statements in greater detail and with concepts that go beyond GAAP (such as title to properties and accounts receivable), serve as the basis for assessing the quality of the financial statements (such as the representation concerning the accuracy of the Acquired Companies' books and records), or use the financial statements as a starting or reference point (such as the absence of certain changes since the date of the financial statements). However, specific line item representations may lead a court to give less significance to the representation concerning overall compliance with GAAP in the case of line items not covered by a specific representation. *See, e.g., Delta Holdings, Inc. v. National Distillers & Chemical Corp.,* 945 F.2d 1226 (2d Cir. 1991), *cert. denied,* 112 S. Ct. 1671 (1992).

The Model Stock Purchase Agreement representation requires the delivery of (1) annual financial statements for a period of years, which may or may not be audited, (2) audited annual financial statements as of the end of the most recent fiscal year, and (3) unaudited financial statements as of the end of an interim period subsequent to the last audited financial statements. The determination of which financial statements should be required will depend upon factors such as availability, relevance to Buyer's commercial evaluation of the acquisition, and the burden and expense on the Sellers that the Buyer is willing to impose and the Sellers are willing to bear. Especially when the Acquired Companies have been operated as part of a larger enterprise and do not have a history of independent financing transactions, separate audited financial statements may not exist and, although the auditors that expressed an opinion concerning the entire enterprise's consolidated financial statements will of necessity have reviewed the financial statements of the Acquired Companies, that review may not have been sufficient for the expression of an opinion about the financial statements of the Acquired Companies by themselves. This occurs most frequently when the Acquired Companies do not represent a major portion of the entire enterprise, so that the materiality judgments made in the examination of the enterprise's financial statements are not appropriate for an examination of the Acquired Companies' financial statements. Although it is not unusual to require the Sellers to cause the Acquired Companies' auditors to do the necessary additional work to express an opinion on one recent set of financial statements for the Acquired Companies, it may not be practical to seek this comfort for earlier periods (for instance, the auditors might not have observed physical inventories in the prior periods). In such a case, the representation concerning the accuracy of the Acquired Companies' books and records (see Section 3.5) is critical because these books and records are the Buyer's main tool for assessing the financial health of the Acquired Companies' businesses (under Section 5.1, the Buyer has a right to inspect these books and records).

The Buyer also may request audited consolidating financial statements, which contain separate financial statements for each of the Acquired Companies and the eliminations necessary to produce the consolidated financial statements. The Sellers can be expected to object to the additional accounting and audit work required to produce those statements, in which materiality judgments reflect the size of the smallest of the Acquired Companies, and to argue that Buyer should be concerned about the financial aspects of the Acquired Companies' business as a whole, not on an entity-by-entity basis. If the Buyer insists on receiving audited consolidating financial statements, the Buyer should be prepared to demonstrate to the Sellers the relevance of that information to the Buyer's evaluation of the acquisition.

If the Buyer is a public company, its counsel should consider the requirements in SEC Regulation S-X, 17 C.F.R. § 210, if any, that apply to post-closing disclosure of audited financial statements for the Acquired Companies; in general, these requirements depend on the relative size of the Buyer and the Acquired Companies.

The Model Stock Purchase Agreement representation does not attempt to characterize the auditors' report; the Buyer's counsel should determine at an early stage whether the report contains any qualifications regarding conformity with GAAP, the auditors' examination having been in accordance with the generally accepted auditing standards, or fair presentation being subject to the outcome of contingencies. Any qualification in the auditors' report should be reviewed with the Buyer's accountants.

In some jurisdictions, including California and New York, auditors cannot be held liable for inaccurate financial reports to persons not in privity with the auditors, with possible exceptions in very limited circumstances. *See Bily v. Arthur Young & Co.,* 11 Cal. Rptr. 2d 51 (1992); *Credit Alliance Corporation v. Arthur Andersen & Co.*, 65 N.Y.2d 536 (1985); *Ultramares Corp. v. Touche,* 255 N.Y. 170 (1931); *see also Security Pacific Credit, Inc. v. Peat Marwick Main & Co.*, 586 N.Y.S.2d 87 (1992) (explaining the circumstances in which accountants may be held liable to third parties); *Gretcas Inc. v. Proud*, 826 F.2d 1560, 1565 (7th Cir. 1987) (holding that, although privity of contract is not required in Illinois, the plaintiff must still demonstrate that a negligent misrepresentation induced detrimental reliance). If the audited financial statements were prepared in the ordinary course, the Buyer probably will not satisfy the requirements for auditors' liability in those jurisdictions in the absence of a "reliance letter" from the auditors addressed to the Buyer. Requests for reliance letters are relatively unusual in acquisitions, and accounting firms are increasingly unwilling to give them.

Issues frequently arise concerning the appropriate degree of assurance regarding the quality of the financial statements. The Buyer's first draft of this representation often includes a statement that the financial statements are true, complete, and correct in an effort to eliminate the leeway for judgments about contingencies (such as to the appropriate size of reserves for subsequent events) and materiality inherent in the concept of fair presentation in accordance with GAAP. The Sellers will likely object that this statement is an unfair request for assurances that the financial statements meet a standard that is inconsistent with the procedures used by accountants to produce them. In addition, the Sellers may be reluctant to represent that interim financial statements are fairly presented in accordance with GAAP, either because of some question about the quality of the information contained (for example, there may be no physical inventory taken at the end of an interim period) or because of the level of disclosure included (such as the absence of a full set of notes to financial statements). The Model Stock Purchase Agreement representation contains an example of a qualification that may be appropriate. It has been suggested that the representation concerning fair presentation in accordance with GAAP should also be qualified with respect to audited financial statements. *See* Augenbraun & Ten Eyck, *Financial Statement Representations in Business Transactions,* 47 Bus. Law. 157 (1991). The Buyer is unlikely to accept this view, especially in its first draft of the acquisition agreement.

The Sellers may be willing to represent only that the financial statements have been prepared from, and are consistent with, the books and records of the Acquired Companies. The Buyer should be aware that this representation provides far less comfort to the Buyer than that provided by the Model Stock Purchase Agreement representation.

Many of the representations in Sections 3.5 through 3.26 reflect the Buyer's attempt to obtain assurances about specific line items in the financial statements that go well beyond fair presentation in accordance with GAAP. Reliance on GAAP may be inadequate if the Acquired Companies are engaged in businesses (such as insurance) in which valuation or contingent liability reserves are especially significant. However, specific line item representations could lead a court to give less significance to the representation concerning overall compliance with GAAP in the case of line items not covered by a specific representation. *See, e.g., Delta Holdings, Inc. v. National Distillers & Chemical Corp.,* 945 F.2d 1226 (2d Cir. 1991), *cert. denied,* 112 S. Ct. 1671 (1992). The specific content of these representations will vary greatly depending on the nature of the Acquired Companies' businesses and assets.

See Chapter V, "Financial Statements," of the *Manual on Acquisition Review.* ■

3.5 Books and Records

The books of account, minute books, stock record books, and other records of the Acquired Companies, all of which have been made available to Buyer, are complete and correct and have been maintained in accordance with sound business practices and the requirements of Section 13(b)(2) of the Securities Exchange Act of 1934, as amended (regardless of whether or not the Acquired Companies are subject to that Section), including the maintenance of an adequate system of internal controls. The minute books of the Acquired Companies contain accurate and complete records of all meetings held of, and corporate action taken by, the stockholders, the Boards of Directors, and committees of the Boards of Directors of the Acquired Companies, and no meeting of any such stockholders, Board of Directors, or committee has been held for which minutes have not been prepared and are not contained in such minute books. At the Closing, all of those books and records will be in the possession of the Acquired Companies.

COMMENT

The books of account of the Acquired Companies are the basis of the financial statements. If the books of account are inaccurate or incomplete, the information provided to the Acquired Companies' auditors (or the Buyer's auditors) will be suspect and the financial statements will be of little value to the Buyer. Therefore, the Buyer often seeks to go behind the financial statements by requesting representations concerning the quality of the Acquired Companies' record keeping. Such representations are especially important when separate audited financial statements have not been prepared for the Acquired Companies, such as when the Acquired Companies are subsidiaries or divisions of a larger enterprise. The Buyer may want to inquire about these matters by requesting the Sellers to deliver copies of management letters and other reports received from the Acquired Companies' auditors over a specified period of time.

Section 13(b)(2) of the Securities Exchange Act of 1934, 15 U.S.C. § 78m(b)(2) (1988), was added by the Foreign Corrupt Practices Act and applies only to public companies; the parenthetical phrase that follows the reference to that Act is necessary if that portion of the representation is to have any meaning in the case of private companies.

Some acquisition agreements omit the portion of the representation relating to the minute books. Such a representation could be especially troublesome to the Sellers if the Acquired Companies are closely held and have conducted their affairs informally. It is in those instances, however, that this representation is most important to the Buyer. The Buyer may want to ask the Sellers to represent that, other than certain listed committees, there have been no other committees of the Company's Board of Directors. If the Company has had management, policy, or similar committees, the Buyer may want to request that the Sellers provide the minutes from meetings of these committees to the Buyer.

See Chapter II, "Basic Corporate Documents," of the *Manual on Acquisition Review.* ■

3.6 Title to Properties; Encumbrances

Part 3.6 of the Disclosure Letter contains a complete and accurate list of all real property, leaseholds, or other interests therein owned by any Acquired Company. [Sellers have delivered or made available to Buyer copies of the deeds and other instruments (as recorded) by which the Acquired Companies acquired such real property and interests, and copies of all title insurance policies, opinions, abstracts, and surveys in the possession of Sellers or the Acquired Companies and relating to such property or interests.] The Acquired Companies own (with good and marketable title in the case of real property, subject only to the matters permitted by the following sentence) all the properties and assets (whether real, personal, or mixed and whether tangible or intangible) that they purport to own [located in the facilities owned or operated by the Acquired Companies or reflected as owned in the books and records of the Acquired Companies], including all of the properties and assets reflected in the Balance Sheet and the Interim Balance Sheet (except for assets held under capitalized leases disclosed or not required to be disclosed in Part 3.6 of the Disclosure Letter and personal property sold since the date of the Balance Sheet and the Interim Balance Sheet, as the case may be, in the Ordinary Course of Business), and all of the properties and assets purchased or otherwise acquired by the Acquired Companies since the date of the Balance Sheet (except for personal property acquired and sold since the date of the Balance Sheet in the Ordinary Course of Business and consistent with past practice) [, which subsequently purchased or acquired properties and assets (other than inventory and short-term investments) are listed in Part 3.6 of the Disclosure Letter]. All material properties and assets reflected in the Balance Sheet and the Interim Balance Sheet are free and clear of all Encumbrances and are not, in the case of real property, subject to any rights of way, building use restrictions, exceptions, variances, reservations, or limitations of any nature except, with respect to all such properties and assets, (a) mortgages or security interests shown on the Balance Sheet or the Interim Balance Sheet as securing specified liabilities or obligations, with respect to which no default (or event that, with notice or lapse of time or both, would constitute a default) exists, (b) mortgages or security interests incurred in connection with the purchase of property or assets after the date of the Interim Balance Sheet (such mortgages and security interests being limited to the property or assets so acquired), with respect to which no default (or event that, with notice or lapse of time or both, would constitute a default) exists, (c) liens for current taxes not yet due, and (d) with respect to real property, (i) minor imperfections of title, if any, none of which is substantial in amount, materially detracts from the value or impairs the use of the property subject thereto, or impairs the operations of any Acquired Company, and (ii) zoning laws and other land use restrictions that do not impair the present or anticipated use of the property subject thereto. All buildings, plants, and structures owned by the Acquired Companies lie wholly within the boundaries of the real property owned by the Acquired Companies and do not encroach upon the property of, or otherwise conflict with the property rights of, any other Person.

COMMENT

Much of this representation has no relevance if the Acquired Companies own no significant real property. The Sellers should consider whether exceptions are necessary for existing use and other restrictions, including environmental matters that may restrict the use or development of the property (the acquisition agreement will often include separate representations concerning environmental matters, such as Section 3.19), but disclosure of environmental restrictions may be necessary here as well. In acquisitions involving very significant real property—or real property intended for development—the Buyer should consider seeking a representation concerning the Acquired Companies' history of zoning and other land use disputes.

See Chapter IV, "Real and Personal Property," of the *Manual on Acquisition Review.* ■

3.7 Condition and Sufficiency of Assets

The buildings, plants, structures, and equipment of the Acquired Companies are structurally sound, are in good operating condition and repair, and are adequate for the uses to which they are being put, and none of such buildings, plants, structures, or equipment is in need of maintenance or repairs except for ordinary, routine maintenance and repairs that are not material in nature or cost. The building, plants, structures, and equipment of the Acquired Companies are sufficient for the continued conduct of the Acquired Companies' businesses after the Closing in substantially the same manner as conducted prior to the Closing.

COMMENT

This representation seeks comfort about the condition and sufficiency of the Acquired Companies' tangible assets. Such matters normally do not involve precise, objective criteria, and both the Sellers and the Buyer should be somewhat uncomfortable with this representation. The Sellers may argue that the Buyer should obtain whatever comfort it needs by appropriate inspection, while the Buyer may want to seek comfort from both inspection and the Sellers' representations. The second sentence is especially significant when the Acquired Companies are closely held or are part of a larger consolidated enterprise. The Buyer may also want a representation concerning transactions with related persons (see Section 3.25) to avoid surprises about key assets that are used by the Acquired Companies but will not be available after the closing (because, for example, they are owned by one of the Sellers or a related person).

See Chapter IV, "Real and Personal Property," of the *Manual on Acquisition Review.* ■

3.8 Accounts Receivable

All accounts receivable of the Acquired Companies that are reflected on the Balance Sheet or the Interim Balance Sheet or on the accounting records of the Acquired Companies as of the Closing Date (collectively, the "Accounts Receivable") represent or will represent valid obligations arising from sales actually made or services actually performed in the Ordinary Course of Business. Unless paid prior to the Closing Date, the Accounts Receivable are or will be as of the Closing Date current and collectible net of the respective reserves shown on the Balance Sheet or the Interim Balance Sheet or on the accounting records of the Acquired Companies as of the Closing Date (which reserves are adequate and calculated consistent with past practice and, in the case of the reserve as of the Closing Date, will not represent a greater percentage of the Accounts Receivable as of the Closing Date than the reserve reflected in the Interim Balance Sheet represented of the Accounts Receivable reflected therein and will not represent a material adverse change in the composition of such Accounts Receivable in terms of aging). Subject to such reserves, each of the Accounts Receivable either has been or will be collected in full, without any set-off, within ninety days after the day on which it first becomes due and payable. There is no contest, claim, or right of set-off, other than returns in the Ordinary Course of Business, under any Contract with any obligor of an Accounts Receivable relating to the amount or validity of such Accounts Receivable. Part 3.8 of the Disclosure Letter contains a complete and accurate list of all Accounts Receivable as of the date of the Interim Balance Sheet, which list sets forth the aging of such Accounts Receivable.

COMMENT

Accounts receivable are assets in the form of balance sheet accounts reflecting amounts due from other parties that were incurred in the ordinary course of business. Typically, the term "accounts receivable" designates trade debtors' accounts; other receivables are separately designated and recorded as special receivables. Accounts receivable are classified under the "current assets" caption on the balance sheet unless they are due more than one year from the balance sheet date (for example, retainage on long-term construction contracts).

The representation concerning accounts receivable provides line-item support to the more general representations regarding the financial statements as a whole. The Buyer should demand this representation when accounts receivable comprise a significant component of the Acquired Companies' assets. If the Sellers argue that adequate protection is provided by the financial statements representations, the Buyer can respond that by the time of the closing, a substantial portion of the accounts receivable reflected in the most recent balance sheet will have been paid and that a specific accounts receivable representation is needed to cover the accounts that the Buyer will acquire at the closing.

The Model Stock Purchase Agreement begins with an assurance that the Acquired Companies' accounts receivable represent valid obligations arising from sales actually made or services actually performed by the Acquired Companies. This is essentially an anti-fraud provision and should be construed as a representation that the accounts receivable reflected on the Acquired Companies' balance sheets and in the books of account are genuine and not fabricated.

In addition to assurances regarding the validity of the Acquired Companies' accounts receivable, the Buyer may seek representations concerning their ultimate collectibility so that it will be adequately compensated if the accounts receivable do not ultimately result in cash equal to the amounts reflected on the Acquired Companies' balance sheets. The Sellers may resist making assurances regarding collectibility by arguing that the Buyer should conduct a thorough pre-closing investigation of the status of the receivables. Similarly, the Sellers may assert that the acquisition is the sale of a going concern and that the possibility of uncollectibility of genuine accounts receivable is simply a risk of doing business that should be transferred to the Buyer at the closing. As a compromise, the parties may negotiate a discount to be applied to the value of the accounts receivable shown on the most recent balance sheets; the purchase price would be reduced by the amount of the discount, and the entire risk of non-collectibility would shift to the Buyer at the closing. In such cases, old accounts are typically discounted more than new accounts.

If the Sellers agree to give assurances of collectibility, they should be sure that the representation relates to the accounts receivable net of any established reserve for uncollectible accounts. The reserve for uncollectible accounts (also known as the allowance for doubtful accounts or the bad debt reserve) is a reserve established to estimate the proportion of the gross amount of the accounts receivable that will not be collected.

Methods of providing the Buyer assurances regarding the collectibility of accounts receivables include (1) a representation of collectibility, net of the corresponding reserve, backed by the Sellers' indemnification obligations, (2) a guaranty that the Sellers will repurchase all pre-closing accounts receivable that remain unpaid after a specified period (such as ninety days) elapses after their creation, and (3) an arrangement in which title to the accounts receivable does not pass and the Buyer collects the accounts on behalf of the Sellers. Regardless of the method selected, the quality of the Buyer's collection efforts will affect the Sellers' post-closing obligations. Because of the inconsistent (and relatively infrequent) interpretations courts have placed on these provisions, precise drafting is critical.

Collectibility—Representations Coupled with Indemnification. In the Model Stock Purchase Agreement representation, the Sellers warrant that the aggregate amount of transferred accounts receivable will be "current and collectible" as of the closing, net of the reserve for uncollectible accounts. The representation further provides that each account will be collected in full, subject to the reserve, without set-off, within ninety days after the date on which it first becomes payable. The indemnification provisions of Section 10 provide that the Sellers will be responsible to the Buyer for any breach of this representation (see Section 10.2). The Buyer should keep in mind that the Sellers' indemnification obligations may be subject to limitations such as thresholds that must be achieved before indemnification is owed and time periods during which claims for indemnification must be made (see Sections 10.5 and 10.6).

Courts have placed various interpretations on contractual representations concerning the collectibility of accounts receivable. *See, e.g., Metro-Goldwyn-Mayer, Inc. v. Ross,* 509 F.2d

930 (2d Cir. 1975); *Forms, Inc. v. American Standard, Inc.,* 546 F. Supp. 314, 321-22 (E.D. Penn. 1982); *see also Resort Car Rental Sys., Inc. v. Chuck Ruwart Chevrolet, Inc.,* 519 F.2d 317 (10th Cir. 1975); *REA Express, Inc. v. Interway Corp.,* 410 F. Supp. 192 (S.D.N.Y.), *rev'd,* 538 F.2d 953 (2d Cir. 1976); *Rocky Mountain Helicopters v. Air Freight,* 773 P.2d 911 (Wyo. 1989). To avoid the kinds of ambiguities that give courts difficulty, the acquisition agreement should specify whether the reserve for uncollectible accounts will be applied on an aggregate or account-by-account basis. The acquisition agreement should also indicate the mechanism for establishing the amount of such reserves (whether by reference to particular financial statements, receivables schedules, or the Acquired Companies' books and records). *See Armco Inc. v. Glenfed Financial Corp.,* 746 F. Supp. 1249 (D.N.J. 1990); *Carolet Corp. v. Garfield,* 157 N.E.2d 876, 880 (Mass. 1959).

Repurchase of Uncollected Accounts by Sellers. An alternative method of providing assurances of collectibility is the Sellers' guaranty that after a stipulated period of time, they will pay to the Buyer the amount that has not been collected on any account. Typically, such a guaranty requires that the Sellers repurchase accounts that remain uncollected, net of applicable reserves, after the passage of the pre-determined period of time from the creation of the accounts. In deciding whether to use the repurchase method, the parties should keep in mind that the quality of the Buyer's collection efforts will affect the Sellers' repurchase obligations and that the Sellers' collection efforts after the re-assignment could interfere with the Buyer's conduct of the newly acquired business, especially with ongoing customer relations.

If the parties use the repurchase method, they should consider how to allocate the reserve for uncollectible accounts. The Buyer may want to allocate the reserve to individual accounts so that each repurchase obligation is of the net amount; the Sellers, however, may insist that their repurchase obligation begin only when the entire reserve has been exhausted. The parties should also agree on specific procedures for re-assignment of uncollected accounts to the Sellers. In particular, they should decide whether the Sellers will be allowed to set off amounts that the Buyer owes the account debtor. *See Hilton v. CET/DDT*

Corp., No. 4, 1990 Tenn. App. LEXIS 40 (Tenn. Ct. App. Jan. 30, 1990).

Collection by Buyer for Sellers' Account. A third alternative provides that title to the accounts receivable remains in the Sellers and the Buyer covenants to collect the accounts on the Sellers' behalf. This method reduces the importance of the accuracy of the financial statements with respect to accounts receivable (including the magnitude of the reserve) because any inability to collect the accounts will not directly affect the Buyer. Nevertheless, the Buyer may want to analyze historical trends in collection of accounts receivable for purposes of pricing the acquisition. This method, as well as the repurchase method, is usually implemented not through a representation, but through a provision elsewhere in the acquisition agreement containing collection and other mechanics, and thus is not subject to the indemnification "basket" in Section 10.6.

Collection Efforts. In each of the three alternatives discussed above, the quality of the Buyer's collection efforts will affect the Sellers' post-closing liability for uncollected accounts. Thus, the Sellers may want to specify the collection efforts, policies, and procedures required of the Buyer. In particular, the Sellers should insist that the Buyer cannot simply allow the accounts to age and thereby force the Sellers to respond in damages or compromise the Sellers' ability to pursue collection after repurchasing the accounts. *See Kominsky, A Primer on Acquisition Hold Harmless Clauses,* 34 Prac. Law. 27, 32 (1988). When procedures are established, the Buyer generally is required to use best efforts to collect in the ordinary course of business, but is not required to resort to collection agencies or litigation. *See Rocky Mountain Helicopters v. Air Freight,* 773 P.2d 911 (Wyo. 1989); *Business Acquisitions* ch. 5, at 173 (Herz & Baller eds., 2d ed. 1981). The Buyer, in return, can negotiate for the option of bringing suit for collection of delinquent receivables and charging the Sellers for any collection and litigation costs. In this case, the Sellers should seek assurances that they will be notified of material proceedings and afforded the opportunity to participate.

The parties may want to outline the parameters of the Buyer's ability to settle or compromise accounts. Although it is usually impractical to require that the Buyer clear individual returns of merchandise with the Sellers, the Sellers may want to prohibit the Buyer from forgiving large outstanding accounts to foster good relations with continuing customers and charging the Sellers with the remaining deficiencies.

The parties may also want to specify procedures to be followed upon receipt of payments on accounts. This issue is of particular concern with respect to on-going relationships with regular customers. The Sellers may insist that the Buyer be required to apply payments to the invoices of pre-closing accounts before applying such payments to current, post-closing invoices. The Buyer could respond that if a customer disputes one invoice but pays another, the customer has not paid the disputed invoice, even though it was incurred before the closing. The Sellers may demand some formal method of monitoring the Buyer's allocation of payments to invoices to ensure an equitable payment process and to prevent collusion with the customer in paying certain invoices and disputing others.

A related concern involves the customer who is a questionable credit risk because it is unable to make current payments without continued business with the Buyer, presumably on similar credit terms. *See* McGaffey, *Buying, Selling and Merging Businesses* 39 (2d ed. 1989). The Sellers will prefer to give the customer every opportunity to make payments on the guaranteed account, but the Buyer may not want to risk extending new credit to facilitate payment of old guaranteed credit, only to end up with a new uncollectible account that is not guaranteed.

Finally, complex issues arise if all or a portion of the accounts receivable are secured by collateral. The acquisition agreement should specify which party has the right of repossession during what time periods and whether the other party has any interest or right to the collateral that must be respected by the repossessing party. *See* Financial Accounting Standards Board, *Accounting Standards Current Text General Standards as of June 1, 1989* R20.404 (1989). In addition, the parties should decide whether the repossessing party has any obligation to repossess and possibly to sell the collateral before charging the other party with any deficiency, and whether the repossessing party must act within established time constraints.

See Chapter V, "Financial Statements," of the *Manual on Acquisition Review.* ■

3.9 Inventory

All inventory of the Acquired Companies, whether or not reflected in the Balance Sheet or the Interim Balance Sheet, consists of a quality and quantity usable and salable in the Ordinary Course of Business, except for obsolete items and items of below-standard quality, all of which have been written off or written down to net realizable value in the Balance Sheet or the Interim Balance Sheet or on the accounting records of the Acquired Companies as of the Closing Date, as the case may be. All inventories not written off have been priced at the lower of cost or [market] [net realizable value] on a [last in, first out] [first in, first out] basis. The quantities of each item of inventory (whether raw materials, work-in-process, or finished goods) are not excessive, but are reasonable in the present circumstances of the Acquired Companies.

COMMENT

Inventories may take many forms. Generally, a manufacturing company's inventories can be classified into three broad categories: raw materials, work in process, and finished goods. The Model Stock Purchase Agreement representation covers all three categories and provides that all inventory is useable and saleable in the ordinary course of business. Before agreeing to make this representation, the Sellers should determine whether work in process is actually saleable and whether raw materials are saleable in the ordinary course of business.

The Model Stock Purchase Agreement representation assumes that the audited financial statements and the accompanying audit reports do not comment adversely on the Acquired Companies' inventory procedures. If an independent audit has not been performed, the Buyer may want to add as a condition to its obligations at the closing either a successful physical inventory or the existence of minimum or maximum inventory levels.

In examining the inventory values shown on the Acquired Companies' financial statements, the Buyer should keep the following considerations in mind. Under GAAP, inventories are usually valued at the lower of cost or market value. A critical factor in calculating financial statement income and the balance sheet value of inventories is the assumption of inventory flow used in inventory accounting. Acceptable methods include First-In-First-Out ("FIFO"), Last-In-First-Out ("LIFO"), and average cost. The Buyer should completely understand the reason for any recent changes in the method used by the Acquired Companies—variations between compared periods may call for restating financial statements to aid comparisons.

Under any method of accounting for inventory flow, inventory valuation requires subjective judgments. The Buyer should attempt to determine whether inventory values have been overstated or understated. Overstatement or understatement may occur because, within the boundaries of GAAP, different kinds of costs can be included either in the cost of goods sold or in general administrative and selling expenses, and whether or not such costs are included in the cost of goods sold affects the value of inventory and the amount of income reported. Also, the preparer of the financial statements must make judgements about the realizable value of obsolete items and the point at which goods in inventory become obsolete. Because of such variables involving inventories, the Buyer may want a post-closing purchase price adjustment based on changes in inventory values after a specified period of time, which gives the Buyer a chance to work with the purchased inventories after the sale but prior to the final settlement of accounts. It is also important when the LIFO method is used that the policy for valuing new inventory items be consistently applied.

Whether the Buyer should seek comfort beyond the financial statement representations will depend on the relative importance of the inventories to the Acquired Companies' businesses. The Buyer should carefully review the Acquired Companies' internal records if significant amounts of finished goods are consigned (consigned goods are assets owned by one firm but kept at another location). In this case, the Buyer may want to specify the location of major inventory stocks. Even without significant consigned inventory, the Buyer might consider including in the first draft of the acquisition agreement a representation concerning the location of inventories.

In acquisitions in which purchased assets will be used as collateral, the lender will typically require specific inventory representations from the borrower. If the Buyer will use borrowed funds to pay the purchase price, the Buyer may want to ask the Sellers to make inventory representations similar or equivalent to those expected to be made by the Buyer to its lender. The Buyer should consider the impact on available credit if the Sellers refuse to make satisfactory representations.

Some industries present special concerns when the acquisition agreement includes provisions requiring inventory verification prior to the closing or a post-closing purchase price adjustment. Special methods are used to estimate inventory in industries with significant natural resource inventories (such as gas, oil, and timber), and the Buyer may want the additional comfort of an independent confirmation of inventory values. In service industries, an inventory amounts to a stock of unbilled services or time, and the Buyer may want to modify the inventory representation to provide for a minimum amount of dollars to be realized from inventory as of a specific date.

The representation that inventories are recorded at the lower of cost or market assumes that the Acquired Companies do not have significant operations in nations with high inflation. In severely inflationary economies, nonmonetary inventories are valued at current replacement cost or restated historical cost. Acquisitions involving inventories in such nations will require more specialized inventory representations.

See Chapter V, "Financial Statements," of the *Manual on Acquisition Review*. ■

3.10 No Undisclosed Liabilities

Except as set forth in Part 3.10 of the Disclosure Letter, the Acquired Companies have no liabilities or obligations of any nature (whether known or unknown and whether absolute, accrued, contingent, or otherwise) except for liabilities or obligations reflected or reserved against in the Balance Sheet or the Interim Balance Sheet and current liabilities incurred in the Ordinary Course of Business since the respective dates thereof.

COMMENT

This representation assures the Buyer that it has been informed of all liabilities (including "contingent" liabilities) of the Acquired Companies. The Sellers may seek to add a knowledge qualification to this representation, arguing that they cannot be expected to identify every conceivable contingent liability to which the Acquired Companies may be subject. The Buyer will typically resist the addition of such a qualification, pointing out that the risk of unknown liabilities is more appropriately borne by the Sellers (who presumably have considerable familiarity with the past and current operations of the Acquired Companies) than by the Buyer.

The Sellers may also seek to narrow the scope of this representation by limiting the types of liabilities that must be disclosed. For example, the Sellers may request that the representation extend only to "liabilities of the type required to be reflected as liabilities on a balance sheet prepared in accordance with GAAP." The Buyer will likely object to this request, arguing that the standards for disclosing liabilities on a balance sheet under GAAP are relatively restrictive and that the Buyer needs to assess the potential impact of *all* types of liabilities on the Acquired Companies, regardless of whether such liabilities are sufficiently definite to merit disclosure in the Acquired Companies' financial statements.

Even if the Buyer successfully resists the Sellers' attempts to narrow the scope of this representation, the Buyer should not overestimate the protection that this representation provides. Although the representation extends to "contingent" liabilities (as well as to other types of liabilities that are not required to be shown as liabilities on a balance sheet under GAAP), the representation focuses exclusively on existing liabilities—it does not cover liabilities that may arise in the future from past events or existing circumstances. Indeed, a number of judicial decisions involving business acquisitions have recognized this critical distinction and have construed the term "liability" (or "contingent liability") narrowly. For example, in *Climatrol Indus. v. Fedders Corp.*, 501 N.E.2d 292 (Ill. App. 1986), the court concluded that a company's defective product does not represent a "contingent liability" of the company unless the defective product has actually injured someone. The court stated:

> As of [the date of the closing of the acquisition in question], there was no liability at all for the product liability suits at issue herein, because no injury had occurred. Therefore, these suits are not amongst the "liabilities . . . whether accrued, absolute, contingent or otherwise, which exist[ed] on the Closing Date," which defendant expressly assumed.

Id. at 294.

Other courts have sharply distinguished between "contingencies" and "contingent liabilities":

> A contingent liability is one thing, a contingency the happening of which may bring into existence a liability is another, and a very different thing. In the former case, there is a liability which will become absolute upon the happening of a certain event. In the latter, there is none until the event happens. The difference is simply that which exists between a conditional debt or liability and none at all.

Id. (citations omitted); *see also Godchaux v. Conveying Techniques, Inc.*, 846 F.2d 306 (5th Cir. 1988) (an employer's withdrawal liability under ERISA comes into existence not when the employer's pension plan first develops an unfunded vested liability, but rather when the employer actually withdraws from the pension plan; therefore, there was no breach of a warranty that the employer "did not have any liabilities of any nature, whether accrued, absolute, contingent, or otherwise"); *Grant-Howard Assocs. v. General Housewares Corp.*, 482 N.Y.S.2d 225, 227 (1984) ("An uninjured party simply is not a 'contingent liability' . . . .").

Even though the terms "liability" and "contingent liability" may be narrowly construed, other provisions in the Model Stock Purchase Agreement protect the Buyer against various contingencies that may not actually constitute "contingent liabilities" as of the closing date. For example, the Model Stock Purchase Agreement contains representations that no event has occurred that may result in a future material adverse change in the business of an Acquired Company (see Section 3.12); that no undisclosed event has occurred that may result in a future violation of law by an Acquired Company (see Section 3.14); that the Sellers have no knowledge of any circumstances that may serve as a basis for the commencement of a future lawsuit against an Acquired Company (see Section 3.15); that no undisclosed event has occurred that would constitute a future default under any of the contracts of the Acquired Companies (see Section 3.17); and that the Sellers know of no facts that materially threaten the Acquired Companies' businesses (see Section 3.24). In addition, the Model Stock Purchase Agreement requires the Sellers to indemnify the Buyer against liabilities that may arise in the future from products manufactured by the Acquired Companies prior to the closing date (see Section 10.2(d)).

If the Buyer seeks even broader protection against undisclosed contingencies, the Buyer should consider proposing a definition of the term "liability" that expressly includes not only "contingent" liabilities, but also "unmatured," "unaccrued," "unliquidated," "unasserted," "conditional," "secondary," "potential," and other similar categories of liabilities. The Buyer should also consider expanding the scope of the Sellers' indemnity obligations under Section 10.2 so that the Sellers are obligated to indemnify the Buyer not only against future product liabilities, but also against other categories of liabilities that may arise after the closing date from circumstances existing before the closing date.

See Chapter V, "Financial Statements," of the *Manual on Acquisition Review*. ■

3.11 Taxes

(a) The Acquired Companies have filed or caused to be filed (on a timely basis since __________) all Tax Returns that are or were required to be filed by or with respect to any of them, either separately or as a member of a group of corporations, pursuant to applicable Legal Requirements. Sellers have delivered [or made available] to Buyer copies of, and Part 3.11 of the Disclosure Letter contains a complete and accurate list of, all such Tax Returns [relating to income or franchise taxes] filed since __________. The Acquired Companies have paid, or made provision for the payment of, all Taxes that have or may have become due pursuant to those Tax Returns or otherwise, or pursuant to any assessment received by Sellers or any Acquired Company, except such Taxes, if any, as are listed in Part 3.11 of the Disclosure Letter and are being contested in good faith and as to which adequate reserves (determined in accordance with GAAP) have been provided in the Balance Sheet and the Interim Balance Sheet.

(b) The United States federal and state income Tax Returns of each Acquired Company subject to such Taxes have been audited by the IRS or relevant state tax authorities or are closed by the applicable statute of limitations for all taxable years through _________. Part 3.11 of the Disclosure Letter contains a complete and accurate list of all audits of all such Tax Returns, including a reasonably detailed description of the nature and outcome of each audit. All deficiencies proposed as a result of such audits have been paid, reserved against, settled, or, as described in Part 3.11 of the Disclosure Letter, are being contested in good faith by appropriate proceedings. Part 3.11 of the Disclosure Letter describes all adjustments to the United States federal income Tax Returns filed by any Acquired Company or any group of corporations including any Acquired Company for all taxable years since __________, and the resulting deficiencies proposed by the IRS. Except as described in Part 3.11 of the Disclosure Letter, no Seller or Acquired Company has given or been requested to give waivers or extensions (or is or would be subject to a waiver or extension given by any other Person) of any statute of limitations relating to the payment of Taxes of any Acquired Company or for which any Acquired Company may be liable.

(c) The charges, accruals, and reserves with respect to Taxes on the respective books of each Acquired Company are adequate (determined in accordance with GAAP) and are at least equal to that Acquired Company's liability for Taxes. There exists no proposed tax assessment against any Acquired Company except as disclosed in the Balance Sheet or in Part 3.11 of the Disclosure Letter. No consent to the application of Section 341(f)(2) of the IRC has been filed with respect to any property or assets held, acquired, or to be acquired by any Acquired Company. All Taxes that any Acquired Company is or was required by Legal Requirements to withhold or collect have been duly withheld or collected and, to the extent required, have been paid to the proper Governmental Body or other Person.

(d) All Tax Returns filed by (or that include on a consolidated basis) any Acquired Company are true, correct, and complete. There is no tax sharing agreement that will require any payment by any Acquired Company after the date of this Agreement. [No Acquired Company is, or within the five-year period preceding the Closing Date has been, an "S" corporation.] [During the consistency period (as defined in Section 338(h)(4) of the IRC with respect to the sale of the Shares to Buyer), no Acquired Company or target affiliate (as defined in Section 338(h)(6) of the IRC with respect to the sale of the Shares to Buyer) has sold or will sell any property or assets to Buyer or to any member of the affiliated group (as defined in Section 338(h)(5) of the IRC) that includes Buyer. Part 3.11 of the Disclosure Letter lists all such target affiliates.]

COMMENT

Section 3.11 both seeks disclosure and provides protection against the unknown. The Buyer's counsel, when drafting these representations, should carefully consider the corporate structure of the Acquired Companies' businesses; if the Acquired Companies are included in a larger consolidated return, the representations should be revised to cover all taxes and tax returns of that group (the constituent corporations in a consolidated group have joint and several liability for the taxes of the entire group), and provisions elsewhere in the acquisition agreement should deal with matters such as responsibility for audit adjustments and for filing returns after the closing for periods prior to the closing for the group that includes the Acquired Companies.

The bracketed representation concerning "S" corporation status in paragraph (d) is important if the Buyer's shareholders want to elect such status for the Buyer after the closing—if an Acquired Company has changed from "S" corporation status to "C" corporation status within the last five years, the Buyer may be unable to adopt "S" corporation status. If, however, an Acquired Company has claimed "S" corporation status, the Buyer should seek to verify the validity of that status, both through representations in the acquisition agreement and through due diligence.

See Chapter VI, "Tax Matters," of the *Manual on Acquisition Review.* ■

3.12 No Material Adverse Change

Since the date of the Balance Sheet, there has not been any material adverse change in the business, operations, properties, prospects, assets, or condition of any Acquired Company, and no event has occurred or circumstance exists that may result in such a material adverse change.

COMMENT

In light of the materiality qualification in this representation, the Sellers would prefer to make this representation on behalf of all Acquired Companies as a whole, rather than with respect to each Acquired Company separately. The Buyer, however, will want to know if any Acquired Company has suffered serious recent setbacks so that it can judge the significance of such problems for the entire acquisition. Similarly, if significant lines or segments of an Acquired Company's business are conducted in divisions (rather than subsidiaries), the Buyer may request this representation for one or more of those divisions.

For a discussion of the advisability of including a separate "no material adverse change" condition in the acquisition agreement, see the Commentary to Section 7.1 under the caption "Desirability of Separate 'No Material Adverse Change' Condition." For a discussion of the implications of various methods of drafting a phrase such as "that may result in such a material adverse change" (which appears at the end of Section 3.12), see the Commentary to Section 3 under the caption "Considerations When Drafting 'Adverse Effect' Language in Representations."

In addition to Section 3.12, which deals generally with material adverse changes affecting the Acquired Companies, Section 3.16 covers several specific matters that are considered significant (though not necessarily adverse) events for the Acquired Companies and may, individually or in the aggregate, constitute material adverse changes. Section 3.16 requires disclosure of such events that occurred after the date of the Company's balance sheet but before the signing of the acquisition agreement, and Section 5.3 requires the Sellers to prevent such events from occurring (to the extent it is within their power to do so) after the signing date but before the closing date (for further discussion, see the Commentary to Section 3.16). Together, Sections 3.12 and 3.16 require the Sellers to disclose to the Buyer updated information concerning important developments in the Acquired Companies' businesses after the date of the balance sheet. ■

3.13 Employee Benefits

(a) As used in this Section 3.13, the following terms have the meanings set forth below.

"Company Other Benefit Obligation" means an Other Benefit Obligation owed, adopted, or followed by an Acquired Company or an ERISA Affiliate of an Acquired Company.

"Company Plan" means all Plans of which an Acquired Company or an ERISA Affiliate of an Acquired Company is or was a Plan Sponsor, or to which an Acquired Company or an ERISA Affiliate of an Acquired Company otherwise contributes or has contributed, or in which an Acquired Company or an ERISA Affiliate of an Acquired Company otherwise participates or has participated. All references to Plans are to Company Plans unless the context requires otherwise.

"Company VEBA" means a VEBA whose members include employees of any Acquired Company or any ERISA Affiliate of an Acquired Company.

"ERISA Affiliate" means, with respect to an Acquired Company, any other person that, together with the Company, would be treated as a single employer under IRC § 414.

"Multi-Employer Plan" has the meaning given in ERISA § 3(37)(A).

"Other Benefit Obligations" means all obligations, arrangements, or customary practices, whether or not legally enforceable, to provide benefits, other than salary, as compensation for services rendered, to present or former directors, employees, or agents, other than obligations, arrangements, and practices that are Plans. Other Benefit Obligations include consulting agreements under which the compensation paid does not depend upon the amount of service rendered, sabbatical policies, severance payment policies, and fringe benefits within the meaning of IRC § 132.

"PBGC" means the Pension Benefit Guaranty Corporation, or any successor thereto.

"Pension Plan" has the meaning given in ERISA § 3(2)(A).

"Plan" has the meaning given in ERISA § 3(3).

"Plan Sponsor" has the meaning given in ERISA § 3(16)(B).

"Qualified Plan" means any Plan that meets or purports to meet the requirements of IRC § 401(a).

"Title IV Plans" means all Pension Plans that are subject to Title IV of ERISA, 29 U.S.C. § 1301 et seq., other than Multi-Employer Plans.

"VEBA" means a voluntary employees' beneficiary association under IRC § 501(c)(9).

"Welfare Plan" has the meaning given in ERISA § 3(1).

(b) (i) Part 3.13(i) of the Disclosure Letter contains a complete and accurate list of all Company Plans, Company Other Benefit Obligations, and Company VEBAs, and identifies as such all Company Plans that are (A) defined benefit Pension Plans, (B) Qualified Plans, (C) Title IV Plans, or (D) Multi-Employer Plans.

(ii) Part 3.13(ii) of the Disclosure Letter contains a complete and accurate list of (A) all ERISA Affiliates of each Acquired Company, and (B) all Plans of which any such ERISA Affiliate is or was a Plan Sponsor, in which any such ERISA Affiliate participates or has participated, or to which any such ERISA Affiliate contributes or has contributed.

(iii) Part 3.13(iii) of the Disclosure Letter sets forth, for each Multi-Employer Plan, as of its last valuation date, the amount of potential withdrawal liability of the Acquired Companies and the Acquired Companies' other ERISA Affiliates, calculated according to information made available pursuant to ERISA § 4221(e).

(iv) Part 3.13(iv) of the Disclosure Letter sets forth a calculation of the liability of the Acquired Companies for post-retirement benefits other than pensions, made in accordance with Financial Accounting Statement 106 of the Financial Accounting Standards Board, regardless of whether any Acquired Company is required by this Statement to disclose such information.

(v) Part 3.13(v) of the Disclosure Letter sets forth the financial cost of all obligations owed under any Company Plan or Company Other Benefit Obligation that is not subject to the disclosure and reporting requirements of ERISA.

(c) Sellers have delivered to Buyer, or will deliver to Buyer within ten days of the date of this Agreement:

(i) all documents that set forth the terms of each Company Plan, Company Other Benefit Obligation, or Company VEBA and of any related trust, including (A) all plan descriptions and summary plan descriptions of Company Plans for which Sellers or the Acquired Companies are required to prepare, file, and distribute plan descriptions and summary plan descriptions, and (B) all summaries and descriptions furnished to participants and beneficiaries regarding Company Plans, Company Other Benefit Obligations, and Company VEBAs for which a plan description or summary plan description is not required;

(ii) all personnel, payroll, and employment manuals and policies;

(iii) all collective bargaining agreements pursuant to which contributions have been made or obligations incurred (including both pension and welfare benefits) by the Acquired Companies and the ERISA Affiliates of the Acquired Companies, and all collective bargaining agreements pursuant to which contributions are being made or obligations are owed by such entities;

(iv) a written description of any Company Plan or Company Other Benefit Obligation that is not otherwise in writing;

(v) all registration statements filed with respect to any Company Plan;

(vi) all insurance policies purchased by or to provide benefits under any Company Plan;

(vii) all contracts with third party administrators, actuaries, investment managers, consultants, and other independent contractors that relate to any Company Plan, Company Other Benefit Obligation, or Company VEBA;

(viii) all reports submitted within the four years preceding the date of this Agreement by third party administrators, actuaries, investment managers, consultants, or other independent contractors with respect to any Company Plan, Company Other Benefit Obligation, or Company VEBA;

(ix) all notifications to employees of their rights under ERISA § 601 et seq. and IRC § 4980B;

(x) the Form 5500 filed in each of the most recent three plan years [with respect to each Company Plan], including all schedules thereto and the opinions of independent accountants;

(xi) all notices that were given by any Acquired Company or any ERISA Affiliate of an Acquired Company or any Company Plan to the IRS, the PBGC, or any participant or beneficiary, pursuant to statute, within the four years preceding the date of this Agreement, including notices that are expressly mentioned elsewhere in this Section 3.13;

(xii) all notices that were given by the IRS, the PBGC, or the Department of Labor to any Acquired Company, any ERISA Affiliate of an Acquired Company, or any Company Plan within the four years preceding the date of this Agreement;

(xiii) with respect to Qualified Plans and VEBAs, the most recent determination letter for each Plan of the Acquired Companies that is a Qualified Plan; and

(xiv) with respect to Title IV Plans, the Form PBGC-1 filed for each of the three most recent plan years.

(d) Except as set forth in Part 3.13(vi) of the Disclosure Letter:

(i) The Acquired Companies have performed all of their respective obligations under all Company Plans, Company Other Benefit Obligations, and Company VEBAs. The Acquired Companies have made appropriate entries in their financial records and statements for all obligations and liabilities under such Plans, VEBAs, and Obligations that have accrued but are not due.

(ii) No statement, either written or oral, has been made by any Acquired Company to any Person with regard to any Plan or Other Benefit Obligation that was not in accordance with the Plan or Other Benefit Obligation and that could have an adverse economic consequence to any Acquired Company or to Buyer.

(iii) The Acquired Companies, with respect to all Company Plans, Company Other Benefits Obligations, and Company VEBAs, are, and each Company Plan, Company Other Benefit Obligation, and Company VEBA is, in full compliance with ERISA, the IRC, and other applicable Laws including the provisions of such Laws expressly mentioned in this Section 3.13, and with any applicable collective bargaining agreement.

(A) No transaction prohibited by ERISA § 406 and no "prohibited transaction" under IRC § 4975(c) have occurred with respect to any Company Plan.

(B) No Seller or Acquired Company has any liability to the IRS with respect to any Plan, including any liability imposed by Chapter 43 of the IRC.

(C) No Seller or Acquired Company has any liability to the PBGC with respect to any Plan or has any liability under ERISA § 502 or § 4071.

(D) All filings required by ERISA and the IRC as to each Plan have been timely filed, and all notices and disclosures to participants required by either ERISA or the IRC have been timely provided.

(E) All contributions and payments made or accrued with respect to all Company Plans, Company Other Benefit Obligations, and Company VEBAs are deductible under IRC § 162 or § 404. No amount, or any asset of any Company Plan or Company VEBA, is subject to tax as unrelated business taxable income.

(iv) Each Company Plan can be terminated within thirty days, without payment of any additional contribution or amount and without the vesting or acceleration of any benefits promised by such Plan.

(v) Since ____________, 19__, there has been no establishment or amendment of any Company Plan, Company VEBA, or Company Other Benefit Obligation.

(vi) No event has occurred or circumstance exists that could result in a material increase in premium costs of Company Plans and Company Other Benefit Obligations that are insured, or a material increase in benefit costs of such Plans and Obligations that are self-insured.

(vii) Other than claims for benefits submitted by participants or beneficiaries, no claim against, or legal proceeding involving, any Company Plan, Company Other Benefit Obligation, or Company VEBA is pending or, to Sellers' Knowledge, is Threatened.

(viii) No Company Plan is a stock bonus, pension, or profit-sharing plan within the meaning of IRC § 401(a).

(ix) Each Qualified Plan of each Acquired Company is qualified in form and operation under IRC § 401(a); each trust for each such Plan is exempt from federal income tax under IRC § 501(a). Each Company VEBA is exempt from federal income tax. No event has occurred or circumstance exists that will or could give rise to disqualification or loss of tax-exempt status of any such Plan or trust.

(x) Each Acquired Company and each ERISA Affiliate of an Acquired Company has met the minimum funding standard, and has made all contributions required, under ERISA § 302 and IRC § 402.

(xi) No Company Plan is subject to Title IV of ERISA.

(xii) The Acquired Companies have paid all amounts due to the PBGC pursuant to ERISA § 4007.

(xiii) No Acquired Company or any ERISA Affiliate of an Acquired Company has ceased operations at any facility or has withdrawn from any Title IV Plan in a manner that would subject to any entity or Sellers to liability under ERISA § 4062(e), § 4063, or § 4064.

(xiv) No Acquired Company or any ERISA Affiliate of an Acquired Company has filed a notice of intent to terminate any Plan or has adopted any amendment to treat a Plan as terminated. The PBGC has not instituted proceedings to treat any Company Plan as terminated. No event has occurred or circumstance exists that may constitute grounds under ERISA § 4042 for the termination of, or the appointment of a trustee to administer, any Company Plan.

(xv) No amendment has been made, or is reasonably expected to be made, to any Plan that has required or could require the provision of security under ERISA § 307 or IRC § 401(a)(29).

(xvi) No accumulated funding deficiency, whether or not waived, exists with respect to any Company Plan; no event has occurred or circumstance exists that may result in an accumulated funding deficiency as of the last day of the current plan year of any such Plan.

(xvii) The actuarial report for each Pension Plan of each Acquired Company and each ERISA Affiliate of each Acquired Company fairly presents the financial condition and the results of operations of each such Plan in accordance with GAAP.

(xviii) Since the last valuation date for each Pension Plan of each Acquired Company and each ERISA Affiliate of an Acquired Company, no event has occurred or circumstance exists that would increase the amount of benefits under any such Plan or that would cause the excess of Plan assets over benefit liabilities (as defined in ERISA § 4001) to decrease, or the amount by which benefit liabilities exceed assets to increase.

(xiv) No reportable event (as defined in ERISA § 4043 and in regulations issued thereunder) has occurred.

(xx) No Seller or Acquired Company has Knowledge of any facts or circumstances that may give rise to any liability of any Seller, any Acquired Company, or Buyer to the PBGC under Title IV of ERISA.

(xxi) No Acquired Company or any ERISA Affiliate of an Acquired Company has ever established, maintained, or contributed to or otherwise participated in, or had an obligation to maintain, contribute to, or otherwise participate in, any Multi-Employer Plan.

(xxii) No Acquired Company or any ERISA Affiliate of an Acquired Company has withdrawn from any Multi-Employer Plan with respect to which there is any outstanding liability as of the date of this Agreement. No event has occurred or circumstance exists that presents a risk of the occurrence of any withdrawal from, or the participation, termination, reorganization, or insolvency of, any Multi-Employer Plan that could result in any liability of either any Acquired Company or Buyer to a Multi-Employer Plan.

(xxiii) No Acquired Company or any ERISA Affiliate of an Acquired Company has received notice from any Multi-Employer Plan that it is in reorganization or is insolvent, that increased contributions may be required to avoid a reduction in plan benefits or the imposition of any excise tax, or that such Plan intends to terminate or has terminated.

(xxiv) No Multi-Employer Plan to which any Acquired Company or any ERISA Affiliate of an Acquired Company contributes or has contributed is a party to any pending merger or asset or liability transfer or is subject to any proceeding brought by the PBGC.

(xxv) Except to the extent required under ERISA § 601 et seq. and IRC § 4980B, no Acquired Company provides health or welfare benefits for any retired or former employee or is obligated to provide health or welfare benefits to any active employee following such employee's retirement or other termination of service.

(xxvi) Each Acquired Company has the right to modify and terminate benefits to retirees (other than pensions) with respect to both retired and active employees.

(xxii) Sellers and all Acquired Companies have complied with the provisions of ERISA § 601 et seq. and IRC § 4980B.

(xxviii) No payment that is owed or may become due to any director, officer, employee, or agent of any Acquired Company will be non-deductible to the Acquired Companies or subject to tax under IRC § 280G or § 4999; nor will any Acquired Company be required to "gross up" or otherwise compensate any such person because of the imposition of any excise tax on a payment to such person.

(xxiv) The consummation of the Contemplated Transactions will not result in the payment, vesting, or acceleration of any benefit.

COMMENT

The law and the accounting standards governing employee benefits continue to evolve. Many rules appear in both ERISA and the IRC; for example, the vesting, benefit accrual, and minimum funding rules are set forth in ERISA §§ 203, 204, and 302, and IRC §§ 411(a), 411(b), and 412, and the COBRA continuation of coverage provisions appear in both ERISA § 601 et seq. and IRC § 4980B. The two statutes sometimes use different words to label the same or similar concepts, such as "party in interest" (ERISA § 3(14)) and "disqualified person" (IRC § 4975(e)(2)). Conversely, the two statutes sometimes assign different meanings to a particular word; for example, the definition of "plan" in ERISA § 3(3) differs from the definition in IRC § 4975(e)(1). Some rules are found only in one statute or the other.

The main potential employee benefit liabilities are:

a. minimum funding liability;
b. termination liability for single-employer pension plans;
c. withdrawal liability for multi-employer pension plans;
d. PBGC insurance premium liability;
e. disqualification of a qualified plan;
f. liability for failure to file, disclose or notify;

g. excise taxes; and

h. liability for violations of fiduciary duties.

The first four categories arise from defined benefit pension plans.

Defined Benefit Plans. Defined benefit pension plans promise the employee an annuity starting at some date in accordance with a formula—for example, the annual payment will equal the product of x% multiplied by the number of years of covered employment multiplied by the average annual earnings in the three highest-paid years. Current contributions are based on estimates of items such as the amount of the annuity that will be owed, the rate of return that is expected to be earned on the assets of the plan, and the anticipated rate of participant attrition.

ERISA Affiliate. Generally, related entities, including non-corporate entities, are jointly and severally liable for pension obligations. *See* ERISA §§ 302(c)(11)(B), 4001(b), 4007, 4041(c)(2)(B), 4062(a), 4068(a) & 4001(a)(14); IRC §§ 412(c)(11)(B), 4971(e). The Buyer should determine whether an Acquired Company has a liability arising from a plan established or maintained by a related entity that is not being acquired.

Minimum Funding. The sponsor of a single-employer defined benefit plan must make a minimum contribution every calendar quarter, unless the plan is fully funded. *See* ERISA § 302; IRC § 412. The employer is subject to a lien in certain circumstances if it fails to meet the minimum funding requirements. *See* ERISA §§ 302(a), 302(c)(6)-(7), 4041(b)(1)(D) & 4241; IRC §§ 412(a) & (c)(6)-(7). The level of funding, as determined under the statutes, may differ substantially from the level determined in accordance with GAAP. The Buyer and its actuary should analyze the assumptions on which the funding of the Acquired Companies' plans is based; plans vary considerably in their assumptions regarding matters such as the return that can be earned on plan assets.

Multi-Employer Plan. Nearly identical definitions of this term are in ERISA § 4001(3) and IRC § 414(f). An employer may promise in a collective bargaining agreement to contribute a particular amount to an industry pension plan per hour of covered employment. Even if the employer makes all promised contributions, the plan may be underfunded. An employer that withdraws from a multi-employer plan, either completely or partially, is liable to the plan for its share of unfunded vested benefits. *See* ERISA § 4201 et seq.; 29 U.S.C. § 1381 et seq.; 56 C.F.R. § 12,228. An employer is entitled to obtain from the plan the information necessary to compute its withdrawal liability. *See* ERISA § 4221(e). An employer will have statutory, as well as perhaps contractual, liability if a multi-employer plan terminates or goes into reorganization. *See* ERISA §§ 4041A & 4243.

Title IV Plans. Title IV covers both single-employer plans and multi-employer plans. The PBGC guarantees the payment of nonforfeitable benefits under defined benefit plans that terminate. *See* ERISA §§ 4022 & 4022A. The employer is liable to the PBGC for premiums. *See* ERISA § 4006. An employer that establishes a single-employer plan is liable to the PBGC for amounts paid under such guaranties, *see* ERISA § 4062 et seq., and subject to a lien in favor of the PBGC to secure such amounts, *see* ERISA § 4068.

Qualified Plans. A deferred compensation or retirement income plan that satisfies the requirements of IRC § 401(a) receives favorable tax treatment in several respects:

a. contributions to the plan are deductible when made;
b. the employee for whose benefit the contribution is made does not have income until he receives a distribution from the plan; and
c. the trust that holds plan assets does not pay tax on income earned by the investment of those assets.

These rules defer, often for decades, the income tax that the employee would otherwise owe on sums contributed for pensions and on the earnings from the investment of those contributions. At the same time, the employer is permitted an immediate deduction. Ordinarily, a plan will obtain a determination letter from the IRS that the terms of the plan qualify under § 401(a). Plans are tested periodically for compliance with various IRC rules. *See, e.g.,* IRC §§ 401(a)(4) & (26), 410(b) & 416. The status of either the Buyer's or an Acquired Company's plan may change as a result of the acquisition.

Requirements to Report, Disclose, and Notify. Both ERISA and the IRC impose requirements that various parties file and distribute reports and give various notices, and both impose sanctions for failure to meet these requirements. *See, e.g.,* ERISA §§ 101 et seq., 502(c)(2) & 4071; IRC §§ 6047(d), 6058(a), 6652 & 6692.

Excise Taxes. The IRC imposes excise taxes for (i) failure to meet funding standards, *see* IRC § 4971; (ii) engaging in prohibited transactions, *see* IRC 4975; (iii) making non-deductible contributions to a plan, *see* IRC § 4972; (iv) failing to distribute excess in a timely manner, *see* IRC § 4979; and (v) receiving reversions of excess assets, *see* IRC § 4980. The IRC also imposes an excise tax on certain parachute payments. *See* IRC §§ 280G & 4999.

The Secretary of Labor may assess a civil penalty against a party in interest that engages in a prohibited transaction. *See* ERISA § 502(i). There are also penalties for failing to provide continuation of coverage in accordance with ERISA § 601 et seq. and IRC § 4980B.

Other Benefit Obligations. This term covers arrangements with persons who are not employees (such as directors) that are not legally binding but the Buyer may feel compelled to continue or that are not plans, such as a practice of entering into consulting agreements with retired directors. *See* 29 C.F.R. § 2510.3-1. The Acquired Companies' arrangements with present and former executives may not have been handled by the department that deals with other employee relationships, and may therefore require special effort for the Buyer to discover.

See Chapter XI, "Labor and Employment Matters," of the *Manual on Acquisition Review.* ■

3.14 Compliance with Legal Requirements; Governmental Authorizations

(a) Except as set forth in Part 3.14 of the Disclosure Letter:

(i) each Acquired Company is, and at all times since _________, 19__ has been, in full compliance with each Legal Requirement that is or was applicable to it or to the conduct or operation of its business or the ownership or use of any of its assets;

(ii) no event has occurred or circumstance exists that (with or without notice or lapse of time) (A) may constitute or result in a violation by any Acquired Company of, or a failure on the part of any Acquired Company to comply with, any Legal Requirement, or (B) may give rise to any obligation on the part of any Acquired Company to undertake, or to bear all or any portion of the cost of, any remedial action of any nature; and

(iii) no Acquired Company has received, at any time since _______, 19__, any notice or other communication (whether oral or written) from any Governmental Body or any other Person regarding (A) any actual, alleged, possible, or potential violation of, or failure to comply with, any Legal Requirement, or (B) any actual, alleged, possible, or potential obligation on the part of any Acquired Company to undertake, or to bear all or any portion of the cost of, any remedial action of any nature.

(b) Part 3.14 of the Disclosure Letter contains a complete and accurate list of each Governmental Authorization that is held by any Acquired Company or that otherwise relates to the business of, or to any of the assets owned or used by, any Acquired Company. Each Governmental Authorization listed or required to be listed in Part 3.14 of the Disclosure Letter is valid and in full force and effect. Except as set forth in Part 3.14 of the Disclosure Letter:

(i) each Acquired Company is, and at all times since ______, 19__ has been, in full compliance with all of the terms and requirements of each Governmental Authorization identified or required to be identified in Part 3.14 of the Disclosure Letter;

(ii) no event has occurred or circumstance exists that may (with or without notice or lapse of time) (A) constitute or result directly or indirectly in a violation of or a failure to comply with any term or requirement of any Governmental Authorization listed or required to be listed in Part 3.14 of the Disclosure Letter, or (B) result directly or indirectly in the revocation, withdrawal, suspension, cancellation, or termination of, or any modification to, any Governmental Authorization listed or required to be listed in Part 3.14 of the Disclosure Letter;

(iii) no Acquired Company has received, at any time since ________, 19__, any notice or other communication (whether oral or written) from any Governmental Body or any other Person regarding (A) any actual, alleged, possible, or potential violation of or failure to comply with any term or requirement of any Governmental Authorization, or (B) any actual, proposed, possible, or potential revocation, withdrawal, suspension, cancellation, termination of, or modification to any Governmental Authorization; and

(iv) all applications required to have been filed for the renewal of the Governmental Authorizations listed or required to be listed in Part 3.14 of the Disclosure Letter have been duly filed on a timely basis with the appropriate Governmental Bodies, and all other filings required to have been made with respect to such Governmental Authorizations have been duly made on a timely basis with the appropriate Governmental Bodies.

The Governmental Authorizations listed in Part 3.14 of the Disclosure Letter collectively constitute all of the Governmental Authorizations necessary to permit the Acquired Companies to lawfully conduct and operate their businesses in the manner they currently conduct and operate such businesses and to permit the Acquired Companies to own and use their assets in the manner in which they currently own and use such assets.

COMMENT

Section 3.14(a) contains the Sellers' "compliance with laws" representation. This representation requires disclosure of past, current, and potential violations of laws and governmental regulations by the Acquired Companies.

Although the scope of this representation is relatively broad, it does not address:

- violations of the terms of governmental licenses or permits held by the Acquired Companies (see Section 3.14(b));
- violations of judicial or other orders applicable to the Acquired Companies (see Section 3.15(c));
- contractual violations by the Acquired Companies (see Section 3.17(b)); or
- violations of laws and other requirements that would be triggered by the acquisition (see Section 3.2(b)).

Other representations in the Model Stock Purchase Agreement address the Acquired Companies' compliance with specific legal requirements—see, for example, Sections 3.11 (tax laws), 3.13 (ERISA), 3.19 (environmental laws), and 3.21 (labor laws).

The Sellers' "compliance with laws" representation focuses on four overlapping categories of violations of legal requirements:

1. past violations (clause (i));
2. pending violations (clause (i));
3. potential or "unmatured" violations (clause (ii)); and
4. violations asserted by governmental authorities and other parties (clause (iii)).

The Sellers may object to the provision in clause (i) of Section 3.14(a) that requires disclosure of past violations, arguing that the Buyer should not be concerned about historical violations that have been cured and are no longer pending. The Buyer may respond by pointing out that it has a legitimate concern that the Acquired Companies' operations have not been based on and do not entail a pattern of legal violations. In addition, without this provision, the Sellers may be able to circumvent the representation by radically altering the Acquired Companies' operations immediately prior to the signing and closing dates in order to bring the Acquired Companies into temporary compliance with applicable legal requirements. The parties may compromise in the selection of the date that marks the beginning of the period with respect to which disclosure of past violations is required.

In some acquisition agreements, the phrase "since ___, 19_" (which appears in both clause (i) and clause (iii) of Section 3.14(a)) is replaced with the phrase "during the ___-year period prior to the date of this Agreement" (or a similar phrase). For an explanation of why the use of this alternative language may be disadvantageous to the Buyer, see the Commentary to Section 3 (under the caption "Considerations When Drafting Representations Incorporating Specific Time Periods").

For a discussion of the significance of the phrase "with or without notice or lapse of time" (which appears in clause (ii) of Section 3.14(a)), see the fifth paragraph of the Commentary to Section 3.2.

Although clause (iii) of Section 3.14(a) (which requires disclosure of notices received from governmental authorities and third parties concerning actual and potential violations) overlaps to some extent with clauses (i) and (ii), clause (iii) is not redundant. Clause (iii) requires disclosure of violations that have been asserted by other parties. The Sellers are required to disclose such asserted violations pursuant to clause (iii) even if there is some uncertainty or dispute over whether the asserted violations have actually been committed.

The references in clauses (ii) and (iii) of Section 3.14(a) to "remedial action" are included because, under some statutory and regulatory provisions, an Acquired Company may become subject to significant monetary or other obligations without necessarily having committed a "violation" of the provision in question.

The parties should recognize that, if information regarding an actual or potential legal violation is included in the Sellers' disclosure letter, this information may be discoverable by adverse parties in the course of litigation involving the Acquired Companies. Accordingly, it is important to use extreme care in preparing the descriptions included in part 3.14 of the Disclosure Letter (see the seventh paragraph of the Commentary to Section 3.2).

The representation in Section 3.14(b) relating to governmental licenses and permits of the Acquired Companies is crucial in highly regulated industries. In these industries, availability and transferability of licenses and permits often dramatically affect the viability of the acquisition. A critical portion of the representation is the Sellers' affirmation that the Acquired Companies have all of the licenses and permits necessary for the conduct of their businesses. Together with the representation concerning the sufficiency of the Acquired Companies' assets (see Section 3.7), this representation gives the Buyer some comfort that all of the essential elements of the businesses will be both present and operable after the closing.

See Chapters IX, "Environmental Laws," and XIII, "Antitrust Laws," of the *Manual on Acquisition Review.* ■

3.15 Legal Proceedings; Orders

(a) Except as set forth in Part 3.15 of the Disclosure Letter, there is no pending Proceeding:

(i) that has been commenced by or against any Acquired Company or that otherwise relates to or may affect the business of, or any of the assets owned or used by, any Acquired Company; or

(ii) that challenges, or that may have the effect of preventing, delaying, making illegal, or otherwise interfering with, any of the Contemplated Transactions.

To the Knowledge of Sellers and the Acquired Companies, (1) no such Proceeding has been Threatened, and (2) no event has occurred or circumstance exists that may give rise to or serve as a basis for the commencement of any such Proceeding. Sellers have delivered to Buyer copies of all pleadings, correspondence, and other documents relating to each Proceeding listed in Part 3.15 of the Disclosure Letter. The Proceedings listed in Part 3.15 of the Disclosure Letter will not have a material adverse effect on the business, operations, assets, condition, or prospects of any Acquired Company.

(b) Except as set forth in Part 3.15 of the Disclosure Letter:

(i) there is no Order to which any of the Acquired Companies, or any of the assets owned or used by any Acquired Company, is subject;

(ii) neither Seller is subject to any Order that relates to the business of, or any of the assets owned or used by, any Acquired Company; and

(iii) [to the Knowledge of Sellers and the Acquired Companies,] no officer, director, agent, or employee of any Acquired Company is subject to any Order that prohibits such officer, director, agent, or employee from engaging in or continuing any conduct, activity, or practice relating to the business of any Acquired Company.

(c) Except as set forth in Part 3.15 of the Disclosure Letter:

(i) each Acquired Company is, and at all times since ______, 19__ has been, in full compliance with all of the terms and requirements of each Order to which it, or any of the assets owned or used by it, is or has been subject;

(ii) no event has occurred or circumstance exists that may constitute or result in (with or without notice or lapse of time) a violation of or failure to comply with any term or requirement of any Order to which any Acquired Company, or any of the assets owned or used by any Acquired Company, is subject; and

(iii) no Acquired Company has received, at any time since __________, 19__, any notice or other communication (whether oral or written) from any Governmental Body or any other Person regarding any actual, alleged, possible, or potential violation of, or failure to comply with, any term or requirement of any Order to which any Acquired Company, or any of the assets owned or used by any Acquired Company, is or has been subject.

COMMENT

Section 3.15(a) contains the Sellers' representations concerning pending and potential lawsuits and other legal proceedings that may affect the Acquired Companies or the consummation of the acquisition. The Sellers may seek to limit the scope of these representations in several respects. For example, the Sellers may point out that the representations in Section 3.15(a) are so broad that they require the Sellers to disclose an acquisition-related lawsuit in which the *Buyer* is the only named defendant. The Sellers may request that these representations be limited to legal proceedings in which the Sellers or the Acquired Companies are actually named as parties or are otherwise directly involved. In making this request, the Sellers may remind the Buyer that they are not proposing to modify the Buyer's ability to terminate the acquisition under Section 7.5, which provides the Buyer with a "walk right" in the event of certain lawsuits against the Buyer.

The Sellers may also point out that the last sentence of Section 3.15(a) effectively requires the Sellers to bear the litigation risks associated with each of the legal proceedings disclosed by the Sellers in their disclosure letter, including routine lawsuits brought against the Acquired Companies in the normal course of their operations. The Sellers may insist that the parties determine, on a case-by-case basis, which of the disclosed proceedings should remain the Sellers' responsibility and which should become the Buyer's responsibility following the closing.

The Buyer should carefully evaluate each disclosed proceeding to determine the probability of an adverse determination and the magnitude of the potential damages. The Buyer should examine both the information provided in the Disclosure Letter and the Company's financial statements and accompanying notes, as well as attorneys' responses to auditors' requests for information. However, if the Buyer reviews privileged materials relating to legal proceedings in which the Acquired Companies are involved, there may be a waiver of the attorney-client privilege (see the fifth paragraph of the Commentary to Section 5.1). For each proceeding, the Buyer should determine whether the potential liability justifies a holdback of a portion of the purchase price or whether indemnification is sufficient. Finally, the Buyer and the Sellers must agree on the manner in which all such proceedings will be conducted up to and after the closing (issues such as who will designate lead counsel and who is empowered to effect a settlement must be resolved).

Section 3.15(b) contains the Sellers' representation concerning the existence of judicial and other orders affecting the operations of the Acquired Companies, and Section 3.15(c) focuses on violations of those orders. Although the representation in Section 3.15(c) is relatively broad, it does not address:

- violations of laws or other legal requirements of general application (see Section 3.14(a));
- violations of the terms of governmental licenses or permits held by the Acquired Companies (see Section 3.14(b));
- contractual violations by the Acquired Companies (see Section 3.17(b)); or
- violations of judicial or other orders that would be triggered by the acquisition (see Section 3.2(b)).

The representation in Section 3.15(c) focuses on four overlapping categories of violations of judicial and other orders:

1. past violations (clause (i));
2. pending violations (clause (i));
3. potential or "unmatured" violations (clause (ii)); and
4. violations asserted by governmental authorities and other parties (clause (iii)).

The Sellers may object to the provision in clause (i) of Section 3.15(c) that requires disclosure of past violations, arguing that the Buyer should not be concerned about historical violations that have been cured and are no longer pending. The Buyer may respond by pointing out that it has a legitimate concern that the Acquired Companies' operations have not been based on and do not entail a pattern of legal violation that the Buyer will be unwilling to continue. In addition, without this provision, the Sellers may be able to circumvent the representation by radically altering the Acquired Companies' operations immediately prior to the signing and closing dates in order to bring the Acquired Companies into temporary compliance with applicable orders. The parties may compromise on this point by selecting a relatively recent date to mark the beginning of the period with respect to which disclosure of past violations is required.

In some acquisition agreements, the phrase "since ____19_" (which appears in both clause (i) and clause (iii) of Section 3.15(c)) is replaced with the phrase "during the ____-year period prior to the date of this Agreement" (or a similar phrase). For an explanation of why the use of this alternative language may be disadvantageous to the Buyer, see the Commentary to Section 3 (under the caption "Considerations When Drafting Representations Incorporating Specific Time Periods").

For a discussion of the significance of the phrase "with or without notice or lapse of time" (which appears in clause (ii) of Section 3.15(c)), see the fifth paragraph of the Commentary to Section 3.2.

Although clause (iii) of Section 3.15(c) (which requires disclosure of notices received from governmental authorities and third parties concerning actual and potential violations) overlaps to some extent with clauses (i) and (ii), clause (iii) is not redundant. Clause (iii) requires disclosure of violations that have been asserted by other parties. The Sellers are required to disclose such asserted violations pursuant to clause (iii) even if there is some uncertainty or dispute over whether the asserted violations have actually been committed.

The parties should recognize that, if information regarding an actual or potential violation of a court order is included in the Sellers' disclosure letter, this information may be discoverable by adverse parties in the course of litigation involving the Acquired Companies. Accordingly, it is important to use extreme care in preparing the descriptions included in part 3.15 of the Disclosure Letter (see the seventh paragraph of the Commentary to Section 3.2).

See Chapter VII, "Litigation," of the *Manual on Acquisition Review.* ■

3.16 Absence of Certain Changes and Events

Except as set forth in Part 3.16 of the Disclosure Letter, since the date of the Balance Sheet, the Acquired Companies have conducted their businesses only in the Ordinary Course of Business and there has not been any:

(a) change in any Acquired Company's authorized or issued capital stock; grant of any stock option or right to purchase shares of capital stock of any Acquired Company; issuance of any security convertible into such capital stock; grant of any registration rights; purchase, redemption, retirement, or other acquisition by any Acquired Company of any shares of any such capital stock; or declaration or payment of any dividend or other distribution or payment in respect of shares of capital stock;

(b) amendment to the Organizational Documents of any Acquired Company;

(c) payment or increase by any Acquired Company of any bonuses, salaries, or other compensation to any stockholder, director, officer, or (except in the Ordinary Course of Business) employee or entry into any employment, severance, or similar Contract with any director, officer, or employee;

(d) adoption of, or increase in the payments to or benefits under, any profit sharing, bonus, deferred compensation, savings, insurance, pension, retirement, or other employee benefit plan for or with any employees of any Acquired Company;

(e) damage to or destruction or loss of any asset or property of any Acquired Company, whether or not covered by insurance, materially and adversely affecting the properties, assets, business, financial condition, or prospects of the Acquired Companies, taken as a whole;

(f) entry into, termination of, or receipt of notice of termination of (i) any license, distributorship, dealer, sales representative, joint venture, credit, or similar agreement, or (ii) any Contract or transaction involving a total remaining commitment by or to any Acquired Company of at least $__________;

(g) sale (other than sales of inventory in the Ordinary Course of Business), lease, or other disposition of any asset or property of any Acquired Company or mortgage, pledge, or imposition of any lien or other encumbrance on any material asset or property of any Acquired Company, including the sale, lease, or other disposition of any of the Intellectual Property Assets;

(h) cancellation or waiver of any claims or rights with alue to any Acquired Company in excess of $__________;

(i) material change in the accounting methods used by any Acquired Company; or

(j) agreement, whether oral or written, by any Acquired Company to do any of the foregoing.

COMMENT

This representation seeks information about actions taken by the Acquired Companies or other events affecting the Acquired Companies since the date of the most current financial statements or the most recent fiscal year of the Company, because such matters may make those financial statements misleading. For example, if employee benefits have been significantly increased, the future cost of such benefits will be greater than is reflected in the financial statements. In addition, this provision requires disclosure of actions taken by an Acquired Company in anticipation of the acquisition.

Most of the subjects dealt with in this representation are also covered by other representations. For example, Section 3.13 contains detailed representations concerning employee benefit plans; Section 3.16(d) focuses on recent changes to such plans, which the Buyer should examine in light of the financial statements. For a discussion of the relationship between the representations in Sections 3.12 and 3.16, see the Commentary to Section 3.12.

In addition to the disclosure function described above, this representation, along with Sections 5.2 and 5.3, serves another purpose. Section 5.3 provides that the Sellers will not, without the prior consent of the Buyer, take any action of the nature described in Section 3.16 during the period between the date of signing the acquisition agreement and the closing. Section 5.2 is a general covenant by the Sellers to operate the Acquired Companies' businesses between those dates only in the ordinary course; Section 5.3 identifies the specific matters covered by Section 3.16 as out of the ordinary course of business.

The date left blank in the first sentence of Section 3.16 should be either the date of the Balance Sheet referred to in Section 3.4 or the date of fiscal year end immediately preceding commencement of the negotiations leading to the acquisition.

Finally, in addition to the matters covered by this representation, which usually are important to the Buyer, there may be other specific matters that pose special risks to the Buyer, and the Buyer may want to include those matters in this representation. ■

3.17 CONTRACTS; NO DEFAULTS

(a) Part 3.17(a) of the Disclosure Letter contains a complete and accurate list, and Sellers have delivered to Buyer true and complete copies, of:

(i) each Applicable Contract that involves performance of services or delivery of goods or materials by one or more Acquired Companies of an amount or value in excess of $____________;

(ii) each Applicable Contract that involves performance of services or delivery of goods or materials to one or more Acquired Companies of an amount or value in excess of $____________;

(iii) each Applicable Contract that was not entered into in the Ordinary Course of Business and that involves expenditures or receipts of one or more Acquired Companies in excess of $____________;

(iv) each lease, rental or occupancy agreement, license, installment and conditional sale agreement, and other Applicable Contract affecting the ownership of, leasing of, title to, use of, or any leasehold or other interest in, any real or personal property (except personal property leases and installment and conditional sales agreements having a value per item or aggregate payments of less than $____________ and with terms of less than one year);

(v) each licensing agreement or other Applicable Contract with respect to patents, trademarks, copyrights, or other intellectual property, including agreements with current or former employees, consultants, or contractors regarding the appropriation or the non-disclosure of any of the Intellectual Property Assets;

(vi) each collective bargaining agreement and other Applicable Contract to or with any labor union or other employee representative of a group of employees;

(vii) each joint venture, partnership, and other Applicable Contract (however named) involving a sharing of profits, losses, costs, or liabilities by any Acquired Company with any other Person;

(viii) each Applicable Contract containing covenants that in any way purport to restrict the business activity of any Acquired Company or any Affiliate of an Acquired Company or limit the freedom of any Acquired Company or any Affiliate of an Acquired Company to engage in any line of business or to compete with any Person;

(ix) each Applicable Contract providing for payments to or by any Person based on sales, purchases, or profits, other than direct payments for goods;

(x) each power of attorney that is currently effective and outstanding;

(xi) each Applicable Contract entered into other than in the Ordinary Course of Business that contains or provides for an express undertaking by any Acquired Company to be responsible for consequential damages;

(xii) each Applicable Contract for capital expenditures in excess of $________________;

(xiii) each written warranty, guaranty, and or other similar undertaking with respect to contractual performance extended by any Acquired Company other than in the Ordinary Course of Business; and

(xiv) each amendment, supplement, and modification (whether oral or written) in respect of any of the foregoing.

Part 3.17(a) of the Disclosure Letter sets forth reasonably complete details concerning such Contracts, including the parties to the Contracts, the amount of the remaining commitment of the Acquired Companies under the Contracts, and the Acquired Companies' office where details relating to the Contracts are located.

(b) Except as set forth in Part 3.17(b) of the Disclosure Letter:

(i) neither Seller (and no Related Person of either Seller) has or may acquire any rights under, and neither Seller has or may become subject to any obligation or liability under, any Contract that relates to the business of, or any of the assets owned or used by, any Acquired Company; and

(ii) [to the Knowledge of Sellers and the Acquired Companies,] no officer, director, agent, employee, consultant, or contractor of any Acquired Company is bound by any Contract that purports to limit the ability of such officer, director, agent, employee, consultant, or contractor to (A) engage in or continue any conduct, activity, or practice relating to the business of any Acquired Company, or (B) assign to any Acquired Company or to any other Person any rights to any invention, improvement, or discovery.

(c) Except as set forth in Part 3.17(c) of the Disclosure Letter, each Contract identified or required to be identified in Part 3.17(a) of the Disclosure Letter is in full force and effect and is valid and enforceable in accordance with its terms.

(d) Except as set forth in Part 3.17(d) of the Disclosure Letter:

(i) each Acquired Company is, and at all times since ______, 19__ has been, in full compliance with all applicable terms and requirements of each Contract under which such Acquired Company has or had any obligation or liability or by which such Acquired Company or any of the assets owned or used by such Acquired Company is or was bound;

(ii) each other Person that has or had any obligation or liability under any Contract under which an Acquired Company has or had any rights is, and at all times since __________, 19__ has been, in full compliance with all applicable terms and requirements of such Contract;

(iii) no event has occurred or circumstance exists that (with or without notice or lapse of time) may contravene, conflict with, or result in a violation or breach of, or give any Acquired Company or other Person the right to declare a default or exercise any remedy under, or to accelerate the maturity or performance of, or to cancel, terminate, or modify, any Applicable Contract; and

(iv) no Acquired Company has given to or received from any other Person, at any time since __________, 19__, any notice or other communication (whether oral or written) regarding any actual, alleged, possible, or potential violation or breach of, or default under, any Contract.

(e) There are no renegotiations of, attempts to renegotiate, or outstanding rights to renegotiate any material amounts paid or payable to any Acquired Company under current or completed Contracts with any Person and [, to the Knowledge of Sellers and the Acquired Companies,] no such Person has made written demand for such renegotiation.

(f) The Contracts relating to the sale, design, manufacture, or provision of products or services by the Acquired Companies have been entered into in the Ordinary Course of Business and have been entered into without the commission of any act alone or in concert with any other Person, or any consideration having been paid or promised, that is or would be in violation of any Legal Requirement.

COMMENT

Section 3.17 requires the Sellers to provide a complete list of the Acquired Companies' contracts that meet specified criteria and to advise the Buyer of any pending, asserted, or potential default under these contracts. Representations concerning such contracts are especially important when contracts are a major asset of the Acquired Companies. For examples of the types of contracts that may fall within the broad scope of the definition of "Applicable Contract," see the second-to-last and third-to-last paragraphs of the Commentary to Section 3.2.

This representation does not address whether any listed contract is void or subject to termination at the option of a third party upon consummation of the acquisition—that issue is covered by Section 3.2(b). Rather, Section 3.17 relates only to existing or pending defaults resulting from the conduct of the Acquired Companies' businesses.

For a discussion of the significance of the phrase "with or without notice or lapse of time" (which appears in clause (iii) of Section 3.17(d)), see the fifth paragraph of the Commentary to Section 3.2.

The Buyer may choose to require the Sellers to list only contracts that are "material" to the Acquired Companies' businesses, were incurred other than in the ordinary course of the businesses, or are void or subject to termination at the option of a third party upon a change in control. If the Buyer uses this alternative, it is important to provide, within the text of the representation itself, a definition of "material." Typically, a definition of materiality is keyed to a threshold dollar amount relating to the Acquired Companies' remaining commitment or liability under each contract.

See Chapter III, "Contracts," of the *Manual on Acquisition Review*. ■

3.18 Insurance

(a) Sellers have delivered to Buyer:

(i) true and complete copies of all policies of insurance to which any Acquired Company is a party or under which any Acquired Company, or any director of any Acquired Company, is or has been covered at any time within the _____ years preceding the date of this Agreement;

(ii) true and complete copies of all pending applications for policies of insurance; and

(iii) any statement by the auditor of any Acquired Company's financial statements with regard to the adequacy of such entity's coverage or of the reserves for claims.

(b) Part 3.18(b) of the Disclosure Letter describes:

(i) any self-insurance arrangement by or affecting any Acquired Company, including any reserves established thereunder;

(ii) any contract or arrangement, other than a policy of insurance, for the transfer or sharing of any risk by any Acquired Company; and

(iii) all obligations of the Acquired Companies to third parties with respect to insurance (including such obligations under leases and service agreements) and identifies the policy under which such coverage is provided.

(c) Part 3.18(c) of the Disclosure Letter sets forth, by year, for the current policy year and each of the _____ preceding policy years:

(i) a summary of the loss experience under each policy;

(ii) a statement describing each claim under an insurance policy for an amount in excess of $_____, which sets forth:

(A) the name of the claimant;

(B) a description of the policy by insurer, type of insurance, and period of coverage; and

(C) the amount and a brief description of the claim; and

(iii) a statement describing the loss experience for all claims that were self-insured, including the number and aggregate cost of such claims.

(d) Except as set forth on Part 3.18(d) of the Disclosure Letter:

(i) All policies to which any Acquired Company is a party or that provide coverage to either Seller, any Acquired Company, or any director or officer of an Acquired Company:

(A) are valid, outstanding, and enforceable;

(B) are issued by an insurer that is financially sound and reputable;

(C) taken together, provide adequate insurance coverage for the assets and the operations of the Acquired Companies [for all risks normally insured against by a Person carrying on the same business or businesses as the Acquired Companies] [for all risks to which the Acquired Companies are normally exposed];

(D) are sufficient for compliance with all Legal Requirements and Contracts to which any Acquired Company is a party or by which any of them is bound;

(E) will continue in full force and effect following the consummation of the Contemplated Transactions; and

(F) do not provide for any retrospective premium adjustment or other experienced-based liability on the part of any Acquired Company.

(ii) No Seller or Acquired Company has received (A) any refusal of coverage or any notice that a defense will be afforded with reservation of rights, or (B) any notice of cancellation or any other indication that any insurance policy is no longer in full force or effect or will not be renewed or that the issuer of any policy is not willing or able to perform its obligations thereunder.

(iii) The Acquired Companies have paid all premiums due, and have otherwise performed all of their respective obligations, under each policy to which any Acquired Company is a party or that provides coverage to any Acquired Company or director thereof.

(iv) The Acquired Companies have given notice to the insurer of all claims that may be insured thereby.

COMMENT

This representation seeks information and assurances regarding the adequacy of the Acquired Companies' insurance coverage and their exposure to uninsured risks. The Buyer should examine the present and prospective cost of the Acquired Companies' insurance, the availability of continued coverage following the acquisition, and whatever insight that the loss runs or claims history may give on matters such as the Acquired Companies' quality control and safety programs. In addition to traditional property and casualty insurance policies, many corporations have large self-insured retentions and complicated retrospective premium programs and may participate in captive insurance company programs. The Buyer needs to understand these alternative risk transfer mechanisms in evaluating the insurance program of the Acquired Companies.

The Buyer may want to continue some or all of the Acquired Companies' existing policies, especially for types of coverages that are difficult or expensive to obtain, such as product liability insurance. If the Buyer wants to continue the Acquired Companies' insurance policies, it should verify that the policies are issued to the Acquired Companies. If the Sellers, rather than the Acquired Companies, are the owners of the policies, the assignment of such policies will require the written consent of the insurer.

Additional provisions may be needed if the Acquired Companies' businesses are covered under policies that also insure other businesses of the Sellers. To the extent that the Acquired Companies have significant exposure to uninsured risks, the parties may allocate such risks in the acquisition agreement.

See Chapter VIII, "Liability and Property Insurance," of the *Manual on Acquisition Review*. ■

3.19 Environmental Matters

Except as set forth in part 3.19 of the disclosure letter:

(a) Each Acquired Company is, and at all times has been, in full compliance with, and has not been and is not in violation of or liable under, any Environmental Law. No Seller or Acquired Company has any basis to expect, nor has any of them or any other Person for whose conduct they are or may be held to be responsible received, any actual or Threatened order, notice, or other communication from (i) any Governmental Body or private citizen acting in the public interest, or (ii) the current or prior owner or operator of any Facilities, of any actual or potential violation or failure to comply with any Environmental Law, or of any actual or Threatened obligation to undertake or bear the cost of any Environmental, Health, and Safety Liabilities with respect to any of the Facilities or any other properties or assets (whether real, personal, or mixed) in which Sellers or any Acquired

Company has had an interest, or with respect to any property or Facility at or to which Hazardous Materials were generated, manufactured, refined, transferred, imported, used, or processed by Sellers, any Acquired Company, or any other Person for whose conduct they are or may be held responsible, or from which Hazardous Materials have been transported, treated, stored, handled, transferred, disposed, recycled, or received.

COMMENT

Although the general representations in Sections 3.14 and 3.15 can incorporate environmental issues, representations concerning compliance with environmental laws are often drafted as a separate section because environmental representations are negotiated separately and the risks and costs of failing to comply with environmental laws can be tremendous. Specific representations concerning environmental issues help the Buyer define or confirm the value of the property being acquired and, together with indemnification and other provisions, offer some protection against the potentially open-ended nature of these liabilities, some of which may not be manifest upon inspection of the property. When the Buyer is financing the acquisition with borrowed funds, secured lenders to the Buyer will have their own concerns.

In addition, the Buyer likely will have to make important determinations of nonapplicability of certain environmental laws. For example, the Buyer may want to confirm that federal or state laws do not require environmental impact assessments of new projects (or that such assessments have been completed) or that state and federal laws relating to wetlands do not apply to the Acquired Companies. An example of a representation that addresses the latter issue is as follows:

> The Facilities do not contain any wetlands, as defined in the Clean Water Act and regulations promulgated thereunder, 33 C.F.R. § 328.3, or similar state or local laws, or other especially sensitive or protected areas or species of flora or fauna. ■

(b) There are no pending or, to the Knowledge of Sellers and the Acquired Companies, Threatened claims, Encumbrances, or other restrictions of any nature, resulting from any Environmental, Health, and Safety Liabilities or arising under or pursuant to any Environmental Law, with respect to or affecting any of the Facilities or any other properties and assets (whether real, personal, or mixed) in which Sellers or any Acquired Company has or had an interest.

COMMENT

The Sellers may want to add a materiality qualification to this representation. Generally, the Buyer will want these provisions to require disclosure of all matters, without such a qualification. Among other reasons, the Buyer may be or become a public company with a responsibility to make environmental disclosures that will require its understanding of all pending and threatened matters. For example, SEC Regulation S-K, Item 103 requires disclosure of a pending administrative or judicial proceeding, or one contemplated by the government, arising under environmental laws and to which the registrant or its subsidiary is a party, or to which any of their property is subject, if "such proceeding involves potential monetary sanctions, unless the registrant reasonably believes that such proceeding will result in no monetary sanctions, or in monetary sanctions, exclusive of interest and costs, of less than $100,000." Regulation S-K, Item 103, Instruction 5, at 3(c), 17 C.F.R. § 229.103 (1993). Obviously, the registrant must have the information necessary to make such an assessment, and the Buyer will want to be aware of these issues prior to the closing. ■

(c) No Seller or Acquired Company has [Knowledge of] any basis to expect, nor has any of them or any other Person for whose conduct they are or may be held responsible, received, any citation, directive, inquiry, notice, Order, summons, warning, or other communication that relates to Hazardous Activity, Hazardous Materials, or any alleged, actual, or potential violation or failure to comply with any Environmental Law, or of any alleged, actual, or potential obligation to undertake or bear the cost of any Environmental, Health, and Safety Liabilities with respect to any of the Facilities or any other properties or assets (whether real, personal, or mixed) in which Sellers or any Acquired Company had an interest, or with respect to any property or facility to which Hazardous Materials generated, manufactured, refined, transferred, imported, used, or processed by Sellers, any Acquired Company, or any other Person for whose conduct they are or may be held responsible, have been transported, treated, stored, handled, transferred, disposed, recycled, or received.

COMMENT

Statutes such as CERCLA and similar state statutes, which are the primary basis for environmental liability, impose strict and retroactive liability. Consequently, the Buyer will not want to limit these representations to violations of the environmental laws, but will want to have the Sellers represent that there are no past or present actions or conditions that could form the basis of an environmental claim against the Acquired Companies or anyone for whose actions the Acquired Companies may be liable. This representation is included in the first sentence of paragraph (c).

These representations also cover persons and entities for whose conduct the Sellers are or may be liable. An important issue for the Buyer, especially in the acquisition of an entire business, is the potential liability of the Acquired Companies relating to their predecessors and subsidiaries, to properties they no longer own or businesses they no longer operate (such as divisions that have been spun off), and to prior agreements to indemnify and assume environmental liabilities. Consequently, the representations include any person or entity whose liability for any environmental claim the Sellers or Acquired Companies have retained or assumed, either contractually or by law.

The Sellers may want to limit the broad scope of the potential sources of communications of possible liability to governmental agencies or property owners by inserting the following phrase after the word "communication":

> "from (x) any Governmental Body, including those administering or enforcing any Environmental Law, or (y) the owner of any real property or other facility,"

The final portion of this representation addresses off-site locations to account for liabilities that arise under CERCLA and analogous state statutes even if the Acquired Companies have taken all actions in a lawful manner. The Sellers likely will attempt to exclude this language or include a knowledge qualification because it is difficult for the Sellers to know about such situations even if they have undertaken extensive investigation. Thus, this representation is in part a risk-shifting mechanism. ■

(d) No Seller or Acquired Company, or any other Person for whose conduct they are or may be held responsible, has any Environmental, Health, and Safety Liabilities with respect to the Facilities or [, to the Knowledge of Sellers and the Acquired Companies,] with respect to any other properties and assets (whether real, personal, or mixed) in which Sellers or any Acquired Company (or any predecessor), has or had an interest, or at any property geologically or hydrologically adjoining the Facilities or any such other property or assets.

(e) There are no Hazardous Materials present on or in the Environment at the Facilities or at any geologically or hydrologically adjoining property, including any Hazardous Materials contained in barrels, above or underground storage tanks, landfills, land deposits, dumps, equipment (whether moveable or fixed) or other containers, either temporary or permanent, and deposited or located in land, water, sumps, or any other part of the Facilities or such adjoining property, or incorporated into any structure therein or thereon. No Seller, Acquired Company, any other Person for whose conduct they are or may be held responsible, or [to the Knowledge of Sellers and the Acquired Companies,] any other Person, has permitted or conducted, or is aware of, any Hazardous Activity conducted with respect to the Facilities or any other properties or assets (whether real, personal, or mixed) in which Sellers or any Acquired Company has or had an interest [except in full compliance with all applicable Environmental Laws].

COMMENT

The Sellers will likely object to these representations because of the broad definitions of Hazardous Activities and Hazardous Materials and the Sellers' unwillingness to make representations concerning prior owners or adjoining property. The bracketed language at the end of paragraph (e) is appropriate when the Acquired Companies' businesses involve any of the listed operations, and for similar reasons may also be appropriate with respect to the Hazardous Materials representation in paragraph (f). ■

(f) There has been no Release or, to the Knowledge of Sellers and the Acquired Companies, Threat of Release, of any Hazardous Materials at or from the Facilities or at any other locations where any Hazardous Materials were generated, manufactured, refined, transferred, produced, imported, used, or processed from or by the Facilities, or from or by any other properties and assets (whether real, personal, or mixed) in which Sellers or any Acquired Company has or had an interest, or [to the Knowledge of Sellers and the Acquired Companies] any geologically or hydrologically adjoining property, whether by Sellers, any Acquired Company, or any other Person.

(g) Sellers have delivered to Buyer true and complete copies and results of any reports, studies, analyses, tests, or monitoring possessed or initiated by Sellers or any Acquired Company pertaining to Hazardous Materials or Hazardous Activities in, on, or under the Facilities, or concerning compliance by Sellers, any Acquired Company, or any other Person for whose conduct they are or may be held responsible, with Environmental Laws.

COMMENT

The Buyers should be aware of any relevant information already in the possession of the Acquired Companies or the Sellers. Such information enables the Buyer, if a public company, to anticipate environmental disclosure issues, including cost estimates.

General Comments to Section 3.19

Generally, the Sellers will want knowledge and materiality qualifications to environmental representations. In addition, the Sellers will often try to limit their liability to that resulting from active violations of the law, as opposed to strict liability and liability for actions by predecessors and other third parties, by limiting the definition of terms such as Environmental Laws and Hazardous Materials to a specific list of existing federal and state laws.

The "innocent purchaser defense" under CERCLA is available only in certain asset acquisitions, not in stock acquisitions.

See Chapter IX, "Environmental Laws," of the *Manual on Acquisition Review*. ■

3.20 EMPLOYEES

(a) Part 3.20 of the Disclosure Letter contains a complete and accurate list of the following information for each employee or director of the Acquired Companies, including each employee on leave of absence or layoff status: employer; name; job title; current compensation paid or payable and any change in compensation since ________, 199__; vacation accrued; and service credited for purposes of vesting and eligibility to participate under any Acquired Company's pension, retirement, profit-sharing, thrift-savings, deferred compensation, stock bonus, stock option, cash bonus, employee stock ownership (including investment credit or payroll stock ownership), severance pay, insurance, medical, welfare, or vacation plan, other Employee Pension Benefit Plan or Employee Welfare Benefit Plan, or any other employee benefit plan or any Director Plan.

(b) No employee or director of any Acquired Company is a party to, or is otherwise bound by, any agreement or arrangement, including any confidentiality, noncompetition, or proprietary rights agreement, between such employee or director and any other Person ("Proprietary Rights Agreement") that in any way adversely affects or will affect (i) the performance of his duties as an employee or director of the Acquired Companies, or (ii) the ability of any Acquired Company to conduct its business, including any Proprietary Rights Agreement with Sellers or the Acquired Companies by any such employee or director. To Sellers' Knowledge, no director, officer, or other key employee of any Acquired Company intends to terminate his employment with such Acquired Company.

(c) Part 3.20 of the Disclosure Letter also contains a complete and accurate list of the following information for each retired employee or director of the Acquired Companies, or their dependents, receiving benefits or scheduled to receive benefits in the future: name, pension benefit, pension option election, retiree medical insurance coverage, retiree life insurance coverage, and other benefits.

COMMENT

Generally, the employment relationship between an employee and employer is on an "at will" basis—that is, it can be terminated at any time by either party for any reason or for no reason. However, the nature and obligation of that relationship can change if the parties have entered into an employment contract for a fixed period of time, and in some states an employment contract can be imputed from personnel policies or employee handbooks. In addition, most states have carved out statutory and judicial exceptions to the employment-at-will doctrine, including public policy exceptions. Therefore, the Buyer should review applicable state law to determine its effect on the employment-at-will relationship.

The Buyer should also learn about the Acquired Companies' employment agreements, benefit arrangements, and pension and insurance obligations. For example, an existing severance pay plan or practice may be construed to entitle employees who continue to work for an Acquired Company to severance pay due to the alleged "termination" of their employment upon the closing of the acquisition. In addition, an Acquired Company may have extensive retiree medical insurance liability or unsatisfied obligations to pay pension or welfare plan payments, which may become the obligation of the Buyer by operation of law.

See Chapter XI, "Labor and Employment Matters," of the *Manual on Acquisition Review.* ■

3.21 Labor Relations; Compliance

Since __________, 19__, no Acquired Company has been or is a party to any collective bargaining or other labor Contract. Since __________, 19__, there has not been, there is not presently pending or existing, and [to Sellers' Knowledge] there is not Threatened, (a) any strike, slowdown, picketing, work stoppage, or employee grievance process, (b) any Proceeding against or affecting any Acquired Company relating to the alleged violation of any Legal Requirement pertaining to labor relations or employment matters, including any charge or complaint filed by an employee or union with the National Labor Relations Board, the Equal Employment Opportunity Commission, or any comparable Governmental Body, organizational activity, or other labor or employment dispute against or affecting any of the Acquired Companies or their premises, or (c) any application for certification of a collective bargaining agent. [To Sellers' Knowledge] No event has occurred or circumstance exists that could provide the basis for any work stoppage or other labor dispute. There is no lockout of any employees by any Acquired Company, and no such action is contemplated by any Acquired Company. Each Acquired Company has complied in all respects with all Legal Requirements relating to employment, equal employment opportunity, nondiscrimination, immigration, wages, hours, benefits, collective bargaining, the payment of social security and similar taxes, occupational safety and health, and plant closing. No Acquired Company is liable for the payment of any compensation, damages, taxes, fines, penalties, or other amounts, however designated, for failure to comply with any of the foregoing Legal Requirements.

COMMENT

The degree of detail of the representations concerning labor relations and compliance with labor laws will vary depending upon the nature and extent of the Acquired Companies' businesses. If any Acquired Company operates in a foreign nation, the Buyer should include specific representations concerning compliance with the labor laws and practices of the applicable foreign jurisdictions.

If the Acquired Companies conduct "double breasted" operations (that is, if the operations of some of the Acquired Companies are subject to collective bargaining agreements and the operations of others are not), the Buyer should analyze in detail the Acquired Companies' collective bargaining agreements and their double-breasted operations to determine whether such operations may be continued and integrated with the Buyer's operations without significant labor dispute.

Some states have special labor relations agencies. For example, in California the Agricultural Labor Relations Board acts pursuant to the Agricultural Labor Relations Act. This Act was patterned after the National Labor Relations Act (NLRA) but has traditionally been enforced in a manner much more favorable to unions than the NLRA. If an Acquired Company's business falls within the jurisdictional reach of such a statute, the Buyer should obtain a complete understanding of the statutory scheme, not only to frame appropriate representations, but also to understand how the statutory framework will affect its conduct of the business following the acquisition.

The Model Stock Purchase Agreement representation states, in effect, that there have been no proceedings instituted in respect of an employee grievance. All collective bargaining agreements, as well as the nonunion employment policies and practices of many companies, provide procedures for handling employee grievances. Often the disclosure and description of grievances are quite burdensome to the Sellers and produce information almost meaningless for the Buyer. The Buyer should obtain an understanding of the Acquired Companies' grievance procedures and collective bargaining agreements in order to define the level of significance to which grievances must rise before disclosure is required. The Buyer should be aware, however, that a large number of pending grievance proceedings, immaterial in the single case, could be symptomatic of deeper problems with the employment relations of the Acquired Companies.

If any Acquired Company is or has been a party to labor contracts or collective bargaining agreements, this provision should require that true and complete copies of those agreements, including all amendments and modifications going back several years, be attached to the Disclosure Letter. The Buyer's counsel should obtain copies of such agreements at an early stage in the negotiations to ascertain their expiration dates and to gain an understanding of the contracts and the impact they will have on the Buyer's operation of the businesses following the closing.

The general catch-all representation concerning compliance with "all laws . . . relating to employment" covers past or contemplated conduct relating to plant closures, layoffs, and compliance (or lack of compliance) with the Worker Adjustment and Retraining Notification Act (29 U.S.C. §§ 2101-2109) and any similar state or local law. The Buyer should consider the effect and significance of such legislation in planning its post-acquisition strategy for the Acquired Companies.

The Buyer should also consider any potential liability for the Acquired Companies' failure to comply with state, federal, and local employment discrimination laws. In particular, the Buyer should require disclosure of any pending or potential discrimination charges or complaints that might arise from the Acquired Companies' actions. Such liability may arise, for example, under the Americans With Disabilities Act ("ADA"), which prohibits employers with twenty-five or more employees (fifteen effective July 26, 1994) from discriminating against otherwise qualified job applicants and workers who have disabilities or become disabled.

See Chapter XI, "Labor and Employment Matters," of the *Manual on Acquisition Review.* ■

3.22 Intellectual Property

(a) *Intellectual Property Assets*—The term "Intellectual Property Assets" includes:

(i) the name [the Company's name], all fictional business names, trading names, registered and unregistered trademarks, service marks, and applications (collectively, "Marks");

(ii) all patents, patent applications, and inventions and discoveries that may be patentable (collectively, "Patents");

(iii) all copyrights in both published works and unpublished works (collectively, "Copyrights");

(iv) all rights in mask works (collectively, "Rights in Mask Works"); and

(v) all know-how, trade secrets, confidential information, customer lists, software, technical information, data, process technology, plans, drawings, and blue prints (collectively, "Trade Secrets"); owned, used, or licensed by any Acquired Company as licensee or licensor.

COMMENT

The definition of "Intellectual Property Assets" encompasses all forms of intellectual property, including the forms expressly identified. Below is a description of the main categories of intellectual property.

Patents: There are three types of United States patents. A "utility patent" may be granted under 35 U.S.C. § 101 for "any new and useful process, machine, manufacture, or composition of matter, or any new and useful improvement thereof." Patents also may be granted under Chapter 15, 35 U.S.C. §§ 161-164 (a "plant patent") for new varieties of plants (other than tuber or plants found in an uncultivated state). Finally, a patent may be granted under Chapter 16, 35 U.S.C. §§ 171-173 (a "design patent") for a new, original, and ornamental design for an article of manufacture.

The patenting process begins with the filing of a patent application in the United States Patent and Trademark Office ("PTO"). Except under certain limited conditions, the inventor (or the inventor's patent attorney) must file the application. A patent application or a patent may be assigned by the owner, whether the owner is the inventor or a subsequent assignee.

The term "patent" as used in the definition of Intellectual Property Assets includes utility, plant, and design patents, as well as pending patent applications and patents granted by foreign jurisdictions, and also includes inventions and discoveries that may be patentable.

Trademarks: A trademark is a word, name, symbol, or slogan used in association with the sale of goods or the provision of services. Generally, all trademarks are created under the common law through use of the mark in offering and selling goods or services. Although both state and federal trademark registration systems exist, trademarks need not be registered at either level. A trademark that is not registered is commonly referred to as an "unregistered mark" or a "common law mark." The term "trademark" as used in the definition of Intellectual Property Assets includes both registered and unregistered marks. If the Acquired Companies have many unregistered trademarks, the Sellers may want to limit the definition to registered trademarks. The Buyer should insist that the definition include any unregistered trademarks that the Buyer identifies as key to the Acquired Companies' businesses and that all goodwill associated with these trademarks is transferred to the Buyer.

Copyrights: 17 U.S.C. § 102(a) provides that "[C]opyright protection subsists . . . in original works of authorship fixed in any tangible medium of expression . . . from which they can be perceived, reproduced, or otherwise communicated." Works of authorship that can be protected by copyright include literary works, musical works, dramatic works, pantomimes and choreographic works, pictorial, graphic, and sculptural works, motion pictures and other audiovisual works, architectural works, and sound recordings. *See* 17 U.S.C. § 102(a). Computer software is considered a "literary work" and can be protected by copyright. Ideas, procedures, processes, systems, methods of operation, concepts, principles, and discoveries cannot be copyrighted. *See* 17 U.S.C. § 102(b). The copyright in a work subsists at the moment of creation by the author—registration of the copyright with the U.S. Copyright Office is not necessary. The term "copyright" as used in the definition of Intellectual Property Assets includes all copyrights, whether or not registered.

Mask Works: Mask works are related to semiconductor products and are protected under 17 U.S.C. § 901 et seq. Because this technology is unique to a particular industry (the microchip industry), the Model Stock Purchase Agreement does not contain a representation concerning mask works.

Trade Secrets: Trade secrets arise and are maintained primarily under the common law, but some states have statutes that define and govern trade secret rights. Trade secrets need not be technical information—they can include customer lists, recipes, or anything of value to the company, provided that it is secret, substantial, and valuable. One common type of trade secret is "know-how": a body of information that is valuable to a business and is not generally known outside the business. The term "trade secret" as used in the definition of Intellectual Property Assets includes both common law and statutory trade secrets of all types, including "know-how." ■

(b) *Agreements*—Part 3.22(b) of the Disclosure Letter contains a complete and accurate list and summary description, including any royalties paid or received by the Acquired Companies, of all Contracts relating to the Intellectual Property Assets to which any Acquired Company is a party or by which any Acquired Company is bound, except for any license implied by the sale of a product and perpetual, paid-up licenses for commonly available software programs with a value of less than $__________ under which an Acquired Company is the licensee. There are no outstanding and, to Sellers' Knowledge, no Threatened disputes or disagreements with respect to any such agreement.

COMMENT

This provision requires the Sellers to list license agreements and other agreements that relate to the Intellectual Property Assets, such as a covenant not to sue in connection with a patent, a noncompetition agreement, a confidentiality agreement, a maintenance and support agreement for any software an Acquired Company is licensed to use, or an agreement to sell or license a particular asset. Disclosure of such agreements enables the Buyer to identify which of the intellectual property assets are subject to a license or other restriction and to determine whether the Acquired Companies have the exclusive right to practice certain technology.

If there is a general representation that all of the Acquired Companies' contracts are valid and binding and in full force and effect and that neither party is in default (see Section 3.17), a separate representation is not needed in this section. If there is not a general representation on contracts, or if it is limited in some way, the Buyer should consider including such a representation in this section, especially if an Acquired Company licenses intellectual property that is important to its business. ■

(c) *Know-How Necessary for the Business*

(i) The Intellectual Property Assets are all those necessary for the operation of the Acquired Companies' businesses as they are currently conducted [or as reflected in the business plan given to Buyer]. One or more of the Acquired Companies is the owner of all right, title, and interest in and to each of the Intellectual Property Assets, free and clear of all liens, security interests, charges, encumbrances, equities, and other adverse claims, and has the right to use without payment to a third party all of the Intellectual Property Assets.

(ii) Except as set forth in Part 3.22(c) of the Disclosure Letter, all former and current employees of each Acquired Company have executed written Contracts with one or more of the Acquired Companies that assign to one or more of the Acquired Companies all rights to any inventions, improvements, discoveries, or information relating to the business of any Acquired Company. No employee of any Acquired Company has entered into any Contract that restricts or limits in any way the scope or type of work in which the employee may be engaged or requires the employee to transfer, assign, or disclose information concerning his work to anyone other than one or more of the Acquired Companies.

COMMENT

The Sellers may object to the disclosure called for in paragraph (c)(i) as too subjective and try to force the Buyer to draw its own conclusion on whether the Acquired Companies' intellectual property assets are sufficient to operate their businesses.

The importance of the representations in paragraphs (d)-(g) depends upon the importance of the various types of intellectual property assets to the Acquired Companies. For example, patents and trade secrets can be the key asset of a technology-driven manufacturing company, while trademarks and copyrights could be the principal asset of the service company. ■

(d) *Patents*

(i) Part 3.22(d) of the Disclosure Letter contains a complete and accurate list and summary description of all Patents. One or more of the Acquired Companies is the owner of all right, title, and interest in and to each of the Patents, free and clear of all liens, security interests, charges, encumbrances, entities, and other adverse claims.

(ii) All of the issued Patents are currently in compliance with formal legal requirements (including payment of filing, examination, and maintenance fees and proofs of working or use), are valid and enforceable, and are not subject to any maintenance fees or taxes or actions falling due within ninety days after the Closing Date.

(iii) No Patent has been or is now involved in any interference, reissue, reexamination, or opposition proceeding. To Sellers' Knowledge, there is no potentially interfering patent or patent application of any third party.

(iv) No Patent is infringed or, to Sellers' Knowledge, has been challenged or threatened in any way. None of the products manufactured and sold, nor any process or know-how used, by any Acquired Company infringes or is alleged to infringe any patent or other proprietary right of any other Person.

(v) All products made, used, or sold under the Patents have been marked with the proper patent notice.

COMMENT

This paragraph requires disclosure of information that will enable the Buyer to determine whether the Acquired Companies have patents for the technology used in their businesses and how long any such patents will remain in force; it will also enable the Buyer to do its own validity and infringement searches, which the Buyer should do if the Sellers' representations are subject to a knowledge qualification. Below is a summary of patent law issues relevant to the representations in this paragraph.

Validity: The Buyer should seek assurances that the Acquired Companies' patents are valid. For a patent to be valid, the invention or discovery must be "useful" and "novel" and must not be "obvious." Very few inventions are not "useful"; well-known examples of inventions that are not "useful" are perpetual motion machines and illegal devices (such as drug paraphernalia). To qualify as "novel," the invention must be new; a patent cannot be granted for an invention already made by another person, even if the person seeking the patent made the invention independently. An invention is "obvious" if the differences between the invention sought to be patented and the prior art are such that the subject matter of the invention as a whole would have been obvious at the time the invention was made to a person having ordinary skill in the art to which the subject matter pertains.

To determine conclusively that an invention is not "obvious" requires knowledge of all prior art. It is difficult even to identify all prior art relevant to the invention, much less to make judgments about what would have been obvious to a person having reasonable skill in such arts. Thus, although the Sellers may in good faith believe that the Acquired Companies' patents are valid, those patents are subject to challenge at any time. If someone can establish that the invention covered by a patent does not meet these three criteria, the patent will be invalid. Because of the difficulty in conclusively determining the validity of a patent, the Sellers will want to add a knowledge qualification to the representation concerning validity. Whether the Buyer agrees to such a qualification is a question of risk allocation.

If the Buyer agrees to a knowledge qualification, it may want to conduct a patent search in the PTO (and, if appropriate, the European Patent Office and other foreign patent offices) to identify all prior art and obtain a validity opinion. However, such searches and analysis of their results can be quite costly.

Term and Maintenance Fees: The Buyer should ensure that the terms of the Acquired Companies' patents have not expired and that all necessary maintenance fees have been paid. The term of a utility patent is generally seventeen years from the date of issuance of the patent, provided that the required maintenance fees are paid by the fourth, eighth, and twelfth years of the patent term. The term of a plant patent is also seventeen years, and the term of a design patent is fourteen years. Maintenance fees need not be paid on plant patents or design patents.

Inventions by Employees: In many jurisdictions in the United States, an invention made by an employee is not necessarily the property of the employer. The Buyer should verify, therefore, that the Acquired Companies have perfected title to all patents or patent applications for inventions made by their employees. In addition, the Acquired Companies should have written agreements with their employees providing that all inventions, patent applications, and patents awarded to employees will be transferred to the Acquired Companies to the extent permissible under state law.

Use of Technology in Foreign Nations: A United States patent has no extraterritorial effect—that is, a United States patent provides the patent owner the right to exclude others from making, using, or selling the invention in the United States only. Thus, the owner of a United States patent can prevent others from making the patented invention outside the United States and shipping it to a customer in the United States, and from making the invention in the United States and shipping it to a customer outside the United States. The patent owner cannot, however, prevent another from making the invention outside the United States and shipping it to a customer also outside the United States. If the Acquired Companies have extensive business in foreign nations, the Buyer should seek assurances that important foreign markets are protected to the greatest extent possible under the intellectual property laws of the applicable foreign jurisdictions.

Enforceability: The Buyer should seek assurances that the Acquired Companies' patents are enforceable. Failure to disclose to the PTO relevant information material to the examination of a patent application can result in the patent being unenforceable. In addition, misuse of a patent (for example, use that results in an antitrust violation) can result in the patent being unenforceable. Finally, because patent rights vary in each nation, representations concerning enforceability require the Sellers to confirm the enforceability of foreign patents separately in each nation.

Infringement: The grant of a patent does not provide any assurance that using the invention will not infringe another person's patent. A patent could be granted, for example, for an improvement to a previously patented device, but the practice of the improvement might infringe the claims of the earlier patent on the device. A patent confers no right of any kind to make, use, or sell the invention; it grants the inventor only the right to exclude others. Therefore, the Buyer should seek assurances that it can use the inventions covered by the Acquired Companies' patents. The Buyer may conduct a patent search in the PTO and obtain an infringement opinion as a step in the process of determining whether certain technology owned (or licensed) by the Acquired Companies infringes any United States patents. In addition, the Buyer may conduct a "right to practice" for expired patents covering inventions that have passed into the public domain.

The Sellers may want to add a knowledge qualification to the representation in clause (iv) because they cannot verify that no one else in the world is practicing the technology covered by an Acquired Company's patent. Whether the Buyer accepts such a qualification is a question of risk allocation.

Marking: Without proper marking of the patented product or the product made using a patented process, damages cannot be collected for infringement of the patent.

Separate Representations for Certain Types of Technology: Some forms of technology are not covered by the traditional patent statutes, and separate statutory schemes have been enacted to afford protection in these areas, which include some types of computer technology and biotechnology. If the Acquired Companies' businesses encompass such technology, the Buyer may want to include specific representations concerning this technology. ■

(e) Trademarks

(i) Part 3.22(e) of Disclosure Letter contains a complete and accurate list and summary description of all Marks. One or more of the Acquired Companies is the owner of all right, title, and interest in and to each of the Marks, free and clear of all liens, security interests, charges, encumbrances, equities, and other adverse claims.

(ii) All Marks that have been registered with the United States Patent and Trademark Office are currently in compliance with all formal legal requirements (including the timely post-registration filing of affidavits of use and incontestability and renewal applications), are valid and enforceable, and are not subject to any maintenance fees or taxes or actions falling due within ninety days after the Closing Date.

(iii) No Mark has been or is now involved in any opposition, invalidation, or cancellation and, to Sellers' Knowledge, no such action is Threatened with the respect to any of the Marks.

(iv) To Sellers' Knowledge, there is no potentially interfering trademark or trademark application of any third party.

(v) No Mark is infringed or, to Sellers' Knowledge, has been challenged or threatened in any way. None of the Marks used by any Acquired Company infringes or is alleged to infringe any trade name, trademark, or service mark of any third party.

(vi) All products and materials containing a Mark bear the proper federal registration notice where permitted by law.

COMMENT

The owner of a trademark can prevent others from using infringing marks and, in some instances, can recover damages for such infringement. Below is a summary of trademark law relevant to the representations in this paragraph.

Registration: Although trademark registration systems are maintained at both the state and federal levels, trademarks need not be registered at either level. State registrations are of little value to businesses either that operate in more than one state or whose market is defined by customers from more than one state.

Two of the major benefits of registration at the federal level are "constructive use" and "constructive notice." The owner of a federal registration is deemed to have used the mark in connection with the goods or services recited in the registration on a nationwide basis as of the filing date of the application. Therefore, any other person who first began using the mark after the trademark owner filed the application is an infringer, regardless of the geographic areas in which the trademark owner and the infringer use their marks. Federal registration also provides constructive notice to the public of the registration of the mark as of the date of issuance of the registration. Because of the importance of federal registration, the representations in paragraph (e)(ii) require the Sellers to ensure that they have obtained federal registration of the Acquired Companies' trademarks.

An application for federal registration of a trademark is filed in the PTO. The PTO maintains two trademark registers: the Principal Register and the Supplemental Register. The Supplemental Register is generally for marks that cannot be registered on the Principal Register. The Supplemental Register does not provide the trademark owner the same rights as those provided by the Principal Register, and it provides no rights in addition to those provided by the Principal Register. The Buyer should determine whether the Acquired Companies' trademarks are on the Principal Register or the Supplemental Register, and if the Buyer learns that an important mark is on the Supplemental Register, the Buyer should find out why it was not registered on the Principal Register. If the mark cannot be registered on the Principal Register, the Buyer should consult trademark counsel to determine the scope of protection for the mark.

After a trademark has been registered with the PTO, the owner should file two affidavits to protect its rights. An affidavit of "incontestability" may be filed within the sixth year of registration of a mark to strengthen the registration by marking it "incontestable." An affidavit of "continuing use" must be filed with the PTO during the sixth year of registration; otherwise, the PTO will automatically cancel the registration at the end of the sixth year. Cancellation of a registration (or abandonment of an application) does not necessarily mean that the trademark owner has abandoned the mark and no longer has rights in the mark—proving abandonment of a mark requires more than merely showing that an application has been abandoned or that a registration has been cancelled. Nevertheless, because of the benefits of federal registration, the representations in paragraph (e)(ii) require the Sellers to have filed continuing use affidavits (as well as incontestability affidavits, which are often combined with continuing use affidavits) for all of the Acquired Companies' trademarks registered more than six years ago.

Term: The Buyer should verify that the terms of the Acquired Companies' federal registrations have not expired. Federal registrations issued on or after November 16, 1989 have a term of ten years; registrations issued prior to that date have a term of twenty years. All federal registrations may be renewed if the mark is still in use when the renewal application is filed. Registrations expiring on or after November 16, 1989 may be renewed for a term of ten years. A registration that was renewed before November 16, 1989 has a renewal term of twenty years. Registrations may be renewed repeatedly. An application for renewal must be filed within the six-month period immediately preceding the expiration of the current term (whether an original or renewal term).

Unregistered Marks: A trademark that is not registered is commonly referred to as an "unregistered mark" or a "common law mark." Generally, the owner of a common law mark can prevent others from using a confusingly similar mark only in the trademark owner's "trading area." Thus, the owner of a common law mark may find, upon expanding use of the mark outside that area, that another has established superior rights there and can stop the trademark owner's expansion. If the Buyer plans to expand the Acquired Companies' businesses to new areas, it should verify that all of the Acquired Companies' important trademarks have been registered at the federal level.

Non-Use and Unauthorized Use: Rights in a trademark can be lost through non-use or through non-authorized use by others. In an extreme example of the latter, long use of a mark by the public to refer to the type of goods marketed by the trademark owner and its competitors can inject the trademark into the public domain. Therefore, the Buyer should determine whether the Acquired Companies are using the marks that are of primary interest to the Buyer, and whether any others using those marks for similar goods or services are doing so under a formal license agreement.

License Agreements: The trademark owner must ensure a certain level of quality of the goods or services sold with the mark. A license agreement thus must provide the licensor with the right to "police" the quality of the goods or services sold with the mark, and the licensor must actually exercise this right—failure to do so works an abandonment of the mark by the licensor. Similarly, an assignment of a mark without an assignment of the assignor's "goodwill" associated with the mark constitutes an abandonment of the mark.

Potentially Interfering Trademarks: Because the representation in paragraph (e)(iv) is qualified by the Sellers' knowledge, the Buyer may want to conduct a trademark search to ensure that there are no potentially interfering trademarks or trademark applications. Several search firms can do a trademark search; limited searching can also be done through databases. A trademark search and analysis of the results should be much less costly than a patent search and analysis.

Infringement: A mark need not be identical to another mark or be used with the same goods or services of the other mark to constitute an infringement. Rather, a mark infringes another mark if it is confusingly similar to it. Several factors are examined to determine whether two marks are confusingly similar, including the visual and phonetic similarities between the marks, the similarities between the goods or services with which the marks are used, the nature of the markets for the goods or services, the trade channels through which the goods or services flow to reach the markets, and the media in which the goods or services are advertised. As with patents, the Sellers may want to add a knowledge qualification to the representations in paragraph (e)(v) because of the difficulty in conclusively determining that no other person is infringing the Acquired Companies' trademarks and that the Acquired Companies' marks do not infringe other trademarks. ■

(f) Copyrights

(i) Part 3.22(f) of the Disclosure Letter contains a complete and accurate list and summary description of all Copyrights. One or more of the Acquired Companies is the owner of all right, title, and interest in and to each of the Copyrights, free and clear of all liens, security interests, charges, encumbrances, equities, and other adverse claims.

(ii) All the Copyrights have been registered and are currently in compliance with formal legal requirements, are valid and enforceable, and are not subject to any maintenance fees or taxes or actions falling due within ninety days after the date of Closing.

(iii) No Copyright is infringed or, to Sellers' Knowledge, has been challenged or threatened in any way. None of the subject matter of any of the Copyrights infringes or is alleged to infringe any copyright of any third party or is a derivative work based on the work of a third party.

(iv) All works encompassed by the Copyrights have been marked with the proper copyright notice.

COMMENT

The first representation in this paragraph provides assurances to the Buyer that the Acquired Companies actually have title to the copyrights for works created by their employees. Such assurances are important because the copyright in a work vests originally in the "author," who is the person who created the work unless the work is a "work made for hire." *See* 17 U.S.C. § 201(a)-(b). A work can be a "work made for hire" in two circumstances: (i) when it is created by an employee in the course of employment, or (ii) when it is created pursuant to a written agreement that states that the work will be a work made for hire, and the work is of a type listed in 17 U.S.C. § 101 under the definition of "work made for hire." To ensure that the Acquired Companies own the copyrights to works created by their employees, the Acquired Companies should have written agreements with their employees providing that all copyrights for works created in the course of employment will be transferred to the Acquired Companies.

Although rights in a copyright may be assigned or licensed in writing, the transfer of copyrights in a work (other than a "work made for hire") may be terminated under the conditions described in 17 U.S.C. § 203. If the Acquired Companies own copyrights by assignment or license, the Buyer should ensure that the copyrights cannot be terminated, or at least that such termination would not be damaging to the Buyer.

The Buyer should verify that the terms of the Acquired Companies' copyrights have not expired. The term of a copyright is as follows:

1. For works created on or after January 1, 1978, the life of the author plus fifty years after the author's death.
2. For joint works created by two or more authors "who did not work for hire," the life of the last surviving author plus fifty years after the death of the last surviving author.
3. For anonymous works, pseudonymous works, and works made for hire, seventy-five years from the date of first publication or 100 years from the year of creation of the work, whichever expires first.

Although it is not necessary to register a copyright with the U.S. Copyright Office for the copyright to be valid, benefits (such as the right to obtain statutory damages, attorneys' fees, and costs) may be obtained in a successful copyright infringement action if the copyright in the work has been registered and a notice of copyright has been placed on the work. Hence the representation in paragraph (f)(ii) requires the Sellers to register all of the Acquired Companies' copyrights.

As with patents and trademarks, the Sellers may want to add a knowledge qualification to the representations in paragraph (f)(iii) because of the difficulty in conclusively determining that no other person is infringing the Acquired Companies' copyrights and that the Acquired Companies do not infringe other copyrights (such determinations would require, among other things, judgments regarding whether another person and the Acquired Company or its employees independently created the same work and whether the allegedly infringing party is making "fair use" of the copyrighted material). Again, whether the Buyer accepts such a qualification is a question of risk allocation. ■

(g) *Trade Secrets*

(i) With respect to each Trade Secret, the documentation relating to such Trade Secret is current, accurate, and sufficient in detail and content to identify and explain it and to allow its full and proper use without reliance on the knowledge or memory of any individual.

(ii) Sellers and the Acquired Companies have taken all reasonable precautions to protect the secrecy, confidentiality, and value of their Trade Secrets.

(iii) One or more of the Acquired Companies has good title and an absolute (but not necessarily exclusive) right to use the Trade Secrets. The Trade Secrets are not part of the public knowledge or literature, and, to Sellers' Knowledge, have not been used, divulged, or appropriated either for the benefit of any Person (other than one or more of the Acquired Companies) or to the detriment of the Acquired Companies. No Trade Secret is subject to any adverse claim or has been challenged or threatened in any way.

COMMENT

As part of the disclosure required by the first clause of this paragraph, the Buyer may want a list of all of the Acquired Companies' trade secrets and the location of each document that contains a complete description of the trade secret. Although a trade secret inventory would assist the parties in identifying the trade secrets that are part of the acquisition, it may be difficult or impossible to create a trade secret inventory, especially if the Sellers are retaining certain parts of the Acquired Companies' businesses. The Buyer could ask the Sellers to identify key trade secrets, which would enable the Buyer to determine whether the Acquired Companies treat information that the Buyer views as key to their businesses as proprietary. However, the Sellers may be reluctant to disclose trade secrets to the Buyer prior to either the closing or a firm commitment by the Buyer to proceed with the acquisition. Moreover, the Buyer's receipt of this information can place the Buyer in a difficult position if the acquisition fails to close and the Buyer subsequently wants to enter the same field or develop a similar product or process. In these circumstances, the Buyer risks suit by the Sellers for theft of trade secrets, and the Buyer may have the burden of proving that it developed the information independently of the information it received from the Sellers, which may be very difficult.

Because the validity of trade secrets depends in part on the efforts made to keep them confidential, the representation in paragraph (g)(ii) provides assurances to the Buyer that the Acquired Companies have treated their trade secrets as confidential. Important methods of maintaining the confidentiality of trade secrets include limiting access to them, marking them as confidential, and requiring everyone to whom they are disclosed to agree in writing to keep them confidential. In particular, the Buyer should verify that the Acquired Companies have treated valuable "know-how" in a manner that gives rise to trade secret protection, such as through the use of confidentiality agreements. In the case of software, the Buyer should determine whether the software is licensed to customers under a license agreement that defines the manner in which the customer may use the software, or whether the software is sold on an unrestricted basis. The Buyer should also investigate any other procedures used by the Acquired Companies to maintain the secrecy of their trade secrets, and the Buyer should determine whether agreements exist that govern the disclosure and use of trade secrets by employees of the Acquired Companies and others who need to learn of them.

See Chapter X, "Intellectual Property," of the *Manual on Acquisition Review*. ■

3.23 Certain Payments

Since ____________, 19__, no Acquired Company or director, officer, agent, or employee of any Acquired Company, or [to Sellers' Knowledge] any other Person associated with or acting for or on behalf of any Acquired Company, has directly or indirectly (a) made any contribution, gift, bribe, rebate, payoff, influence payment, kickback, or other payment to any Person, private or public, regardless of form, whether in money, property, or services (i) to obtain favorable treatment in securing business, (ii) to pay for favorable treatment for business secured, (iii) to obtain special concessions or for special concessions already obtained, for or in respect of any Acquired Company or any Affiliate of an Acquired Company, or (iv) in violation of any Legal Requirement, (b) established or maintained any fund or asset that has not been recorded in the books and records of the Acquired Companies.

COMMENT

The nature of the Acquired Companies' businesses will determine whether this representation should be included in the acquisition agreement. If an Acquired Company conducts extensive offshore business, the Buyer may want to make oral inquiry early in the negotiations. If any Acquired Company is engaged in the entertainment business, such as the recording business, the Buyer should obtain assurances that there is no "payola" or similar improper inducement to promote the Acquired Company's products (or find out about it if it exists).

If this representation is used, the Buyer should require the Sellers to deliver, both through the Disclosure Letter and to the Buyer's representatives prior to the closing, copies of any "business practices," "ethics," or "conflicts of interest" policies of the Acquired Companies, the reports and questionnaires that may have been periodically submitted by employees pursuant to these policies, and details relating to breaches of these policies and actions taken in response to any such breaches. If the Buyer has its own policies, in addition to requiring disclosure of the Acquired Companies' policies, the Buyer may want to include representations that the policies have been in place for a given period of time and that there have been no breaches of the policies (other than as described in the Disclosure Letter).

If the Buyer is engaged in the same businesses as the Acquired Companies, the Buyer may have its own views on the conduct of these businesses and may be prepared, subject to whatever level of due diligence inquiry it decides to make, to proceed with the acquisition without much concern about the Acquired Companies' prior and existing practices. On the other hand, a careful Buyer may conclude, following its due diligence investigation, that there has been a course of conduct of such a questionable nature that the Buyer elects to walk away from the acquisition.

Several aspects of this representation may produce endless discussions and negotiations. The Sellers may point out that this representation covers Christmas gifts to employees, business gifts of relatively low value (such as diaries, calendars, and bottles of wine), and customary charitable contributions. This is an example of an objection based on the lack of materiality qualifications in the Sellers' representations—see the Commentary to Section 3 under the caption "The Absence of Materiality Qualifications." Moreover, the Buyer may want to know the purposes of "contributions" described in clauses (i), (ii), and (iii).

Another area for recurring debate is the Sellers' desire to limit the representation to cover only "illegal" payments. The Buyer should reject this approach because even legal payments may be of concern to the Buyer.

If the Buyer insists that the Sellers make this representation, the Buyer will want full details about disclosed payments. The Buyer normally will want indemnification rights against the Sellers if any loss, liability, or exposure arises after the closing as a result of questionable payments, whether or not such payments are disclosed. The Sellers may agree to make the representation only if it does not cover the acts of "employees," because they cannot know what the lowest echelon employee may have done to curry favor with an inspector. Resolution of these issues ultimately is a question of risk allocation: should the Sellers have indemnification obligations for bribes or payoffs, or should the Buyer bear the risk that the Acquired Companies have liability for such acts that materializes after the Closing? ■

3.24 Disclosure

(a) No representation or warranty of Sellers in this Agreement and no statement in the Disclosure Letter omits to state a material fact necessary to make the statements herein or therein, in light of the circumstances in which they were made, not misleading.

(b) No notice given pursuant to Section 5.5 will contain any untrue statement or omit to state a material fact necessary to make the statements therein or in this Agreement, in light of the circumstances in which they were made, not misleading.

COMMENT

These representations assure the Buyer that the specific disclosures made in the Sellers' representations and in the Disclosure Letter do not, and no supplement to the Disclosure Letter will (see Section 5.7), contain any misstatements or omissions. There is no materiality qualification (except for omissions) because the representations elsewhere in Section 3 contain any applicable materiality standard—to include an additional materiality standard here would be redundant. For example, Section 3.1 represents that the Company is qualified to do business in all jurisdictions in which the failure to be so qualified would have a material adverse effect; if Section 3.24(a) provided that there is no untrue statement of a "material" fact, one would have to determine first whether the consequences of a failure to qualify were "material" under Section 3.1, and then whether the untrue statement itself was "material" under Section 3.24. Section 3.24 contains no requirement of knowledge or scienter by the Sellers (any such requirements would be in the representations elsewhere in Section 3) and no requirement of reliance by the Buyer. As a result, Section 3.24 imposes a higher standard of accuracy on the Sellers than the applicable securities laws.

Section 3.24(a) contains a materiality standard with respect to information omitted from the representations in the acquisition agreement and from the Disclosure Letter because the representations concerning omitted information are independent from the representations elsewhere in Section 3. Although the omissions representations are derived from Section 12(2) of the Securities Act and Section 10b-5 of the Securities Exchange Act of 1934, the representations are contractual in nature, do not require any proof of reliance on the part of the Buyer, and do not require any proof of negligence or knowledge on the part of either Seller. Thus, the acquisition agreement imposes a contractual standard of strict liability, in contrast with (i) Section 10b-5, which predicates liability for misrepresentation or nondisclosure on reliance by the Buyer and conduct involving some form of scienter by the Sellers to be held responsible, (ii) Section 12(2) of the Securities Act, which provides a defense to the Sellers if they can prove that they "did not know, and in the exercise of reasonable care could not have known, of such untruth or omission," and (iii) common law fraud, which is usually predicated upon the Sellers' actual intent to mislead the Buyer. *See B. S. Int'l Ltd. v. Licht,* 696 F. Supp. 813, 827 (D.R.I. 1988); Bromberg & Lowenfels, 4 *Securities Fraud & Commodities Fraud* § 8.4 (1988).

The Buyer should ensure that it receives the Disclosure Letter (subject to necessary modifications) before signing the acquisition agreement. If the Sellers insist on signing the acquisition agreement before delivering the Disclosure Letter, the Buyer should demand that the acquisition agreement require delivery of the Disclosure Letter by a specific date far enough before the closing to permit a thorough review of the Disclosure

Letter and an analysis of the consequences of disclosed items, and that the Buyer has the right to terminate the agreement if there any disclosures it finds objectionable in its sole discretion. *See* Freund, *Anatomy of a Merger* 171-72 (1975). ■

(c) There is no fact known to either Seller that has specific application to either Seller or any Acquired Company (other than general economic or industry conditions) and that materially adversely affects [or, as far as either Seller can reasonably foresee, materially threatens,] the assets, business, prospects, financial condition, or results of operations of the Acquired Companies (on a consolidated basis) that has not been set forth in this Agreement or the Disclosure Letter.

COMMENT

Section 3.24(c) is a representation that there is no material information regarding the Acquired Companies that has not been disclosed to the Buyer. This representation is common in the Buyer's first draft of the acquisition agreement. The Sellers may argue that the representation expands, in ways that cannot be foreseen, the detailed representations and warranties in the acquisition agreement and is neither necessary nor appropriate. The Buyer can respond that the Sellers are in a better position to evaluate the significance of all facts relating to the Acquired Companies. ■

3.25 Relationships with Related Persons

No Seller or any Related Person of Sellers or of any Acquired Company has, or since [the first day of the next to last completed fiscal year of the Acquired Companies] has had, any interest in any property (whether real, personal, or mixed and whether tangible or intangible), used in or pertaining to the Acquired Companies' businesses. No Seller or any Related Person of Sellers or of any Acquired Company is, or since [the first day of the next to last completed fiscal year of the Acquired Companies] has owned (of record or as a beneficial owner) an equity interest or any other financial or profit interest in, a Person that has (i) had business dealings or a material financial interest in any transaction with any Acquired Company [other than business dealings or transactions conducted in the Ordinary Course of Business with the Acquired Companies at substantially prevailing market prices and on substantially prevailing market terms], or (ii) engaged in competition with any Acquired Company with respect to any line of the products or services of such Acquired Company (a "Competing Business") in any market presently served by such Acquired Company [except for less than one percent of the outstanding capital stock of any Competing Business that is publicly traded on any recognized exchange or in the over-the-counter market]. Except as set forth in Part 3.25 of the Disclosure Letter, no Seller or any Related Person of Sellers or of any Acquired Company is a party to any Contract with, or has any claim or right against, any Acquired Company.

COMMENT

The first sentence of this representation provides assurances that the Sellers and related persons do not have any interest in property used in the Acquired Companies' businesses. The broad definition of "Related Person" covers indirect relationships, which may be very important to the Buyer. If there are many interrelationships among individuals who are related persons of the Sellers or of the Acquired Companies, as well as of other entities that are affiliated with the Acquired Companies, a significant amount of disclosure may be required and a rather detailed and elaborate series of representations may be needed to cover various relationships.

In acquisitions involving large corporations, the Sellers may not be able to make this representation without a list of exceptions so long that the representation becomes meaningless. Moreover, depending on the size of the corporations and the relationship of the parties, the representation may not be necessary or relevant. A more appropriate alternative may be to require, solely for the purpose of disclosure, that the Disclosure Letter describe such relationships.

Many corporations have "conflict of interest" policies that require periodic questionnaires to be completed and signed by certain levels of management and employees. The Buyer should demand disclosure of any such policies and that true and complete copies of all such current policies [or all such policies in effect during the past five years] be attached to the Disclosure Letter. The Buyer should also request detailed descriptions of any breaches or remedial or disciplinary action taken. The Buyer may want to require as a condition to the closing that all employees who are subject to the policy complete and sign current questionnaires.

The final sentence in the Model Stock Purchase Agreement representation can be revised to exclude the Sellers' rights to their respective shares of the purchase price and to the pre-closing compensation and other distributions they currently receive from the Acquired Companies. The Buyer should, however, require as a closing condition that the Sellers sign releases of all claims against the Acquired Companies.

If the Sellers' disclosures reveal that officers, directors, or major shareholders of the Acquired Companies or related persons that the Sellers hold beneficial interests in competing businesses, the Buyer should determine whether the interest in question constituted a corporate opportunity for the Acquired Companies and why the opportunity was not taken by the Acquired Companies. ■

3.26 Brokers or Finders

Sellers and their agents have incurred no obligation or liability, contingent or otherwise, for brokerage or finders' fees or agents' commissions or other similar payment in connection with this Agreement.

COMMENT

There are many types of intermediaries who may facilitate an acquisition through a variety of services ranging from introducing the parties (a finder) to assisting in every stage of the transaction (a broker). The Model Stock Purchase Agreement representation expresses the usual format for finders' or brokers' fees when no finder or broker is involved. If obligations for brokers' or finders' fees or agents' commissions have been incurred, the acquisition agreement should specify whether the Sellers, the Buyer, or an Acquired Company will bear the financial liability for these payments. If an Acquired Company will assume this obligation, the parties should carefully consider the tax ramifications (such as whether the payments would be deemed a constructive dividend). ■

4. REPRESENTATIONS AND WARRANTIES OF BUYER

COMMENT

The Model Stock Purchase Agreement contains nearly ninety pages (including Commentary) of representations by the Sellers and only three pages of representations by the Buyer. This is due to the assumption that the Buyer is purchasing all the stock of the Acquired Companies for a combination of cash and promissory notes. In an acquisition in which the purchase price is paid at the closing in cash, the Sellers are interested primarily in the Buyer's due organization, the power of the Buyer and the authority of the Buyer's agents to execute a binding acquisition agreement, and the Buyer's obligations to finders or brokers.

When promissory notes or stock in the Buyer represent a substantial part of the purchase price, the Sellers may want to learn as much about the Buyer's financial condition as the Buyer wants to know about the financial condition of the Acquired Companies, and the Sellers may ask for representations concerning the accuracy of the Buyer's financial statements and the ranking of the notes in the Buyer's debt hierarchy, especially if the Buyer is newly organized or has a questionable future. Moreover, the Sellers may want a representation concerning the absence of contingent liabilities that could have a materially adverse effect on the Buyer's ability to pay. In rare cases of stock-for-stock mergers between two companies of roughly equal size, financial strength, and stability, the representations may be virtually the same for each party. In such cases both the Buyer's and the Sellers' counsel should use judgment and not fall into "symmetrical schizophrenia." *See* Freund, *Anatomy of a Merger* 283 (1975). ■

Buyer represents and warrants to Sellers as follows:

4.1 Organization and Good Standing

Buyer is a corporation duly organized, validly existing, and in good standing under the laws of the State of _______________.

COMMENT

This representation parallels that given by the Sellers in Section 3.1. This representation is relevant to the Buyer's ability to enter into the acquisition agreement and complete the acquisition. The Sellers have no real interest in other matters concerning the Buyer, such as whether it is qualified to do business in foreign jurisdictions. ■

4.2 Authority; No Conflict

(a) This Agreement constitutes the legal, valid, and binding obligation of Buyer, enforceable against Buyer in accordance with its terms. Upon the execution and delivery by Buyer of the Escrow Agreement, the Employment Agreements, and the Promissory Notes (collectively, the "Buyer's Closing Documents"), the Buyer's Closing Documents will constitute the legal, valid, and binding obligations of Buyer, enforceable against Buyer in accordance with their respective terms. Buyer has the absolute and unrestricted right, power, and authority to execute and deliver this Agreement and the Buyer's Closing Documents and to perform its obligations under this Agreement and the Buyer's Closing Documents.

(b) Except as set forth in Schedule 4.2, neither the execution and delivery of this Agreement [by Buyer] nor the consummation or performance of any of the Contemplated Transactions [by Buyer] will give any Person the right to prevent, delay, or otherwise interfere with any of the Contemplated Transactions pursuant to:

(i) any provision of Buyer's Organizational Documents;

(ii) any resolution adopted by the board of directors or the stockholders of Buyer;

(iii) any Legal Requirement or Order to which Buyer may be subject; or

(iv) any Contract to which Buyer is a party or by which Buyer may be bound.

Except as set forth in Schedule 4.2, Buyer is not and will not be required to obtain any Consent from any Person in connection with the execution and delivery of this Agreement or the consummation or performance of any of the Contemplated Transactions.

COMMENT

The representations in the first two sentences parallel those in the first two sentences of Section 3.2, modified to refer to a corporation rather than to individuals. The representation that the acquisition agreement is enforceable against the Buyer in accordance with its terms is not normally qualified by reference to equitable remedies or bankruptcy laws, as would be the case in a legal opinion. The no-conflict representation is similar to that in Section 3.2 referring to the Sellers and the Acquired Companies, and portions of the Commentary to Section 3.2 apply here as well. ■

4.3 Investment Intent

Buyer is acquiring the Shares for its own account and not with a view to their distribution within the meaning of Section 2(11) of the Securities Act.

COMMENT

The sale of shares in an acquisition such as that contemplated by the Model Stock Purchase Agreement is normally exempt from the registration requirements of the Securities Act under the so-called $4(1\frac{1}{2})$ exemption, which applies to a private sale between non-issuers and non-underwriters.

The Sellers may want to establish that they have performed their disclosure obligations under applicable securities laws, in which case the Sellers will propose a provision such as the following:

> Buyer confirms that Sellers have made available to Buyer and its representatives and agents the opportunity to ask questions of the officers and management employees of the Acquired Companies and to acquire such additional information about the business and financial condition of the Acquired Companies as Buyer has requested, and all such information has been received.

However, the Buyer will probably not want to include such a provision in its initial draft and in any event will want to clarify that such language does not affect the liability of the Sellers for breaches of their representations and warranties. ■

4.4 Certain Proceedings

There is no pending Proceeding that has been commenced against Buyer and that challenges, or may have the effect of preventing, delaying, making illegal, or otherwise interfering with, any of the Contemplated Transactions. To Buyer's Knowledge, no such Proceeding has been Threatened.

COMMENT

See the Commentary to Sections 3.15 and 8.5. ■

4.5 Brokers or Finders

Buyer and its officers and agents have incurred no obligation or liability, contingent or otherwise, for brokerage or finders' fees or agents' commissions or other similar payment in connection with this Agreement and will indemnify and hold Sellers harmless from any such payment alleged to be due by or through Buyer as a result of the action of Buyer or its officers or agents.

COMMENT

See the Commentary to Section 3.26. ■

5. COVENANTS OF SELLERS PRIOR TO CLOSING DATE

COMMENT

Sections 3 and 4 contain the representations made by the parties to each other. Although some acquisition agreements intermingle covenants and conditions with representations, the Model Stock Purchase Agreement segregates the representations in Sections 3 and 4 from the covenants to be performed prior to the closing in Sections 5 and 6 and from the conditions to the parties' obligations to complete the acquisition in Sections 7 and 8. Article 11 contains certain additional covenants that do not relate solely to the obligations of the parties during the period between signing and closing, but, also to the post-closing obligations and rights of the parties.

Because the Model Stock Purchase Agreement provides for the purchase of all of the outstanding stock of the Company from its shareholders, neither the Company nor any of the other Acquired Companies is a party to the acquisition agreement (see the Commentary to the preamble). Thus, even though many of the obligations imposed by Section 5 will be performed by the Acquired Companies, the Model Stock Purchase Agreement necessarily imposes these obligations on the Sellers rather than the Acquired Companies.

A breach of the covenants in Section 5, like any other covenant, under normal contract principles will result in liability by the breaching party (the Sellers) to the non-breaching party (the Buyer) for damages. Section 10.1 provides that the covenants survive the closing and thus the Sellers are obligated to indemnify the Buyer after the closing for breaches of the covenants in Section 5. ■

5.1 Access and Investigation

Between the date of this Agreement and the Closing Date, Sellers will, and will cause each Acquired Company and its Representatives to, (a) afford Buyer and its Representatives and prospective lenders and their Representatives (collectively, "Buyer's Advisors") full and free access to each Acquired Company's personnel, properties (including subsurface testing), contracts, books and records, and other documents and data, (b) furnish Buyer and Buyer's Advisors with copies of all such contracts, books and records, and other existing documents and data as Buyer may reasonably request, and (c) furnish Buyer and Buyer's Advisors with such additional financial, operating, and other data and information as Buyer may reasonably request.

COMMENT

Section 5.1 provides the Buyer and its representatives with access to the Acquired Companies' personnel, properties, and records so that the Buyer can continue its investigation of the Acquired Companies, confirm the accuracy of the Sellers' representations, and verify satisfaction of the conditions to its obligation to complete the acquisition, such as the absence of a material adverse change in the financial conditions, results of operations, businesses, or prospects of the Acquired Companies.

The access right provided for in Section 5.1 extends to prospective lenders and their representatives. Even though the acquisition contemplated by the Model Stock Purchase Agreement does not contain a financing condition (see the third paragraph of the Commentary to Section 7), the Buyer may be required to obtain new or additional financing to allow it to complete the acquisition. A prospective lender may want to engage environmental consultants, asset appraisers, and other consultants to present their findings before making a definitive lending commitment.

The access right in clause (a) of Section 5.1 is accompanied by the rights in clause (b) to obtain copies of existing documents and in clause (c) to obtain data not yet reduced to writing or data storage.

In many acquisitions, the Buyer's investigation occurs both before and after the signing of the acquisition agreement. While the Model Stock Purchase Agreement provides for comprehensive representations from the Sellers, the importance of these representations increases if the Buyer is unable to complete its investigation prior to execution of the acquisition agreement. In those circumstances, the representations can be used to elicit information that the Buyer will be unable to ferret out on its own prior to execution (see the Commentary to Section 3 under the caption "Purposes of the Sellers' Representations"). In addition, if, as a result of the Buyer's post-signing investigation, the Buyer discovers a material inaccuracy in the Sellers' representations, the Buyer can terminate the acquisition (or consummate the acquisition and, subject to the possible limitations described in the Commentary to Section 10.1, recover damages against the Sellers). Conversely, if the Buyer has been able to conduct a significant portion of its investigation prior to execution and is comfortable with the results of that investigation, the Buyer may have greater latitude in responding to the Sellers' requests to pare down the Seller's representations.

The Sellers may want to negotiate certain limitations on the scope of the Buyer's investigation. For example, the Sellers may have disclosed that the Company is involved in a dispute with a competitor or is the subject of a governmental investigation. While the Buyer clearly has a legitimate interest in ascertaining as much as it can about the dispute or investigation, both the Sellers and the Buyer should exercise caution in granting access to certain information for fear that such access would deprive the Company of its attorney-client privilege. *See* Hundley, *White Knights, Pre-Nuptial Confidences and the Morning After: The Effects of Transaction-Related Disclosures on the Attorney-Client and Related Privileges*, 5 DePaul Bus. L.J. 59 (1993).

The Buyer's right of access is not limited to testing the Sellers' representations and confirming the satisfaction of conditions. The Buyer may want to learn more about the operation of the Acquired Companies in order to make appropriate plans for the Acquired Companies after the closing. In particular, the

Buyer may want to have some of its personnel investigate the Acquired Companies to prepare for the integration of the Buyer's and the Acquired Companies' product lines, marketing strategies, and administrative functions.

During the investigation, the Buyer has access to a great deal of information concerning the Acquired Companies. If the information reveals a material inaccuracy in the Sellers' representations as of the date of the acquisition agreement, the Buyer has several options. If the inaccuracy results in the Sellers not being able to satisfy the applicable closing condition in Section 7.1, the Buyer can terminate the acquisition. The Buyer may, however, want to complete the acquisition despite the inaccuracy if it can obtain an adjustment in the purchase price. If the Sellers refuse to reduce the purchase price, the Buyer must either terminate the acquisition or close and pursue its indemnification rights based on the inaccuracy of the Sellers' representation (see the Commentary to Section 7.1 and Appendix A, scenario 2).

If the Buyer's investigation does not reveal an inaccuracy that actually exists, because the inaccuracy is subtle or because the Buyer's personnel did not read all the relevant information or realize the full import of apparently inconsequential matters, the Buyer may not be able to exercise its right to terminate the acquisition, but upon discovery of such an inaccuracy after the closing, the Buyer should be entitled to pursue its indemnification rights. Section 10.1 attempts to preserve the Buyer's remedies for breach of the Sellers' representations regardless of any knowledge acquired by the Buyer before the signing of the acquisition agreement or between the signing of the acquisition agreement and the closing; this approach reflects the view that the risks of the acquisition were allocated by the representations when the acquisition agreement was signed. The Model Stock Purchase Agreement thus attempts to give the Buyer benefit of its bargain regardless of the results of its investigation and regardless of any information furnished to the Buyer by the Sellers or the Acquired Companies (but see the Commentary to Section 10.1). ■

5.2 Operation of the Businesses of the Acquired Companies

Between the date of this Agreement and the Closing Date, Sellers will, and will cause each Acquired Company to:

(a) conduct the business of such Acquired Company only in the Ordinary Course of Business;

(b) use their Best Efforts to preserve intact the current business organization of such Acquired Company, keep available the services of the current officers, employees, and agents of such Acquired Company, and maintain the relations and good will with suppliers, customers, landlords, creditors, employees, agents, and others having business relationships with such Acquired Company;

(c) confer with Buyer concerning operational matters of a material nature; and

(d) otherwise report periodically to Buyer concerning the status of the business, operations, and finances of such Acquired Company.

COMMENT

Section 5.2(a) requires the Sellers to operate the Acquired Companies only in the "Ordinary Course of Business" (as defined in Section 1). This provision prohibits the Sellers from taking certain actions that could adversely affect the value of the Acquired Companies to the Buyer or interfere with the Buyer's plans for the Acquired Companies' businesses.

If the Buyer is uncomfortable with the leeway that the ordinary course of business restriction leaves the Sellers, the Buyer may want to provide a list of activities it considers to be outside of the ordinary course of business and perhaps set dollar limits on the Acquired Companies' right to take specific types of action without the Buyer's approval. Note, however, that Section 5.3 incorporates a number of specific prohibitions by reference to Section 3.16.

Because many companies are not accustomed to operating under such restrictions, the Sellers may have to implement new procedures to ensure that the restrictions will be honored. Depending on the nature of the restricted activity, the Sellers should ensure that the appropriate persons within the Acquired Company (such as directors, officers, and employees) are aware of the obligations imposed on the Acquired Companies and that procedures are implemented and monitored at the appropriate levels.

When the acquisition agreement is signed, the Buyer typically expects to become involved in material decisions concerning the Acquired Companies. Thus, clauses (c) and (d) of Section 5.2 require the Sellers to confer with the Buyer on operational matters of a material nature and to cause the Acquired Companies to report periodically to the Buyer on the status of their businesses, operations, and finances. The reach of clause (c) is broader than that of clause (a) because the Sellers must confer with Buyer on operational matters of a material nature even if such matters do not involve action outside the ordinary course of business. On matters falling into this category, however, the Buyer has only a right to be conferred with; the Sellers and the Acquired Company retain freedom to make the decisions. The Sellers have the obligation to take the initiative in conferring with the Buyer under clause (c) and in reporting to the Buyer under clause (d). For example, if an Acquired Company were a retail company, clause (c) would require Sellers to confer with the Buyer about large purchases of seasonal inventory within the ordinary course of business. However, the decision whether to purchase such inventory would remain with the Acquired Company.

In negotiating the covenants in Sections 5.2 and 5.3, the Buyer should consider whether the exercise of the power granted to the Buyer by expansive covenants may result in the Buyer incurring potential liability under statutory or common law. For example, because of the expansive reach of many environmental laws (see Section 3.19 and "Environmental Law" (as defined in Section 1)), the Buyer should be cautious in exercising the powers granted by expansive covenants to make business decisions having environmental impact. Similarly, if the Company is financially troubled, the Buyer may want to be circumspect in the degree of control it exercises over the Company lest the acquisition fail to close and claims akin to "lender liability" be asserted against the Buyer. If the Company is publicly held, the Buyer should consider the impact of control person liability under Section 20(a) of the Exchange Act and Section 15(a) of the Securities Act in determining the extent of the rights it should seek under Section 5.2. *See Radol v. Thomas*, 556 F. Supp. 586, 592 (S.D. Ohio 1983), *aff'd*, 772 F.2d (6th Cir. 1985), *cert. denied*, 477 U.S. 903 (1986). *See generally* Blumberg & Strasser, *The Law of Corporate Groups—Statutory Law—Specific* chs. 2-7 (1992 & Supp. 1993); Blumberg & Strasser, *The Law of Corporate Groups—General Statutory Law* chs. 19-28 (1989 & Supp. 1993). ■

5.3 Negative Covenant

Except as otherwise expressly permitted by this Agreement, between the date of this Agreement and the Closing Date, Sellers will not, and will cause each Acquired Company not to, without the prior consent of Buyer, take any affirmative action, or fail to take any reasonable action within their or its control, as a result of which any of the changes or events listed in Section 3.16 is likely to occur.

COMMENT

Section 5.2 requires the Sellers to cause each Acquired Company to conduct its business between the signing of the acquisition agreement and the closing only in the ordinary course of business. Section 5.3 eliminates any risk to the Buyer that the items specified in Section 3.16 could be deemed to be within the ordinary course of business by expressly prohibiting the Acquired Companies from taking such actions without the Buyer's prior consent.

The Buyer should understand, however, that Section 5.3 prevents only the taking of affirmative actions and the failure to take actions within the control of the Sellers and the Acquired Companies, as a result of which the changes or events listed in Section 3.16 may occur. Some of the changes and events described in Section 3.16 (such as the suffering of damage or loss of property as a result of an earthquake) are not within the control of the Acquired Companies. Section 5.3 does not require the Sellers to cause the Acquired Companies not to suffer damage from events described in Section 3.16 that are beyond their control—such a covenant is impossible to perform. Accordingly, if one of the Acquired Companies suffers damage or loss of property between the signing of the acquisition agreement and the closing, and that damage or loss was not the result of the Acquired Company's failure to take steps within its control to prevent that damage or loss, the Buyer would have the right to terminate the acquisition, but the Buyer would not have the right to obtain damages from the Sellers unless the Buyer had obtained a warranty from the Sellers that the representations in Section 3 would be accurate as of the closing date (see the Commentary to Section 7.1 under the caption "Supplemental 'Bring Down' Representation"). If, however, the Acquired Company could have prevented the damage or loss (because, for example, the loss resulted from a fire that was caused by the Acquired Company's negligent storage of hazardous substances), the Buyer not only would have the right to terminate the acquisition, but also would have the right to pursue damages from the Sellers (regardless of whether the Buyer elects to proceed with the acquisition).

In addition to the items listed in Section 3.16, there may be other items of concern to the Buyer between the signing of the acquisition agreement and the closing. Such items could be added to either Section 5.2 or Section 5.3.

Note that Section 5.8, operating in conjunction with Section 7.1, requires the Sellers to use their best efforts to ensure that the representation in Section 3.16 is accurate as of the closing date. Thus, Sections 5.3 and 5.8 overlap to some degree. ■

5.4 Required Approvals

As promptly as practicable after the date of this Agreement, Sellers will, and will cause each Acquired Company to, make all filings required by Legal Requirements to be made by them in order to consummate the Contemplated Transactions (including all filings under the HSR Act). Between the date of this Agreement and the Closing Date, Sellers will, and will cause each Acquired Company to, (a) cooperate with Buyer with respect to all filings that Buyer elects to make or is required by Legal Requirements to make in connection with the Contemplated Transactions, and (b) cooperate with Buyer in obtaining all consents identified in Schedule 4.2 (including taking all actions requested by Buyer to cause early termination of any applicable waiting period under the HSR Act).

COMMENT

Section 5.4 works in conjunction with Section 6.1. Section 5.4 requires the Sellers to make all necessary filings as promptly as practicable and to cooperate with the Buyer in obtaining the approvals required by the Buyer from governmental bodies and private parties (including, for example, lenders) needed to complete the acquisition. Section 5.4 does not contain a proviso similar to that in Section 6.1 limiting the Seller's obligations, because normally the potential incremental burdens on the Sellers are not as great as those that could be imposed on the Buyer.

The need for governmental approvals is more likely to arise in acquisitions of assets including items such as permits and licenses. Even in stock acquisitions, however, governmental notifications or approvals may be necessary if an Acquired Company conducts business in a regulated industry (see the ninth paragraph of the Commentary to Section 3.2). *See generally* Blumberg & Strasser, *The Law of Corporate Groups—Statutory Law—Specific* chs. 2-7 (1992 & Supp. 1993); Blumberg & Strasser, *The Law of Corporate Groups—General Statutory Law* chs. 19-28 (1989 & Supp. 1993).

The HSR Act requires the Sellers and the Buyer (or their ultimate parent entities) to make separate filings. Accordingly, Sections 5.4 and 6.1 impose the filing obligation on the Sellers and the Buyer and provide that each party will cooperate with the other party in connection with these filings. There may be circumstances, however, in which it is appropriate to give one party control over certain aspects of the approval process. For example, under the HSR Act, the acquisition cannot be consummated until the applicable waiting period expires. Although the parties have the ability to request early termination of the waiting periods, the Buyer may have more at stake in making the decision because of the accompanying earlier public disclosure of the acquisition. Accordingly, Section 5.4 gives the Buyer control over the decision to request early termination of the HSR Act waiting periods.

Responsibility for the HSR Act filing fee is allocated in Section 11.1. ■

5.5 Notification

Between the date of this Agreement and the Closing Date, each Seller will promptly notify Buyer in writing if such Seller or any Acquired Company becomes aware of any fact or condition that causes or constitutes a Breach of any of Sellers' representations and warranties as of the date of this Agreement, or if such Seller or any Acquired Company becomes aware of the occurrence after the date of this Agreement of any fact or condition that would (except as expressly contemplated by this Agreement) cause or constitute a Breach of any such representation or warranty had such representation or warranty been made as of the time of occurrence or discovery of such fact or condition. Should any such fact or condition require any change in the Disclosure Letter if the Disclosure Letter were dated the date of the occurrence or discovery of any such fact or condition, Sellers will promptly deliver to Buyer a supplement to the Disclosure Letter specifying such change. During the same period, each Seller will promptly notify Buyer of the occurrence of any Breach of any covenant of Sellers in this Section 5 or of the occurrence of any event that may make the satisfaction of the conditions in Section 7 impossible or unlikely.

COMMENT

Section 5.5 requires the Sellers to notify the Buyer if they discover that a representation made when they signed the acquisition agreement was inaccurate or that a representation will be inaccurate as if made on the closing date because of occurrences after the acquisition agreement was signed. This notification is not simply for the Buyer's information. Section 7.1 makes it a condition to the Buyer's obligation to complete the acquisition that the Sellers' representations were materially correct when the acquisition agreement was signed and that they are materially correct as "brought down" to the closing date. Section 5.5 also requires the Sellers to provide a supplement to the Disclosure Letter, which clarifies which representations are affected by the newly discovered or subsequently occurring fact.

Supplements to the Sellers' disclosure letter generally are not taken into account for purposes of determining whether the Buyer has a "walk right" under Section 7.1 (see the Commentary to Section 7.1 under the heading "Effect of Disclosure Letter Supplements"; see also Appendix A, scenarios 2, 3, and 5). Such supplements are also not taken into account for purposes of determining whether the Buyer has an indemnification right under clause (a) of Section 10.2 (see Appendix A, scenarios 2 and 4).

In contrast, supplements to the Disclosure Letter sometimes are taken into account in determining whether the Buyer has an indemnification right under clause (b) of Section 10.2. In particular, a disclosure letter supplement will be taken into account if the Sellers concede, in the "bring down" certificate delivered to the Buyer at the closing (see Section 2.4(a)(v)), that the Buyer has a "walk right" under Section 7.1 as a result of the matters disclosed in the Disclosure Letter supplement. See Section 10.2(b) and the eighth paragraph of the Commentary to Section 10.2; see also Appendix A, scenarios 5 and 9, and the

Commentary to Section 2.4 under the caption "Sellers' Closing Certificate."

The provision in Section 5.5 requiring notice of events that render unlikely the satisfaction of closing conditions also gives the Buyer an opportunity to limit its ongoing expenses and decide whether to abandon the acquisition. ■

5.6 Payment of Indebtedness by Related Persons

Except as expressly provided in this Agreement, Sellers will cause all indebtedness owed to an Acquired Company by either Seller or any Related Person of either Seller to be paid in full prior to Closing.

COMMENT

Closely held companies frequently make loans to their shareholders. When the Sellers cease to be shareholders of the Company, however, the rationale for such loans also ceases. Unless an Acquired Company is a financial institution, the Buyer probably would not view loans to the Sellers as an appropriate use of corporate assets. Indeed, the representations concerning related persons (see Section 3.25) force the Sellers to disclose any such loans, because the Buyer presumably would not approve of them.

If the Buyer is inclined to allow loans by an Acquired Company to the Sellers to remain outstanding after the closing, the Buyer should be aware that it may be difficult to collect such indebtedness if there is a post-closing dispute involving an alleged breach of representation by the Sellers. ■

5.7 No Negotiation

Until such time, if any, as this Agreement is terminated pursuant to Section 9, Sellers will not, and will cause each Acquired Company and each of their Representatives not to, directly or indirectly solicit, initiate, or encourage any inquiries or proposals from, discuss or negotiate with, provide any non-public information to, or consider the merits of any unsolicited inquiries or proposals from, any Person (other than Buyer) relating to any transaction involving the sale of the business or assets (other than in the Ordinary Course of Business) of any Acquired Company, or any of the capital stock of any Acquired Company, or any merger, consolidation, business combination, or similar transaction involving any Acquired Company.

COMMENT

Section 5.7 is commonly called a "no shop" provision. This provision was originally developed for acquisitions of public companies, as an adjunct to the Sellers' best efforts obligations, to prevent another buyer from interfering with the acquisition during the period between the signing of the acquisition agreement and the closing. In a stock acquisition, a "no shop" provision may be unnecessary because the acquisition agreement is a legally binding undertaking of the Sellers to consummate the acquisition, subject only to the satisfaction of the various closing conditions—thus, the Sellers are liable for damages if they breach the acquisition agreement to pursue a transaction with another buyer, and the other buyer may be liable for tortious interference with the acquisition agreement. Nonetheless, the Buyer has a legitimate interest in preventing the Sellers from seeking to obtain a better offer, and the "no shop" provision may provide a basis for the Buyer to obtain injunctive relief if Sellers do so.

Section 5.7 is not qualified by a "fiduciary out" exception. In several cases involving the acquisition of public companies, courts have held that the fiduciary duty of the board of directors to the shareholders of the target company overrode the target company's contractual obligation to use its best efforts to consummate the transaction. *See ConAgra, Inc. v. Cargill, Inc.*, 382 N.W.2d 576 (Neb. 1986); *Great Western Producers Co-Op v. Great Western United Corp.*, 613 P.2d 873 (Colo. 1986); *cf. Jewel Companies v. Pay Less Drug Stores*, 741 F.2d 1555 (9th Cir. 1984). The result of these cases has been that express "fiduciary out" exceptions to "no shop" provisions ordinarily are included in acquisition agreements for public companies.

In a stock acquisition, a "fiduciary out" exception is not appropriate because shareholder approval is not needed. The Sellers, who own all of the outstanding stock, have given the only required approval by executing the acquisition agreement. A "fiduciary out" exception also is not appropriate in a merger, a share exchange, or a sale of substantially all of the assets if the directors and the shareholders of the Company are the same, the number of shareholders is small enough to obtain shareholder approval prior to the signing of the acquisition agreement, or all of the shareholders sign the acquisition agreement. ■

5.8 Best Efforts

Between the date of this Agreement and the Closing Date, Sellers will use their Best Efforts to cause the conditions in Sections 7 and 8 to be satisfied.

COMMENT

Section 5.8 is a powerful provision. It establishes a contractual obligation of the Sellers to use their "Best Efforts" (as broadly defined in Section 1) to cause the conditions to each party's obligation to complete the acquisition to be satisfied. The conditions in Section 8 (conditions to the Sellers' obligation) as well as those in Section 7 (conditions to the Buyer's obligation), are included in this provision because, even though the Sellers may elect not to complete the acquisition if a Section 8 condition (such as the Sellers' obtaining a necessary release or consent) is not satisfied, the Buyer will want the Sellers to use their best efforts to cause such a condition to be satisfied (that is, to obtain the necessary release or consent).

The definition of "Best Efforts" in Section 1 makes it clear that the Sellers are obligated to do more than merely act in good faith—they must exert the efforts that a prudent person who desires to complete the acquisition would use in similar circumstances to ensure that the closing occurs within the time frame contemplated by the parties.

Thus, for example, Section 5.8 requires the Sellers to use their best efforts to ensure that their representations are accurate in all material respects as of the closing date as if made on that date, because Section 7.1(a) makes such accuracy a condition to the Buyer's obligation to complete the acquisition. Section 5.8 also requires the Sellers to use their best efforts to obtain all of the consents necessary for the Sellers and the Buyer to complete the acquisition, because Sections 7.3 and 8.3 make the obtaining of such consents conditions to the parties' obligations to consummate the acquisition.

Because Section 5.8 is a covenant, if the closing does not occur because one of the conditions in Section 7 or Section 8 is not satisfied, the Sellers may have liability to the Buyer for breach of contract if they have not used their best efforts to cause the condition to be satisfied (see the second and third paragraphs of the Commentary to Section 7). ■

6. COVENANTS OF BUYER PRIOR TO CLOSING DATE

6.1 Approvals of Governmental Bodies

As promptly as practicable after the date of this Agreement, Buyer will, and will cause each of its Related Persons to, make all filings required by Legal Requirements to be made by them to consummate the Contemplated Transactions (including all filings under the HSR Act). Between the date of this Agreement and the Closing Date, Buyer will, and will cause each Related Person to, cooperate with Sellers with respect to all filings that Sellers are required by Legal Requirements to make in connection with the Contemplated Transactions, and (ii) cooperate with Sellers in obtaining all consents identified in Part 3.2 of the Disclosure Letter; provided that this Agreement will not require Buyer to dispose of or make any change in any portion of its business or to incur any other burden to obtain a Governmental Authorization.

COMMENT

Section 6.1 mirrors Section 5.4. Section 6.1 requires the Buyer to make (or cause to be made) all filings required to consummate the acquisition. The HSR Act requires a filing to be made by the Buyer's "ultimate parent entity." Accordingly, if the Buyer is a subsidiary of another company, that company will be required to make the HSR Act filing. The provision at the end of Section 6.1 makes it clear that the Buyer's obligation is limited to efforts to persuade officials (in a legal manner) to grant approvals. The Buyer retains sole discretion to determine, for example, whether to dispose of one of its existing businesses to obtain antitrust approval. The provision at the end of Section 6.1 has no counterpart in Section 5.4; the Sellers would not expect to be asked to dispose of another business to obtain approval to dispose of the Acquired Companies.

If the Buyer is not a U.S. person, the Exon-Florio Amendment to the 1988 Defense Production Act may make advisable a filing with the Committee on Foreign Investment in the United States, an inter-executive department group constituted by Executive Order of the President. ■

6.2 Best Efforts

Except as set forth in the proviso to Section 6.1, between the date of this Agreement and the Closing Date, Buyer will use its Best Efforts to cause the conditions in Sections 7 and 8 to be satisfied.

COMMENT

Section 6.2 establishes "Best Efforts" (as defined in Section 1) as an affirmative contractual duty of the Buyer and is parallel to Section 5.8, which establishes the Sellers' best efforts duties. The Buyer should be cautious in inserting or agreeing to this provision if its obligation to consummate the acquisition is subject to a "financing out" (see the fourth paragraph of the Commentary to Section 7); if there is such an "out," the Buyer should carefully define what constitutes best efforts in this context (for example, which lenders it must seek financing from and what financing terms it must accept). ■

7. CONDITIONS PRECEDENT TO BUYER'S OBLIGATION TO CLOSE

Buyer's obligation to purchase the Shares and to take the other actions required to be taken by Buyer at the Closing is subject to the satisfaction, at or prior to the Closing, of each of the following conditions (any of which may be waived by Buyer, in whole or in part):

COMMENT

Section 7 sets forth the conditions precedent to the Buyer's obligation to consummate the acquisition of the Sellers' shares. If any one of the conditions in Section 7 is not satisfied as of the scheduled closing date, the Buyer may decline to proceed with the acquisition (without incurring liability to the Sellers) and may terminate the acquisition agreement in accordance with Section 9. A party's right to refuse to consummate the acquisition when a closing condition remains unsatisfied is often referred to as a "walk right" or an "out."

It is critical for the parties and their attorneys to appreciate the fundamental differences between closing conditions, on the one hand, and representations and covenants, on the other. While every representation and covenant of the Sellers also operates as a closing condition (subject in most cases to a materiality qualification) through Sections 7.1 and 7.2, some of the closing conditions in Section 7 do *not* constitute representations or covenants of the Sellers. If the Sellers fail to satisfy any of these closing conditions, the Buyer will have the right to terminate the acquisition, but unless there has also been a separate breach by the Sellers of a representation or covenant, the Sellers will not be liable to the Buyer for their failure to satisfy the condition. However, because of the Sellers' obligation (in Section 5.8) to use their best efforts to satisfy all of the conditions in Section 7, even if a particular closing condition does not constitute a representation or covenant of the Sellers, the Sellers will be liable if they fail to use their best efforts to satisfy the condition.

The importance of the distinction between conditions and covenants can be illustrated by examining the remedies that may be exercised by the Buyer if the Sellers fail to obtain the estoppel certificates referred to in Section 7.4(b). Because the delivery of the estoppel certificates is a *condition* to the Buyer's obligation to consummate the acquisition, the Buyer may elect to terminate the acquisition as a result of the Sellers' failure to procure the certificates. However, the delivery of the estoppel certificates is not an absolute *covenant* of the Sellers. Accordingly, the Sellers' failure to obtain the estoppel certificates will not, in and of itself, render the Sellers liable to the Buyer. If the Sellers made no attempt to obtain the estoppel certificates, however, the Sellers could be liable to the Buyer under Section 5.8 for failing to use their best efforts to satisfy the applicable closing condition. For an excellent discussion of the relationships and interplay between the representations, pre-closing covenants, closing conditions, termination provisions, and indemnification provisions in an acquisition agreement, see Freund, *Anatomy of a Merger* 153-68 (1975), and *Business Acquisitions* ch. 31, at 1256 (Herz & Baller eds., 2d ed. 1981).

Although Section 7 includes many of the closing conditions commonly found in acquisition agreements, it does not provide an exhaustive list of all possible closing conditions. Examples of additional conditions that the Buyer may want to add to Section 7 include:

- a "due diligence out" (making the Buyer's obligation to purchase the Sellers' shares subject to the Buyer's satisfactory completion of a "due diligence" investigation relating to the business of the Acquired Companies); and
- a "financing out" (making the Buyer's obligation to purchase the Sellers' shares subject to the Buyer's receipt of

a third-party loan or other financing in an amount sufficient to enable the Buyer to complete the purchase of the shares).

The Buyer may find it difficult to persuade the Sellers to include additional conditions of this type, because such conditions give the Buyer very broad "walk rights" and place the Buyer in a position similar to that of the holder of an option to purchase the Sellers' shares. For a discussion of "due diligence outs" and "financing outs," see Kling & Nugent Simon, *Negotiated Acquisitions of Companies, Subsidiaries and Divisions* §§ 14.10, 14.11[4] (1992). A number of other closing conditions that the Buyer may seek to include in Section 7 are discussed in the Commentary to Sections 7.1 and 7.4.

The Buyer may waive any of the conditions to its obligation to close the acquisition. However, the Buyer will not be deemed to have waived any of these conditions unless the waiver is in writing (see Section 11.7). This requirement avoids disputes about whether a particular condition has actually been waived. ■

7.1 Accuracy of Representations

(a) All of Sellers' representations and warranties in this Agreement (considered collectively), and each of these representations and warranties (considered individually), must have been accurate in all material respects as of the date of this Agreement, and must be accurate in all material respects as of the Closing Date as if made on the Closing Date, without giving effect to any supplement to the Disclosure Letter.

(b) Each of Sellers' representations and warranties in Sections [3.3, 3.4, 3.12, and 3.24] must have been accurate in all respects as of the date of this Agreement, and must be accurate in all respects as of the Closing Date as if made on the Closing Date, without giving effect to any supplement to the Disclosure Letter.

COMMENT

Pursuant to this section, all of the Sellers' representations function as closing conditions. Thus, the Sellers' representations serve a dual purpose — they provide the Buyer with a possible basis not only for recovering damages against the Sellers (see Section 10.2), but also for exercising "walk rights." See the Commentary to Section 3 under the caption "Purposes of the Sellers' Representations."

***Materiality Qualification in Section 7.1(a)*:** Section 7.1(a) allows the Buyer to refuse to complete the acquisition only if there are *material* inaccuracies in the Sellers' representations. A materiality qualification is needed in Section 7.1 because most of the Sellers' representations do not contain any such qualification (see the Commentary to Section 3 under the caption "The Absence of 'Materiality' Qualifications"). The materiality qualification in Section 7.1(a) prevents the Buyer from using a trivial breach of the Sellers' representations as an excuse for terminating the acquisition (see Appendix A, scenarios 4, 8, and 9).

Section 7.1(a) provides that the materiality of any inaccuracies in the Sellers' representations is to be measured both by considering each of the representations on an individual basis and by considering all of the representations on a collective basis. Accordingly, even though there may be no individual representation that is materially inaccurate when considered alone, the Buyer will be able to terminate the acquisition if several different representations contain immaterial inaccuracies that, considered together, reach the overall materiality threshold.

The materiality qualification in Section 7.1 can be expressed in different ways. In some acquisition agreements, the materiality qualification is expressed as a specific dollar amount, which operates as a cumulative "basket" akin to the indemnification "basket" in Section 10.6.

***Absence of Materiality Qualification in Section 7.1(b)*:** A few of the Sellers' representations (such as the "no material adverse change" representation in Section 3.12 and the "disclosure" representation in Section 3.24) already contain express materiality qualifications. It is appropriate to require that these representations be accurate "in all respects" (rather than merely "in all *material* respects") in order to avoid "double materiality" problems. Section 7.1(b), which does not contain a materiality qualification, accomplishes this result. Section 3.4 is included among the representations that must be accurate in all respects under Section 7.1(b) because GAAP contains its own materiality standards. For a further discussion of "double materiality" issues, see Freund, *Anatomy of a Merger* 35-36, 245-46 (1975), and Kling & Nugent Simon, *Negotiated Acquisitions of Companies, Subsidiaries and Divisions* § 14.02[3] (1992).

In addition, some of the Sellers' representations that do not contain express materiality qualifications may be so fundamental that the Buyer will want to retain the ability to terminate the acquisition if they are inaccurate in *any* respect. Consider, for example, the Sellers' capitalization representation in Section 3.3, which states that the Company has no stock outstanding other than the stock owned by the Sellers. Assume that the Sellers hold 100,000 shares of the Company's stock and that, shortly before the scheduled closing date, the Buyer discovers that a third party owns a single share of the Company's stock. The Buyer may consider it highly undesirable to acquire shares of a company that will have even one minority stockholder, no matter how insignificant the size of the minority stockholder's interest. Accordingly, the Buyer may want to terminate the acquisition in this situation. However, the Sellers will likely argue that their representation concerning the Company's capitalization is accurate in all *material* respects (because their shares comprise more than 99.99% of the outstanding shares of the Company) and that the Buyer must proceed with the acquisition. To avoid a dispute about the meaning of the term "material" in such a situation, the Buyer may seek to include the capitalization representation (and other fundamental representations made by the Sellers) among the representations that must be accurate in *all* respects pursuant to Section 7.1(b).

Even though there is no materiality qualification in Section 7.1(b), a court might establish its own materiality standard to prevent the Buyer from terminating the acquisition because of a trivial inaccuracy in one of the representations identified in Section 7.1(b). *See Business Acquisitions* ch. 31, n.24 (Herz & Baller eds., 2d ed. 1981).

***Time as of Which Accuracy of Representations Is Determined*:** Each paragraph in Section 7.1 contains two clauses. The first clause focuses on the accuracy of the Sellers' representations on the date of the acquisition agreement, while the second clause refers specifically to the closing date. Pursuant to this second clause—referred to as the "bring down" clause—the Sellers' representations are "brought down" to the closing date to determine whether they would be accurate if made on that date.

Although it is unlikely that the Sellers would object to the inclusion of a standard "bring down" clause, they may object to the first clause in Section 7.1, which requires the Sellers' representations to have been accurate on the original signing date.

This clause permits the Buyer to terminate the acquisition because of a representation that was materially inaccurate when made, even if the inaccuracy has been fully cured by the scheduled closing date (see Appendix A, scenario 3). If the Sellers object to this clause, the Buyer may point out that the elimination of this clause would permit the Sellers to sign the acquisition agreement knowing that their representations are inaccurate at that time (on the expectation that they will be able to cure the inaccuracies before the closing). This possibility could seriously undermine the disclosure function of the Sellers' representations (see the Commentary to Section 3 under the caption "Purposes of the Sellers' Representations"). *See generally* Kling & Nugent Simon, *Negotiated Acquisitions of Companies, Subsidiaries and Divisions* § 14.02[1] (1992).

***Effect of Disclosure Letter Supplements*:** Section 7.1 specifies that supplements to the Disclosure Letter have no effect for purposes of determining the accuracy of the Sellers' representations. This ensures the Buyer that its "walk rights" will be preserved notwithstanding any disclosures made by the Sellers after the signing of the acquisition agreement.

The importance of the qualification negating the effect of supplements to the Disclosure Letter can be illustrated by a simple example. Assume that a material lawsuit is brought against the Company after the signing date and that the Sellers promptly disclose the lawsuit to the Buyer in a Disclosure Letter supplement as required by Section 5.5. Assume further that the lawsuit remains pending on the scheduled closing date. In these circumstances, the representation in Section 3.15(a) (which states that, except as disclosed in the Disclosure Letter, there are no legal proceedings pending against any Acquired Company) will be deemed accurate as of the closing date if the Disclosure Letter supplement is taken into account, but will be deemed materially inaccurate if the supplement is not taken into account. Because Section 7.1 provides specifically that supplements to the Disclosure Letter are not to be given effect, the Buyer will be able to terminate the acquisition in this situation (see Appendix A, scenario 5). Although supplements to the Disclosure Letter are not given effect for purposes of determining whether the Buyer has a "walk right" under Section 7.1, such supplements are given effect (in some circumstances) for purposes of determining whether the Buyer has a right to indemnification after the closing (see Sections 2.4(a)(v) and 10.2(b) and Appendix A, scenario 5).

Operation of the "Bring Down" Clause: It is important that the parties and their counsel understand how the "bring down" clause in Section 7.1 operates. Consider, for example, the application of this clause to the representation in Section 3.4 concerning the Acquired Companies' financial statements. This representation states that the financial statements "fairly present the financial condition . . . of the Acquired Companies as at the respective dates thereof." Does the "bring down" clause in Section 7.1 require, as a condition to the Buyer's obligation to close, that these historical financial statements also fairly reflect the Acquired Companies' financial condition as of the closing date?

The answer to this question is "no." The inclusion of the phrase "as at the respective dates thereof" in the representation precludes the representation from being "brought down" to the closing date pursuant to Section 7.1. Nevertheless, to eliminate any possible uncertainty about the proper interpretation of the "bring down" clause, the Sellers may insist that the language of this clause be modified to include a specific exception for representations "expressly made as of a particular date."

The Sellers may also seek to clarify that certain representations speak specifically as of the signing date and are not to be "brought down" to the closing date. For example, the Sellers may be concerned that the representation in Section 3.17(a)(i) (which states that the Disclosure Letter accurately lists all of the Acquired Companies' contracts involving the delivery of goods worth more than a specified dollar amount) would be rendered inaccurate as of the closing date if the Acquired Companies were to enter into a significant number of such contracts as part of their routine business operations between the signing date and the closing date. (Note that, because Section 7.1 does not give effect to supplements to the Sellers' disclosure letter, the Sellers would not be able to eliminate the Buyer's "walk right" in this situation simply by listing the new contracts in a disclosure letter supplement.) Because it would be unfair to give the Buyer a "walk right" tied to routine actions taken in the normal course of the Acquired Companies' business operations, the Sellers may request that the representation in Section 3.17(a)(i) be introduced by the phrase "as of the date of this Agreement" so that it will not be "brought down" to the closing date. *See* Freund,

Anatomy of a Merger 154 (1975). The Buyer may respond that, if the new contracts do not have a material adverse effect on the Acquired Companies' businesses, the representation in Section 3.17(a)(i) would remain accurate in all *material* respects and the Buyer therefore could not use the technical inaccuracy resulting from the "bring down" of this representation as an excuse to terminate the acquisition.

The Sellers may also request that the "bring down" clause be modified to clarify that the Buyer will not have a "walk right" if any of the Sellers' representations is rendered inaccurate as a result of an occurrence specifically contemplated by the acquisition agreement. The requested modification entails inserting the words "except as contemplated or permitted by this Agreement" (or some similar qualification) in Section 7.1. To illustrate the appropriateness of the requested modification, the Sellers may point to the representation concerning the absence of encumbrances affecting their shares (see Section 3.3), which might be technically inaccurate on the closing date as a result of encumbrances arising from the Buyer's own right to acquire the shares pursuant to the acquisition agreement. Thus, the Sellers would argue, unless the requested qualification is included in the "bring down" clause, the Buyer may have the right to terminate the acquisition as a result of the inaccuracy in the Sellers' "no encumbrances" representation—an obviously inappropriate result.

The Buyer may object to the qualification requested by the Sellers because of the difficulty inherent in ascertaining whether a particular inaccuracy arose as a result of something "contemplated" or "permitted" by the acquisition agreement. *See* Kling & Nugent Simon, *Negotiated Acquisitions of Companies, Subsidiaries and Divisions* § 14.02[4] (1992). The Buyer may argue that, if the Sellers are truly concerned about technical inaccuracies in their representations, they should bear the burden of specifically disclosing these inaccuracies in their disclosure letter, rather than relying on a potentially overbroad qualification in the "bring down" clause.

***"Bring Down" of Representations That Include "Adverse Effect" Language*:** See the Commentary to Section 3.

***"Bring Down" of Representations Incorporating Specific Time Periods*:** See the Commentary to Section 3.

Desirability of Separate "No Material Adverse Change" Condition: Some acquisition agreements contain a separate closing condition giving the Buyer a "walk right" if there has been a "material adverse change" in the Acquired Companies' businesses since the date of the agreement. The Model Stock Purchase Agreement does not include a separate condition of this type because the Buyer receives comparable protection by virtue of the Sellers' "no material adverse change" representation in Section 3.12 (which operates as a closing condition pursuant to Section 7.1).

The Buyer should be aware, however, that there is a potentially significant difference between the representation in Section 3.12 and a typical "no material adverse change" condition. While the representation in Section 3.12 focuses on the time period beginning on the date of the most recent audited balance sheet of the Acquired Companies (see Section 3.4), a "no material adverse change" condition normally focuses on the period beginning on the date on which the acquisition agreement is signed (which may be months after the balance sheet date). Because of this difference, the Buyer can obtain broader protection by adding a separate "no material adverse change" condition to Section 7.

The following example illustrates the extra protection that the Buyer can obtain by including a separate "no material adverse change" condition. Assume that the Company's business has improved between the balance sheet date and the signing date, but has deteriorated significantly between the signing date and the scheduled closing date. Assume further that the net cumulative change in the Company's business between the balance sheet date and the scheduled closing date is *not* materially adverse (because the magnitude of the improvement between the balance sheet date and the signing date exceeds the magnitude of the deterioration between the signing date and the scheduled closing date). In this situation, the Buyer *would* have a "walk right" if a separate "no material adverse change" condition (focusing on the time period from the signing date through the scheduled closing date) were included in the acquisition agreement, but would *not* have a "walk right" if left to rely exclusively on the "bring down" of the representation in Section 3.12.

If a separate "no material adverse change" condition is included in the acquisition agreement, the Sellers may seek to ensure that the "no material adverse change" representation speaks only as of the signing date and is not separately "brought down" to the closing date through the condition that certain representations be true in all respects on the closing date as if made on the closing date. This can be accomplished by replacing the phrase "Since the date of the Balance Sheet" (which appears at the beginning of Section 3.12) with the phrase "From the date of the Balance Sheet through the date of this Agreement." See the Commentary to Section 7.1 under the caption "Operation of the 'Bring Down' Clause"; see also the Commentary to Section 3 under the caption "Considerations When Drafting Representations Incorporating Specific Time Periods."

***Supplemental "Bring Down" Representation*:** The Buyer may seek to supplement the "bring down" clause in Section 7.1 by having the Sellers make a separate "bring down" representation in Section 3. By making such a representation, the Sellers would be providing the Buyer with binding assurances that the representations in the acquisition agreement will be accurate as of the closing date as if made on that date (without taking into account any disclosure letter supplement delivered by the Sellers to the Buyer between the signing date and the closing date).

The Sellers will likely resist the Buyer's attempt to include a "bring down" representation because such a representation could subject them to liability for events beyond their control. For example, assume that there is a major earthquake a short time after the signing date, and that the earthquake materially and adversely affects the Acquired Companies' properties within the meaning of Section 3.16(v). If there were a "bring down" representation in Section 3 (in addition to the "bring down" clause in Section 7.1), the Buyer not only would be permitted to terminate the acquisition because of the destruction caused by the earthquake, but also would be entitled to sue and recover damages from the Sellers for their breach of the "bring down" representation (in other words, the Buyer would have the right to "walk and sue" in this situation). Although the Sellers would presumably consider this an inappropriate result, the Buyer may defend its request for a "bring down" representation by arguing that the Buyer is entitled to the benefit of its original bargain—the bargain that it struck when it signed the acquisition agreement—notwithstanding the subsequent occurrence of events beyond the Sellers' control. Thus, the Buyer would argue, the Sellers should be prepared to guarantee, by means of a "bring down" representation, that the state of affairs existing on the signing date will remain in existence on the closing date.

If the Buyer succeeds in its attempt to include a "bring down" representation in the acquisition agreement, the Sellers may be left in a vulnerable position. Even when the Sellers notify the Buyer before the closing that one of the Sellers' representations has been rendered materially inaccurate as of the closing date because of a post-signing event beyond the Sellers' control, the Buyer would retain the right to "close and sue"—the right to consummate the purchase of the Sellers' shares and immediately bring a lawsuit demanding that the Sellers indemnify the Buyer against any losses resulting from the Sellers' breach of the "bring down" representation. The Buyer should be aware, however, that courts may not necessarily enforce the Buyer's right to "close and sue" in this situation (see the cases cited in the Commentary to Section 10.1).

Although the Model Stock Purchase Agreement does not include a separate "bring down" representation in Section 3, it does include a separate "bring down" provision as part of the Sellers' indemnification obligations in Section 10.2(b). The "bring down" provision in Section 10.2(b), however, does not have the same effect as a typical "bring down" representation. While supplements to the Sellers' disclosure letter are not given effect in the context of a typical "bring down" representation, such supplements *are* given effect under Section 10.2(b) if the Sellers concede in their "bring down" certificate (delivered pursuant to Section 2.4(a)(v)) that the Buyer has a "walk right" under Section 7.1. See Section 10.2(b) and the eighth paragraph of the Commentary to Section 10.2; see also Sections 2.4(a)(v), 5.5, and 7.1 and the related Commentary.

Effect of "Knowledge" Qualifications in Representations: See the Commentary to Section 3. ■

7.2 Sellers' Performance

(a) All of the covenants and obligations that Sellers are required to perform or to comply with pursuant to this Agreement at or prior to the Closing (considered collectively), and each of these covenants and obligations (considered individually), must have been duly performed and complied with in all material respects.

(b) Each document required to be delivered pursuant to Section 2.4 must have been delivered, and each of the other covenants and obligations in Sections [5.4 and 5.8] must have been performed and complied with in all respects.

COMMENT

Pursuant to Section 7.2, all of the Sellers' pre-closing covenants function as closing conditions. Thus, if the Sellers materially breach any of their pre-closing covenants, the Buyer will have a "walk right" (in addition to its right to sue and recover damages from the Sellers because of the breach).

Section 7.2 is similar in structure to Section 7.1 (under which the Sellers' representations operate as closing conditions). Like Section 7.1, Section 7.2 consists of two paragraphs: one paragraph (Section 7.2(a)) contains a materiality qualification, and the other (Section 7.2(b)) does not. For purposes of determining whether breaches of the Sellers' covenants are material under Section 7.2(a), the covenants are considered both individually and collectively (as are the Sellers' representations under Section 7.1(a)). Moreover, the covenants identified in Section 7.2(b) (like the representations identified in Section 7.1(b)) fall into two categories:

1. covenants that already contain an express materiality qualification or that otherwise specify a standard of performance less stringent than absolute performance (such as the covenant in Section 5.8, which incorporates a "best efforts" standard); and
2. covenants that are of sufficient importance to justify giving the Buyer a "walk right" if they are breached in *any* respect (such as the covenants in Section 2.4). ■

7.3 CONSENTS

Each of the Consents identified in subparts _____ and _____ of Part 3.2 of the Disclosure Letter, and each Consent identified in Schedule 4.2, must have been obtained and must be in full force and effect.

COMMENT

Under Section 7.3, the Buyer's obligation to purchase the Sellers' shares is conditioned upon the delivery of certain specified consents (which may include both governmental approvals and contractual consents). For a discussion of the types of consents that might be needed for the sale of a company's outstanding stock, see the Commentary to Sections 3.2(b) and 5.4.

There are two categories of consents identified in Section 7.3. The first category consists of consents that are needed because of legal or contractual requirements applicable to the Acquired Companies or the Sellers. The consents in this category (which are required to be disclosed by the Sellers in part 3.2 of the Disclosure Letter) might include, for example, a consent required to be obtained by the Company from a third-party landlord under a lease containing a "change in control" provision.

The second category of consents identified in Section 7.3 includes consents that are needed because of requirements applicable to the Buyer. The consents in this category (which are required to be disclosed by the Buyer in Schedule 4.2) might include, for example, a consent required to be obtained by the Buyer from a third-party lender under a loan agreement providing that the lender must approve any major acquisition by the Buyer.

Because Section 3.2(b) contains no materiality qualifications, some relatively unimportant consents may be listed in the Disclosure Letter. Accordingly, Section 7.3 will not necessarily condition the Buyer's obligation to close on the receipt of *all* of the consents identified in the Disclosure Letter. Before executing the acquisition agreement, the parties must jointly determine which of the specified consents are significant enough to justify allowing the Buyer to terminate the acquisition if they ultimately cannot be obtained, and only those consents will be listed in Section 7.3 (see the Commentary to Section 8.3).

The condition in Section 7.3 does not overlap with the "bring down" of the Sellers' representation in Section 3.2, because Section 3.2(b) contains an express carve-out for the consents identified in the Disclosure Letter. Assume, for example, that one of the consents listed in the Disclosure Letter cannot be obtained by the scheduled closing date. In this situation, the Buyer would *not* automatically have a "walk right" under the "bring down" clause in Section 7.1(a), because the representation in Section 3.2(b) (which provides that no consents are needed except as disclosed in the Disclosure Letter) would remain accurate as of the closing date. However, if the withheld consent were included among the consents specifically listed in Section 7.3, then the Buyer *would* have a "walk right" under that section.

There is no need to refer to the HSR Act in Section 7.3 because Section 2.3 already specifies that the closing cannot take place until the waiting period prescribed by that Act has expired or been terminated. ■

7.4 Additional Documents

Each of the following documents must have been delivered to Buyer:

(a) an opinion of ______________________________, dated the Closing Date, in the form of Exhibit 7.4(a);

(b) estoppel certificates executed on behalf of ______________ and __________________, dated as of [a date not more than ___ days prior to] the Closing Date, each in the form of Exhibit 7.4(b); and

(c) such other documents as Buyer may reasonably request for the purpose of (i) enabling its counsel to provide the opinion referred to in Section 8.4(a), (ii) evidencing the accuracy of any of Sellers' representations and warranties, (iii) evidencing the performance by either Seller of, or the compliance by either Seller with, any covenant or obligation required to be performed or complied with by such Seller, (iv) evidencing the satisfaction of any condition referred to in this Section 7, or (v) otherwise facilitating the consummation or performance of any of the Contemplated Transactions.

COMMENT

Pursuant to Section 7.4, the Buyer's obligation to purchase the Sellers' shares is conditioned upon the Sellers' delivery to the Buyer of certain specified documents, including a legal opinion of the Sellers' counsel and estoppel certificates relating to certain key contracts of the Acquired Companies.

Section 7.4 works in conjunction with Section 2.4. Section 2.4 identifies various documents that the Sellers have covenanted to deliver at the closing. These documents include various instruments signed by the Sellers (such as the Escrow Agreement, the Release, the Employment Agreement, and the Noncompetition Agreement). The delivery of these documents is separately made a condition to the Buyer's closing obligation in Section 7.2(b).

In contrast, the documents identified in Section 7.4 are executed by parties other than the Sellers. Because the Sellers cannot guarantee that these other parties will deliver the specified documents at the closing, the delivery of these documents is not made an absolute covenant of the Sellers, but rather is merely a closing condition. (For a discussion of the differences between covenants and conditions, see the second and third paragraphs of the Commentary to Section 7.) Pursuant to Section 5.8, however, the Sellers are obligated to use their best efforts to obtain all of the documents identified in Section 7.4.

The Sellers may seek to clarify that the condition in Section 7.4(b) will be deemed satisfied even if the legal opinion delivered to the Buyer is not a "clean" opinion (that is, it contains specific exceptions not reflected in Exhibit 7.4(b)). In support of this request, the Sellers may point out that all of the matters covered by the legal opinion are also covered by their representations. Thus, they might argue, the availability of a "walk" right should not depend on whether the legal opinion given to the Buyer is "clean," but rather on whether the exceptions stated in the opinion are sufficiently material to preclude the condition in Section 7.1 ("Accuracy of Representations") from being satisfied.

The Buyer may deem it appropriate to request the delivery of certain additional documents as a condition to its obligation to consummate the acquisition. These additional documents may include, for example, an employment agreement signed by a key employee of the Company (who is not a stockholder of the Company), an updated title insurance policy (which may be particularly important if the Acquired Companies have substantial real estate holdings), and a letter from the Acquired Companies' independent auditors as to certain matters. (For a discussion of the use of accountants' "comfort letters" in acquisitions, see Freund, *Anatomy of a Merger* 301-04 (1975); Kling & Nugent Simon, *Negotiated Acquisitions of Companies, Subsidiaries and Divisions* § 14.06[2] (1992); and Statement on Auditing Standards No. 72 ("Letters for Underwriters and Certain Other Requesting Parties").) Although the Buyer might be able to demand various additional documents after the signing of the acquisition agreement under the "catch-all" language of Section 7.4(c), it is better to identify specifically all important closing documents in the acquisition agreement. ■

7.5 No Proceedings

Since the date of this Agreement, there must not have been commenced or Threatened against Buyer, or against any Person affiliated with Buyer, any Proceeding (a) involving any challenge to, or seeking damages or other relief in connection with, any of the Contemplated Transactions, or (b) that may have the effect of preventing, delaying, making illegal, or otherwise interfering with any of the Contemplated Transactions.

COMMENT

Section 7.5 contains the Buyer's "litigation out." This provision gives the Buyer a "walk right" if any material litigation relating to the acquisition is commenced or threatened against the Buyer or an affiliated party.

Section 7.5 relates only to litigation against the Buyer and its affiliates. Litigation against an Acquired Company or the Sellers is separately covered by the "bring down" of the Sellers' litigation representation in Section 3.15(a) pursuant to Section 7.1(a). The Sellers' litigation representation in Section 3.15(a) is drafted very broadly so that it extends not only to litigation involving the Acquired Companies or the Sellers, but also to litigation brought or threatened against other parties (including the Buyer) in connection with the acquisition. Thus, the "bring down" of Section 3.15(a) overlaps with the Buyer's "litigation out" in Section 7.5. However, the Sellers may object to the broad scope of the representation in Section 3.15(a) and may attempt to modify this representation so that it covers only litigation against the Acquired Companies and the Sellers (and not litigation against other parties). If the Sellers succeed in so narrowing the scope of Section 3.15(a), the Buyer will not be able to rely on the "bring down" of the Sellers' litigation representation to provide the Buyer with a "walk right" if a lawsuit relating to the acquisition is brought against the Buyer. In this situation, a separate "litigation out" (such as the one in Section 7.5) covering legal proceedings against the Buyer and its affiliates will be especially important to the Buyer.

The scope of the Buyer's "litigation out" is often the subject of considerable negotiation between the parties. The Sellers may seek to narrow this condition by arguing that threatened (and even pending) lawsuits are sometimes meritless, and perhaps also by suggesting the possibility that the Buyer might be tempted to encourage a third party to threaten a lawsuit against the Buyer as a way of ensuring that the Buyer will have a "walk right." Indeed, the Sellers may take the extreme position that the

Buyer should be required to purchase their shares even if there is a significant pending lawsuit challenging the Buyer's acquisition of the shares—in other words, the Sellers may seek to ensure that the Buyer will not have a "walk right" unless a court issues an injunction prohibiting the Buyer from purchasing their shares. If the Buyer accepts the Sellers' position, Section 7.5 will have to be reworded to parallel the less expansive language of Section 8.5.

There are many possible compromises that the parties may reach in negotiating the scope of the Buyer's "litigation out." For example, the parties may agree to permit the Buyer to terminate the acquisition if there is acquisition-related litigation pending against the Buyer, but not if such litigation has merely been threatened. Alternatively, the parties may decide to give the Buyer a right to terminate the acquisition if a governmental body has brought or threatened to bring a lawsuit against the Buyer in connection with the acquisition, but not if a private party has brought or threatened to bring such a lawsuit.

Section 7.5 covers threatened as well as pending litigation. Under the broad definition of the term "Threatened" in Section 1, a lawsuit may be deemed to have been threatened against the Buyer even if the Buyer has not received any formal written notice of the prospective plaintiff's intention to file suit.

For the Buyer to terminate the acquisition under Section 7.5, a legal proceeding must have been commenced or threatened "since the date of this Agreement." The quoted phrase is included in Section 7.5 because it is normally considered inappropriate to permit the Buyer to terminate the acquisition as a result of a lawsuit that was originally brought before the Buyer signed the acquisition agreement. Indeed, the Buyer represents to the Sellers that no such lawsuit relating to the acquisition was brought against the Buyer before the signing date (see Section 4.4).

The Buyer may, however, want to delete the quoted phrase so that it can terminate the acquisition if, after the signing date, there is a significant adverse development in a lawsuit previously brought against the Buyer in connection with the acquisition. Similarly, the Buyer may want to add a separate closing condition giving the Buyer a "walk right" if there is a significant adverse development after the signing date in any legal proceeding that the Sellers originally identified in their Disclosure

Letter as pending against any of the Acquired Companies as of the signing date. ■

7.6 No Claim Regarding Stock Ownership or Sale Proceeds

There must not have been made or Threatened by any Person any claim asserting that such Person (a) is the holder or the beneficial owner of, or has the right to acquire or to obtain beneficial ownership of, any stock of, or any other voting, equity, or ownership interest in, any of the Acquired Companies, or (b) is entitled to all or any portion of the Purchase Price payable for the Shares.

COMMENT

Section 7.6 overlaps to some extent with Section 7.5 and with the "bring down" of the Sellers' litigation representation in Section 3.15(a). However, while Sections 7.5 and 3.15(a) focus on pending and threatened legal proceedings, Section 7.6 focuses more broadly on "claims," including claims that have not developed into actual or threatened litigation as of the scheduled closing date.

The Sellers may object to the inclusion of the condition in Section 7.6 because this condition permits the Buyer to terminate the acquisition in the face of a meritless or trivial claim by a third party. The Buyer may respond that its "walk right" under Section 7.6 is triggered only by claims that relate to the ownership of the Acquired Companies' stock or to the payment of the purchase price for the Sellers' shares—claims that go to the very heart of the acquisition—and that the Buyer may not be able to determine at the time of the closing whether such claims have merit or are material. Thus, the Buyer would argue, the mere existence of such claims should allow the Buyer to terminate the acquisition. ■

7.7 No Prohibition

Neither the consummation nor the performance of any of the Contemplated Transactions will, directly or indirectly (with or without notice or lapse of time), materially contravene, or conflict with, or result in a material violation of, or cause Buyer or any Person affiliated with Buyer to suffer any material adverse consequence under, (a) any applicable Legal Requirement or Order, or (b) any Legal Requirement or Order that has been published, introduced, or otherwise [formally] proposed by or before any Governmental Body.

COMMENT

Section 7.7 allows the Buyer to terminate the acquisition if the Buyer or any affiliated party would violate any law, regulation, or other legal requirement as a result of the acquisition. This Section supplements the Sellers' "no conflict" representation in Section 3.2(b)(ii) and the Sellers' "compliance with legal requirements" representation in Section 3.15(a), both of which operate as closing conditions pursuant to Section 7.1(a). However, unlike the representations in Sections 3.2(b)(ii) and 3.15(a) (which focus exclusively on legal requirements applicable to the Acquired Companies and the Sellers), Section 7.7 focuses on legal requirements applicable to the Buyer and its affiliates.

Section 7.7 refers to proposed legal requirements as well as to those already in effect. Thus, if legislation is proposed that would prohibit or impose material restrictions on the Buyer's control or ownership of the stock of the Company, the Buyer will be able to terminate the acquisition on the scheduled closing date, even though the proposed legislation might never become law. (Note that the term "Contemplated Transactions" is defined broadly in Section 1 to include the Buyer's "ownership of the Shares and exercise of control over the Acquired Companies.") The Sellers may seek to limit the scope of Section 7.7 to legal requirements that are in effect on the scheduled closing date.

The Buyer may exercise its "walk right" under Section 7.7 if the acquisition would cause it to "suffer any material adverse consequence" under any applicable law, even though there might be no actual "violation" of the law in question. Thus, for example, the Buyer would be permitted to terminate the acquisition under Section 7.7 because of the enactment of a statute prohibiting the Buyer from voting or receiving dividends with respect to the shares to be purchased under the acquisition agreement, even though the statute in question might not actually impose an outright prohibition on the Buyer's acquisition or ownership of such shares.

The Buyer should be aware that Section 7.7 does not allow the Buyer to terminate the acquisition merely because of an adverse change in the general regulatory climate in which the Acquired Companies operate. The Buyer cannot terminate the acquisition under Section 7.7 unless the acquisition itself (or one of the other contemplated transactions) would trigger a material violation or a material adverse consequence under an applicable or proposed legal requirement.

The Sellers may take the position that Section 7.7 should extend only to legal requirements that have been adopted or proposed since the date of the acquisition agreement, arguing that the Buyer should not be entitled to terminate the acquisition as a result of an anticipated violation of a statute that was already in place (and that the Buyer presumably knew to be in place) when the Buyer signed the agreement. The Buyer may respond that, even if a particular statute is already in effect as of the signing date, there may subsequently be significant changes in the interpretation of the statute or in the government's enforcement of the statute, and that such changes should be sufficient to justify the Buyer's refusal to complete the acquisition. Indeed, the Buyer may seek to expand the scope of Section 7.7 to ensure that the Buyer will have a "walk right" if any such change in the interpretation or enforcement of a legal requirement creates a mere risk that such a violation might occur or be asserted, even though there may be some uncertainty about the correct interpretation of the legal requirement in question. ■

8. CONDITIONS PRECEDENT TO SELLERS' OBLIGATION TO CLOSE

Sellers' obligation to sell the Shares and to take the other actions required to be taken by Sellers at the Closing is subject to the satisfaction, at or prior to the Closing, of each of the following conditions (any of which may be waived by Sellers, in whole or in part):

COMMENT

Section 8 sets forth the conditions precedent to the Sellers' obligation to sell their shares to the Buyer. The failure to satisfy any of these conditions will give the Sellers a "walk right" and the right to terminate the acquisition agreement under Section 9.

The structure of Section 8 is similar to the structure of Section 7, and there is a degree of symmetry between the two sections. Specifically:

Section 8.1 corresponds generally to Section 7.1;
Section 8.2 corresponds generally to Section 7.2;

Section 8.3 corresponds generally to Section 7.3;
Section 8.4 corresponds generally to Section 7.4; and
Section 8.5 corresponds generally to Sections 7.5 and 7.7.

In reality, however, the "walk rights" given to the Sellers are much narrower than the "walk rights" given to the Buyer. This reflects the view that, if the Sellers receive their cash payments (along with appropriately executed promissory notes and employment agreements) at the closing, they will have received the full "benefit of their bargain" and, with few exceptions, should be unconditionally obligated to proceed with the acquisition. ■

8.1 Accuracy of Representations

All of Buyer's representations and warranties in this Agreement (considered collectively), and each of these representations and warranties (considered individually), must have been accurate in all material respects as of the date of this Agreement and must be accurate in all material respects as of the Closing Date as if made on the Closing Date.

COMMENT

See the Commentary to Section 7.1. Because the Buyer's representations are far less extensive than the Sellers' representations, the Sellers' "walk right" under Section 8.1 is considerably narrower than the Buyer's corresponding "walk right" under Section 7.1. ■

8.2 Buyer's Performance

(a) All of the covenants and obligations that Buyer is required to perform or to comply with pursuant to this Agreement at or prior to the Closing (considered collectively), and each of these covenants and obligations (considered individually), must have been performed and complied with in all material respects.

(b) Buyer must have delivered each of the documents required to be delivered by Buyer pursuant to Section 2.4 and must have made the cash payments required to be made by Buyer pursuant to Sections 2.4(b)(i) and 2.4(b)(ii).

COMMENT

See the Commentary to Section 7.2. Because the Buyer's pre-closing covenants are less extensive than those of the Sellers, the Sellers' "walk right" under Section 8.2 is not as broad as the Buyer's corresponding "walk right" under Section 7.2. ■

8.3 Consents

Each of the Consents identified in Subpart _____ of Part 3.2 of the Disclosure Letter must have been obtained and must be in full force and effect.

COMMENT

See the Commentary to Section 7.3. The consents referred to in Section 8.3 will not necessarily be the same as those referred to in Section 7.3, because it is sometimes appropriate to make the receipt of a particular consent a condition to the obligation of only one party. *See* Freund, *Anatomy of a Merger* 299 (1975). For example, assume that the Company is leasing an important facility from a third-party landlord under a lease that requires the landlord's approval of any "change in control" of the Company (such as the change in control that will occur when the Sellers sell their shares to the Buyer). Because the receipt of the landlord's approval will presumably be a condition to the Buyer's closing obligation (by virtue of Section 7.3), the Buyer can terminate the acquisition if the landlord's approval has not been obtained by the scheduled closing date. However, the Buyer may decide on the scheduled closing date that the facility covered by the lease is not sufficiently important to the Company's operations (and that the potential liability of the Company for failing to obtain the landlord's approval is not sufficiently great) to justify the Buyer's exercise of its "walk right" under Section 7.3. Accordingly, the Buyer may elect to waive the applicable closing condition.

In these circumstances, assuming that the Sellers have not personally guaranteed the Company's obligations under the lease and that the landlord's remedies are limited to terminating the lease and recovering damages from the Company (and not from the Sellers), the Sellers arguably should not have a "walk right." (Note that the Sellers' representation in Section 3.2 contains an express exception for consents disclosed in the Disclosure Letter; therefore, this representation will not be rendered inaccurate by virtue of the failure to obtain the landlord's approval, and the Sellers will not be liable to the Buyer if the

Buyer elects to waive the applicable closing condition and proceeds with the acquisition despite the landlord's refusal to approve the "change in control" of the Company.) Similarly, the Sellers should not necessarily have a "walk right" if there is a failure to obtain any of the consents identified on Schedule 4.2 (which lists consents needed to be obtained because of legal and contractual requirements applicable specifically to the Buyer). ■

8.4 Additional Documents

Buyer must have caused the following documents to be delivered to Sellers:

(a) an opinion of ______________________, dated the Closing Date, in the form of Exhibit 8.4(a); and

(b) such other documents as Sellers may reasonably request for the purpose of (i) enabling their counsel to provide the opinion referred to in Section 7.4(a), (ii) evidencing the accuracy of any representation or warranty of Buyer, (iii) evidencing the performance by Buyer of, or the compliance by Buyer with, any covenant or obligation required to be performed or complied with by Buyer, (ii) evidencing the satisfaction of any condition referred to in this Section 8, or (v) otherwise facilitating the consummation of any of the Contemplated Transactions.

COMMENT

See the Commentary to Section 7.4. ■

8.5 No Injunction

There must not be in effect any Legal Requirement or any injunction or other Order that (a) prohibits the sale of the Shares by Sellers to Buyer, and (b) has been adopted or issued, or has otherwise become effective, since the date of this Agreement.

COMMENT

See the Commentary to Sections 7.5 and 7.7. The Sellers' "walk right" under Section 8.5 is considerably narrower than the Buyer's "walk rights" under Sections 7.5 and 7.7. For example, the Sellers will not have the right to terminate the acquisition merely because there is pending or threatened litigation against the Sellers that challenges the acquisition; rather, the Sellers can terminate the acquisition under Section 8.5 only if there is an actual injunction (or other comparable prohibition) in place, and only if the injunction was originally issued after the signing of the acquisition agreement. ■

9. TERMINATION

9.1 TERMINATION EVENTS

This Agreement may, by notice given prior to or at the Closing, be terminated:

(a) by either Buyer or Sellers if a material Breach of any provision of this Agreement has been committed by the other party and such Breach has not been waived;

(b) (i) by Buyer if any of the conditions in Section 7 has not been satisfied as of the Closing Date or if satisfaction of such a condition is or becomes impossible (other than through the failure of Buyer to comply with its obligations under this Agreement) and Buyer has not waived such condition on or before the Closing Date; or (ii) by Sellers, if any of the conditions in Section 8 has not been satisfied of the Closing Date or if satisfaction of such a condition is or becomes impossible (other than through the failure of Sellers to comply with their obligations under this Agreement) and Sellers have not waived such condition on or before the Closing Date;

(c) by mutual consent of Buyer and Sellers; or

(d) by either Buyer or Sellers if the Closing has not occurred (other than through the failure of any party seeking to terminate this Agreement to comply fully with its obligations under this Agreement) on or before ________________, or such later date as the parties may agree upon.

COMMENT

Under basic principles of contract law, one party has the right to terminate its obligations under an agreement in the event of a material breach by the other party or the nonfulfillment of a condition precedent to the terminating party's obligation to perform. An acquisition agreement does not require a special provision simply to confirm this principle. However, Section 9 serves two additional purposes: first, it makes it clear that a non-defaulting party may terminate its further obligations under the acquisition agreement before the closing if it is clear that a condition to that party's obligations cannot be fulfilled by the closing date; second, it confirms that the right of a party to terminate the acquisition agreement does not necessarily mean that the parties do not have continuing liabilities and obligations to each other, especially if one party has breached the agreement.

The first basis for termination is straightforward—one party may terminate its obligations under the acquisition agreement if the other party has committed a material default or breach. While there may be a dispute between the parties that results in litigation, this provision makes it clear that a non-defaulting party can walk away from the acquisition if the other party has committed a material breach. To the extent that there is any ambiguity in the law of contracts that might require that the parties consummate the acquisition and litigate over damages later, this provision eliminates that ambiguity.

Under clause (b), each party has the right to terminate if conditions to the terminating party's obligation to close are not fulfilled, unless such nonfulfillment has been caused by the terminating party. Unlike clause (a), this provision enables a party to terminate the acquisition agreement without regard to whether the other party is at fault, if one or more of the conditions to closing in Sections 7 and 8 are not fulfilled through no fault of either party. For example, it is a condition to each party's obligation to close that the representations and warranties of the other party be correct in all material respects at the closing (see Sections 7.1 and 8.1). This condition might fail due to outside forces over which neither party has control, such as a significant new lawsuit. The party for whose benefit such a condition was provided should have the right to terminate the acquisition agreement, and clause (b) provides this right. If the condition cannot be fulfilled in the future, that party need not wait until the scheduled closing date to exercise its right to terminate. Also, unlike clause (a), clause (b) has no materiality test. The materiality and reasonableness qualifications, where appropriate, are incorporated into the closing conditions of Sections 7 and 8.

Clauses (a) and (b) may overlap to some extent in that the breach of a representation will often also result in the failure to satisfy a condition and neither provision contains a right by the breaching party to cure the breach. However, either party (more likely the Sellers) may suggest that a non-breaching party should not be able to terminate the agreement if the breaching party cures all breaches before the scheduled closing date. This may be reasonable in some circumstances, but both parties (especially the Buyer) should carefully consider the ramifications of giving the other party a blanket right to cure any breaches regardless of their nature.

The third basis for termination, the mutual consent of the parties, makes it clear that the parties do not the need the consent of any third-party beneficiaries (despite the disclaimer of any third-party beneficiaries in Section 11.10) to terminate the acquisition agreement.

The final basis for termination is the "drop dead" date provision. Section 2.3 provides that the closing will take place on the later of a specified date or the expiration of the HSR waiting period. Section 2.3 states that failure to close on the designated closing date does not, by itself, constitute a termination of the obligations under the acquisition agreement. Clause (d) of Section 9.1 complements Section 2.3 by enabling the parties to choose a date beyond which either party may call off the deal simply because it has taken too long to get it done. Again, like clause (b), this right of termination does not depend upon one party being at fault. Of course, if there is fault, Section 9.2 preserves the rights of the party not at fault. However, even if no one is at fault, one party should be entitled to call a halt to the acquisition at some outside date. Sometimes the "drop dead" date will be obvious from the circumstances of the acquisition. In other cases it may be quite arbitrary. In any event, it is a good idea for the parties to resolve the issue when the acquisition agreement is signed. ■

9.2 Effect of Termination

Each party's right of termination under Section 9.1 is in addition to any other rights it may have under this Agreement or otherwise, and the exercise of a right of termination will not be an election of remedies. If this Agreement is terminated pursuant to Section 9.1, all further obligations of the parties under this Agreement will terminate, except that the obligations in Sections 11.1 and 11.3 will survive; provided, however, that if this Agreement is terminated by a party because of the Breach of the Agreement by the other party or because one or more of the conditions to the terminating party's obligations under this Agreement is not satisfied as a result of the other party's failure to comply with its obligations under this Agreement, the terminating party's right to pursue all legal remedies will survive such termination unimpaired.

COMMENT

Section 9.2 provides that if the acquisition agreement is terminated through no fault of the non-terminating party, neither party has any further obligations under the acquisition agreement. The exceptions acknowledge that the parties will have continuing obligations to pay their own expenses (see Section 11.1) and to preserve the confidentiality of the other party's information (see Section 11.3).

The parties should consider the possibility of preserving the continued viability of other provisions in the acquisition agreement. For example, Sections 3.26 and 4.4 are reciprocal representations by the parties that there are no broker's fees. While any broker's fee most likely would be due only upon the successful closing of the acquisition, it is possible that a broker will demand payment of a fee after termination, in which case the parties may want this representation to continue in full force and effect. Another example is Section 11.5, which provides for the jurisdiction and venue of any action arising out of the acquisition agreement. While this provision would probably remain in effect regardless of the exceptions in Section 9.2, it is possible that the obligations of the parties in Section 11.5 would terminate along with the acquisition agreement.

If the terminating party asserts that the acquisition agreement has been terminated due to a breach by the other party, the terminating party's rights are preserved under Section 9.2. This provision deals only with the effect of termination by a party under the terms of this Section and does not define the rights and liabilities of the parties under the acquisition agreement except in the context of a termination provided for in Section 9.1. ■

10. INDEMNIFICATION; REMEDIES

COMMENT

Section 10 of the Model Stock Purchase Agreement provides for indemnification and other monetary remedies. Generally, the

Buyer of a privately-held company seeks to impose on the Sellers financial responsibility for breaches of the Sellers' representations in the acquisition agreement and for other specified matters that may not be the subject of representations. The conflict between the Buyer's desire for that protection and the Sellers' desire not to have continuing responsibility for a business that they no longer own often results in intense negotiation. Thus, there is no such thing as a set of "standard" indemnification provisions. However, there is a standard set of issues to be dealt with in the indemnification provisions of an acquisition agreement. Section 10 of the Model Stock Purchase Agreement addresses these issues in a way that favors the Buyer. The Commentary identifies areas in which the Sellers may propose a different resolution.

The organization of Section 10 of the Model Stock Purchase Agreement is as follows. Section 10.1 provides that the parties' representations survive the closing of the acquisition and are thus available as the basis for post-closing monetary remedies. It also attempts to negate defenses based on knowledge and implied waiver. Section 10.2 defines the matters for which the Sellers will have post-closing monetary liability. It is not limited to matters arising from inaccuracies in the Sellers' representations. In one respect, identified in the Commentary to Section 10.2, Section 10.2 suggests a change in existing practices. Section 10.3 provides a specific monetary remedy for environmental matters. It is included as an example of a provision that deals specifically with contingencies that may not be adequately covered by the more general indemnification provisions. The types of contingencies that may be covered in this manner vary from transaction to transaction. Section 10.4 defines the matters for which the Buyer will have post-closing monetary liability. In a cash acquisition, the scope of this provision is very limited; indeed, it is often omitted entirely. Section 10.5 defines the time periods during which post-closing monetary remedies may be sought. Sections 10.6 and 10.7 define *de minimis* levels of damage for which post-closing monetary remedies are not available. Section 10.8 provides collection techniques for the Buyer; an escrow of a portion of the purchase price and setoff rights against notes delivered as part of the purchase price. Section 10.9 provides procedures to be followed in seeking monetary remedies for, and in the defense of, third party claims. Section 10.10 provides the procedure for seeking monetary remedies for matters not involving third party claims.

The Commentary in Section 10 uses the term "indemnification" to refer to indemnification and other monetary remedies, without distinction. ■

10.1 SURVIVAL; RIGHT TO INDEMNIFICATION NOT AFFECTED BY KNOWLEDGE

All representations, warranties, covenants, and obligations in this Agreement, the Disclosure Letter, the supplements to the Disclosure Letter, the certificate delivered pursuant to Section 2.4(a)(v), and any other certificate or document delivered pursuant to this Agreement will survive the Closing. The right to indemnification, payment of Damages or other remedy based on such representations, warranties, covenants, and obligations will not be affected by any investigation conducted with respect to, or any Knowledge acquired (or capable of being acquired) at any time, whether before or after the execution and delivery of this Agreement or the Closing Date, with respect to the accuracy or inaccuracy of or compliance with, any such representation, warranty, covenant, or obligation. The waiver of any condition based on the accuracy of any representation or warranty, or on the performance of or compliance with any covenant or obligation, will not affect the right to indemnification, payment of Damages, or other remedy based on such representations, warranties, covenants, and obligations.

COMMENT

The representations made by the Sellers in acquisitions of private companies are typically, although not universally, intended to provide a basis for post-closing liability if they prove to be inaccurate. In acquisitions of public companies without controlling stockholders, the Sellers' representations typically terminate at the closing and thus serve principally as information gathering mechanisms, closing conditions, and a basis for liability if the closing does not occur (see the Commentary to Section 3 under the caption "Purposes of the Sellers' Representations"). If the Sellers of a private company are numerous and include investors who have not actively participated in the Company's business (such as venture capital investors in a development stage company), they may analogize their situation to that of the stockholders of a public company and argue that their representations should not survive the closing.

If the Sellers' representations are intended to provide a basis for post-closing liability, it is common for the acquisition agreement to include an express survival clause to avoid the possibility that a court might import the real property law principle that obligations merge in the delivery of a deed and hold that the representations merge with the sale of the shares and thus cannot form the basis of a remedy after the closing. *Cf. Business Acquisitions* ch. 31, at 1279-80 (Herz & Baller eds., 2d ed. 1981). Although no such case is known, the custom of explicitly providing for survival of representations in business acquisitions is sufficiently well established that it is unlikely to be abandoned.

Even in the relatively rare cases in which the Sellers of a private company are able to negotiate an acquisition agreement that provides that their representations will not survive the closing and otherwise expressly excludes any right to indemnification based on those representations, the Sellers may still be subject to post-closing liability based on those representations under the antifraud provisions of the federal securities laws and under principles of common law fraud. The sale of the stock of a privately held company is a sale of securities for purposes of the federal securities laws. *See Landreth Timber Co. v. Landreth,* 471 U.S. 681 (1984). The actions of a corporate officer or other agent in negotiating a merger or sale may be imputed to the Sellers to establish the scienter required for a cause of action under the antifraud provisions of the federal securities laws and for common law fraud. *See Reinfeld v. Riklis,* 722 F. Supp. 1077 (S.D.N.Y. 1990).

Section 10.1 provides that knowledge of an inaccuracy by the indemnified party is not a defense to the claim for indemnity, which permits the Buyer to assert an indemnification claim not only for inaccuracies first discovered after the closing, but also for inaccuracies disclosed or discovered before the closing. This approach is often the subject of considerable debate. The Sellers may argue that the Buyer should be required to disclose a known breach of the Sellers' representations before the closing and waive it, renegotiate the purchase price, or refuse to close. The Buyer may respond that it is entitled to rely on the representations made when the acquisition agreement was signed—which presumably entered into the Buyer's determination of the price that it is willing to pay—and that the Sellers should not be able to limit the Buyer's options to waiving the breach or terminating the acquisition agreement. The Buyer can argue that it has purchased the Sellers' representations and the related right to indemnification and is entitled to a purchase price adjustment for an inaccuracy in those representations, regardless of the Buyer's knowledge. In addition, the Buyer can argue that any recognition of a defense based on the Buyer's knowledge could convert each claim for indemnification into an extensive discovery inquiry into the state of the Buyer's knowledge.

If the Buyer is willing to accept some limitation on its entitlement to indemnification based on its knowledge, it should carefully define the circumstances in which knowledge is to have this effect. For example, the acquisition agreement could distinguish between knowledge that the Buyer had before signing the acquisition agreement, knowledge acquired through the Buyer's pre-closing investigation, and knowledge resulting from the Sellers' pre-closing disclosures, and could limit the class of persons within the Buyer's organization whose knowledge is relevant (for example, the actual personal knowledge of named senior officers having responsibility for the transaction). Aggressive Sellers may request a contractual provision requiring that the Buyer disclose its discovery of an inaccuracy immediately and elect at that time to waive the inaccuracy or terminate the acquisition agreement. The Buyer should be wary of such a provision, which prevents it from making its decision on the basis of the cumulative effect of all inaccuracies discovered before the closing.

The Buyer's ability to assert a fraud claim based on federal or state securities laws or the common law after the closing may be adversely affected if the Buyer discovers an inaccuracy before the closing but fails to disclose the inaccuracy to the Sellers until after the closing. In such a case, the Sellers may assert that the Buyer did not rely on the representation, or that its claim is barred by waiver or estoppel.

The doctrine of substituted performance can come into play when both parties recognize before the closing that the Sellers cannot fully perform their obligations. If the Sellers offer to perform, albeit imperfectly, can the Buyer accept without waiving its right to sue on the Sellers' breach? The common law has long been that if a breaching party *expressly conditions* its substitute performance on such a waiver, the non-breaching party may not accept the substitute performance, even with an express reservation of rights, and also retain its right to sue under the original contract. *See United States v. Lamont*, 155 U.S. 303, 309-10 (1984); *Restatement, (Second) of Contracts* § 278, comment a. Thus, if the Sellers offer to close on the condition that the Buyer waive its right to sue on the Sellers' breach, under the common law the Buyer must choose whether to close or to sue, but cannot close and sue. Although the acquisition agreement may contain an express reservation of the Buyer's right to close and sue, it is unclear whether courts will respect such a provision and allow the Buyer to close and sue the Sellers for indemnification.

The survival of an indemnification claim after the Buyer's discovery during pre-closing investigations of a possible inaccuracy in the Sellers' representations was the issue in *CBS, Inc. v. Ziff-Davis Publishing Co.,* 553 N.E.2d 997 (N.Y. 1990). The buyer of a business advised the seller before the closing of facts that had come to the buyer's attention and, in the buyer's judgment, constituted a breach of a representation. The seller denied the existence of a breach and insisted on closing. The buyer asserted that closing on its part with this knowledge would not constitute a waiver of its rights. After the closing, the buyer sued the seller on the alleged breach of the representation. The New York Court of Appeals held that, in contrast to a tort action based on fraud or misrepresentation, which requires the plaintiff's belief in the truth of the information warranted, the critical question in a contractual claim based on an express representation is "whether [the buyer] believed [it] was purchasing the [seller's] promise as to its truth." The court stated:

> The express warranty is as much a part of the contract as any other term. Once the express warranty is shown to have been relied on as part of the contract, the right to be indemnified in damages for its breach does not depend on proof that the buyer thereafter believed that the assurances of fact made in the warranty would be fulfilled. The right to indemnification depends only on establishing that the warranty was breached.

Id. at 1001 (citations omitted).

Although the *Ziff-Davis* opinion was unequivocal, the unusual facts of this case (a pre-closing assertion of a breach of a representation by the buyer and the seller's assertion that no breach existed and threat to litigate if the buyer refused to close), the contrary views of the lower courts, and a vigorous dissent in the Court of Appeals all suggest that the issue should not be regarded as completely settled. A recent decision of the Court of Appeals for the Second Circuit (applying New York law) has increased the uncertainty by construing *Ziff-Davis* as limited to cases in which the Sellers do not acknowledge any breach at the closing and thus as inapplicable to situations in which the Sellers disclose an inaccuracy in a representation before the closing. *See Galli v. Metz,* 973 F.2d 145, 150-51 (2d Cir. 1992). The *Galli* court explained:

> In *Ziff-Davis,* there was a dispute at the time of closing as to the accuracy of particular warranties. *Ziff-Davis* has far less force where the parties agree at closing that certain warranties are not accurate. Where a buyer closes on a contract in the full knowledge and acceptance of facts disclosed by the seller which would constitute a breach of warranty under the terms of the contract, the buyer should be foreclosed from later asserting the breach. In that situation, unless the buyer expressly preserves his rights (as CBS did in *Ziff-Davis*), we think the buyer has waived the breach.

Id.

It is not apparent from the *Galli* opinion whether the agreement in question contained a provision similar to Section 10.1 purporting to avoid such a waiver; under an agreement containing such a provision, the Buyer could attempt to distinguish *Galli* on that basis. It is also unclear whether *Galli* would apply to a situation in which the disclosed inaccuracy was not (or was not agreed to be) sufficiently material to excuse the Buyer from completing the acquisition (see Section 7.1 and the related comment).

The Eighth Circuit seems to agree with the dissent in *Ziff-Davis* and holds, in essence, that if the Buyer acquires knowledge of a breach from any source (not just the Sellers' acknowledgment of the breach) before the closing, the Buyer waives its right to sue. *See Hendricks v. Callahan*, 972 F.2d 190, 195-96 (8th Cir. 1992) (applying Minnesota law and holding that a buyer's personal knowledge of an outstanding lien defeats a claim under either a property title warranty or a financial statement warranty even though the lien was not specifically disclosed or otherwise exempted).

Given the holdings of *Galli* and *Hendricks*, the effect of the survival and non-waiver language in Section 10.1 is uncertain. Section 10.1 protects the Buyer if, in the face of a known dispute, the Sellers close believing or asserting that they are offering full performance under the acquisition agreement when, as adjudged later, they have not. However, reliance on Section 10.1 may be risky in cases in which there is no dispute over the inaccuracy of a representation—a Buyer that proceeds with the closing and later sues for indemnification can expect to be met with a defense based on waiver and non-reliance, with an uncertain outcome.

In a typical negotiated business acquisition, which involves knowledgeable principals represented by sophisticated counsel, a court should give effect to an acquisition agreement provision that the Buyer is entitled to rely on its right to indemnification and payment of damages based on the Sellers' representations even if the Buyer learns that they are inaccurate before the closing. Representations are often viewed by the parties as a risk allocation and price adjustment mechanism, not necessarily as assurances regarding the accuracy of the facts that they state, and should be given effect as such. *Galli* should be limited to situations in which the acquisition agreement is ambiguous with respect to the effect of the Buyer's knowledge. ■

10.2 Indemnification and Payment of Damages by Sellers

Sellers, jointly and severally, will indemnify and hold harmless Buyer, the Acquired Companies, and their respective Representatives, stockholders, controlling persons, and affiliates (collectively, the "Indemnified Persons") for, and will pay to the Indemnified Persons the amount of, any loss, liability, claim, damage (including incidental and consequential damages), expense (including costs of investigation and defense and reasonable attorneys' fees) or diminution of value, whether or not involving a third-party claim (collectively, "Damages"), arising, directly or indirectly, from or in connection with:

(a) any Breach of any representation or warranty made by Sellers in this Agreement (without giving effect to any supplement to the Disclosure Letter), the Disclosure Letter, the supplements to the Disclosure Letter, or any other certificate or document delivered by Sellers pursuant to this Agreement;

(b) any Breach of any representation or warranty made by Sellers in this Agreement as if such representation or warranty were made on and as of the Closing Date without giving effect to any supplement to the Disclosure Letter, other than any such Breach that is disclosed in a supplement to the Disclosure Letter and is expressly identified in the certificate delivered pursuant to Section 2.4(a)(v) as having caused the condition specified in Section 7.1 not to be satisfied;

(c) any Breach by either Seller of any covenant or obligation of such Seller in this Agreement;

(d) any product shipped or manufactured by, or any services provided by, any Acquired Company prior to the Closing Date;

(e) any matter disclosed in Part _____ of the Disclosure Letter; or

(f) any claim by any Person for brokerage or finder's fees or commissions or similar payments based upon any agreement or understanding alleged to have been made by any such Person with either Seller or any Acquired Company (or any Person acting on their behalf) in connection with any of the Contemplated Transactions.

The remedies provided in this Section 10.2 will not be exclusive of or limit any other remedies that may be available to Buyer or the other Indemnified Persons.

COMMENT

Although the inaccuracy of a representation that survives the closing may give rise to a claim for damages for breach of the acquisition agreement without any express indemnification provision, it is customary in the acquisition of a privately held company for the Buyer to be given a clearly specified right of indemnification for breaches of representations, covenants, and obligations and for certain other liabilities. Although customary in concept, the scope and details of the indemnification provisions are often the subject of intense negotiation.

Indemnification provisions should be carefully tailored to the type and structure of the acquisition, the identity of the parties, and the specific business risks associated with the Acquired Companies. The Model Stock Purchase Agreement indemnification provisions may require significant adjustment before being applied to a merger or asset purchase, because the transfer of liabilities by operation of law in each case is different. Other adjustments may be required for a purchase from a consolidated group of companies, a foreign corporation, or a joint venture, because in each case there may be different risks and difficulties in obtaining indemnification. Still other adjustments will be required to address risks associated with the nature of the Acquired Companies' businesses and their past manner of operation.

Certain business risks and liabilities may not be covered adequately by traditional representations and may be covered by specific indemnification provisions (such as Section 10.2(d)). Similar provision may also be made for indemnification for the liability arising from a disclosed lawsuit or other contingency affecting an Acquired Company, which, as a result of its disclosure in response to Section 3.15(a), would not give rise to a claim for breach of a representation (see Section 10.2(e)). The extent to which these types of provisions are included depends on the circumstances of each acquisition and is often subject to negotiation.

In the absence of explicit provision to the contrary, the Buyer's remedies for inaccuracies in the Sellers' representations may not be limited to those provided by the indemnification provisions; the Buyer may also have causes of action based on breach of contract, fraud and misrepresentation, federal securities laws, and other federal and state statutory claims until the expiration of the applicable statute of limitations. The Sellers therefore may want to add a clause providing that the indemnification provisions are the sole remedy for any claims relating to the sale of the shares. This clause could also limit the parties' rights to monetary damages only, at least after the closing. The Model Stock Purchase Agreement states that indemnification is not the exclusive remedy, but the limitations on when claims may be asserted (Section 10.5) and the deductible or "basket" provisions (Sections 10.6 and 10.7) apply to the parties' liability "for indemnification or otherwise."

Liabilities arising under the federal securities laws cannot be waived by an exclusivity clause. *See* Section 14 of the Securities Act of 1933, 15 U.S.C. § 77n (1988); Section 29 of the Securities Exchange Act of 1934, 15 U.S.C. § 78cc (1988). Other claims, including those based on common law fraud, may also survive an exclusivity clause under applicable state law.

The scope of the indemnification provisions is important. The Buyer generally will want the indemnification provisions to cover breaches of representations in the Disclosure Letter, any supplements to the Disclosure Letter, and any other certificates delivered pursuant to the acquisition agreement, but may not want the indemnification provisions to cover breaches of non-competition agreements, ancillary service agreements, and similar agreements related to the acquisition, for which there would normally be separate breach of contract remedies, separate limitations (if any) regarding timing and amounts of any claims for damages, and perhaps equitable remedies.

Section 10.2(a) provides for indemnification for any breach of the Sellers' representations in the acquisition agreement and the Disclosure Letter as of the signing date. The Sellers may seek to exclude from the indemnity a breach of the representations in the original acquisition agreement if the breach is disclosed by a supplement to the Disclosure Letter before the closing. This provides an incentive for the Sellers to update the Disclosure Letter carefully, although it also limits the Buyer's remedy to refusing to complete the acquisition if a material breach of the original representations is discovered and disclosed by the Sellers (see Appendix A, scenario 2). For a discussion of related issues, see the Commentary to Section 10.1.

Section 10.2(b) provides for indemnification for an undisclosed breach of the Sellers' representations as of the closing date (see Appendix A, scenario 7). This represents customary practice. However, the Model Stock Purchase Agreement departs from customary practice by providing that, if a disclosure letter supplement discloses inaccuracies in the Sellers' representations as of the closing date, this disclosure will be disregarded for purposes of an indemnification claim (that is, the Sellers will still be subject to indemnification liability for such inaccuracies) unless the Sellers concede that these inaccuracies resulted in failure of a condition to the Buyer's obligations and thus permit the Buyer to elect not to close (see Appendix A, scenarios 5 and 9). Although unusual, this structure is designed to protect the Buyer against changes that occur after the execution of the acquisition agreement and before the closing. Without such a provision, the Buyer would be obligated to acquire a business that did not at the time of the closing conform to the Sellers' representations, and the Buyer would have no right to indemnification for these adverse changes. If the Sellers concede that the condition was not satisfied and the Buyer nevertheless elects to close, the disclosed inaccuracies as of the closing date will not provide a basis for indemnification.

The Model Stock Purchase Agreement provides for indemnification for any inaccuracy in the documents delivered pursuant to the acquisition agreement. Broadly interpreted, this could apply to any documents reviewed by the Buyer during its due diligence investigation. The Buyer may believe that it is entitled to this degree of protection, but the Sellers can argue that (a) if the Buyer wants to be assured of a given fact, that fact should be included in the representations in the acquisition agreement, and (b) to demand that all documents provided by the Sellers be factually accurate, or to require the Sellers to correct inaccuracies in them, places unrealistic demands on the Sellers and would needlessly hamper the due diligence process. As an alternative, the Sellers may represent that they are not aware of any material inaccuracies or omissions in certain specified documents reviewed by the Buyer during the due diligence process.

Section 10.2 provides for joint and several liability, which the Buyer will typically request and the Sellers, seeking to limit their exposure to several liability (usually in proportion to each Seller's percentage ownership), may oppose. Occasionally, different liability will be imposed on different Sellers, depending on the representations at issue. For example, the Sellers may be jointly and severally liable for representations concerning the Acquired Companies, but only individually liable for the representations concerning their respective ownership of the stock being sold. The Sellers may separately agree to allocate responsibility among themselves in a manner different from that provided in the acquisition agreement (for example, a Seller who has been active in the business may be willing to accept a greater share of the liability than one who has not).

Factors of creditworthiness may influence the Buyer in selecting the persons from whom to seek an indemnity. If one of the Sellers is part of a consolidated group of companies, that Seller may request that the indemnity be limited to, and the Buyer may be satisfied with an indemnity from, a single member of the Seller's consolidated group (often the ultimate parent), as long as the Buyer is reasonably comfortable with the credit of the indemnitor. In other circumstances, the Buyer may seek an indemnity (or guaranty of an indemnity) from an affiliate of the Seller (for example, an individual who is the sole shareholder of a Seller that is a thinly capitalized holding company). For other ways of dealing with an indemnitor whose credit is questionable, see the Commentary to Section 10.8.

The persons indemnified may include virtually everyone on the Buyer's side of the acquisition, including directors, officers, and stockholders who may become defendants in litigation involving the Acquired Companies or who may suffer a loss resulting from their association with problems at the Acquired Companies. It may be appropriate to include fiduciaries of the Buyer's employee benefit plans if such plans have played a role in the acquisition, such as when an employee stock ownership plan participates in a leveraged buyout. These persons are not, however, expressly made third-party beneficiaries of the indemnification provisions, which may therefore be read as giving the Buyer a contractual right to cause the Sellers to indemnify such persons, and Section 11.10 provides that no third-party rights are created by the acquisition agreement. Creation of third-party beneficiary status may prevent the Buyer from amending the indemnification provisions or compromising claims for indemnification without obtaining the consent of the third-party beneficiaries.

The definition of "Damages" is very broad and includes, among other things, losses unrelated to third-party claims. However, the common law definition of the term "indemnification" describes a restitutionary cause of action in which a plaintiff sues a defendant for reimbursement of payments made by the plaintiff to a third party. A court may hold, therefore, that a drafter's unadorned use of the term "indemnify" (usually coupled with "and hold harmless") refers only to compensation for losses due to third-party claims. *See Pacific Gas & Electric Co. v. G.W. Thomas Drayage & Rigging Co.,* 442 P.2d 641, 646 n.9 (Cal. 1968) (indemnity clause in a contract ambiguous on the issue; failure to admit extrinsic evidence on the point was error); *see also Mesa Sand & Gravel Co. v. Landfill,* 759 P.2d 757, 760 (Colo. Ct. App. 1988), *rev'd in part on other grounds*, 776 P.2d 362 (Colo. 1989) (indemnification clause covers only payments made to third parties). *But see Atari Corp. v. Ernst & Whinney,* 981 F.2d 1025, 1031 (9th Cir. 1992) (limiting *Pacific Gas & Electric* and relying on Black's Law Dictionary; the term "indemnification" is not limited to repayment of amounts expended on third party claims); *Edward E. Gillen Co. v. United States,* 825 F.2d 1155, 1157 (7th Cir. 1987) (same). Modern usage and practice have redefined the term "indemnification" in the acquisition context to refer to compensation for all losses and expenses, from any source, caused by a breach of the acquisition agreement (or other specified events). The courts presumably will respect express contract language that incorporates the broader meaning. In Section 10.2 of the Model Stock Purchase Agreement, the express language that a third-party claim is not required makes the parties' intent unequivocally clear that compensable damages may exist absent a third-party claim and if no payment has been made by the Buyer to any person.

The amount to be indemnified is generally the dollar value of the out-of-pocket payment or loss. That amount may not fully compensate the Buyer, however, if the loss relates to an item that was the basis of a pricing multiple. For example, if the Buyer agreed to pay $10,000,000, which represented five times earnings, but it was discovered after the closing that annual earnings were overstated by $200,000 because inventories were overstated by that amount, indemnification of $200,000 for the inventory shortage would not reimburse the Buyer fully for its $1,000,000 overpayment. The acquisition agreement could specify the basis for the calculation of the purchase price (which may be hotly contested by the Sellers) and provide specifically for indemnification for overpayments based on that pricing methodology. The Buyer should proceed cautiously in this area, since the corollary to the argument that it is entitled to indemnification based on a multiple of earnings is that any matter that affects the balance sheet but not the earnings statement (for example, fixed asset valuation) should not be indemnified at all. Furthermore, raising the subject in negotiations may lead to an express provision excluding the possibility of determining damages on this basis. The inclusion of diminution of value as an element of damages gives the Buyer flexibility to seek recovery on this basis without an express statement of its pricing methodology.

The Sellers often argue that the appropriate measure of damages is the amount of the Buyer's out-of-pocket payment, less any tax benefit that the Buyer receives as a result of the loss, liability, or expense. If this approach is accepted, the logical extension is to include in the measure of damages the tax cost to the Buyer of receiving the indemnification payment (including tax costs resulting from a reduction in basis, and the resulting reduction in depreciation and amortization or increase in gain recognized on a sale, if the indemnification payment is treated as an adjustment of purchase price). The resulting provisions, and the impact on the Buyer's administration of its tax affairs, are highly complex and the entire issue of adjustment for tax benefits and costs is often omitted to avoid this complexity. The Sellers may also argue that the acquisition agreement should explicitly state that damages will be net of any insurance proceeds or payments from any other responsible parties. If the Buyer is willing to accept such a limitation, it should be careful to ensure that it is compensated for any cost it incurs due to insurance or other third-party recoveries, including those that may result from retrospective premium adjustments, experience-based premium adjustments, and indemnification obligations. Aggressive Sellers may also seek to reduce the damages to which the Buyer is entitled by any so-called "found assets" (assets of an Acquired Company not reflected on its financial statements). The problems inherent in valuing such assets and in determining whether they add to the value of the Acquired Company in a way not already taken into account in the purchase price lead most Buyers to reject any such proposal.

Occasionally, the Buyer insists that damages include interest from the date the Buyer first is required to pay any expense through the date the indemnification payment is received. Such a provision may be appropriate if the Buyer expects to incur substantial expenses before the Buyer's right to indemnification has been established, and also lessens the Sellers' incentive to dispute the claim for purposes of delay.

If the acquisition agreement contains post-closing adjustment mechanisms, the Sellers should ensure that the indemnification provisions do not require the Sellers to compensate the Buyer for matters already taken into account through the post-closing adjustment process. This can be done by providing that the damages subject to indemnification for a matter that was also the subject of a post-closing adjustment are reduced by the amount of the corresponding purchase price reduction.

Generally, indemnification is not available for claims made that later prove to be groundless (for example, a groundless allegation by a Company employee that before the closing she was promised a large bonus). Thus, the Buyer could incur substantial expenses in investigating and litigating a claim without being able to obtain indemnification. In this respect, the indemnification provisions in many acquisition agreements provide less protection than indemnities given in other situations such as securities underwriting agreements. The definition of "Breach" in Section 1, which is used in Section 10.2, takes a more aggressive approach by including "any claim (by any Person) . . . that is . . . inconsistent with such representation." Section 10.2(f) takes a similar approach with respect to brokerage claims. ■

10.3 Indemnification and Payment of Damages by Sellers—Environmental Matters

In addition to the provisions of Section 10.2, Sellers, jointly and severally, will indemnify and hold harmless Buyer, the Acquired Companies, and the other Indemnified Persons for, and will pay to Buyer, the Acquired Companies, and the other Indemnified Persons the amount of, any Damages (including costs of cleanup, containment, or other remediation) arising, directly or indirectly, from or in connection with:

(a) any Environmental, Health, and Safety Liabilities arising out of or relating to: (i) (A) the ownership, operation, or condition at any time on or prior to the Closing Date of the Facilities or any other properties and assets (whether real, personal, or mixed and whether tangible or intangible) in which Sellers or any Acquired Company has or had an interest, or (B) any Hazardous Materials or other contaminants that were present on the Facilities or such other properties and assets at any time on or prior to the Closing Date; or (ii) (A) any Hazardous Materials or other contaminants, wherever located, that were, or were allegedly, generated, transported, stored, treated, Released, or otherwise handled by Sellers or any Acquired Company or by any other Person for whose conduct they are or may be held responsible at any time on or prior to the Closing Date, or (B) any Hazardous Activities that were, or were allegedly, conducted by Sellers or any Acquired Company or by any other Person for whose conduct they are or may be held responsible; or

(b) any bodily injury (including illness, disability, and death, and regardless of when any such bodily injury occurred, was incurred, or manifested itself), personal injury, property damage (including trespass, nuisance, wrongful eviction, and deprivation of the use of real property), or other damage of or to any Person, including any employee or former employee of Sellers or any Acquired Company or any other Person for whose conduct they are or may be held responsible, in any way arising from or allegedly arising from any Hazardous

Activity conducted or allegedly conducted with respect to the Facilities or the operation of the Acquired Companies prior to the Closing Date, or from Hazardous Material that was (i) present or suspected to be present on or before the Closing Date on or at the Facilities (or present or suspected to be present on any other property, if such Hazardous Material emanated or allegedly emanated from any of the Facilities and was present or suspected to be present on any of the Facilities on or prior to the Closing Date) or (ii) Released or allegedly Released by Sellers or any Acquired Company or any other Person for whose conduct they are or may be held responsible, at any time on or prior to the Closing Date.

Buyer will be entitled to control any Cleanup, any related Proceeding, and, except as provided in the following sentence, any other Proceeding with respect to which indemnity may be sought under this Section 10.3. The procedure described in Section 10.9 will apply to any claim solely for monetary damages relating to a matter covered by this Section 10.3.

COMMENT

This provision for indemnification for environmental matters supplements and largely overlaps the indemnification provided in Section 10.2, which addresses inaccuracies in or inconsistencies with the Sellers' representations (including those relating to environmental matters in Section 3.19). There are several reasons why a Buyer may seek to include separate indemnification for environmental matters instead of relying on the general indemnification based on the Sellers' representations. Environmental matters are often the subject of a risk allocation agreement with respect to unknown and unknowable liabilities, and Sellers who are willing to assume those risks may nevertheless be reluctant to make representations concerning factual matters of which they cannot possibly have knowledge. An indemnification obligation that goes beyond the scope of the representation implements such an agreement. In addition, the nature of, and the potential for disruption arising from, environmental cleanup activities often leads the Buyer to seek different procedures for handling claims with respect to environmental matters. A Buyer will often feel a greater need to control the cleanup and related proceedings than it will to control other types of litigation.

The effectiveness of contractual provisions such as indemnification in protecting the Buyer against environmental liabilities is difficult to evaluate. Such liabilities may be discovered at any time in the future and are not cut off by any statute of limitations that refers to the date of release of hazardous materials. In contrast, a contractual provision may have an express temporal limitation, and in any event should be expected to decrease in usefulness over time as parties go out of existence or become difficult to locate (especially when the Sellers are individuals). The Buyer may be reluctant to assume that the Sellers will be available and have adequate resources to meet an obligation that matures several years after the acquisition. In addition, environmental liabilities may be asserted by governmental agencies and third parties, which are not bound by the acquisition agreement and are not bound to pursue only the indemnitor.

Finally, it is often difficult to assess the economic adequacy of an environmental indemnity. Even with an environmental audit, estimates of the cost of remediation or compliance may prove to be considerably understated years later when the process is completed, and the Sellers' financial ability to meet that obligation at that time cannot be assured. These limitations on the usefulness of indemnification provisions may lead, as a practical matter, to the negotiation of a price reduction or an increased escrow of funds or letter of credit to meet indemnification obligations, in conjunction with some limitation on the breadth of the provisions themselves. Often, the amount of monies saved by the Buyer at the time of the closing will be far more certain than the amount it may receive years later under an indemnification provision.

While a responsible party's liability to the government and third parties under CERCLA cannot be transferred to another party by contract (*see* 42 U.S.C. § 9607(e)), express contractual allocation has generally been held to be enforceable between the parties to the contract, and an indemnification provision would thus be enforceable between the Buyer and the Sellers. *See, e.g., Mardan Corp. v. CGC Music, Ltd.*, 804 F.2d 1454 (9th Cir. 1986). There is, however, some authority to the effect that indemnity agreements between potentially responsible parties under CERCLA are unenforceable. *See CPC Int'l, Inc. v. Aerojet-General Corp.*, 759 F. Supp. 1269 (W.D. Mich. 1991); *AM Int'l Inc. v. International Forging Equip.*, 743 F. Supp. 525 (N.D. Ohio 1990).

One consequence of treating an unknown risk through an indemnity instead of a representation is that the Buyer may be required to proceed with the acquisition even if a basis for the liability in question is discovered prior to the closing, because the existence of a liability subject to indemnification will not by itself cause a failure of the condition specified in Section 7.1. The representations in Section 3.19 substantially overlap this indemnity in order to avoid that consequence.

The issue of control of cleanup and other environmental matters is often controversial. The Buyer may argue for control based upon the unusually great potential that these matters have for interference with business operations. The Sellers may argue for control based upon their financial responsibility under the indemnification provision.

If the Sellers are unwilling to commit to such broad indemnification provisions, or if the Buyer is not satisfied with such provisions because of specific environmental risks that are disclosed or become known through the due diligence process or are to be anticipated from the nature of the Acquired Companies' businesses, several alternatives exist for resolving the risk allocation problems that may arise. For example, the Sellers may ultimately agree to a reduction in the purchase price in return for deletion or limitation of their indemnification obligations.

The Sellers are likely to have several concerns with the indemnification provisions in Section 10.3. Many of these concerns are discussed in the Commentary to Section 3.19, such as the indemnification for third-party actions and with respect to substances that may be considered hazardous in the future or with respect to future environmental laws. The Sellers may also be interested in having the Buyer indemnify them for liabilities arising from the operation of the Acquired Companies' businesses after the closing date, although it is often difficult for Sellers to articulate the basis on which they may have liability for these matters.

The Sellers may object to obligations regarding future environmental laws and concomitant liabilities arising from common law decisions interpreting such laws. From the Buyer's perspective, however, the reference to future laws is needed to account for strict liability statutes such as CERCLA that impose liability retroactively. The Sellers may insist that the representations in Section 3.19 clearly be limited to existing or prior laws.

Although representations and indemnification provisions address many environmental issues, it is typical for the Buyer to undertake an environmental due diligence process prior to acquiring any interest from the Sellers. Phase I of such a process usually includes a review of pertinent records, site visits, and interviews with selected personnel. Based upon the results of the Phase I process, a Phase II audit may be developed and implemented. A Phase II audit normally involves investigation, sampling, and analysis of potential areas of concern. ■

10.4 Indemnification and Payment of Damages by Buyer

Buyer will indemnify and hold harmless Sellers, and will pay to Sellers the amount of any Damages arising, directly or indirectly, from or in connection with (a) any Breach of any representation or warranty made by Buyer in this Agreement or in any certificate delivered by Buyer pursuant to this Agreement, (b) any Breach by Buyer of any covenant or obligation of Buyer in this Agreement, or (c) any claim by any Person for brokerage or finder's fees or commissions or similar payments based upon any agreement or understanding alleged to have been made by such Person with Buyer (or any Person acting on its behalf) in connection with any of the Contemplated Transactions.

COMMENT

In general, the indemnification by the Buyer is similar to that of the Sellers. The significance of the Buyer's indemnity will depend to a large extent on the type of consideration being paid and, as a result, on the breadth of the Buyer's representations. If the consideration paid to the Sellers is equity securities of the Buyer, the Sellers may seek broad representations and indemnification comparable to that given by the Sellers, including indemnification that covers specific known problems. In all cash transactions, however, the Buyer's representations are usually minimal and the Buyer generally runs little risk of liability for post-closing indemnification. It is not unusual for the Buyer's first draft to omit this provision entirely. ■

10.5 Time Limitations

If the Closing occurs, Sellers will have no liability (for indemnification or otherwise) with respect to any representation or warranty, or covenant or obligation to be performed and complied with prior to the

Closing Date, other than those in Sections 3.3, 3.11, 3.13, and 3.19, unless on or before ______________ Buyer notifies Sellers of a claim specifying the factual basis of that claim in reasonable detail to the extent then known by Buyer; a claim with respect to Section 3.3, 3.11, 3.13, or 3.19, or a claim for indemnification or reimbursement not based upon any representation or warranty or any covenant or obligation to be performed and complied with prior to the Closing Date, may be made at any time. If the Closing occurs, Buyer will have no liability (for indemnification or otherwise) with respect to any representation or warranty, or covenant or obligation to be performed and complied with prior to the Closing Date, unless on or before _______ Sellers notify Buyer of a claim specifying the factual basis of that claim in reasonable detail to the extent then known by Sellers.

COMMENT

It is customary for an acquisition agreement to specify the time period within which a claim for indemnification must be made. The Sellers want to have uncertainty eliminated after a period of time, and the Buyer wants to have a reasonable opportunity to discover any basis for indemnification. The time period will vary depending on factors such as the type of business, the adequacy of financial statements, the Buyer's plans for retaining existing management, the Buyer's ability to perform a thorough investigation prior to the acquisition, the method of determination of the purchase price, and the relative bargaining strength of the parties. A two-year period may be sufficient for most liabilities because it will permit at least one post-closing audit and because, as a practical matter, many hidden liabilities will be uncovered within two years. However, an extended or unlimited time period for stock ownership, capitalization, products liability, taxes, ERISA issues, and environmental issues is not unusual.

The appropriate standard for some types of liabilities may be the period of time during which a private or governmental plaintiff could bring a claim for actions taken or circumstances existing prior to the closing. For example, indemnification for tax liabilities often extends for as long as the relevant statute of limitations for collection of the tax extends. If this approach is taken, the limitation should be drafted to include extensions of the statute of limitations (which are frequently granted in tax audits), situations in which there is no statute of limitations (such as those referred to in Section 6501(c) of the Internal Revenue Code of 1986), and a brief period after expiration of the statute of limitations to permit a claim for indemnification to be made if the tax authorities act on the last possible day.

If the Sellers are to retain certain specified liabilities (such as ERISA claims), the provisions pursuant to which they agree to retain or assume such liabilities should not be affected by any limitations on the time or amount of general indemnification payments, although any expenses relating to recovery against the Sellers could be subject to the limitations of time and amount.

The Buyer should consider the relationship between the time periods within which a claim for indemnification may be made and the time periods for other post-closing transactions. For example, if there is an escrow, the Buyer will want to have the escrow last until any significant claims for indemnification have been paid or finally adjudicated. Similarly, if part of the purchase price is to be paid by promissory note, or if there is to be an "earn-out" pursuant to which part of the consideration for the shares is based on future performance, the Buyer will want to be able to offset claims for indemnification against any payments that it owes on the promissory note or earn-out (see Section 10.8).

In drafting time limitations, the Buyer's counsel should consider whether they should apply only to claims for indemnification (see the Commentary to Section 10.2). ■

10.6 Limitations on Amount—Sellers

Sellers will have no liability (for indemnification or otherwise) with respect to the matters described in clause (a), clause (b) or, to the extent relating to any failure to perform or comply prior to the Closing Date, clause (c) of Section 10.2 until the total of all Damages with respect to such matters exceeds $______________, and then only for the amount by which such Damages exceed $__________. Sellers will have no liability (for indemnification or otherwise) with respect to the matters described in clause (d) of Section 10.2 until the total of all Damages with respect to such matters exceeds $___________, and then only for the amount by which such Damages exceed $________. However, this Section 10.6 will not apply to any Breach of any of Sellers' representations and warranties of which either Seller had Knowledge at any time prior to the date on which such representation and warranty is made or any intentional Breach by either Seller of any covenant or obligation, and Sellers will be jointly and severally liable for all Damages with respect to such Breaches.

COMMENT

Section 10.6 provides the Sellers with a safety net, or "basket," but does not establish a ceiling, or "cap." The basket is a minimum amount that must be exceeded before any indemnification is owed—in effect, it is a deductible. A more aggressive Buyer may wish to provide for a "threshold" deductible that, once crossed, entitles the indemnified party to recover all damages, rather than merely the excess over the basket. The purpose of the basket or "threshold" deductible is to recognize that representations concerning an ongoing business are unlikely to be perfectly accurate and to avoid disputes over insignificant amounts.

In the Model Stock Purchase Agreement, the Sellers' representations are generally not subject to materiality qualifications, and the full dollar amount of damages caused by a breach must be indemnified, subject to the effect of the basket established by this Section. This framework avoids "double-dipping"—that is, the situation in which the Sellers contend that the breach exists only to the extent that it is material, and then the material breach is subjected to the deduction of the basket. If the acquisition agreement contains materiality qualifications to the Sellers' representations, the Buyer should consider a provision to the effect that such a materiality qualification will not be taken into account in determining the magnitude of the damages occasioned by the breach for purposes of calculating whether the basket has been filled; otherwise, the immaterial items may be material in the aggregate, but not applied to the basket.

The Buyer may want the Sellers' obligation to fund certain types of indemnities to be absolute and not subject to the basket. For example, the Buyer may insist that the Sellers pay all tax liabilities from a pre-closing period or the damages resulting from a disclosed lawsuit without regard to the basket. The parties also may negotiate different baskets for different types of liabilities; the Buyer should consider the aggregate effect of those baskets (the Model Stock Purchase Agreement includes a separate basket for product liability claims).

The Sellers may also seek to provide for a maximum indemnifiable amount, which is frequently the purchase price. The Sellers' argument for such a provision is that they had limited liability as stockholders and should be in no worse position having sold the Company than they were in when they owned it; this argument may not be persuasive to a Buyer that views the Acquired Companies as a component of its overall business strategy, intends to invest additional capital in the Acquired Companies, or is unwilling to see its subsidiaries' obligations dishonored. If a maximum amount is established, it usually does not apply to liabilities for taxes, environmental matters, or ERISA matters—for which the Buyer may have liability under applicable law—or defects in the ownership of the stock. The parties may also negotiate separate limits for different kinds of liabilities.

Often baskets and thresholds do not apply to breaches of representations of which a Seller had knowledge or a willful failure by a Seller to comply with a covenant or obligation—the rationale is that the Sellers should not be allowed to reduce the purchase price or the amount of the basket or threshold by behavior that is less than forthright. Similarly, the Buyer will argue that any limitation as to the maximum amount should not apply to Sellers who engage in intentional wrongdoing. ■

10.7 Limitations on Amount—Buyer

Buyer will have no liability (for indemnification or otherwise) with respect to the matters described in clause (a) or (b) of Section 10.4 until the total of all Damages with respect to such matters exceeds $______________, and then only for the amount by which such Damages exceed $ ______________. However, this Section 10.7 will not apply to any Breach of any of Buyer's representations and warranties of which Buyer had Knowledge at any time prior to the date on which such representation and warranty is made or any intentional Breach by Buyer of any covenant or obligation, and Buyer will be liable for all Damages with respect to such Breaches.

COMMENT

In its first draft, the Buyer often suggests a basket below which it is not required to respond in damages to breaches of its representations, typically the same dollar amount as that used for the Sellers' basket. ■

10.8 Escrow; Right of Set-Off

Upon notice to Sellers specifying in reasonable detail the basis for such set-off, Buyer may set off any amount to which it may be entitled under this Section 10 against amounts otherwise payable under the Promissory Notes or may give notice of a Claim in such amount under the Escrow Agreement. The exercise of such right of set-off by Buyer in good faith, whether or not ultimately determined to be justified, will not constitute an event of default under the Promissory Notes or any instrument securing a Promissory Note. Neither the exercise of nor the failure to exercise such right of set-off or to give a notice of a Claim under the Escrow Agreement will constitute an election of remedies or limit Buyer in any manner in the enforcement of any other remedies that may be available to it.

COMMENT

Regardless of the clarity of the acquisition agreement on the allocation of risk and the Buyer's right of indemnification, the Buyer may have difficulty enforcing the indemnity—especially against Sellers who are individuals—unless it places a portion of the purchase price in escrow, holds back a portion of the purchase price (often in the form of a note, an earn-out, or payments under consulting or non-competition agreements) with a right of set-off, or obtains other security (such as a letter of credit) to secure performance of the Sellers' indemnification obligations. These techniques shift bargaining power in post-closing disputes from the Sellers to the Buyer and usually will be resisted by the Sellers.

An escrow provision may give the Buyer the desired security, especially when there are several Sellers and the Buyer will have difficulty in obtaining jurisdiction over the Sellers or in collecting on the indemnity without an escrow. Sellers who are jointly and severally liable may also favor an escrow in order to ensure that other Sellers share in any indemnity payment. The amount and duration of the escrow will be determined by negotiation, based on the parties' analyses of the magnitude and probability of potential claims and the period of time during which they may be brought. The Sellers may insist that the size of the required escrow diminish in stages over time. The Buyer should be careful that there is no implication that the escrow is the exclusive remedy for breaches and nonperformance, although a request for an escrow is often met with a suggestion by the Sellers that claims against the escrow be the Buyer's exclusive remedy.

The Buyer may also seek an express right of set-off against sums otherwise payable to the Sellers. The Buyer obtains more protection from an express right of set-off against deferred purchase price payments due under a promissory note than from a deposit of the same amounts in an escrow because the former leaves the Buyer in control of the funds and thus gives the Buyer more leverage in resolving disputes with the Sellers. The Buyer may also want to apply the set-off against payments under employment, consulting, or non-competition agreements (although state law may prohibit set-offs against payments due under employment agreements). The comfort received by the Buyer from an express right of set-off depends on the schedule of the payments against which it can withhold. Even if the Sellers agree to express set-off rights, the Sellers may attempt to prohibit set-offs prior to definitive resolution of a dispute and to preserve customary provisions that call for acceleration of any payments due by the Buyer if the Buyer wrongfully attempts set-off. Also, the Sellers may seek to require that the Buyer exercise its set-off rights on a pro rata basis in proportion to the amounts due to each Seller. If the promissory note is to be pledged to a bank, the bank as pledgee will likely resist set-off rights (especially because the inclusion of express set-off rights will make the note non-negotiable). As in the case of an escrow, the suggestion of an express right of set-off often leads to discussions of exclusive remedies.

Rather than inviting counterproposals from the Sellers by including an express right of set-off in the acquisition agreement, the Buyer's counsel may decide to omit such a provision and instead rely on the Buyer's common law right of counterclaim and set-off. Even without an express right of set-off in the acquisition agreement or related documents such as a promissory note or an employment, consulting, or non-competition agreement, the Buyer can, as a practical matter, withhold amounts from payments due to the Sellers under the acquisition agreement or the related documents on the ground that the Buyer is entitled to indemnification for these amounts from the Sellers under the acquisition agreement. The question then is whether, if the Sellers sue the Buyer for its failure to make full payment to the Sellers, the Buyer will be able to counterclaim that it is entitled to set off the amounts for which it believes it is entitled to indemnification.

The common law of counterclaim and set-off varies from state to state, and when deciding whether to include or forgo an express right of set-off in the acquisition agreement, the Buyer's counsel should examine the law governing the acquisition agreement. The Buyer's counsel should determine whether the applicable law contains requirements such as a common transaction, mutuality of parties, and a liquidated amount and, if so, whether those requirements would be met in the context of a dispute under the acquisition agreement and related documents. Generally, counterclaim is mandatory when both the payment due to the plaintiff and the amount set off by the defendant relate to the same transaction, *see United States v. Southern California Edison Co.*, 229 F. Supp. 268, 270 (S.D. Cal. 1964); when different transactions are involved, the court may, in its discretion, permit a counterclaim, *see Rochester Genesee Regional Transp. Dist., Inc. v. Trans World Airlines, Inc.*, 383 N.Y.S.2d 856, 857 (1976), but is not obligated to do so, *see Columbia Gas Transmission v. Larry H. Wright, Inc.*, 443 F. Supp. 14 (S.D. Ohio 1977); *Townsend v. Bentley*, 292 S.E.2d 19 (N.C. App. 1982). Although a promissory note representing deferred purchase price payments would almost certainly be considered part of the same transaction as the acquisition, it is less certain that the execution of an employment, consulting, or non-competition agreement, even if a condition to the closing of the acquisition, and its subsequent performance would be deemed part of the same transaction as the acquisition.

In addition, a counterclaim might not be possible if the parties obligated to make and entitled to receive the various payments are different (that is, if there is not "mutuality of parties"). For example, a counterclaim might not be permitted if the Sellers have consulting agreements with the Company (which after the acquisition is a wholly-owned subsidiary of the Buyer) and the Company, at the direction of the Buyer, withholds from consulting payments because the Buyer is entitled to indemnification from the Sellers under the acquisition agreement (note, however, that Section 10.2 of the Model Stock Purchase Agreement provides that both the Buyer and the Company have indemnification rights against the Sellers).

An express right of set-off should address the possible consequences of an unjustified set-off. Section 10.8 allows the Buyer to set off amounts for which the Buyer in good faith believes that it is entitled to indemnification from the Sellers against payments due to the Sellers under the promissory note without bearing the risk that, if the Sellers ultimately prevail on the indemnification claim, they will be able to accelerate the promissory note or obtain damages or injunctive relief. ■

10.9 Procedure for Indemnification—Third Party Claims

(a) Promptly after receipt by an indemnified party under Section 10.2, 10.4, or (to the extent provided in the last sentence of Section 10.3) Section 10.3 of notice of the commencement of any Proceeding against it, such indemnified party will, if a claim is to be made against an indemnifying party under such Section, give notice to the indemnifying party of the commencement of such claim, but the failure to notify the indemnifying party will not relieve the indemnifying party of any liability that it may have to any indemnified party, except to the extent that the indemnifying party demonstrates that the defense of such action is prejudiced by the indemnifying party's failure to give such notice.

(b) If any Proceeding referred to in Section 10.9(a) is brought against an indemnified party and it gives notice to the indemnifying party of the commencement of such Proceeding, the indemnifying party will, unless the claim involves Taxes, be entitled to participate in such Proceeding and, to the extent that it wishes (unless (i) the indemnifying party is also a party to such Proceeding and the indemnified party determines in good faith that joint representation would be inappropriate, or (ii) the indemnifying party fails to provide reasonable assurance to the indemnified party of its financial capacity to defend such Proceeding and provide indemnification with respect to such Proceeding), to assume the defense of such Proceeding with counsel satisfactory to the indemnified party and, after notice from the indemnifying party to the indemnified party of its election to assume the defense of such Proceeding, the indemnifying party will not, as long as it diligently conducts such defense, be liable to the indemnified party under this Section 10 for any fees of other counsel or any other expenses with respect to the defense of such Proceeding, in each case subsequently incurred by the indemnified party in connection with the defense of such Proceeding, other than reasonable costs of investigation. If the indemnifying party assumes the defense of a Proceeding, (i) it will be conclusively established for purposes of this Agreement that the claims made in that Proceeding are within the scope of and subject to indemnification; (ii) no compromise or settlement of such claims may be effected by the indemnifying party without the indemnified party's consent unless (A) there is no finding or admission of any violation of Legal Requirements or any violation of the rights of any Person and no effect on any other claims that may be made against the indemnified party, and (B) the sole relief provided is monetary damages that are paid in full by the indemnifying party; and (iii) the indemnified party will have no liability with respect to any compromise or settlement of such claims effected without its consent. If notice is given to an indemnifying party of the commencement of any Proceeding and the indemnifying party does not, within ten days after the indemnified party's notice is given, give notice to the indemnified party of its election to assume the defense of such Proceeding, the indemnifying party will be bound by any determination made in such Proceeding or any compromise or settlement effected by the indemnified party.

(c) Notwithstanding the foregoing, if an indemnified party determines in good faith that there is a reasonable probability that a Proceeding may adversely affect it or its affiliates other than as a result of monetary damages for which it would be entitled to indemnification under this Agreement, the indemnified party may, by notice to the indemnifying party, assume the exclusive right to defend, compromise, or settle such Proceeding, but the indemnifying party will not be bound by any determination of a Proceeding so defended or any compromise or settlement effected without its consent (which may not be unreasonably withheld).

(d) Sellers hereby consent to the non-exclusive jurisdiction of any court in which a Proceeding is brought against any Indemnified Person for purposes of any claim that an Indemnified Person may have under this Agreement with respect to such Proceeding or the matters alleged therein, and agree that process may be served on Sellers with respect to such a claim anywhere in the world.

COMMENT

It is common to permit an indemnifying party to have some role in the defense of the claim. There is considerable room for negotiation of the manner in which that role is implemented. Because the Buyer is more likely to be an indemnified party than an indemnifying party, the Model Stock Purchase Agreement provides procedures that are favorable to the indemnified party.

The indemnified party normally will be required to give the indemnifying party notice of third-party claims for which indemnity is sought. The Model Stock Purchase Agreement requires such notice only after a proceeding is commenced, and provides that the indemnified party's failure to give notice does not affect the indemnifying party's obligations unless the failure to give notice results in prejudice to the defense of the proceeding. The Sellers may want to require notice of threatened proceedings and of claims that do not yet involve proceedings and to provide that prompt notice is a condition to indemnification; the Buyer likely will be very reluctant to introduce the risk and uncertainty inherent in a notice requirement based on any event other than the initiation of formal proceedings.

The Model Stock Purchase Agreement permits the indemnifying party to participate in and assume the defense of proceedings for which indemnification is sought, but imposes significant limitations on its right to do so. The indemnifying party is not entitled to participate in or assume the defense of proceedings involving taxes, because these proceedings frequently involve multiple issues—of which only some may be subject to indemnification—that the Buyer will want to be able to manage and settle without interference. This may not be acceptable to the Sellers, and acquisition agreements often provide elaborate procedures for dealing with tax claims. The indemnifying party's right to assume the defense of other proceedings is subject to (a) a conflict of interest test if the claim is also made against the indemnifying party, (b) a requirement that the indemnifying party demonstrate its financial capacity to conduct the defense and provide indemnification if it is unsuccessful, and (c) a requirement that the defense be conducted with counsel satisfactory to the indemnified party. The Sellers will often resist the financial capacity requirement and seek either to modify the requirement that counsel be satisfactory with a reasonableness qualification or to identify satisfactory counsel in the acquisition agreement (the Sellers' counsel should carefully consider in whose interest they are acting if they specify themselves). The Sellers may also seek to require that, in cases in which they do not assume the defense, all indemnified parties be represented by the same counsel (subject to conflict of interest concerns).

The Sellers may seek to modify the provision that the indemnifying party is bound by the indemnified party's defense or settlement of a proceeding if the indemnifying party does not assume the defense of that proceeding within ten days after notice of the proceeding. The Sellers may request a right to assume the defense of the proceeding at a later date and a requirement for advance notice of a proposed settlement.

An indemnified party usually will be reluctant to permit an indemnifying party to assume the defense of a proceeding while reserving the right to argue that the claims made in that proceeding are not subject to indemnification. Accordingly, the Model Stock Purchase Agreement excludes that possibility. However, the Sellers may object that the nature of the claims could be unclear at the start of a proceeding and may seek the right to reserve their rights in a manner similar to that often permitted to liability insurers.

An indemnifying party that has assumed the defense of a proceeding will seek the broadest possible right to settle the matter. The Model Stock Purchase Agreement imposes strict limits on that right; the conditions relating to the effect on other claims and the admission of violations of legal requirements are often the subject of negotiation.

Section 10.9(c) permits the indemnified party to retain control of a proceeding that presents a significant risk of injury beyond monetary damages that would be borne by the indemnifying party, but the price of that retained control is that the indemnifying party will not be bound by determinations made in that proceeding. The Buyer may want to maintain control of a proceeding seeking equitable relief that could have an impact on its business that would be difficult to measure as a monetary loss, or a proceeding involving product liability claims that extend beyond the Acquired Companies' businesses (a tobacco company that acquires another tobacco company, for example, is unlikely to be willing to surrender control of any of its products liability cases).

Section 10.9(d) permits the Buyer to minimize the risk of inconsistent determinations by asserting its claim for indemnification in the same proceeding as the claims against the Buyer.

Environmental indemnification often presents special procedural issues because of the wide range of remediation techniques that may be available and the potential for disruption of the Acquired Companies' businesses. These matters are often dealt with in separate provisions (see Section 10.3). ■

10.10 Procedure for Indemnification—Other Claims

A claim for indemnification for any matter not involving a third-party claim may be asserted by notice to the party from whom indemnification is sought.

COMMENT

This Section emphasizes the parties' intention that indemnification remedies provided in the acquisition agreement are not limited to third-party claims. Some courts have implied such a limitation in the absence of clear contractual language to the contrary. See the Commentary to Section 10.2. ■

11. GENERAL PROVISIONS

11.1 Expenses

Except as otherwise expressly provided in this Agreement, each party to this Agreement will bear its respective expenses incurred in connection with the preparation, execution, and performance of this Agreement and the Contemplated Transactions, including all fees and expenses of agents, representatives, counsel, and accountants. [_____ will pay all amounts payable to [finder or investment banker] in connection with this Agreement and the Contemplated Transactions.] Buyer will pay one-half and Sellers will pay one-half of the HSR Act filing fee. Sellers will cause the Acquired Companies not to incur any out-of-pocket expenses in connection with this Agreement [except for professional fees not in excess of $_______]. In the event of termination of this Agreement, the obligation of each party to pay its own expenses will be subject to any rights of such party arising from a breach of this Agreement by another party.

COMMENT

The Buyer and the Sellers often agree that expenses will be paid by the party incurring the expense. The Model Stock Purchase Agreement adopts this view. The second sentence in brackets should be made consistent with the representations in Section

3.26 and 4.4 concerning brokers or finders. The Buyers will want the Sellers to pay most of the expenses with the Sellers' own resources and not with the Company's funds. The Sellers will prefer to charge some expenses to the Company and may be accustomed to cause the Company to pay a large amount of expenses in acquisitions. The Company's tax deduction for the Sellers' expenses may be limited. The bracketed language beginning on the seventh line caps the amount of fees that can be charged to the Company. The parties should consider state law when resolving this issue because the Company's incurring expenses that do not directly benefit the Company may be grounds for creditors and others to object to the acquisition under state fraudulent conveyance laws.

The last sentence of Section 11.1 avoids a conflict between a judgment for damages due to a breach of the acquisition agreement and any obligation to pay expenses by providing that a judgment for a breach will supersede obligations under Section 11.1. ■

11.2 Public Announcements

Any public announcement or similar publicity with respect to this Agreement or the Contemplated Transactions will be issued, if at all, at such time and in such manner as Buyer determines. Unless consented to by Buyer in advance or required by Legal Requirements, prior to the Closing Sellers shall, and shall cause the Acquired Companies to, keep this Agreement strictly confidential and may not make any disclosure of this Agreement to any Person. Sellers and Buyer will consult with each other concerning the means by which the Acquired Companies' employees, customers, and suppliers and others having dealings with the Acquired Companies will be informed of the Contemplated Transactions, and Buyer will have the right to be present for any such communication.

COMMENT

The Model Stock Purchase Agreement provides that the Buyer will control the timing and content of public announcements. The Sellers may suggest that control of public announcements be at least mutual. The Buyer and the Sellers may want to have the covenant to maintain the confidentiality of the acquisition agreement be mutual as well. Because the Buyer's and the Sellers' interests in confidentiality and controlling public announcements are nearly equal in most cases, the Buyer may want to provide in the initial draft that these covenants are mutual. If an Acquired Company has a few key suppliers or customers, the Buyer may want to have the right to approve communications with those suppliers or customers or even to be present during discussions with them regarding contemplated transactions.

The Buyer sometimes will negotiate for the additional right to visit with key customers or suppliers to obtain business information or to gain assurances that their relationship with the Acquired Companies will continue. Such a provision should be made consistent with the Sellers' obligations to obtain consents to assignments. The Buyer may want to add provisions to Section 5.11 permitting the Buyer to be present or take an active hand in obtaining consents of certain key suppliers or customers.

For publicly traded companies, the timing of a public announcement regarding the acquisition may be governed by federal securities laws. If the Company is a public company, in most cases the Buyer will not be able to control the timing of certain public announcements. ■

11.3 Confidentiality

Between the date of this Agreement and the Closing Date, Buyer and Sellers will maintain in confidence, and will cause the directors, officers, employees, agents, and advisors of Buyer and the Acquired Companies to maintain in confidence, [and not use to the detriment of another party or an Acquired Company] any [written, oral, or other information obtained in confidence from] [written information stamped "confidential" when originally furnished by] another party or an Acquired Company in connection with this Agreement or the Contemplated Transactions, unless (a) such information is already known to such party or to others not bound by a duty of confidentiality or such information becomes publicly available through no fault of such party, (b) the use of such information is necessary or appropriate in making any filing or obtaining any consent or approval required for the consummation of the Contemplated Transactions, or (c) the furnishing or use of such information is required by [or necessary or appropriate in connection with] legal proceedings.

If the Contemplated Transactions are not consummated, each party will return or destroy as much of such written information as the other party may reasonably request. [Whether or not the Closing takes place, Sellers waive, and will upon Buyer's request cause the Acquired Companies to waive, any cause of action, right, or claim arising out of the access of Buyer or its representatives to any trade secrets or other confidential information of the Acquired Companies except for the intentional competitive misuse by Buyer of such trade secrets or confidential information.]

COMMENT

This Section imposes a confidentiality obligation between the date of signing and the closing date. The Buyer should consider whether information furnished after the acquisition agreement is signed is subject to this confidentiality covenant. The language prohibiting use of confidential information protects information about the Acquired Companies' customers, markets, operating margins, and similar matters while the parties are trying to complete the acquisition. This provision will be especially important to the Sellers if the Buyer's obligation to close is contingent on obtaining financing or subject to other contingencies not related to the condition of the Acquired Companies.

The parties should consider the scope of the information subject to the confidentiality covenant. The Model Stock Purchase Agreement presents the alternatives of all information or only information that is stamped confidential when originally furnished to the Buyer. Stamping every document confidential may be impractical for the Sellers, but the Buyer may object to deeming all information confidential.

The bracketed language in the second paragraph provides that the Sellers will not bring any action against the Buyer for use of confidential or trade secret information of the Acquired Companies arising from the Buyer's access to such information. The Sellers will strenuously resist this provision if they fear that the Buyer would take strategic advantage of its knowledge of confidential and trade secret information after deciding not to complete the acquisition. ■

11.4 Notices

All notices, consents, waivers, and other communications under this Agreement must be in writing and will be deemed to have been duly given when (a) delivered by hand (with written confirmation of receipt), (b) sent by telecopier (with written confirmation of receipt), provided that a copy is mailed by registered mail, return receipt requested, or (c) when received by the addressee, if sent by a nationally recognized overnight delivery service (receipt requested), in each case to the appropriate addresses and telecopier numbers set forth below (or to such other addresses and telecopier numbers as a party may designate by notice to the other parties):

Sellers:	______________________
	______________________
	______________________
	Attention: ______________
	Facsimile No.: __________
with a copy to:	______________________
	______________________
	______________________
	Attention: ______________
	Facsimile No.: __________
Buyer:	______________________
	______________________
	______________________
	Attention: ______________
	Facsimile No.: __________
with a copy to:	______________________
	______________________
	______________________
	Attention: ______________
	Facsimile No.: __________

COMMENT

The Model Stock Purchase Agreement notice provision states that communications between the parties must be in writing and provides three alternative means for delivering such communication (personally, via facsimile, or via overnight courier). The Model Stock Purchase Agreement does *not* permit notice by ordinary mail because of the possibility that notices sent in this manner will be delayed or lost, to the detriment of both parties. Under the Model Stock Purchase Agreement, notice will be effective when received if delivered by hand or by overnight courier or when receipt is confirmed if it is sent by facsimile (provided that a copy is mailed). The drafter may prefer to have notice be effective when the party sending a notice has taken all steps that may be reasonably required to inform the other party of such notice. Thus, notice can be effective when deposited for delivery with the appropriate delivery service or after a period of time.

The parties should be sure to include street addresses to ensure proper delivery by courier. The notice provision should be modified if some parties prefer to receive or send notices only by registered or certified mail.

The use of facsimile for giving notices is increasingly common. The parties should consider whether some notices should not be sent via facsimile, which is a relatively nonconfidential form of transmission. In international acquisitions, the parties may want the ability to send notices via telex or the alternative of sending confirmatory notice to a United States Post Office Box. ■

11.5 Jurisdiction; Service of Process

Any action or proceeding seeking to enforce any provision of, or based on any right arising out of, this Agreement may be brought against any of the parties in the courts of the State of __________, County of ____________, or, if it has or can acquire jurisdiction, in the United States District Court for the ________ District of ________, and each of the parties consents to the jurisdiction of such courts (and of the appropriate appellate courts) in any such action or proceeding and waives any objection to venue laid therein. Process in any action or proceeding referred to in the preceding sentence may be served on any party anywhere in the world.

COMMENT

This provision is designed to ensure that jurisdiction can be obtained for any litigation arising from the acquisition. The Model Stock Purchase Agreement recognizes that a federal district court might not have jurisdiction over a claim related to the acquisition, but provides that each party consents to federal court jurisdiction if such jurisdiction can be acquired. The Model Stock Purchase Agreement also waives objections to venue, which gives certainty to the forum of any litigation. If the acquisition agreement includes an arbitration provision, the jurisdiction and service of process provisions should be made consistent with an arbitration provision.

The last sentence of Section 11.5 establishes that service of process may be obtained on any party anywhere in the world and establishes a basis for acquiring in personam jurisdiction.

If there are many Sellers, the Buyer may want to provide that a large group of Sellers appoint an agent for service of process. Such a provision can be as follows:

> Sellers hereby irrevocably appoint ____________________, [address], as their lawful agent in the state of _______ to receive and forward on their behalf service of all necessary processes in any action, suit, or proceeding arising under this Agreement or [insert any other agreements] that may be brought against any of Sellers in any court (including federal courts) in the state of ______________. Such service of process or notice received thereof by the agent will have the same force and effect as if served upon Sellers (Sellers will pay all costs and expenses and circulate forms as may be required by _________ to act in this capacity).

Foreign Sellers should consider whether consent to service of process within the United States will alter their taxpaying status. Sellers who do not operate on a nationwide basis should consider whether consent to service constitutes doing business in a state if the consent to jurisdiction is the sole contact with that state.

The Model Stock Purchase Agreement does not contain an alternate dispute resolution ("ADR") provision (other than that related to the purchase price adjustment formula in Section 2.5) and contemplates litigation as the principal means of dispute resolution. Existing practice with respect to ADR provisions is varied and changing. A Buyer's reasonable first draft may contemplate that litigation is the appropriate dispute resolution mechanism because the Buyer is more likely than the Sellers to assert claims under the acquisition agreement. The prospect of litigation may give the Buyer greater leverage in resolving such claims than would the prospect of mandatory ADR. However, in choosing between litigation and ADR, the Buyer should consider factors such as the cost, the time until resolution, the scope of discovery, its ongoing relationship with the Sellers, confidentiality of the dispute, and the need for expertise in resolving the dispute.

The Buyer may prefer the broad scope of discovery available in litigation. Although discovery is available under some kinds of ADR procedures, it is generally more limited. Because many of the facts necessary for favorable resolution of the Buyer's claims may be in the Sellers' possession (especially if a dispute centers on representations and warranties containing knowledge qualifications), these facts may not be available without full discovery. Recourse to court sanctions for failing to respond properly to discovery requests may be important to the Buyer.

Many attorneys and clients feel that ADR has the effect of leveling the playing field by giving more certainty and speed to the outcome. If the Buyer is the wealthier party, it may prefer litigation.

Nonetheless, the Buyer may prefer ADR in certain circumstances. If the Buyer and the Sellers have a continuing business relationship, they may desire to avoid or minimize adversarial proceedings by using ADR. ADR also makes it easier to preserve the confidentiality of a controversy. If the parties believe that special expertise is necessary to resolve the dispute, an ADR process can provide an expert panel.

ADR in the context of business transactions can take a variety of forms. Although arbitration is perhaps the most well known, other forms of ADR include mediation, conciliation, summary or "mini" trials, and structured negotiation. ADR may be binding on the parties or may be merely an agreement to attempt to resolve an issue in good faith prior to litigation. For a general discussion of the types of ADR and the issues involved, see *Alternate Dispute Resolution* (Coopers & Meyerson eds., 1991). For guidance on drafting ADR provisions, see American Arbitration Association, *Drafting Dispute Resolution Clauses: A Practical Guide* (1993). ■

11.6 Further Assurances

The parties agree (a) to furnish upon request to each other such further information, (b) to execute and deliver to each other such other documents, and (c) to do such other acts and things, all as the other party may reasonably request for the purpose of carrying out the intent of this Agreement and the documents referred to in this Agreement.

COMMENT

A further assurances provision is common in acquisition agreements. Often there are permits, licenses, and consents that can be obtained as a routine matter either after the execution of the acquisition agreement or after the closing. The further assurances provision assures each party that routine matters will be accomplished and that the other party will not withhold signatures required for transferring assets or consenting to transfers of business licenses in an attempt to extract additional consideration.

In addition to the covenants in Section 11.6, the acquisition agreement may contain other covenants that involve matters that cannot be conditions precedent to the closing because of time or other considerations, but that the Buyer views as an important part of the acquisition. These additional covenants may arise out of exceptions to the Sellers' representations noted in the Disclosure Letter. For example, the Sellers may covenant to remove a title encumbrance, finalize a legal proceeding, or resolve an environmental problem. Ordinarily there is a value placed upon each post-closing covenant so that if the Seller does not perform, the Buyer is compensated by an escrow or hold-back arrangement. Post-closing covenants may also include a covenant by the Sellers to pay certain debts and obligations of the Acquired Companies to third parties not assumed by the Buyer, or deliver promptly to the Buyer any cash or other property that Sellers may receive after the closing that the acquisition agreement requires them to transfer to the Buyer.

Finally, the Buyer may want either to include provisions in the acquisition agreement or to enter into a separate agreement with the Sellers requiring the Sellers to perform certain services during the transition of ownership of the Acquired Companies. Such provisions (or such an agreement) typically describe the nature of the Sellers' services, the amount of time (in hours per week and number of days or weeks) the Sellers must devote to such services, and the compensation, if any, they will receive for performing such services. Because such agreements are highly dependent on the circumstances of each acquisition, the Model Stock Purchase Agreement does not contain such provisions. ■

11.7 Waiver

The rights and remedies of the parties to this Agreement are cumulative and not alternative. Neither the failure nor any delay by any party in exercising any right, power, or privilege under this Agreement or the documents referred to in this Agreement will operate as a waiver of such right, power, or privilege, and no single or partial exercise of any such right, power, or privilege will preclude any other or further exercise of such right, power, or privilege or the exercise of any other right, power, or privilege. To the maximum extent permitted by applicable law, (a) no claim or right arising out of this Agreement or the documents referred to in this Agreement can be discharged by one party, in whole or in part, by a waiver or renunciation of the claim or right unless in writing signed by the other party; (b) no waiver that may be given by a party will be applicable except in the specific instance for which it is given; and (c) no notice to or demand on one party will be deemed to be a waiver of any obligation of such party or of the right of the party giving such notice or demand to take further action without notice or demand as provided in this Agreement or the documents referred to in this Agreement.

COMMENT

A waiver provision is common in acquisition agreements. A waiver provision specifies that the rights of the parties are cumulative in order to avoid construction that one remedy is sufficient. For example, if a party first requests an injunction and later requests money damages, the waiver provision eliminates any chance that the party will be deemed to have waived its right to money damages when it requested an injunction.

The waiver provision also defeats arguments that the course of performance or course of dealing with respect to the acquisition agreement dictates the outcome of disputes between the parties and that an immaterial delay prejudices the rights of the delaying party. Counsel should consider the relationship between the second sentence of Section 11.7 and the "time is of the essence provision" in Section 11.13. ■

11.8 Entire Agreement and Modification

This Agreement supersedes all prior agreements between the parties with respect to its subject matter (including the Letter of Intent between Buyer and Sellers dated ________, 199__) and constitutes (along with the documents referred to in this Agreement) a complete and exclusive statement of the terms of the agreement between the parties with respect to its subject matter. This Agreement may not be amended except by a written agreement executed by the party to be charged with the amendment.

COMMENT

This Section provides that the acquisition agreement (along with the documents referred to in the acquisition agreement) contains the entire understanding of the Buyer and the Sellers regarding the acquisition so that, unless otherwise specified, all prior agreements (whether written or oral) between the parties relating to the acquisition are superseded by (and not incorporated into) the terms of the acquisition agreement and any conflicts between previous agreements and the acquisition agreement are eliminated. Accordingly, if any pre-existing agreements between the parties regarding the acquisition (such as the Confidentiality Agreement or certain provisions in the Letter of Intent) are to remain in effect, this Section should make specific reference to these agreements. The Model Stock Purchase Agreement addresses confidentiality (see Section 11.3) and "no-shop" (see Section 5.7) obligations; thus, there is no need for the Letter of Intent to remain in effect. For an example of the codification of non-integration clauses, see Cal. Civ. Proc. Code § 1856.

This Section also states that the acquisition agreement may be amended only by a written agreement signed by the party to be charged with the amendment. This Section reflects the principle that a contract required by the Statute of Frauds to be in writing may not be orally modified, and follows Section 2-209(2) of the Uniform Commercial Code, which provides that "[a] signed agreement which excludes modification or recision except by a signed writing cannot be otherwise modified or rescinded." *Cf.* Cal. Civ. Code § 1698; *Deering Ice Cream Corp. v. Columbo, Inc.*, 598 A.2d 454, 456 (Me. 1988) ("The parties never memorialized any meeting of the minds on modifying their contract in the form required by the contract documents."). However, the rule prohibiting oral modification of contracts within the Statute of Frauds has not been applied in cases in which there has been partial performance of an oral agreement to modify the written contract, especially if one party's conduct induces another to rely on the modification agreement. *See, e.g., Rose v. Spa Realty Assoc.*, 42 N.Y.2d 338, 340-41 (1977); *Ridley Park Shopping Ctr., Inc. v. Sun Ray Drug Co.*, 180 A.2d 1 (Pa. 1962); *Paul v. Bellavia*, 536 N.Y.S.2d 472, 474 (App. Div. 1988); *cf.* Jossis, *Contracts as Bilateral Commitments: A New Concern About Contract Modification*, Dis. Paper No. 128, Harvard Law School (July 1993). ■

11.9 Disclosure Letter

(a) The disclosures in the Disclosure Letter, and those in any Supplement thereto, must relate only to the representations and warranties in the Section of the Agreement to which they expressly relate and not to any other representation or warranty in this Agreement.

(b) In the event of any inconsistency between the statements in the body of this Agreement and those in the Disclosure Letter (other than an exception expressly set forth as such in the Disclosure Letter with respect to a specifically identified representation or warranty), the statements in the body of this Agreement will control.

COMMENT

Section 11.9(a) represents the Buyer's opening position in a debate that occurs frequently in negotiations of acquisition agreements: what effect does a disclosure made with respect to one representation have on other representations? The Buyer typically seeks to limit the effect of such a disclosure to the specific representation to which the disclosure refers, arguing that the impact of the matter disclosed cannot be evaluated in the absence of the context given by the particular representation. For example, the Buyer may view differently a contract disclosed in response to a representation that calls for a list of material contracts than one disclosed in response to a representation concerning transactions with related parties—the latter situation increases the likelihood that the economic terms of the contract are not at arm's length. The Sellers will frequently argue that it is unfair for them to be penalized for a failure to identify each of the many representations in a long-form acquisition agreement—which typically overlap—to which a disclosed state of facts relate. Indeed, the Sellers often prefer not to characterize the disclosures made in the Disclosure Letter by reference to any representations and attempt to qualify all representations by the

Disclosure Letter (for example, Section 3 would begin "Sellers represent and warrant to Buyer as follows, except as otherwise set forth in the Disclosure Letter:"). A frequent compromise is to modify Section 11.9(a) by adding at the end "except to the extent that the relevance to such other representation and warranty is manifest on the face of the Disclosure Letter."

The parenthetical clause in Section 11.9(b) prevents the Sellers from renegotiating the representations in the acquisition agreement by adding knowledge or materiality qualifications to the Disclosure Letter. ■

11.10 Assignments, Successors, and no Third-Party Rights

Neither party may assign any of its rights under this Agreement without the prior consent of the other parties[, which will not be unreasonably withheld,] except that Buyer may assign any of its rights under this Agreement to any Subsidiary of Buyer. Subject to the preceding sentence, this Agreement will apply to, be binding in all respects upon, and inure to the benefit of the successors and permitted assigns of the parties. Nothing expressed or referred to in this Agreement will be construed to give any Person other than the parties to this Agreement any legal or equitable right, remedy, or claim under or with respect to this Agreement or any provision of this Agreement. This Agreement and all of its provisions and conditions are for the sole and exclusive benefit of the parties to this Agreement and their successors and assigns.

COMMENT

This Section requires the other party's consent before a party may assign its rights under the acquisition agreement (except that the Buyer may assign its rights to a subsidiary without the Sellers' consent). This provision is necessary because the modern rule is that, absent an express provision to the contrary, contract rights are freely assignable. *See, e.g., Scott v. Fox Bros. Enter., Inc.*, 667 P.2d 773 (Cal. Ct. App. 1983); Murray, *Murray on Contracts* § 138 (3d ed. 1990). Although the terms of the agreement will be binding upon, and will inure to the benefit of, the successors and assigns of the parties, the assignment will not release the assignor from its duties and obligations unless the obligee consents to the assignment. *See, e.g.*, Cal. Civ. Code § 1457; *Murray on Contracts* § 140. For business, financial, strategic, or even emotional reasons, the Sellers may try to limit the Buyer's right of assignment by requiring the Sellers' prior consent even for assignments to the Buyer's subsidiaries.

The right of a third party to be considered a third-party beneficiary and enjoy rights under a contract depends on the intention of the contracting parties. *See* Corbin, *Corbin on Contracts* § 776 (Supp. 1993); *see also Norton v. First Fed. Sav.*, 624 P.2d 854, 855 (Ariz. 1989); *Sheetz, Aiken & Aiken, Inc. v. Spann, Hall, Ritchie, Inc.*, 512 So.2d 99, 101-02 (Ala. 1987); *Strutz v. State Farm Mutual Ins. Co.*, 609 A.2d 569, 570 (Pa. Super. 1992). Moreover, states may have specific statutes requiring that "[i]n order for a contract to be enforceable by a third party, the contract must be made expressly for the benefit of the third person." *Eastern Aviation Group, Inc. v. Airborne Express, Inc.*, 8 Cal. Rptr. 2d 355, 357 (Cal. Ct. App. 1992) (interpreting Cal. Civ. Code § 1559). Section 11.10 expressly states that the parties do not intend to benefit, or create any rights, remedies, or claims in, any third parties.

Under Section 9.2, the parties do not need the consent of any third-party beneficiary to terminate the acquisition agreement. For a discussion of the indemnification procedure relating to third-party claims, see the Commentary to Section 10.9. ■

11.11 Severability

If any provision of this Agreement is held invalid or unenforceable by any court of competent jurisdiction, the other provisions of this Agreement will remain in full force and effect. Any provision of this Agreement held invalid or unenforceable only in part or degree will remain in full force and effect to the extent not held invalid or unenforceable.

COMMENT

Whether a contract is entire or severable depends upon the parties' intention, the subject matter of the agreement, and the circumstances of the transaction. *See, e.g., Christian v. Christian*, 365 N.E.2d 849 (N.Y. 1977); *Keene v. Harling*, 392 P.2d 273 (Cal. 1964); *Heilwood Fuel Company v. Manor Real Estate Co.*, 175 A.2d 880 (Pa. 1961); *Knight v. Hamilton*, 233 S.W.2d 969 (Ky. 1950). Under Section 11.10, if a provision of the acquisition agreement is held unenforceable, the remaining provisions are separated from the invalid or unenforceable provision and remain in effect. *Cf. Christian*, 365 N.E.2d at 856 ("Here the parties had a right to and did, by expressly stipulating that if any provision of the separation agreement be held invalid or unenforceable all other[s] shall nevertheless continue in full force, make the agreement within reasonable limits dividable, and there is little room for construction.").

However, the language in Section 11.11 may not be effective if the invalid provision constitutes an essential element of the contract. According to the *Restatement, (Second) of Contracts* § 184:

> (1) If less than all of an agreement is unenforceable . . . a court may nevertheless enforce the rest of the agreement in favor of a party who did not engage in serious misconduct if the performance as to which the agreement is unenforceable is not an essential part of the agreed exchange.
>
> (2) A court may treat only a part of a term as unenforceable under the rule stated in Subsection (1) if the party who seeks to enforce the term obtained it in good faith and in according with reasonable standards of fair dealing.

As the commentary to this section of the *Restatement* explains:

> If the performance as to which the agreement is unenforceable is an essential part of the agreed exchange, the inequality will be so great as to make the entire agreement unenforceable. Under Subsection (1), however, if that performance is not an essential part of the agreed exchange, a court may enforce all but the part that contravenes public policy. For example, a promise not to compete that is unreasonably in restraint of trade will often not invalidate the entire agreement of which it is a part. Whether the performance is an essential part of the agreed exchange depends on its relative importance in light of the entire agreement between the parties.

The parties may also want to consider inserting a provision calling for judicial reformation of the agreement to modify the invalid provision to achieve the parties' intention. This practice is common with respect to covenants not to compete. The Buyer should consider whether it will want to rescind the entire acquisition agreement if a major, yet non-essential, provision of the agreement is held to be invalid or unenforceable. ■

11.12 Section Headings, Construction

The headings of Sections in this Agreement are provided for convenience only and will not affect its construction or interpretation. All references to "Section" or "Sections" refer to the corresponding Section or Sections of this Agreement. All words used in this Agreement will be construed to be of such gender or number as the circumstances require. Unless otherwise expressly provided, the word "including" does not limit the preceding words or terms.

COMMENT

The first three sentences of this Section are self-explanatory. The last sentence is designed to eliminate the need for repetitive and cumbersome use of the phrase "including, but not limited to," or "including, without limitation," in every instance in which a broad term is followed by a list of items encompassed by that term. The Revised Model Business Corporation Act, Section 1.40 contains a similar definition: " 'Including' denotes a partial definition." In certain jurisdictions, however, the rule of ejusdem generis has been applied to construe the meaning of a broad phrase to include only matters that are of a similar nature to those specifically described. *See, e.g., Forward Industries, Inc. v. Rolm of New York Corp.*, 506 N.Y.S.2d 453, 455 (App. Div. 1986) (requiring the phrase "Other cause beyond the control" to be limited to events of the same kind as those events specifically enumerated); *see also Buono Sales, Inc. v. Chrysler Motors Corp.*, 363 F.2d 43 (3d Cir.), *cert. denied*, 385 U.S. 971 (1966); *Thaddeus Davids Co. v. Hoffman-LaRoche Chemical Works*, 166 N.Y.S. 179 (App. Div. 1917). ■

11.13 Time of Essence

With regard to all dates and time periods set forth or referred to in this Agreement, time is of the essence.

COMMENT

To take advantage of, among other things, the "drop dead" date termination provision in Section 9.1(d), the Model Stock Purchase Agreement contains a "time is of the essence" provision in Section 11.13. An express statement of this provision is important because time will not be of the essence in a contract unless it is specifically provided or the circumstances clearly indicate that it was the intention of the parties. *See, e.g., Mailloux v. Dickey*, 523 A.2d 66, 69 (N.H. 1986) ("As a general rule, time is not considered to be of the essence unless the contract specifically states it is."); *Hollars v. Randall*, 554 N.E.2d 1177, 1179 (Ind. Ct. App. 1990) ("Courts asked to give equitable relief generally do not consider time to be of the essence unless the terms of the agreement or the conduct of the parties indicated that the intent of the parties was to make it so."); *Bogojavlensky v. Logan*, 124 A.2d 412, 415 (Pa. Super. 1956) ("Time is not of the essence in a contract unless it is specifically so provided or unless the circumstances clearly indicate that it was the intent of the parties.").

Courts differ, however, about whether the failure of a party to comply with its obligations under an agreement in a timely manner will permit the enforcement of the remedies provided for in the agreement. Relying on a state statute and precedent dating to 1897, the North Dakota Supreme Court in *E.E.E. Inc. v. Hanson*, 318 N.W.2d 101 (N.D. 1982), allowed a party to enforce its rights under a "time is of the essence" provision:

> [N]ormally, parties to a contract are allowed to write the terms of the contract themselves . . . . A court may be called upon to interpret a contract written by the parties thereto but the court's authority to interpret a contract does not give a court the authority to modify it . . . . Here, because the parties took special pains to assure that the contract reflected their intent that time was of the essence . . . there can be no doubt of their intent and we cannot ignore it under the guise of interpreting the contract.

Id. at 104-05; *see also Sun Bank of Miami v. Lester*, 404 So. 2d 141, 143 (Fla. Ct. App. 1981). However, enforcement of "time is of the essence" provisions often has been subject to application of principles of equity. For example, courts have held that such a provision will not be given effect if it causes a forfeiture. *See Kaiman Realty, Inc. v. Carmichael*, 655 P.2d 872, 874 (Haw. 1982) ("[A] 'time is of the essence' clause is an agreement of sale will not foreclose equitable relief where, absent gross negligent or bad faith conduct of the vendee, forfeiture would be harsh and unreasonable."); *Rothenberg v. Follman*, 172 N.W.2d 845, 850 (Mich. 1969) ("[T]he fact that the parties have stipulated that time is of the essence is but one of the factors to be taken into consideration in determining whether equity will intervene to set aside a forfeiture. Where the forfeiture is disproportionately large and the other facts, circumstances and equities cry out for relief, a court of equity may, nevertheless, intervene."); *see also Restatement, (Second) of Contracts* § 242(c) cmt. d; *Sun Bank of Miami*, 404 So. 2d at 141 (Ferguson, J., dissenting).

Finally, a party should remember that by its conduct it may negate the effectiveness of a "time is of the essence" provision if a waiver is found. In *Porterco, Inc. v. Igloo Products Corp.*, 955 F.2d 1164 (8th Cir. 1992), the court observed:

> Provisions in a contract which specify, or limit the time of performance, even where time is of the essence of the contract may be waived. Further, such a waiver may be express or implied . . . .
>
> A waiver of the time of performance of a contract will result from any act that induces the opposite party to believe that exact performance within the time designated in the contract will not be insisted upon.

Id. at 1171. Section 11.7 of the Model Stock Purchase Agreement, which provides that a party's delay in exercising any of its rights, powers, the privileges under the agreement will not operate as a waiver, may be of little help to the party seeking to enforce rights under Section 11.13 because, as the *Porterco* court observed, "it is within the jury's power to find that such a provision was itself waived or modified by the parties' agreement or conduct." *Id.* at 1172. ■

11.14 Governing Law

This Agreement will be governed by the laws of the State of _______ without regard to conflicts of laws principles.

COMMENT

This Section allows the parties to select the law that will govern the contractual rights and obligations of the Buyer and the Sellers. Without such a provision, the court must assess the underlying interest of each jurisdiction to determine which jurisdiction has the greatest interest in the outcome of the matter. As for which states the parties may select the *Restatement, (Second) of Conflicts of Laws* § 187 provides:

§ 187. Law of the State Chosen by the Parties

> (1) The law of the state chosen by the parties to govern their contractual rights and duties will be applied if the particular issue is one which the parties could have resolved by an explicit provision in their agreement directed to that issue.
>
> (2) The law of the state chosen by the parties to govern their contractual rights and duties will be applied, even if the particular issue is one which the parties could not have resolved by an explicit provision in their agreement directed to that issue, unless either
>
> > (a) the chosen state has no substantial relationship to the parties or the transaction and there is no other reasonable basis for the parties' choice, or
> >
> > (b) application of the law of the chosen state would be contrary to a fundamental policy of a state which has a materially greater interest than the chosen state in the determination of the particular issue and which, under the rule of § 188, would be the state of the applicable law in the absence of an effective choice of law by the parties.
>
> (3) In the absence of a contrary indication of intention, the reference is to the local law of the state of the chosen law.

In *Nedlloyd Lines B.V. v. Superior Court of San Mateo County (Seawinds Ltd.)*, 834 P.2d 1148 (Cal. 1992), the Supreme Court of California applied these principles to uphold a choice of law provision requiring a contract between commercial entities to finance and operate an international shipping business to be governed by the laws of Hong Kong, a jurisdiction having a substantial connection with the parties:

> Briefly restated, the proper approach under Restatement section 187, subdivision (2) is for the court first to deter-

> mine either: (1) whether the chosen state has a substantial relationship to the parties or their transaction, or (2) whether there is any other reasonable basis for the parties' choice of law. If neither of these tests is met, that is the end of the inquiry, and the court need not enforce the parties' choice of law. . . . If, however, either test is met, the court must next determine whether the chosen state's law is contrary to a fundamental policy of California. . . . If there is no such conflict, the court shall enforce the parties' choice of law. If, however, there is a fundamental conflict with California law, the court must then determine whether California has a "materially greater interest than the chosen state in the determination of the particular issue." If California has a materially greater interest than the chosen state, the choice of law shall not be enforced, for the obvious reason that in such circumstance we will decline to enforce a law contrary to this state's fundamental policy.

Id. at 1151; *see also Kronovet v. Lipchin*, 415 A.2d 1096, 1104 n.16 (Md. Ct. App. 1980) (noting that "courts and commentators now generally recognize the ability of parties to stipulate in the contract that the law of a particular state or states will govern construction, enforcement and the essential validity of their contract" but recognizing that "the parties' ability to choose governing law on issues of contract validity is not unlimited and will not be given effect unless there is a 'substantial' or 'vital' relationship between the chosen sites and issues to be decided.").

However, choice of law provisions have not been uniformly upheld by the courts. *See, e.g., Rosenmiller v. Bordes*, 607 A.2d 465, 469 (Del. Ch. 1991) (holding that, notwithstanding an express choice of New Jersey law in the agreement, Delaware had a greater interest than New Jersey in regulating stockholder voting rights in Delaware corporations, and therefore the parties' express choice of New Jersey law could not apply to this issue).

In some jurisdictions, statutes validate a choice of law provision even if the law chosen bears no relationship to the transaction. ■

11.15 COUNTERPARTS

This Agreement may be executed in one or more counterparts, each of which will be deemed to be an original copy of this Agreement and all of which, when taken together, will be deemed to constitute one and the same agreement.

COMMENT

This Section, which permits execution of the acquisition agreement in counterparts, is common in acquisition agreements. It is inserted for the convenience of the parties and facilitates execution of the acquisition agreement when the signatories are not available at the same time or place.

This Section does not alter the effective date specified on the initial page of the acquisition agreement. The articles of incorporation or the charter, bylaws, and minutes will determine which persons have the authority to execute the agreement on behalf of corporations that are parties to the transaction. ■

IN WITNESS WHEREOF, the parties have executed and delivered this Agreement as of the date first written above.

Buyer:

By: ____________________

Sellers:

____
A

____
B

EXHIBITS

Exhibit 1

Disclosure Letter

PRELIMINARY NOTE

The form and content of the Disclosure Letter should be negotiated concurrently with the negotiation of the Model Stock Purchase Agreement, and the two documents should be executed contemporaneously. Where this is not practicable in whole or in part, or it is contemplated that the disclosures in the Disclosure Letter may be supplemented or amended, modifications of both the Model Stock Purchase Agreement and the Disclosure Letter may be appropriate. For example, the Buyer may seek provisions to the effect that the information set forth in the Disclosure Letter is subject to acceptance and approval by the Buyer, which acceptance may be acknowledged only by the Buyer's execution of the Disclosure Letter, and that the Buyer has a specified number of days after receipt of the Disclosure Letter to terminate the Model Stock Purchase Agreement.

As an alternative to using a separate Disclosure Letter, the parties may append schedules to the Model Stock Purchase Agreement referencing the particular Section or Sections of the Model Stock Purchase Agreement to which they relate. The net effect is the same, the Disclosure Letter (or the schedules, as the case may be) serve to limit, modify or expand the representations and warranties of the Sellers set forth in Section 3 of the Model Stock Purchase Agreement.

[Date]

[NAME] ____________________

[COMPANY] ____________________

[ADDRESS] ____________________

[CITY & STATE] ____________________

Gentlemen:

We refer to the Stock Purchase Agreement (the "Agreement") to be entered into today between the undersigned individuals ("Sellers") and ____________________ ("Buyer") pursuant to which Sellers are to sell and Buyer is to purchase all of the issued and outstanding capital stock of ________________ (the "Company") as provided in the Agreement.

This letter constitutes the Disclosure Letter referred to in Section 3 of the Agreement. The representations and warranties of Sellers in Section 3 of the Agreement are made and given subject to the disclosures in this Disclosure Letter. The disclosures in this Disclosure Letter are to be taken as relating to the representations and warranties in the section of the Agreement to which they expressly relate and to no other representation or warranty in the Agreement.

Terms defined in the Agreement are used with the same meaning in this Disclosure Letter. References to Appendices are to the Appendices to this Disclosure Letter.

By reference to Section 3 of the Agreement (using the numbering in such Section), the following matters are disclosed:

. . . . . .

[NAME]________________

[DATE]

Page 2

[describe particularly any exceptions]

Very truly yours,

____

____

Sellers

Buyer acknowledges receipt of the Disclosure Letter of which this is a duplicate (including the Appendices referred to therein).

Dated: ________________________

BUYER:

By: __________________________

COMMENT

In circumstances where securities of the Buyer or the Company are, or will be, publicly traded, the Model Stock Purchase Agreement may have to be filed with the United States Securities and Exchange Commission ("SEC") (*see* Regulation S-K, Item 601(b)(2)) and with the "blue sky" authorities of various states. Similarly, under certain circumstances, depending upon the nature of the business or size of the Buyer or the Company, the Model Stock Purchase Agreement may have to be filed with the Justice Department, bank regulatory authorities or similar regulatory authorities.

In many circumstances, information filed with regulatory authorities is publicly available. Although the filing party may request confidential treatment of information which it files, such treatment may not be granted. *See e.g.*, Rule 406 under the Securities Act of 1933, as amended; Rule 24b-2 under the Securities Exchange Act of 1934, as amended. If confidential treatment is granted, the grant is subject to challenge under the Freedom of Information Act ("FOIA"). Furthermore, even when confidential treatment is granted and the grant survives a FOIA challenge, regulatory authorities are generally not prohibited from sharing the filed documents with other regulatory agencies. *Id.*

Information that constitutes an exception to a representation and warranty may relate to an act or omission on the part of the filing party. The act or omission may give rise to potential criminal or civil penalties or may constitute an admission or "road map" for a plaintiff with respect to pending or potential civil litigation. In these circumstances, if the Sellers disclose the act or omission and the disclosure becomes public or becomes available to regulatory authorities, the Sellers or the Company's officers or directors may become subject to liability or damages. However, if the Sellers do not disclose the act or omission, they are exposed to potential liability to the Buyer.

It can be argued that the Disclosure Letter is not technically required to be filed with regulatory authorities on the ground that the Disclosure Letter does not form a part of the Model Stock Purchase Agreement, as do the Exhibits. Therefore, the use of the Disclosure Letter may reduce the possibility that information concerning exceptions will come into the public domain or otherwise become available to regulatory authorities. This does not mean that the Disclosure Letter will never have to be filed with a regulatory authority. Filing may be required either because of a specific regulation or because of the materiality of the information in the disclosure letter. For example, if a disclosure contained in the Disclosure Letter is material to the registrant, disclosure may otherwise be required under Rule 10b-5 under the Securities Exchange Act of 1934, as amended. Similarly, certain regulations may be broad enough to require the filing of the Disclosure Letter. Therefore, while the filing of the Disclosure Letter with regulatory authorities can be found not to be required, the decision whether to file must be made in view of the nature of the information in the Disclosure Letter and the applicable regulations.

Exhibit 2.4(a)(ii)

Release

PRELIMINARY NOTE

The Release is to be delivered by each of the Sellers on behalf of themselves and their Related Persons. One of the objectives in obtaining the Release is to effect a clean break from the prior owners. In this regard, one should consider the interrelationship between the Release and certain of the representations and warranties in the Model Stock Purchase Agreement such as the absence of claims by Related Persons (including severance arrangements), and the existence or absence of any claims for indemnification under the Acquired Companies' organizational documents or by contract. By reviewing the representations and warranties, the Disclosure Letter and the scope of the Release, the Buyer ought to be in a better position to assess the potential for post-closing liability arising from pre-closing events, thereby evaluating some of the risk of the transaction. The Buyer's agreement to purchase the Sellers' stock in the Company is sufficient consideration to support the Release.

RELEASE

This Release is being executed and delivered in accordance with Section 2.4(a)(ii) of the Stock Purchase Agreement dated ___________, 199____ (the "Agreement") between ___________, a ___________ corporation ("Buyer"), ___________ ("A") and ___________ ("B"). Capitalized terms used in this Release without definition have the respective meanings given to them in the Agreement.

Each Seller acknowledges that execution and delivery of this Release is a condition to Buyer's obligation to purchase the outstanding capital stock of the Company pursuant to the Agreement and that Buyer is relying on this Release in consummating such purchase.

Each Seller, for good and valuable consideration the receipt and sufficiency of which is hereby acknowledged and intending to be legally bound, in order to induce Buyer to purchase the outstanding capital stock of the Company pursuant to the Agreement, hereby agrees as follows:

Each Seller, on behalf of himself and each of his Related Persons, hereby releases and forever discharges the Buyer, the Company and each of the other Acquired Companies, and each of their respective individual, joint or mutual, past, present and future Representatives, affiliates, stockholders, controlling persons, Subsidiaries, successors and assigns (individually, a "Releasee" and collectively, "Releasees") from any and all claims, demands, Proceedings, causes of action, Orders, obligations, contracts, agreements, debts and liabilities whatsoever, whether known or unknown, suspected or unsuspected, both at law and in equity, which each of the Sellers or any of their respective Related Persons now has, have ever had or may hereafter have against the respective Releasees arising contemporaneously with or prior to the Closing Date or on account of or arising out of any matter, cause or event occurring contemporaneously with or prior to the Closing Date, including, but not limited to, any rights to indemnification or reimbursement from the Company or any other Acquired Company, whether pursuant to their respective Organizational Documents, contract or otherwise and whether or not relating to claims pending on, or asserted after, the Closing Date; *provided, however,* that nothing contained herein shall operate to release any obligations of Buyer arising under the Agreement or any obligation of any Acquired Company which obligation has been disclosed in Part ____ [e.g., identified transactions with Related Persons of Sellers or any Acquired Company which are to remain in effect after the Closing] of the Disclosure Letter.

Each Seller hereby irrevocably covenants to refrain from, directly or indirectly, asserting any claim or demand, or commencing, instituting or causing to be commenced, any proceeding of any kind against any Releasee, based upon any matter purported to be released hereby.

Without in any way limiting any of the rights and remedies otherwise available to any Releasee, each Seller[, jointly and severally,] shall indemnify and hold harmless each Releasee from and against all loss, liability, claim, damage (including incidental and consequential damages) or expense (including costs of investigation and defense and reasonable attorney's fees) whether or not involving third party claims, arising directly or indirectly from or in connection with (i) the assertion by or on behalf of the Sellers or any of their Related Persons of any claim or other matter purported to be released pursuant to this Release and (ii) the assertion by any third party of any claim or demand against any Releasee which claim or demand arises directly or indirectly from, or in connection with, any assertion by or on behalf of the Sellers or any of their Related Persons against such third party of any claims or other matters purported to be released pursuant to this Release.

If any provision of this Release is held invalid or unenforceable by any court of competent jurisdiction, the other provisions of this Release will remain in full force and effect. Any provision of this Release held invalid or unenforceable only in part or degree will remain in full force and effect to the extent not held invalid or unenforceable.

This Release may not be changed except in a writing signed by the person(s) against whose interest such change shall operate. This Release shall be governed by and construed under the laws of the State of ________ without regard to principles of conflicts of law.

All words used in this Release will be construed to be of such gender or number as the circumstances require.

IN WITNESS WHEREOF, each of the undersigned have executed and delivered this Release as of this ___ day of ________, 199_.

____

[Name of Releasor]

____

[Name of Releasor]

COMMENT

The scope and extent of the Release depends on the intent of the parties as expressed in the instrument. By its terms, the Release covers all claims which the releasing parties had, or arising from any cause or matter that existed, as of the closing date against any of the released parties. It includes claims that the releasing parties may have for indemnification or reimbursement from an Acquired Company. Without such a release, if the Buyer asserts claims against the Sellers, the Sellers might assert that the Buyer's claims relate to actions taken by them in their capacities as directors and officers of an Acquired Company and present a claim for indemnification and advancement of costs of defense against the Buyer's claims. *See TBG Inc. v. Richard A. Bendis*, 1991 U.S. Dist. Lexis 2765, 1991 U.S. Dist. Lexis 4417, 1991 U.S. Dist. Lexis 14303 (D. Kansas, 1991).

This instrument does not release any claims which the Sellers might have under the Model Stock Purchase Agreement (such as a claim under the Buyer's promissory note) or that the parties have agreed will be an obligation of an Acquired Company, as reflected in the Model Stock Purchase Agreement or the Disclosure Letter (such as transactions with related persons which remain in effect after the closing). Any obligations which the parties intend to survive the purchase of the stock by the Buyer should be clearly set forth in the Release.

If the transaction involves a public company, the breadth of the definition of the released parties should be considered. An appropriate limitation is to release the identified persons (agents, representatives, employees, officers, directors, affiliates, stockholders) only for actions they have taken acting in such capacities.

The Release also includes a covenant not to sue with respect to any matter purported to be released. This covenant clearly is part of the Release (which extinguishes any cause of action that the releasing parties might have had against any of the released parties). In addition to the affirmative defense of the Release, the covenant may give a released party a cause of action for breach of covenant. The "hold harmless" provision is standard language in a covenant not to sue.

Additional language or formalities may be required under applicable state law. For example, if the Release is subject to

California law, it should contain an express waiver of Section 1542 of the California Civil Code (to the effect that a general release does not extend to claims which a creditor does not "know or suspect to exist" in his favor, which if known by him would have materially affected his settlement with the debtor). The Release contains a severability provision reflecting the parties' intention that if a provision of the Release is held invalid or unenforceable, the remaining provisions are separated from the invalid or unenforceable provision and remain in effect.

Exhibit 2.4(a)(iii)

Employment Agreement

PRELIMINARY NOTE

The Buyer will frequently seek to obtain the services of one or more of the Sellers, especially if the Sellers have special knowledge about the operations, customers, or suppliers of the business or technical expertise that is needed in the business. The Employment Agreement assumes that A, one of the two Sellers has technical expertise that will be needed for a period of time by the Company, which is referred to in the Employment Agreement as the Employer. Therefore, the Employer is seeking to employ A for a period of at least three years to be its Vice President and Chief Operating Officer with substantial management responsibilities.

The Employment Agreement strongly favors the Employer in certain respects such as the Employer's broad termination rights and the Executive's limited post-termination remedies. Although the Buyer's attorney might ordinarily be inclined to draft an employment agreement that strongly favors the Employer, the first draft of an employment agreement may be distributed at a sensitive point in the negotiations of the acquisition, and, as a result, the Buyer may opt for a more even-handed agreement that will not alienate the Executive or jeopardize the overall transaction.

Before execution of the Model Stock Purchase Agreement, the Executive's attorney should investigate the Executive's compensation and benefits package and the compensation and benefits of comparable executives of the Buyer. The Buyer's attorney should also have this information before preparing the first draft of the Employment Agreement.

EMPLOYMENT AGREEMENT

This Employment Agreement (this "Agreement") is made as of ____, 199__ by ____________________, a _____________ corporation (the "Employer"), and ____________, an individual resident in ____________ (the "Executive").

RECITALS

Concurrently with the execution and delivery of this Agreement, _________________, a ______________ corporation (the "Buyer"), is purchasing from the Executive and ____________ ("B"), all of the issued shares of stock of the Employer, pursuant to a Stock Purchase Agreement dated _________________, 199__ between the Executive, B, and the Buyer (the "Stock Purchase Agreement"). The Buyer and the Employer desire the Executive's continued employment with the Employer, and the Executive wishes to accept such continued employment, upon the terms and conditions set forth in this Agreement.

AGREEMENT

The parties, intending to be legally bound, agree as follows:

---

1. DEFINITIONS

For the purposes of this Agreement, the following terms have the meanings specified or referred to in this Section 1.

"Agreement"—this Employment Agreement, including Exhibits ____ and ____ hereto, as amended from time to time.

"Basic Compensation"—Salary and Benefits.

"Benefits"—as defined in Section 3.1(b).

"Board of Directors"—the board of directors of the Employer.

"Confidential Information"—any and all:

(a) trade secrets concerning the business and affairs of the Employer, product specifications, data, know-how, formulae, compositions, processes, designs, sketches, photographs, graphs, drawings, samples, inventions and ideas, past, current, and planned research and development, current and planned manufacturing or distribution methods and processes, customer lists, current and anticipated customer requirements, price lists, market studies, business plans, computer software and programs (including object code and source code), computer software and database technologies, systems, structures, and architectures (and related formulae, compositions, processes, improvements, devices, know-how, inventions, discoveries, concepts, ideas, designs, methods and information, ________________), and any other information, however documented, that is a trade secret within the meaning of ____________ § ____-__-___ [applicable state trade secret law]; and

(b) information concerning the business and affairs of the Employer (which includes historical financial statements, financial projections and budgets, historical and projected sales, capital spending budgets and plans, the names and backgrounds of key personnel, personnel training and techniques and materials, and ______________), however documented; and

(c) notes, analysis, compilations, studies, summaries, and other material prepared by or for the Employer containing or based, in whole or in part, on any information included in the foregoing.

COMMENT

The Buyer's first draft may have a rather broad definition of confidential information such as the language above, which closely corresponds to the definition of Confidential Information in the Confidentiality Agreement. The Executive, however, likely will ask for exceptions to the scope of Confidential Information. See the Confidentiality Agreement and Letter of Intent for more detailed discussions of this subject.

"disability"—as defined in Section 6.2.

"Effective Date"—the date stated in the first paragraph of the Agreement.

"Employee Invention"—any idea, invention, technique, modification, process, or improvement (whether patentable or not), any industrial design (whether registerable or not), any mask work, however fixed or encoded, that is suitable to be fixed, embedded or programmed in a semiconductor product (whether recordable or not), and any work of authorship (whether or not copyright protection may be obtained for it) created, conceived, or developed by the Executive, either solely or in conjunction with others, during the Employment Period, or a period that includes a portion of the Employment Period, that relates in any way to, or is useful in any manner in, the business then being conducted or proposed to be conducted by the Employer, and any such item created by the Executive, either solely or in conjunction with others, following termination of the Executive's employment with the Employer, that is based upon or uses Confidential Information. The term "Employee Invention" includes the inventions, techniques, and specially commissioned works described in Exhibit ____. [The term "Employee Invention" does not include, however, the inventions, techniques and works described in Exhibit ____.]

COMMENT

This definition, which is used in Section 7.2(b), under which the Executive agrees that any employee inventions belong to the Employer, may be the subject of negotiation. The Employer will generally want the definition to be very broad so that it includes any ideas, inventions, techniques, and "works for hire" developed by the Executive during the term of his employment. The Executive may seek to narrow the definition so that ideas, inventions, and techniques developed before the term of his employment, or apart from his employment, are excluded. State law may affect the Employer's ability to require the assignment of Employee inventions. See the Commentary to Section 7.2(b). In some cases, it may be advisable for the Employer to list in an exhibit to the agreement specific projects that are foreseeable at the time of entering into the agreement. Such a list may better secure for the Employer the status of the invention as a "specially commissioned work made for hire." *See* 17 U.S.C. § 101 (Subsection 2 work made for hire). The Buyer's initial draft probably would not include the bracketed language, which carves out certain inventions, techniques, and works developed by the Executive on his own time from the definition of "Employee Invention." However, the Executive, if he has strong bargaining power, may insist on such a carve-out. The definition of "Employee Invention" and the provisions that use this term are very deal specific and must be tailored to the particular transaction.

"Employment Period"—the term of the Executive's employment under this Agreement.

"Fiscal Year"—the Employer's fiscal year, as it exists on the Effective Date or as changed from time to time.

"for cause"—as defined in Section 6.3.

"for good reason"—as defined in Section 6.4.

"Incentive Compensation"—as defined in Section 3.2.

"Noncompetition Agreement"—as defined in Section 6.3.

"person"—any individual, corporation (including any non-profit corporation), general or limited partnership, limited liability company, joint venture, estate, trust, association, organization, or governmental body.

"Post-Employment Period"—as defined in Section 8.2.

"Proprietary Items"—as defined in Section 7.2(a)(iv).

"Salary"—as defined in Section 3.1(a).

2. EMPLOYMENT TERMS AND DUTIES

2.1 Employment

The Employer hereby employs the Executive, and the Executive hereby accepts employment by the Employer, upon the terms and conditions set forth in this Agreement.

2.2 Term

Subject to the provisions of Section 6, the term of the Executive's employment under this Agreement will be three years, beginning on the Effective Date and ending on the third anniversary of the Effective Date.

COMMENT

If the Employer has a continuing need for the Executive's services (for example, because of his technical knowledge, knowledge of the business, or relationships with customers, suppliers, or other executives), the Employment Agreement will often be, as in Section 2.2, for a fixed term of years but will also include an "evergreen" feature (that is, the term of the agreement will continue for an unlimited number of one-year or multi-year periods after the initial term unless terminated by either party before the beginning of a renewal term).

2.3 Duties

The Executive will have such duties as are assigned or delegated to the Executive by the Board of Directors or Chief Executive Officer, and will initially serve as [Vice President and Chief Operating Officer] of the Employer. The Executive will devote his [entire business] time, attention, skill, and energy [exclusively] to the business of the Employer, will use his [best] [good faith] efforts to promote the success of the Employer's business, and will cooperate fully with the Board of Directors in the advancement of the best interests of the Employer. [Nothing in this Section 2.3, however, will prevent the Executive from engaging in additional activities in connection with personal investments and community affairs that are not inconsistent with the Executive's duties under this Agreement.] If the Executive is elected as a director of the Employer or as a director or officer of any of its affiliates, the Executive will fulfill his duties as such director or officer without additional compensation.

COMMENT

In an acquisition context, the term of the Employment Agreement and the Executive's duties depend on the nature of the transaction and the negotiating leverage between the Executive (here one of the Sellers) and the Buyer. If the Executive's duties will be more limited or part-time, the time that the Executive must devote to the Employer's business may be stated as a certain minimum or maximum number of hours per week or month, the term may consist of a fixed term of months or years, and the events upon which the employment agreement may be terminated by the Employer may be more limited. On the other hand, if the Executive will actively manage the business and may earn incentive compensation based on the results of his efforts, he may want more control over the operations of the business so that he can be more assured of earning the incentive compensation. The bracketed language in Section 2.3 illustrates a few of the negotiable issues with respect to the Executive's duties.

Federal income tax issues may arise if payments to the Executive under the Employment Agreement actually represent disguised payments for the Executive's stock. Compensation to the Executive will be deductible, under Section 162 of the Internal Revenue Code, only to the extent that it represents reasonable compensation for services rendered. Purchase price payments for stock, however, are not deductible or amortizable for federal income tax purposes.

In many acquisitions in which one of the Sellers will serve as a director or officer of the Buyer or the Company, the Employment Agreement will contain a promise by the Employer to indemnify the Seller with respect to the performance of his duties as director or officer to the maximum extent permitted by law or as permitted under the Employer's bylaws. Some agreements require the Employer to maintain directors and officers liability insurance and to advance to the Executive the costs of defense of any lawsuit against him with respect to his service as director or officer.

3. COMPENSATION

3.1 Basic Compensation

(A) *Salary.* The Executive will be paid an annual salary of $______________, subject to adjustment as provided below (the "Salary"), which will be payable in equal periodic installments according to the Employer's customary payroll practices, but no less frequently than monthly. The Salary will be reviewed by the Board of Directors [or Chief Executive Officer] not less frequently than annually, and may be adjusted upward or downward in the sole discretion of the Board of Directors [or Chief Executive Officer], but in no event will the Salary be less than $______________ per year.

COMMENT

Salary provisions vary with each transaction. The above provision is merely an example of a salary provision that might be included in the Employer's first draft.

In many employment agreements, salary increases are subject to the discretion of the Employer's board of directors or chief executive officer, depending on the Executive's position with the Employer. In other agreements, the salary may be increased or decreased, subject to a minimum base compensation, by some type of objective index such as a consumer price index. An executive, especially one who has entered into an employment agreement in connection with the sale of his stock, may insist on an increase in salary each year based on some objective index or other criteria.

In some cases, if salary is not automatically increased, but is subject to periodic review, the Executive is permitted to terminate the employment agreement "for good reason" if he has not received an increase of a certain dollar amount or percentage over a specified period of time. A termination for good reason generally will be without prejudice to the Executive's right to continue to receive incentive compensation for a specified period of time, such as a prorated portion of the Employer's fiscal year during which the termination occurs.

(B) *Benefits.* The Executive will, during the Employment Period, be permitted to participate in such pension, profit sharing, bonus, life insurance, hospitalization, major medical, and other employee benefit plans of the Employer that may be in effect from time to time, to the extent the Executive is eligible under the terms of those plans (collectively, the "Benefits").

COMMENT

In many cases, after negotiations between the parties, the benefits to be received by the Executive will be specified in the Employment Agreement. The Executive will often want to preserve or enhance his existing benefits, such as life, medical, and disability insurance. However, the Employer may be reluctant to preserve perquisites that, although not unusual, are incompatible with the Employer's policies.

The amount of time that must elapse before the Executive becomes eligible for certain benefits under the Employer's plans may be the subject of substantial negotiations, especially in an asset purchase in which the Buyer is not assuming the Executive benefit plans of the Company. The Executive may want coverage under the Employer's various benefit plans to begin on the first day of employment. This may conflict with the terms of eligibility under the Employer's plans. In some cases, subject to the non-discrimination rules of ERISA, the Employer's benefit plans can be amended to provide coverage to the Executive from the first day of his employment.

When the Company will become a subsidiary of the Buyer, which is one of the facts assumed in the Model Stock Purchase Agreement, the Executive may desire to have benefits provided by the Buyer rather than the Company, if the Buyer is a more substantial company.

3.2 Incentive Compensation

As additional compensation (the "Incentive Compensation") for the services to be rendered by the Executive pursuant to this Agreement, the Employer will pay the Executive with respect to each Fiscal Year during the Employment Period, commencing on or after __________, 199__, an amount equal to __________ percent (__%) of the Employer's net after-tax operating income during such Fiscal Year.

[(a) For purposes of this Agreement, "net after-tax operating income" will be the Employer's income from ordinary business operations (which will not include capital gains and other extraordinary income or gains and will not be reduced by extraordinary losses), less federal and state income taxes, expenses, and other charges (except such taxes, expenses, and charges attributable to capital gains and other extraordinary income or gains excluded from the definition of "net after-tax operating income"), all as reflected on the Employer's books, and will be calculated without taking the payment of such Incentive Compensation into account for any purpose. The "net after-tax operating income" will be determined by the certified public accounting firm regularly engaged by the Employer, and such determination will be binding on the Employer and the Executive.]

(b) The Employer will cause to be prepared, at its own expense and within a reasonable period of time after the end of each Fiscal Year during the term of this Agreement, [unaudited] financial statements showing the Employer's net after-tax operating income as provided above. [Such financial statements must have been audited by the certified public accounting firm regularly engaged by the Employer, which must have expressed an opinion that these financial statements have been prepared in accordance with generally accepted accounting principles consistently applied.] Subject to Section 6 below, the Executive will be paid the Incentive Compensation within [____________________] months after the end of the Fiscal Year to which the Incentive Compensation relates.

COMMENT

Incentive compensation is another subject that is very deal specific. Incentive compensation may be based on a variety of factors or formulae. Compensation based on a percentage of the Employer's net after-tax operating income is an example of one type of incentive compensation. The definition of "net after tax operating income" (or a similar term) is very important and may vary based on the transaction. If the Employer is a Subchapter S corporation (as defined under the Internal Revenue Code) or a limited liability company, the term "net after-tax operating income" would be inappropriate because, as a general rule, Subchapter S corporations and limited liability companies do not pay federal income tax on their income. The Executive may seek to exclude from the formula that determines incentive compensation matters resulting from the acquisition, such as interest on acquisition debt, increases in depreciation resulting from purchase accounting adjustments, and any allocations by the Buyer. Financial statements on which incentive compensation will be based may be audited or unaudited subject to the agreement of the parties. If the Employer's operations will be merged or otherwise integrated with those of another corporation after the transaction, it may be more difficult to determine incentive compensation based solely on the Employer's income.

4. FACILITIES AND EXPENSES

4.1 General

The Employer will furnish the Executive office space, equipment, supplies, and such other facilities and personnel as the Employer deems necessary or appropriate for the performance of the Executive's duties under this Agreement. The Employer will pay the Executive's dues in such professional societies and organizations as the [Chairman of the Board or Chief Executive Officer] deems appropriate, and will pay on behalf of the Executive (or reimburse the Executive for) reasonable expenses incurred by the Executive at the request of, or on behalf of, the Employer in the performance of the Executive's duties pursuant to this Agreement, and in accordance with the Employer's employment policies, including reasonable expenses incurred by the

Executive in attending conventions, seminars, and other business meetings, in appropriate business entertainment activities, and for promotional expenses. The Executive must file expense reports with respect to such expenses in accordance with the Employer's policies.

COMMENT

The types of fringe benefits granted to an executive and the expenses for which the Employer will reimburse the Executive vary based on the particular transaction. The Employer usually requires the Executive to submit expense reports that will meet the requirements of the Employer's policies and Section 274 of the Internal Revenue Code for the substantiation of certain types of expenses such as business meals, use of an automobile, and travel and entertainment expenses. Failure to meet the substantiation requirements of Section 274 may result in the disallowance of a deduction of the expense by the Employer for federal income tax purposes. As a result, the Employer may desire to include a provision that requires the Executive to reimburse the Employer for any expenses that are disallowed under federal, state, or local income tax laws because of a failure to meet the substantiation requirements.

4.2 Automobile

The Employer will include the Executive in the Employer's automobile allowance policy. The Executive will own his own automobile, and maintain and insure it at his own expense, for his business use in connection with his employment under this Agreement. The Executive will at his own expense maintain liability insurance on any automobile used in connection with the Employer's business, including excess liability (umbrella) insurance coverage in an amount not less than _____ million dollars per occurrence, with underlying insurance coverage as required by such excess liability insurance policy, and the Executive will furnish proof of such insurance to the Employer as requested by the Employer. The Executive must file expense reports with respect to such automobile in accordance with the Employer's policies.

COMMENT

The Executive may want a particular make or model of automobile, whether furnished by the Employer or the Executive, and the provisions regarding the automobile may be more detailed than the clause set forth above. In many cases, a more "customized" provision will be negotiated, including a specified dollar amount or per mile amount of reimbursement. However, federal income tax laws place limitations on the deductibility of automobile expenses.

5. VACATIONS AND HOLIDAYS

The Executive will be entitled to [four] weeks' paid vacation each [Fiscal Year] in accordance with the vacation policies of the Employer in effect for its executive officers from time to time. Vacation must be taken by the Executive at such time or times as approved by the Chairman of the Board or Chief Executive Officer. The Executive will also be entitled to the paid holidays [and other paid leave] set forth in the Employer's policies. Vacation days and holidays during any Fiscal Year that are not used by the Executive during such Fiscal Year may [not] be used in any subsequent Fiscal Year.

6. TERMINATION

6.1 Events of Termination

The Employment Period, the Executive's Basic Compensation and Incentive Compensation, and any and all other rights of the Executive under this Agreement or otherwise as an employee of the Employer will terminate (except as otherwise provided in this Section 6):

(a) upon the death of the Executive;

(b) upon the disability of the Executive (as defined in Section 6.2) immediately upon notice from either party to the other;

(c) for cause (as defined in Section 6.3), immediately upon notice from the Employer to the Executive, or at such later time as such notice may specify; or

(d) for good reason (as defined in Section 6.4) upon not less than thirty days' prior notice from the Executive to the Employer.

COMMENT

Termination provisions generally correspond to the intended role of the Executive and to the projected term of employment as well as to the amount of compensation in question.

6.2 Definition of Disability

For purposes of Section 6.1, the Executive will be deemed to have a "disability" if, for physical or mental reasons, the Executive is unable to perform [the essential functions of] the Executive's duties under this Agreement for 120 consecutive days, or 180 days during any twelvemonth period, as determined in accordance with this Section 6.2. The disability of the Executive will be determined by a medical doctor selected by written agreement of the Employer and the Executive upon the request of either party by notice to the other. If the Employer and the Executive cannot agree on the selection of a medical doctor, each of them will select a medical doctor and the two medical doctors will select a third medical doctor who will determine whether the Executive has a disability. The determination of the medical doctor selected under this Section 6.2 will be binding on both parties. The Executive must submit to a reasonable number of examinations by the medical doctor making the determination of disability under this Section 6.2, and the Executive hereby authorizes the disclosure and release to the Employer of such determination and all supporting medical records. If the Executive is not legally competent, the Executive's legal guardian or duly authorized attorney-in-fact will act in the Executive's stead, under this Section 6.2, for the purposes of submitting the Executive to the examinations, and providing the authorization of disclosure, required under this Section 6.2.

COMMENT

The disability provisions of the Employment Agreement are often negotiated by the parties. The Employer may want its board of directors or a physician selected by the Employer to determine whether the Executive is disabled. The Executive will often object to a determination of disability by the board of directors or a physician selected only by the Employer, and will generally want the right to approve the physician who will make the determination of disability.

Attorneys drafting disability termination clauses should be sensitive to the requirements of the Americans with Disabilities Act. The bracketed language with respect to essential functions has been inserted to address these concerns.

In some cases, the definition of disability will correspond to the definition of total disability under the Executive's disability insurance coverage so that the termination of employment and commencement of disability insurance benefits will coincide.

6.3 Definition of *"For Cause"*

For purposes of Section 6.1, the phrase "for cause" means: (a) the Executive's [material] breach of this Agreement [or the Noncompetition Agreement entered into on the date hereof between the Buyer and the Executive (the "Noncompetition Agreement")]; (b) the Executive's failure to adhere to any written Employer policy if the Executive has been given a reasonable opportunity to comply with such policy or cure his failure to comply (which reasonable opportunity must be granted during the ten-day period preceding termination of this Agreement); (c) the appropriation (or attempted appropriation) of a material business opportunity of the Employer, including attempting to secure or securing any personal profit in connection with any transaction entered into on behalf of the Employer; (d) the misappropriation (or attempted misappropriation) of any of the Employer's funds or property; or (e) the conviction of, the indictment for (or its procedural equivalent), or the entering of a guilty plea or plea of no contest with respect to, a felony, the equivalent thereof, or any other crime with respect to which imprisonment is a possible punishment.

COMMENT

The Employer generally wants flexibility in being able to terminate the Executive including substantial breadth in the definition of "for cause." The Executive wants to limit the Employer's rights to terminate the agreement for cause and desires to have an opportunity to cure a breach.

If the Employment Agreement favors the Employer, it may consist solely of a clause permitting the Employer to terminate the agreement for any behavior or conduct of the Executive that, in the judgment of the Employer's board of directors, is detrimental to or harms the business or reputation of the Employer. Executives will usually vigorously resist such a clause, especially in the context of an acquisition. Alternatively, the Employer could stipulate that failure of the Executive to achieve mutually-agreed business goals constitutes grounds for termination. This allows the Employer to terminate an Executive who has "retired at his desk" without requiring continuing payments under the

Employment Agreement. The Executive will want limited, and more objective, criteria for termination.

Executives are often very sensitive with respect to the Employer's right to terminate for certain criminal matters, such as merely being charged with a crime or the conviction of a misdemeanor. However, the Employer may be concerned about adverse publicity for the Employer if the Executive is charged with or convicted of certain crimes or misdemeanors.

6.4 Definition of *"For Good Reason"*

For purposes of Section 6.1, the phrase "for good reason" means any of the following: (a) The Employer's material breach of this Agreement; (b) the assignment of the Executive without his consent to a position, responsibilities, or duties of a materially lesser status or degree of responsibility than his position, responsibilities, or duties at the Effective Date; or (c) the relocation of the Employer's principal executive offices outside the metropolitan [______________, ______________] area; or (d) the requirement by the Employer that the Executive be based anywhere other than the Employer's principal executive offices, in either case without the Executive's consent.

COMMENT

A termination of the Employment Agreement "for good reason" is generally included in the Employer's first draft only at the insistence of the Executive who has sufficient bargaining leverage. It is intended to cover instances in which the Employer "constructively terminates" the Executive by taking certain actions, without the Executive's consent, that result in lesser status or responsibilities or hardships for the Executive. If the Executive terminates the Employment Agreement "for good reason," the Executive will be entitled to compensation and benefits for a specified period of time. If the Employment Agreement also permits the Executive to terminate the agreement without cause, the Executive will generally receive greater compensation and benefits if he terminates "for good reason" rather than without cause.

An additional ground for termination "for good reason" might include a change in control of the Employer or its parent corporation and the Executive may be provided with a "golden parachute" if this occurs. The Executive may seek to secure his "golden parachute" by way of a letter of credit, for example.

6.5 Termination Pay

Effective upon the termination of this Agreement, the Employer will be obligated to pay the Executive (or, in the event of his death, his designated beneficiary as defined below) only such compensation as is provided in this Section 6.5[, and in lieu of all other amounts and in settlement and complete release of all claims the Executive may have against the Employer]. For purposes of this Section 6.5, the Executive's designated beneficiary will be such individual beneficiary or trust, located at such address, as the Executive may designate by notice to the Employer from time to time or, if the Executive fails to give notice to the Employer of such a beneficiary, the Executive's estate. Notwithstanding the preceding sentence, the Employer will have no duty, in any circumstances, to attempt to open an estate on behalf of the Executive, to determine whether any beneficiary designated by the Executive is alive or to ascertain the address of any such beneficiary, to determine the existence of any trust, to determine whether any person or entity purporting to act as the Executive's personal representative (or the trustee of a trust established by the Executive) is duly authorized to act in that capacity, or to locate or attempt to locate any beneficiary, personal representative, or trustee.

(A) *Termination by the Executive for Good Reason.* If the Executive terminates this Agreement for good reason, the Employer will pay the Executive (i) the Executive's Salary for the remainder, if any, of the calendar month in which such termination is effective [and for twelve consecutive calendar months thereafter], and (ii) that portion of the Executive's Incentive Compensation, if any, for the Fiscal Year during which the termination is effective, prorated through the date of termination. Notwithstanding the preceding sentence, if the Executive obtains other employment prior to the end of the six months following the month in which the termination is effective, he must promptly give notice thereof to the Employer, and the Salary payments under this Agreement for any period after the Executive obtains other employment will be reduced by the amount of the cash compensation received and to be received by the Executive from the Executive's other employment for services performed during such period.

COMMENT

The Employment Agreements may provide, instead of the preceding provision, that if the Employer terminates the agreement without cause during the initial term, the Employer will continue to pay salary or incentive compensation, or both, during the remainder of the initial term, as if the agreement had not been terminated. Such a provision is used when the payments to the Executive under the Employment Agreement constitute, in effect, a portion of the total consideration for the purchase of the business, or when the Executive has substantial bargaining leverage. When the Employer is required to pay salary and incentive compensation for the remainder of the initial term in the case of a termination by the Employer without cause, the Employer may want to require, as a condition to the Executive's receipt of such continued income, that the Executive furnish to the Employer a complete release of all claims that the Executive may have against the Employer.

The Employment Agreement does not provide for payments that are contingent on any change in the ownership or effective control of the Employer or in the ownership of a substantial portion of the Employer's assets (so-called "golden parachute" payments). Attorneys should be aware that "excess parachute payments" are non-deductible to the Employer under Section 280G of the Internal Revenue Code and the recipient of an excess parachute payment is subject to a 20% excise tax under Section 4999 of the Internal Revenue Code.

(B) *Termination by the Employer for Cause.* If the Employer terminates this Agreement for cause, the Executive will be entitled to receive his Salary only through the date such termination is effective, but will not be entitled to any Incentive Compensation for the Fiscal Year during which such termination occurs or any subsequent Fiscal Year.

(C) *Termination upon Disability.* If this Agreement is terminated by either party as a result of the Executive's disability, as determined under Section 6.2, the Employer will pay the Executive his Salary through the remainder of the calendar month during which such termination is effective [and for the lesser of (i) ____ consecutive months thereafter, or (ii) the period until disability insurance benefits commence under the disability insurance coverage furnished by the Employer to the Executive].

COMMENT

The Executive is usually concerned that there be no gap in income between the termination of compensation from the Employer and the beginning of disability insurance benefits. The Executive should be familiar with the terms of his disability insurance coverage when negotiating the Employment Agreement. Careful planning may be required so that the Executive's disability insurance is not adversely affected because of provisions in the Employment Agreement that conflict with the disability insurance policy.

(D) *Termination upon Death.* If this Agreement is terminated because of the Executive's death, the Executive will be entitled to receive his Salary through the end of the calendar month in which his death occurs, and that part of the Executive's Incentive Compensation, if any, for the Fiscal Year during which his death occurs, prorated through the end of the calendar month during which his death occurs.

(E) *Benefits.* The Executive's accrual of, or participation in plans providing for, the Benefits will cease at the effective date of the termination of this Agreement, and the Executive will be entitled to accrued Benefits pursuant to such plans only as provided in such plans. [The Executive will not receive, as part of his termination pay pursuant to this Section 6, any payment or other compensation for any vacation, holiday, sick leave, or other leave unused on the date the notice of termination is given under this Agreement.]

COMMENT

The Executive may want to negotiate an extension of benefits, in the event of a termination without cause or for good reason, that may be difficult or expensive for the Executive to obtain after the termination, such as medical and dental benefits for the Executive's family and life and disability insurance. However, under the Consolidated Omnibus Reconciliation Act (COBRA), the Employer may be required, for a period of eighteen months after the termination, to provide, at the Executive's expense, a continuation of medical coverage for the Executive and the Executive's spouse and dependents.

The Employer's attorneys should be very careful about including the bracketed language. Many states have enacted statutes requiring that compensation due to the Executive, including, in some states, vacation pay and other fringe benefits, be paid within a specified number of days after the Executive resigns or is terminated. The Employer's failure to comply with such a statute may subject the Employer to penalties and attorneys' fees in addition to payment of the compensation. *See* 90 A.L.R.2d 606 (1963); 11 A.L.R.5th 715 (1993).

7. NON-DISCLOSURE COVENANT; EMPLOYEE INVENTIONS

7.1 Acknowledgments by the Executive

The Executive acknowledges that (a) during the Employment Period and as a part of his employment, the Executive will be afforded access to Confidential Information; (b) public disclosure of such Confidential Information could have an adverse effect on the Employer and its business; (c) because the Executive possesses substantial technical expertise and skill with respect to the Employer's business, the Employer desires to obtain exclusive ownership of each Employee Invention, and the Employer will be at a substantial competitive disadvantage if it fails to acquire exclusive ownership of each Employee Invention; (d) the Buyer has required that the Executive make the covenants in this Section 7 as a condition to its purchase of the Employer's stock; and (e) the provisions of this Section 7 are reasonable and necessary to prevent the improper use or disclosure of Confidential Information and to provide the Employer with exclusive ownership of all Employee Inventions.

7.2 Agreements of the Executive

In consideration of the compensation and benefits to be paid or provided to the Executive by the Employer under this Agreement, the Executive covenants as follows:

(A) *Confidentiality*.

(i) During and following the Employment Period, the Executive will hold in confidence the Confidential Information and will not disclose it to any person except with the specific prior written consent of the Employer or except as otherwise expressly permitted by the terms of this Agreement.

(ii) Any trade secrets of the Employer will be entitled to all of the protections and benefits under ____________________ Section ______ [applicable state trade secret law] and any other applicable law. If any information that the Employer deems to be a trade secret is found by a court of competent jurisdiction not to be a trade secret for purposes of this Agreement, such information will, nevertheless, be considered Confidential Information for purposes of this Agreement. The Executive hereby waives any requirement that the Employer submit proof of the economic value of any trade secret or post a bond or other security.

(iii) None of the foregoing obligations and restrictions applies to any part of the Confidential Information that the Executive demonstrates was or became generally available to the public other than as a result of a disclosure by the Executive.

(iv) The Executive will not remove from the Employer's premises (except to the extent such removal is for purposes of the performance of the Executive's duties at home or while traveling, or except as otherwise specifically authorized by the Employer) any document, record, notebook, plan, model, component, device, or computer software or code, whether embodied in a disk or in any other form (collectively, the "Proprietary Items"). The Executive recognizes that, as between the Employer and the Executive, all of the Proprietary Items, whether or not developed by the Executive, are the exclusive property of the Employer. Upon termination of this Agreement by either party, or upon the request of the Employer during the Employment Period, the Executive will return to the Employer all of the Proprietary Items in the Executive's possession or subject to the Executive's control, and the Executive shall not retain any copies, abstracts, sketches, or other physical embodiment of any of the Proprietary Items.

COMMENT

The non-disclosure covenant of the Employment Agreement may be very important to the Employer in protecting its trade secrets and other proprietary information. Although the Executive may have an obligation under statute or common law, even in the absence of a written agreement, to refrain from disclosing the Employer's trade secrets, a written agreement concerning confidentiality can better protect the Employer by clearly defining the matters that the Employer seeks to protect and by broadening the scope of protection beyond what is afforded by statute or common law. However, the matters to be protected must generally be commercially valuable to the Employer, and the Employer must have made reasonable efforts to protect their secrecy. Another advantage of a non-disclosure covenant is that in many jurisdictions, such a covenant is evidence that the Employer has taken reasonable measures to protect the secrecy of the purported trade secrets. To the extent possible, the non-disclosure covenant should clearly describe the matters for which confidentiality is sought rather than merely providing a very general statement of protection.

The exception requested by the Executive for confidential information obtained by the Executive on a non-confidential basis has not been included in the provision above because (1) the Executive might receive such information as agent for the Employer, and (2) in an acquisition in which the Executive is a principal of the Company, the Executive might have received information on a non-confidential basis prior to the acquisition which the Employer now treats as confidential.

The frequently seen exception for materials independently developed by the Executive is not included in the Employment Agreement because of the potential for disputes over what was independently developed.

For more in-depth commentary on these issues, see the Commentary to the Confidentiality Agreement.

(B) *Employee Inventions.* Each Employee Invention will belong exclusively to the Employer. The Executive acknowledges that all of the Executive's writing, works of authorship, specially commissioned works listed in Exhibit ____, and other Employee Inventions are works made for hire and the property of the Employer, including any copyrights, patents, [semiconductor mask protection,] or other intellectual property rights pertaining thereto. If it is determined that any such works are not works made for hire, the Executive hereby assigns to the Employer all of the Executive's right, title, and interest, including all rights of copyright, patent, [semiconductor mask protection,] and other intellectual property rights, to or in such Employee Inventions. The Executive covenants that he will promptly:

(i) disclose to the Employer in writing any Employee Invention;

(ii) assign to the Employer or to a party designated by the Employer, at the Employer's request and without additional compensation, all of the Executive's right to the Employee Invention for the United States and all foreign jurisdictions;

(iii) execute and deliver to the Employer such applications, assignments, and other documents as the Employer may request in order to apply for and obtain patents or other registrations with respect to any Employee Invention in the United States and any foreign jurisdictions;

(iv) sign all other papers necessary to carry out the above obligations; and

(v) give testimony and render any other assistance [but without expense to the Executive] in support of the Employer's rights to any Employee Invention.

COMMENT

This Section provides that any ideas, inventions, techniques, modifications, processes, mask works, and original works of authorship, such as works made for hire, and designs conceived or developed by the Executive, whether individually or together with others, during his term of employment, will belong exclusively to the Employer. The second sentence recites that Employee Inventions are "works made for hire," which in some cases will vest in the Employer greater rights than would accrue by mere assignment under the Copyright Act or Semiconductor Chip Protection Act. *See, e.g.,* 17 U.S.C. §§ 201(b), 203(a) & 302(c). Work produced by the Executive within the scope of his employment will generally be considered as a work made for hire. However, the United States Supreme Court has adopted a literal construction of the definition of works made for hire that substantially limits its scope. *See Community for Creative Non-Violence v. Reid,* 490 U.S. 730 (1989). Therefore, should the second sentence of Section 7.2(b) fail to create work made for hire status when otherwise not available, the third sentence effects an express assignment of any protectable intellectual property rights to the Employer. Under 17 U.S.C. § 203, the Executive may terminate such assignments after thirty-five years.

In the absence of an agreement, there is generally no common law duty of the Executive to assign an invention or work of authorship to the Employer. *See, e.g., Great Lakes Press Corp. v. Froom,* 695 F. Supp. 1440, 1445 (W.D.N.Y. 1987); *Ingersoll-Rand Co. v. Ciavatta,* 542 A.2d 879, 885-87 (N.J. 1988). However, some states have enacted statutes that render unenforceable or void as against public policy contractual provisions that require the assignment to the Employer of inventions that were developed by the Executive outside of the field of the Employer's business, outside the scope of the Executive's duties, on the Executive's own time, and without use of the Employer's resources. *See, e.g.*, CAL. LAB. CODE §§ 2870, 2872 (West 1989); Del. Code Ann. tit. 19, § 805 (1991); Ill. Ann. Stat. ch. 140, para. 302 (Smith-Hurd 1986); Minn. Stat. § 181.78 (1990); N.C. Gen. Stat. § 66-57.1 (1990); Wash. Rev. Code Ann. §§ 49.44.140, 49.44.150 (West 1990). Because these types of covenants are often the subject of litigation, consultation with an attorney who is experienced in litigating issues arising from these covenants may be advisable.

7.3 Disputes or Controversies

The Executive recognizes that should a dispute or controversy arising from or relating to this Agreement be submitted for adjudication to any court, arbitration panel, or other third party, the preservation of the secrecy of Confidential Information may be jeopardized. All pleadings, documents, testimony, and records relating to any such adjudication will be maintained in secrecy and will be available for inspection by the Employer, the Executive, and their respective attorneys and experts, who will agree, in advance and in writing, to receive and maintain all such information in secrecy, except as may be limited by them in writing.

COMMENT

Although the above provision seeks to preserve the confidentiality of Confidential Information in the context of a dispute between the parties, if there is substantial concern over whether a court will protect the confidentiality of the Confidential Information, the parties may want to arbitrate any disputes under the agreement.

8. NON-COMPETITION AND NON-INTERFERENCE

8.1 Acknowledgments by the Executive

The Executive acknowledges that: (a) the services to be performed by him under this Agreement are of a special, unique, unusual, extraordinary, and intellectual character; (b) the Employer's business is [national in scope and its products are marketed throughout the United States]; (c) the Employer competes with other businesses that are or could be located in any part of [the United States]; (d) the Buyer has required that the Executive make the covenants set forth in this Section 8 as a condition to the Buyer's purchase of the Executive's stock in the Employer; and (e) the provisions of this Section 8 are reasonable and necessary to protect the Employer's business.

8.2 Covenants of the Executive

In consideration of the acknowledgments by the Executive, and in consideration of the compensation and benefits to be paid or provided to the Executive by the Employer, the Executive covenants that he will not, directly or indirectly:

(a) during the Employment Period, except in the course of his employment hereunder, and during the Post-Employment Period, engage or invest in, own, manage, operate, finance, control, or participate in the ownership, management, operation, financing, or control of, be employed by, associated with, or in any manner connected with, lend the Executive's name or any similar name to, lend Executive's credit to or render services or advice to, any business whose products or activities compete in whole or in part with the products or activities of the Employer [anywhere within the United States]; provided, however, that the Executive may purchase or otherwise acquire up to (but not more than) one percent of any class of securities of any enterprise (but without otherwise participating in the activities of such enterprise) if such securities are listed on any national or regional securities exchange or have been registered under Section 12(g) of the Securities Exchange Act of 1934;

(b) whether for the Executive's own account or for the account of any other person, at any time during the Employment Period and the Post-Employment Period, solicit business of the same or similar type being carried on by the Employer, from any person known by the Executive to be a customer of the Employer, whether or not the Executive had personal contact with such person during and by reason of the Executive's employment with the Employer;

(c) whether for the Executive's own account or the account of any other person (i) at any time during the Employment Period and the Post-Employment Period, solicit, employ, or otherwise engage as an employee, independent contractor, or otherwise, any person who is or was an employee of the Employer at any time during the Employment Period or in any manner induce or attempt to induce any employee of the Employer to terminate his employment with the Employer; or (ii) at any time during the Employment Period and for three years thereafter, interfere with the Employer's relationship with any person, including any person who at any time during the Employment Period was an employee, contractor, supplier, or customer of the Employer; or

(d) at any time during or after the Employment Period, disparage the Employer or any of its shareholders, directors, officers, employees, or agents.

For purposes of this Section 8.2, the term "Post-Employment Period" means the _____ year period beginning on the date of termination of the Executive's employment with the Employer.

If any covenant in this Section 8.2 is held to be unreasonable, arbitrary, or against public policy, such covenant will be considered to be divisible with respect to scope, time, and geographic area, and such lesser scope, time, or geographic area, or all of them, as a court of competent jurisdiction may determine to be reasonable, not arbitrary, and not against public policy, will be effective, binding, and enforceable against the Executive.

The period of time applicable to any covenant in this Section 8.2 will be extended by the duration of any violation by the Executive of such covenant.

The Executive will, while the covenant under this Section 8.2 is in effect, give notice to the Employer, within ten days after accepting any other employment, of the identity of the Executive's employer. The Buyer or the Employer may notify such employer that the Executive is bound by this Agreement and, at the Employer's election, furnish such employer with a copy of this Agreement or relevant portions thereof.

COMMENT

The noncompetition covenant of the Employment Agreement must be drafted with care to comply with any relevant state statutes and to withstand close scrutiny by the courts, which are reluctant to uphold any restraints of trade. One important factor is whether the covenant not to compete is supported by consideration. Some states hold that continued employment does not constitute sufficient consideration for a covenant not to compete. *See, e.g., PEMCO Corp. v. Rose,* 257 S.E.2d 885, 889 (W. Va. 1979); *Maintenance Specialties, Inc. v. Gottus,* 314 A.2d

279, 281 (Pa. 1974). In such cases, the covenant must be supported by additional consideration, such as a salary increase, bonus, or promotion. However, since the Executive who agrees not to compete is also a stockholder selling the stock of his corporation, the court may find that the consideration for the sale of the business includes the consideration for the sale of goodwill and the withdrawal from competition. *See, e.g., Russell v. Jim Russell Supply Inc.,* 558 N.E.2d 115, 120 (Ill. App. 1990).

The Buyer's counsel should consider whether the Employment Agreement should also contain a covenant not to compete if the Model Stock Purchase Agreement contains such a covenant or as in this case, a Noncompetition Agreement is executed.

Courts are more likely to enforce more restrictive provisions in a noncompetition agreement ancillary to the sale of a business than a noncompetition covenant in an employment agreement. *See, e.g., Fogle v. Shah*, 539 N.E.2d 500, 502 (Ind. Ct. App. 1989); *Bowen v. Carlsbad Ins. & Real Estate*, 724 P.2d 223, 225 (N.M. 1986). The courts emphasize that the restrictive covenants ancillary to the sale of a business are more likely to be fair and reasonable because of the roughly equal bargaining powers between the parties, as compared with the imbalance that usually exists in the employer-employee relationship. *See, e.g., J.B.N. Morris v. Homco Int'l, Inc.,* 853 F.2d 337, 341 (5th Cir. 1988); *Marathon Petroleum Co. v. Chronister Oil Co.,* 687 F. Supp. 437, 439 (C.D. Ill. 1988); *Madison Bank & Trust v. First Nat'l Bank of Huntsville,* 635 S.W.2d 268, 270-71 (Ark. 1982); *Annis v. Tomberlin & Shelnutt Assocs.,* 392 S.E.2d 717, 721 (Ga. App. 1990). Courts are generally unwilling to deprive an employee of his livelihood by enforcing an oppressive covenant not to compete, as opposed to enforcing a covenant by a knowledgeable and sophisticated selling stockholder of a business who then becomes an executive.

If both the Model Stock Purchase Agreement (or Noncompetition Agreement) and the Employment Agreement contain a covenant not to compete, the two covenants must be carefully coordinated so that they are not inconsistent. Courts may treat less restrictive provisions in an employment agreement as overriding harsher provisions in an acquisition agreement in order to avoid an adverse effect on the employee's ability to earn a living. *See, e.g., Wilmot H. Simonson Co. v. Green Textiles Assoc.,* 755 F.2d 217, 220 (1st Cir. 1985).

In an action to enforce a covenant not to compete in the Employment Agreement, a court will most likely balance the reasonable need of the Employer to be protected from competition with the right of the Executive to earn a living. Thus, covenants not to compete must generally be definite and reasonable with respect to the time period of the restraint, the geographic area covered, and the types of activities proscribed. The Employer's counsel should examine carefully the different state laws that could apply to the noncompetition covenant. For example, the above covenant applies throughout the United States. Under the laws of many states, for such a covenant to be enforceable, it must not cover a geographic area broader than necessary to protect the reasonable needs of the Employer. In some states covenants covering the entire United States are deemed void, unless the business of the Employer and the responsibilities of the Executive and truly national in scope. Many businesses are regional or local in scope and, therefore, will be entitled only to covenants not to compete that, from a geographic standpoint, more nearly match the geographic scope of the business. For discussions of geographic restrictions in, and the duration of, covenants not to compete in employment agreements, see 43 A.L.R.2d 94 and 41 A.L.R.2d 15.

The above covenant contains a provision permitting the court to reduce the time, scope, or geographic area of the covenant not to compete if it determines that any of these covenants are unreasonable as drafted. Although courts in many states will, through their equity power, tailor the terms of a covenant not to compete even in the absence of such a "blue-lining" provision, it is advisable to insert such a provision in the agreement if the court would not, on its own initiative, tailor the provision. In some states, however, courts will not tailor a covenant not to compete even with a "blue lining" clause in the agreement. In such states, covenants not to compete will be unenforceable if the court finds that they are unreasonable as written.

For a more in-depth discussion of state laws concerning employee noncompete covenants, see *Covenants Not to Compete: A State-by-State Survey*, by the ABA Section of Labor and Employment Law, published by The Bureau of National Affairs, Inc.

Payments made for a covenant not to compete have significant federal income tax consequences. Such payments are includable in the gross income of the recipient and, to the extent they are reasonable in amount, are amortizable by the payor over a fifteen-year period. In the past, there would have been considerable tension between the Sellers and the Buyer as to how much of the purchase price should be allocated to the Sellers' goodwill or going-concern value and how much should be allocated to a covenant not to compete. Payments for goodwill or going-concern value are usually favored by the Sellers because they generally produce long-term capital gain to the Sellers rather than ordinary income, which results from covenant not to compete payments. On the other hand, the Buyer would have usually preferred payments for a covenant not to compete because they were amortizable for tax purposes during the term of the covenant whereas payments for goodwill or going-concern value were not amortizable. However, the Omnibus Budget Reconciliation Act of 1993 permits purchased goodwill and covenants not to compete to be amortized over a fifteen-year period regardless of the duration of the covenant (usually a much shorter time period), which reduces the Buyer's incentive to allocate a portion of the purchase price to the noncompete covenant. The Sellers will still prefer to receive payment for goodwill rather than a covenant not to compete because of the possibility of obtaining long-term capital gain treatment.

If any person who owns 10% or more of an entity transfers an interest in the entity and, in connection with the transfer, that person (or a related person) enters into an employment contract, covenant not to compete, or other agreement with the transferee, that person and the transferee must furnish the IRS with certain information about the transaction. *See* Section 1060(e) of the Internal Revenue Code of 1986, as amended. A seller and buyer in an asset acquisition or certain other transactions should review the other provisions of Section 1060 and the regulations under Section 1060 for rules regarding the allocation of purchase price to the assets being sold, including goodwill.

9. GENERAL PROVISIONS

9.1 Injunctive Relief and Additional Remedy

The Executive acknowledges that the injury that would be suffered by the Employer as a result of a breach of the provisions of this Agreement (including any provision of Sections 7 and 8) would be irreparable and that an award of monetary damages to the Employer for such a breach would be an inadequate remedy. Consequently, the Employer will have the right, in addition to any other rights it may have, to obtain injunctive relief to restrain any breach or threatened breach or otherwise to specifically enforce any provision of this Agreement, and the Employer will not be obligated to post bond or other security in seeking such relief. [Without limiting the Employer's rights under this Section 9 or any other remedies of the Employer, if the Executive breaches any of the provisions of Section 7 or 8, the Employer will have the right to cease making any payments otherwise due to the Executive under this Agreement.]

COMMENT

In some cases, depending on the solvency of the Executive and the potential difficulty under the applicable state law of obtaining injunctive relief for breaches of the Noncompetition Agreement, the Employer may elect to forego provisions with respect to injunctive relief and, in lieu thereof, provide for liquidated damages. If the Employer selects the more traditional provisions allowing for injunctive relief, the Employer should be aware that any offset by the Employer for damages it claims as a result of a violation of the noncompetition covenant could weaken its position in requesting injunctive relief. See the Commentary to Section 9.3. The Employer may want to include the bracketed language to make clear that it may cease making payments to the Executive under the agreement if the Executive breaches Sections 7 or 8.

9.2 Covenants of Sections 7 and 8 Are Essential and Independent Covenants

The covenants by the Executive in Sections 7 and 8 are essential elements of this Agreement, and without the Executive's agreement to comply with such covenants, the Buyer would not have purchased the Executive's stock under the Stock Purchase Agreement and the Employer would not have entered into this Agreement or employed or continued the employment of the Executive. The Employer and the Executive have independently consulted their respective counsel and have been advised in all respects concerning the reasonableness and propriety of such covenants, with specific regard to the nature of the business conducted by the Employer.

The Executive's covenants in Sections 7 and 8 are independent covenants and the existence of any claim by the Executive against the Employer under this Agreement or otherwise, or against the Buyer, will not excuse the Executive's breach of any covenant in Section 7 or 8.

If the Executive's employment hereunder expires or is terminated, this Agreement will continue in full force and effect as is necessary or appropriate to enforce the covenants and agreements of the Executive in Sections 7 and 8.

[9.3 Offset

The Employer will be entitled to offset against any and all amounts owing to the Executive under this Agreement the amount of any and all claims that the Buyer may have against the Executive under the Stock Purchase Agreement [or the Noncompetition Agreement]].

COMMENT

The Employer's first draft may contain an offset provision, such as the one above, which is likely to be vigorously resisted by the Executive. The legality of such a provision must be determined under the applicable state law. In many states, such a provision may be unenforceable and may subject the Employer to penalties and attorneys' fees for failure to pay wages within a period specified by statute after the Executive's resignation or termination. *See* 90 A.L.R.2d 606; 11 A.L.R.5th 715.

The offset provision should probably not refer to the Noncompetition Agreement if, under the applicable state law, the effect of such an offset option would weaken the Buyer's position that its remedy at law for damages is inadequate and that it is entitled to injunctive relief. In some noncompetition agreements, however, as discussed in the Commentary to Section 9.1, a liquidated damages provision is provided in lieu of injunctive relief and an offset provision might be appropriate.

9.4 Representations and Warranties by the Executive

The Executive represents and warrants to the Employer that the execution and delivery by the Executive of this Agreement do not, and the performance by the Executive of the Executive's obligations hereunder will not, with or without the giving of notice or the passage of time, or both: (a) violate any judgment, writ, injunction, or order of any court, arbitrator, or governmental agency applicable to the Executive; or (b) conflict with, result in the breach of any provisions of or the termination of, or constitute a default under, any agreement to which the Executive is a party or by which the Executive is or may be bound.

9.5 Obligations Contingent on Performance

The obligations of the Employer hereunder, including its obligation to pay the compensation provided for herein, are contingent upon the Executive's performance of the Executive's obligations hereunder.

9.6 Waiver

The rights and remedies of the parties to this Agreement are cumulative and not alternative. Neither the failure nor any delay by either party in exercising any right, power, or privilege under this Agreement will operate as a waiver of such right, power, or privilege, and no single or partial exercise of any such right, power, or privilege will preclude any other or further exercise of such right, power, or privilege or the exercise of any other right, power, or privilege. To the maximum extent permitted by applicable law, (a) no claim or right arising out of this Agreement can be discharged by one party, in whole or in part, by a waiver or renunciation of the claim or right unless in writing signed by the other party; (b) no waiver that may be given by a party will be applicable except in the specific instance for which it is given; and (c) no notice to or demand on one party will be deemed to be a waiver of any obligation of such party or of the right of the party giving such notice or demand to take further action without notice or demand as provided in this Agreement.

9.7 Binding Effect; Delegation of Duties Prohibited

This Agreement shall inure to the benefit of, and shall be binding upon, the parties hereto and their respective successors, assigns, heirs, and legal representatives, including any entity with which the Employer may merge or consolidate or to which all or substantially all of its assets may be transferred. The duties and covenants of the Executive under this Agreement, being personal, may not be delegated.

9.8 Notices

All notices, consents, waivers, and other communications under this Agreement must be in writing and will be deemed to have been duly given when (a) delivered by hand (with written confirmation of receipt), (b) sent by facsimile (with written confirmation of receipt), provided that a copy is mailed by registered mail, return receipt requested, or (c) when received by the addressee, if sent by a nationally recognized overnight delivery service (receipt requested), in each case to the appropriate addresses and facsimile numbers set forth below (or to such other addresses and facsimile numbers as a party may designate by notice to the other parties):

If to Employer: ______________________________
____
____
Attention: ______________________
Facsimile No.: ___________________

With a copy to: ______________________________
____
____
Attention: ______________________
Facsimile No.: ___________________

If to the Executive: ______________________________
____
____
Attention: ______________________
Facsimile No.: ___________________

With a copy to: ______________________________
____
____
Attention: ______________________
Facsimile No.: ___________________

9.9 Entire Agreement; Amendments

This Agreement, the Stock Purchase Agreement, and the documents executed in connection with the Stock Purchase Agreement, contain the entire agreement between the parties with respect to the subject matter hereof and supersede all prior agreements and understandings, oral or written, between the parties hereto with respect to the subject matter hereof. This Agreement may not be amended orally, but only by an agreement in writing signed by the parties hereto.

9.10 Governing Law

This Agreement will be governed by the laws of the State of________ without regard to conflicts of laws principles.

COMMENT

The Employer's counsel should be cautious in drafting provisions in the Employment Agreement regarding choice of law, choice of forum, and designation of agent for service of process so that they will not be determined to be unconscionable or overreaching.

For a discussion of choice of law provisions with respect to covenants not to compete, see 70 A.L.R.2d 1292.

The parties may also want to consider binding arbitration, non-binding arbitration, mediation, or another alternative dispute resolution mechanism, and the procedures that will apply to such alternative dispute resolution mechanism.

9.11 Jurisdiction

Any action or proceeding seeking to enforce any provision of, or based on any right arising out of, this Agreement may be brought against either of the parties in the courts of the State of ________________, County of ______________, or, if it has or can acquire jurisdiction, in the United States District Court for the __________ District of ___________, and each of the parties consents to the jurisdiction of such courts (and of the appropriate appellate courts) in any such action or proceeding and waives any objection to venue laid therein. Process in any action or proceeding referred to in the preceding sentence may be served on either party anywhere in the world.

COMMENT

Employers should be very wary of relying on consent to jurisdiction provisions in the Employment Agreement. Generally speaking, if the Employer is seeking to enforce, by injunction, the covenant not to compete, a suit will usually be brought in the state where the Executive resides or is doing business, so that the court will have jurisdiction over the Executive for the purpose of issuing and enforcing injunctive relief.

The parties may want to consider, when permitted by statute or rules of court, allowing service of process by certified mail. Alternatively, the Employer may insist that the Executive designate an agent for service of process in a particular state or jurisdiction. For an example of such a provision, see the Commentary to Section 11.5 of the Model Stock Purchase Agreement.

9.12 Section Headings, Construction

The headings of Sections in this Agreement are provided for convenience only and will not affect its construction or interpretation. All references to "Section" or "Sections" refer to the corresponding Section or Sections of this Agreement unless otherwise specified. All words used in this Agreement will be construed to be of such gender or number as the circumstances require. Unless otherwise expressly provided, the word "including" does not limit the preceding words or terms.

9.13 Severability

If any provision of this Agreement is held invalid or unenforceable by any court of competent jurisdiction, the other provisions of this Agreement will remain in full force and effect. Any provision of this Agreement held invalid or unenforceable only in part or degree will remain in full force and effect to the extent not held invalid or unenforceable.

9.14 Counterparts

This Agreement may be executed in one or more counterparts, each of which will be deemed to be an original copy of this Agreement and all of which, when taken together, will be deemed to constitute one and the same agreement.

[9.15 Waiver of Jury Trial

THE PARTIES HERETO HEREBY WAIVE A JURY TRIAL IN ANY LITIGATION WITH RESPECT TO THIS AGREEMENT.]

IN WITNESS WHEREOF, the parties have executed and delivered this Agreement as of the date above first written above.

EMPLOYER:	EXECUTIVE:
By: ______________________	______________________

Exhibit 2.4(a)(iv)

Noncompetition Agreement

PRELIMINARY NOTE

The Buyer may want to prevent the Sellers from competing with the Acquired Companies once the Sellers are no longer associated with them. This can be accomplished by means of a restrictive covenant in the Model Stock Purchase Agreement, by means of a separate Noncompetition Agreement, or, as in the case of the fact pattern of the Model Stock Purchase Agreement, if the Sellers are employed after the purchase is consummated, by means of a post-employment restrictive covenant in the Employment Agreements. Any of these methods, either alone or in combination, can be used in a transaction of the type contemplated by the Model Stock Purchase Agreement. It is important that all noncompetition provisions in documents used in the transaction be consistent. It is also important to note that there are differences between a post-employment restrictive covenant in an employment agreement and a noncompetition agreement entered into in conjunction with an acquisition, and that a noncompetition agreement made in conjunction with an acquisition is more likely to be enforced. *See* the Commentary to Section 4 of the Noncompetition Agreement.

NONCOMPETITION AGREEMENT

This Noncompetition Agreement (this "Agreement") is made as of __________, 199__, by and between ________________________, a __________ corporation ("Buyer"), and ____________________, residing at ______________________ ("Seller").

COMMENT

If one of the Sellers will be entering into the Employment Agreement with the Company, the Buyer's counsel should consider whether both the Model Stock Purchase Agreement (either directly or, as in this instance, by means of the Noncompetition Agreement) and the Employment Agreement should contain a covenant not to compete. See the Preliminary Note and the Commentary to Section 4 of this Noncompetition Agreement and the Commentary to Section 8.2 of the Employment Agreement.

RECITALS

Concurrently with the execution and delivery of this Agreement, Buyer is purchasing from Seller and ______________________ residing at ______________________ ("A") all of the outstanding shares (the "Shares") of common stock, par value $__ per share, of ______________________ (the "Company") pursuant to the terms and conditions of a stock purchase agreement made as of ________, 19__, (the "Stock Purchase Agreement"). Section 2.4(a)(iv) of the Stock Purchase Agreement requires that noncompetition agreements be executed and delivered by each of Seller and A as a condition to the purchase of the Shares by Buyer.

AGREEMENT

The parties, intending to be legally bound, agree as follows:

---

1. DEFINITIONS

Capitalized terms not expressly defined in this Agreement shall have the meanings ascribed to them in the Stock Purchase Agreement.

2. ACKNOWLEDGMENTS BY SELLER

Seller acknowledges that (a) Seller has occupied a position of trust and confidence with the Acquired Companies prior to the date hereof and has become familiar with the following, any and all of which constitute confidential information of the Acquired Companies, (collectively the "Confidential Information"): (i) any and all trade secrets concerning the business and affairs of the Acquired Companies, product specifications, data, know-how, formulae, compositions, processes, designs, sketches, photographs, graphs, drawings, samples, inventions and ideas, past, current and planned research and development, current and planned manufacturing and distribution methods and processes, customer lists, current and anticipated customer requirements, price lists, market studies, business plans, computer software and programs (including object code and source code), computer software and database technologies, systems, structures and architectures (and related processes, formulae, compositions, improvements, devices, know-how, inventions, discoveries, concepts, ideas, designs, methods and information, ___________________, of the Acquired Companies and any other information, however documented, of the Acquired Companies that is a trade secret within the meaning of ____________ § —[applicable state trade secret law]; (ii) any and all information concerning the business and affairs of the Acquired Companies (which includes historical financial statements, financial projections and budgets, historical and projected sales, capital spending budgets and plans, the names and backgrounds of key personnel, personnel training and techniques and materials, and ______________), however documented; and (iii) any and all notes, analysis, compilations, studies, summaries, and other material prepared by or for the Acquired Companies containing or based, in whole or in part, on any information included in the foregoing, (b) the business of the Acquired Companies is [national] [international] in scope, (c) its products and services are marketed throughout the [United States] [World]; (d) the Acquired Companies compete with other businesses that are or could be located in any part of the [United States] [World]; (e) Buyer has required that Seller make the covenants set forth in Sections 3 and 4 of this Agreement as a condition to the Buyer's purchase of the Shares owned by Seller and A; (f) the provisions of Sections 3 and 4 of this Agreement are reasonable and necessary to protect and preserve the Acquired Companies' business, and (g) the Acquired Companies would be irreparably damaged if Seller were to breach the covenants set forth in Sections 3 and 4 of this Agreement.

3. CONFIDENTIAL INFORMATION

Seller acknowledges and agrees that all Confidential Information known or obtained by Seller, whether before or after the date hereof, is the property of the Acquired Companies. Therefore, Seller agrees that Seller will not, at any time, disclose to any unauthorized Persons or use for his own account or for the benefit of any third party any Confidential Information, whether Seller has such information in Seller's memory or embodied in writing or other physical form, without Buyer's written consent, unless and to the extent that the Confidential Information is or becomes generally known to and available for use by the public other than as a result of Seller's fault or the fault of any other Person bound by a duty of confidentiality to Buyer or the Acquired Companies. Seller agrees to deliver to Buyer at the time of execution of this Agreement, and at any other time Buyer may request, all documents, memoranda, notes, plans, records, reports, and other documentation, models, components, devices, or computer software, whether embodied in a disk or in other form (and all copies of all of the foregoing), relating to the businesses, operations, or affairs of the Acquired Companies and any other Confidential Information that Seller may then possess or have under Seller's control.

COMMENT

The nondisclosure covenant is just as important in protecting the Buyer as the noncompetition covenant. Although the Seller may have a common law and statutory obligation not to disclose the Acquired Companies' trade secrets and other confidential information, a written agreement can clearly define the matters for which protection is sought and has an *in terrorem* effect. The Buyer should therefore exercise care in identifying trade secrets that may be particularly sensitive to the Acquired Companies. Such trade secrets may include customer preferences and pricing information, customer lists, and customer contacts. Identifying and including specific trade secrets within the written agreement makes the courts more apt to enforce the non-disclosure covenant. *See Leo Silfen, Inc. v. Cream*, 29 N.Y.2d 387, 328 N.Y.S.2d 423, 273 N.E.2d 636, 629 (1972) (finding the absence of an express nondisclosure agreement was relevant in not protecting a customer list); *Webcraft Technologies, Inc. v. McCaw*, 674 F. Supp. 1039, 1045 (S.D.N.Y.1987). *See* the Commentary to Section 2 of the Confidentiality Agreement.

4. NONCOMPETITION

As an inducement for Buyer to enter into the Stock Purchase Agreement and as additional consideration for the consideration to be paid to Seller under the Stock Purchase Agreement [and the consideration to be paid under this Agreement,] Seller agrees that:

(a) For a period of [five] years after the Closing:

(i) Seller will not, directly or indirectly, engage or invest in, own, manage, operate, finance, control, or participate in the ownership, management, operation, [financing,] or control of, be employed by, associated with, or in any manner connected with, lend Seller's name or any similar name to, lend Seller's credit to, or render services or advice to, any business whose products or activities compete in whole or in part with the products or activities of the Company, [anywhere within the United States]; provided, however, that Seller may purchase or otherwise acquire up to (but not more than) one percent of any class of securities of any enterprise (but without otherwise participating in the activities of such enterprise) if such securities are listed on any national or regional securities exchange or have been registered under Section 12(g) of the Securities Exchange Act of 1934. Seller agrees that this covenant is reasonable with respect to its duration, geographical area, and scope.

(ii) Seller will not, directly or indirectly, either for himself or any other Person, (A) induce or attempt to induce any employee of an Acquired Company to leave the employ of such Acquired Company, (B) in any way interfere with the relationship between an Acquired Company and any employee of such Acquired Company, (C) employ, or otherwise engage as an employee, independent contractor, or otherwise, any employee of an Acquired Company, or (D) induce or attempt to induce any customer, supplier, licensee, or business relation of an Acquired Company to cease doing business with such Acquired Company, or in any way interfere with the relationship between any customer, supplier, licensee, or business relation of an Acquired Company.

(iii) Seller will not, directly or indirectly, either for himself or any other Person, solicit the business of any Person known to Seller to be a customer of an Acquired Company, whether or not Seller had personal contact with such Person[, with respect to products or activities which compete in whole or in part with the products or activities of the Company];

(b) In the event of a breach by Seller of any covenant set forth in Subsection 4(a) of this Agreement, the term of such covenant will be extended by the period of the duration of such breach;

(c) Seller will not, at any time during or after the five year period, disparage Buyer or the Acquired Companies, or any of their shareholders, directors, officers, employees, or agents; and

(d) Seller will, for a period of [five] years after the Closing, within ten days after accepting any employment, advise Buyer of the identity of any employer of Seller. Buyer or an Acquired Company may serve notice upon each such employer that Seller is bound by this Agreement and furnish each such employer with a copy of this Agreement or relevant portions thereof.

COMMENT

Agreements not to compete are agreements in restraint of trade and historically have not been favored by the courts. The courts are more prone, however, to enforce such agreements if they are reasonable in geographic scope and duration and are necessary to protect interests such as trade secrets and goodwill. *See Wilson v. Electro Marine Systems. Inc.*, 915 F.2d 1110, 1115 (7th Cir. 1990) (New York and Illinois law). In addition, some states have statutes specifically dealing with the subject. Agreements not to compete given in connection with the sale of a business are more likely to be enforced than those contained in an employment agreement, because the seller of a business usually has more bargaining power than an employee and is receiving consideration other than wages for the covenant. Additionally, a covenant not to compete made to a purchaser serves to preserve the value of what the purchaser has bought, while a covenant to an employer serves only to protect the information or relationships that the employee might acquire by virtue of the fact that the employer hired the employee. *See* Blake,

Employee Agreements Not to Compete, 73 Harv. L. Rev. 625, 646-647 (1960); Note, *The Validity of Covenants Not to Compete: Common law rules in Illinois law*, 1978 Ill. L. Forum 249, 253; *O'Sullivan v. Conrad*, 358 N.E. 2d 926, 929 (1976); *Business Records Corp. v. Lueth*, 981 F.2d 957 (7th Cir. 1992). The question of enforceability is a local one, and the laws of each relevant jurisdiction must be examined. *See* also the Commentary to Section 8.2 of the Employment Agreement.

[5. COMPENSATION

As additional consideration for the covenants in Section 4 of this Agreement, the Company will pay Seller the sum of $__________ Dollars ($______) payable [with the execution of this Agreement.][as follows:

(a) The sum of __________ Dollars ($______) simultaneously with the execution of this Agreement; and

(b) The sum of __________ Dollars ($______) on each of the first [five] anniversary dates of the Closing.]

COMMENT

This optional provision provides for the allocation of part of the purchase price to the covenant not to compete. The amount of the purchase price allocated to a covenant not to compete is deductible by the Buyer and includible in the income of the Sellers as ordinary income. Under the Omnibus Budget Reconciliation Act of 1993 a covenant not to compete is amortizable over a fifteen year period. The Sellers will prefer not to have any of the purchase price allocated to the covenant not to compete to avoid ordinary income treatment. In an asset acquisition, prior to the Omnibus Budget Reconciliation Act, goodwill was not amortizable for federal income tax purposes. As a result, the Buyer always would have wanted part of the purchase price allocated to a covenant not to compete, while the Sellers would not have. Since goodwill is now amortizable over a fifteen year period, the incentive for the Buyer to insist that part of the purchase price be allocated to the covenant not to compete is reduced. See the Commentary to Section 8.2 of the Employment Agreement. Also see that Commentary for the information return requirements for buyers and sellers under Section 1060 of the Internal Revenue Code relating to the consideration for covenants not to compete.

6. REMEDIES

If Seller breaches the covenants set forth in Sections 3 or 4 of this Agreement, Buyer and the Acquired Companies will be entitled to the following remedies:

(a) Damages from Seller;

[(b) To offset against any and all amounts owing to Seller under [the Stock Purchase Agreement][Subsection 5(b) of this Agreement] any and all amounts which Buyer or the Acquired Companies claim under Subsection 6(a) of this Agreement;] and

(c) In addition to its right to damages and any other rights it may have, to obtain injunctive or other equitable relief to restrain any breach or threatened breach or otherwise to specifically enforce the provisions of Sections 3 and 4 of this Agreement, it being agreed that money damages alone would be inadequate to compensate the Buyer and the Acquired Companies and would be an inadequate remedy for such breach.

(d) The rights and remedies of the parties to this Agreement are cumulative and not alternative.

COMMENT

Provisions for forfeiture of the unpaid amount of the consideration for a covenant not to compete if the covenant is breached may be enforceable in some states even though the covenant may not be enforceable. Such a provision also provides a floor for the award of monetary damages to the Buyer and the Acquired Companies. However, inclusion of a provision for a monetary award may affect the ability to obtain injunctive relief, because it may weaken the argument that monetary damages are inadequate. See the Commentary to Section 9.1 of the Employment Agreement. The Sellers will resist the right to offset in Subsection 6(b). It is included in a form most favorable to the Buyer, because this is a Buyer's reasonable first draft. (However, such a provision may be unenforceable in some states.) The Buyer may have to compromise by agreeing to an escrow arrangement pending resolution of the Buyer's claims.

Some agreements provide for liquidated damages on a per diem basis as an alternative to the measure of damages in Subsection 6(a).

7. SUCCESSORS AND ASSIGNS

This Agreement will be binding upon Buyer, the Acquired Companies and Seller and will inure to the benefit of Buyer and the Acquired Companies and their affiliates, successors and assigns and Seller and Seller's assigns, heirs and legal representatives.

8. WAIVER

The rights and remedies of the parties to this Agreement are cumulative and not alternative. Neither the failure nor any delay by any party in exercising any right, power, or privilege under this Agreement will operate as a waiver of such right, power, or privilege, and no single or partial exercise of any such right, power, or privilege will preclude any other or further exercise of such right, power, or privilege or the exercise of any other right, power, or privilege. To the maximum extent permitted by applicable law, (a) no claim or right arising out of this Agreement can be discharged by one party, in whole or in part, by a waiver or renunciation of the claim or right unless in writing signed by the other party; (b) no waiver that may be given by a party will be applicable except in the specific instance for which it is given; and (c) no notice to or demand on one party will be deemed to be a waiver of any obligation of such party or of the right of the party giving such notice or demand to take further action without notice or demand as provided in this Agreement.

9. GOVERNING LAW

This Agreement will be governed by the laws of the State of _______ without regard to conflicts of laws principles.

COMMENT

The law to be applied to a covenant not to compete can determine whether the covenant will be enforced, because the law of some states is more liberal than the law of other states regarding covenants not to compete. The forum in which the covenant is litigated is also important, because a state court might not enforce a covenant that is against that state's public policy, even though valid under the law of the state whose law governs the question of validity. Applicable state laws should also be consulted to determine enforceability of these choices of law and consent to venue provisions. *See Webcraft Technologies*, 674 F. Supp. at 1044 (discussing the public policy concerns a court examines in order to resolve a choice of law issue pertaining to a covenant not to compete). See the Commentary to Section 9.10 of the Employment Agreement.

10. JURISDICTION; SERVICE OF PROCESS

Any action or proceeding seeking to enforce any provision of, or based on any right arising out of, this Agreement may be brought against any of the parties in the courts of the State of ______________, County of ________________, or, if it has or can acquire jurisdiction, in the United States District Court for the ____________________ District of _______________, and each of the parties consents to the jurisdiction of such courts (and of the appropriate appellate courts) in any such action or proceeding and waives any objection to venue laid therein. Process in any action or proceeding referred to in the preceding sentence may be served on any party anywhere in the world.

11. SEVERABILITY

Whenever possible each provision and term of this Agreement will be interpreted in a manner to be effective and valid but if any provision or term of this Agreement is held to be prohibited by or invalid, then such provision or term will be ineffective only to the extent of such prohibition or invalidity, without invalidating or affecting in any manner whatsoever the remainder of such provision or term or the remaining provisions or terms of this Agreement. If any of the covenants set forth in Section 4 of this Agreement are held to be unreasonable, arbitrary, or against public policy, such covenants will be considered divisible with respect to scope, time, and geographic area, and in such lesser scope, time and geographic area, will be effective, binding and enforceable against Seller.

COMMENT

This provision may enable a court to "blue line," even though the court would not tailor the covenant on its own initiative. See the Commentary to Section 8.2 of the Employment Agreement.

12. COUNTERPARTS

This Agreement may be executed in one or more counterparts, each of which will be deemed to be an original copy of this Agreement and all of which, when taken together, will be deemed to constitute one and the same agreement.

13. SECTION HEADINGS, CONSTRUCTION

The headings of Sections in this Agreement are provided for convenience only and will not affect its construction or interpretation. All references to "Section" or "Sections" refer to the corresponding Section or Sections of this Agreement unless otherwise specified. All words used in this Agreement will be construed to be of such gender or number as the circumstances require. Unless otherwise expressly provided, the word "including" does not limit the preceding words or terms.

14. NOTICES

All notices, consents, waivers, and other communications under this Agreement must be in writing and will be deemed to have been duly given when (a) delivered by hand (with written confirmation of receipt), (b) sent by facsimile (with written confirmation of receipt), provided that a copy is mailed by registered mail, return receipt requested, or (c) when received by the addressee, if sent by a nationally recognized overnight delivery service (receipt requested), in each case to the appropriate addresses and facsimile numbers set forth below (or to such other addresses and facsimile numbers as a party may designate by notice to the other parties):

Seller: ______________________________

____

Attention: ______________________________

Facsimile No.: ______________________________

with a copy to: ______________________________
____
Attention: ______________________________
Facsimile No.: ______________________________

Buyer: ______________________________
____
Attention: ______________________________
Facsimile No.: ______________________________

with a copy to: ______________________________
____
Attention: ______________________________
Facsimile No.: ______________________________

Company: ______________________________
____
Attention: ______________________________
Facsimile No.: ______________________________

with a copy to: ______________________________
____
Attention: ______________________________
Facsimile No.: ______________________________

15. ENTIRE AGREEMENT

This Agreement[, the Employment Agreement] and the Stock Purchase Agreement constitute the entire agreement between the parties with respect to the subject matter of this Agreement and supersede all prior written and oral agreements and understandings between Buyer and Seller with respect to the subject matter of this Agreement. This Agreement may not be amended except by a written agreement executed by the party to be charged with the amendment.

IN WITNESS WHEREOF, the parties have executed and delivered this Agreement as of the date first above written.

BUYER:

By: ______________________

SELLERS:

____
A

____
B

COMPANY:

By: ______________________________

Exhibit 2.4(b)

Non-Negotiable Promissory Note

PRELIMINARY NOTE

The Commentary to Section 2.4 of the Model Stock Purchase Agreement briefly describes the form of the Buyer's promissory notes to be delivered to the Sellers. It includes a discussion of the principal reason that the Buyer will desire that the notes be in nonnegotiable form: the protection of the Buyer's set-off rights. A nonnegotiable note would enable the Buyer to exercise its right to set-off provided in the Model Stock Purchase Agreement by withholding payments due under the note in the event circumstances arise which entitle the Buyer to make a claim against the Sellers under the Model Stock Purchase Agreement. The Buyer's right to set-off contained in the Promissory Note is a particularly potent remedy since, in addition to having control over the funds, a good faith exercise of the right will not constitute an Event of Default under Section 2.1(a), regardless of the fact that such exercise may ultimately be determined to be unjustified.

NON-NEGOTIABLE PROMISSORY NOTE

$_____________ _____________, 199_

FOR VALUE RECEIVED, _______________, a ____________ corporation ("Maker"), promises to pay to _______________, an individual resident in _____________ ("Payee"), in lawful money of the United States of America, the principal sum of _______________ Dollars ($_____________), together with interest in arrears on the unpaid principal balance at an annual rate equal to _____%, in the manner provided below. Interest shall be calculated on the basis of a year of 365 or 366 days, as applicable, and charged for the actual number of days elapsed.

This Note has been executed and delivered pursuant to and in accordance with the terms and conditions of the Stock Purchase Agreement, dated ______________, 199_, by and between Maker, Payee and _______________, (the "Agreement"), and is subject to the terms and conditions of the Agreement, which are, by this reference, incorporated herein and made a part hereof. Capitalized terms used in this Note without definition shall have the respective meanings set forth in the Agreement.

1. PAYMENTS

1.1 Principal and Interest

The principal amount of this Note shall be due and payable in _______ equal consecutive [annual] [quarterly] installments commencing on _______________, 19__, [and on ___________ of each year thereafter] [and on _________________, _________________ and _________________ of each year thereafter] until paid in full. Interest on the unpaid principal balance of this Note shall be due and payable [annually] [quarterly], together with each payment of principal.

1.2 Manner of Payment

All payments of principal and interest on this Note shall be made by [certified or bank cashier's] check at _______________________, ___________________, __________________ or at such other place in the United States of America as Payee shall designate to Maker in writing [or by wire transfer of immediately available funds to an account designated by Payee in writing]. If any payment of principal or interest on this Note is due on a day which is not a Business Day, such payment shall be due on the next succeeding Business Day, and such extension of time shall be taken into account in calculating the amount of interest payable under this Note. "Business Day" means any day other than a Saturday, Sunday or legal holiday in the State of ______________.

1.3 Prepayment

Maker may, without premium or penalty, at any time and from time to time, prepay all or any portion of the outstanding principal balance due under this Note, provided that each such prepayment is accompanied by accrued interest on the amount of principal prepaid calculated to the date of such prepayment. Any partial prepayments shall be applied to installments of principal in inverse order of their maturity.

1.4 Right of Set-Off

Maker shall have the right to withhold and set-off against any amount due hereunder the amount of any claim for indemnification or payment of damages to which Maker may be entitled under the Agreement, as provided in Section 10.8 thereof.

2. DEFAULTS

2.1 Events of Default

The occurrence of any one or more of the following events with respect to Maker shall constitute an event of default hereunder ("Event of Default"):

(a) If Maker shall fail to pay when due any payment of principal or interest on this Note and such failure continues for fifteen (15) days after Payee notifies Maker therein writing; *provided, however*, that the exercise by Maker in good faith of its right of set-off pursuant to Section 1.4 above, whether or not ultimately determined to be justified, shall not constitute an Event of Default.

(b) If, pursuant to or within the meaning of the United States Bankruptcy Code or any other federal or state law relating to insolvency or relief of debtors (a "Bankruptcy Law"), Maker shall (i) commence a voluntary case or proceeding; (ii) consent to the entry of an order for relief against it in an involuntary case; (iii) consent to the appointment of a trustee, receiver, assignee, liquidator or similar official; (iv) make an assignment for the benefit of its creditors; or (v) admit in writing its inability to pay its debts as they become due.

(c) If a court of competent jurisdiction enters an order or decree under any Bankruptcy Law that (i) is for relief against Maker in an involuntary case, (ii) appoints a trustee, receiver, assignee, liquidator or similar official for Maker or substantially all of Maker's properties, or (iii) orders the liquidation of Maker, and in each case the order or decree is not dismissed within [120] days.

2.2 Notice by Maker

Maker shall notify Payee in writing within [five] days after the occurrence of any Event of Default of which Maker acquires knowledge.

2.3 Remedies

Upon the occurrence of an Event of Default hereunder (unless all Events of Default have been cured or waived by Payee), Payee may, at its option, (i) by written notice to Maker, declare the entire unpaid principal balance of this Note, together with all accrued interest thereon, immediately due and payable regardless of any prior forbearance, and (ii) exercise any and all rights and remedies available to it under applicable law, including, without limitation, the right to collect from Maker all sums due under this Note. Maker shall pay all reasonable costs and expenses incurred by or on behalf of Payee in connection with Payee's exercise of any or all of its rights and remedies under this Note, including, without limitation, reasonable attorneys' fees.

3. MISCELLANEOUS

3.1 Waiver

The rights and remedies of Payee under this Note shall be cumulative and not alternative. No waiver by Payee of any right or remedy under this Note shall be effective unless in a writing signed by Payee. Neither the failure nor any delay in exercising any right, power or privilege under this Note will operate as a waiver of such right, power or privilege and no single or partial exercise of any such right, power or privilege by Payee will preclude any other or further exercise of such right, power or privilege or the exercise of any other right, power or privilege. To the maximum extent permitted by applicable law, (a) no claim or right of Payee arising out of this Note can be discharged by Payee, in whole or in part, by a waiver or renunciation of the claim or right unless in a writing, signed by Payee; (b) no waiver that may be given by Payee will be applicable except in the specific instance for which it is given; and (c) no notice to or demand on Maker will be deemed to be a waiver of any obligation of Maker or of the right of Payee to take further action without notice or demand as provided in this Note. Maker hereby waives presentment, demand, protest and notice of dishonor and protest.

3.2 Notices

Any notice required or permitted to be given hereunder shall be given in accordance with Section 11.4 of the Agreement.

3.3 Severability

If any provision in this Note is held invalid or unenforceable by any court of competent jurisdiction, the other provisions of this Note will remain in full force and effect. Any provision of this Note held invalid or unenforceable only in part or degree will remain in full force and effect to the extent not held invalid or unenforceable.

3.4 Governing Law

This Note will be governed by the laws of the State of ___________ without regard to conflicts of laws principles.

3.5 Parties in Interest

This Note shall bind Maker and its successors and assigns. This Note shall not be assigned or transferred by Payee without the express prior written consent of Maker, except by will or, in default thereof, by operation of law.

3.6 Section Headings, Construction

The headings of Sections in this Note are provided for convenience only and will not affect its construction or interpretation. All references to "Section" or "Sections" refer to the corresponding Section or Sections of this Note unless otherwise specified.

All words used in this Note will be construed to be of such gender or number as the circumstances require. Unless otherwise expressly provided, the words "hereof" and "hereunder" and similar references refer to this Note in its entirety and not to any specific section or subsection hereof.

IN WITNESS WHEREOF, Maker has executed and delivered this Note as of the date first stated above.

[MAKER]

By: ______________________________
Title: ____________________________

COMMENT

The requirements for a negotiable instrument are set out in Section 3-104 of the Uniform Commercial Code. The "magic words" needed for negotiability are missing in at least two respects: the Promissory Note designates the identified Seller as the sole payee, thereby failing to meet the requirement of UCC Section 3-104(1)(d) of being "payable to order or to bearer"; and in the second paragraph the Promissory Note states that it is subject to the terms and conditions of the Model Stock Purchase Agreement, thereby rendering the Buyer's promise conditional and making the Promissory Note nonnegotiable. See UCC Sections 3-104(1)(b) and 3-105(2)(a).

The terms of the Promissory Note to be taken by the Sellers, however, will be negotiated based upon the relative bargaining powers of the principals to the transaction. The Sellers usually want the Promissory Note to be negotiable, so that it might be sold or pledged to a bank or financial institution to obtain immediate liquidity. If the Promissory Note is nonnegotiable, by definition there cannot be a holder in due course. *See* UCC Section 3-302. However, if the Promissory Note is negotiable and a Seller negotiates the note to a holder in due course, the Buyer would be unable to make any claims against the note arising out of a breach of warranty by the Sellers. *See* UCC Section 3-305. One potential solution to the competing interests of the parties may be a parallel series of negotiable and nonnegotiable notes pursuant to which the deferred portion of the purchase price payable to the Sellers would be split between negotiable and nonnegotiable notes in such amounts and with such maturity dates as reflect the relative bargaining power of the parties.

In addition to the question of negotiability, issues which are likely to be raised by the Sellers include whether the Promissory Note will be secured, the availability of a guarantor, and the priority of the Buyer's obligation relative to the Buyer's other indebtedness. The question of security depends upon the creditworthiness of the Buyer and the availability of unencumbered assets. Potential collateral might include a pledge by the Buyer of the shares acquired in the transaction, although the Sellers might insist on additional collateral to protect against the possibility of diminished value in the event the Sellers have to take back the stock which has diminished in value. The Buyer, on the other hand, will be reluctant to secure a note for only part of the purchase price with collateral worth, on the date of closing, more than the principal amount of the Promissory Note. If the Promissory Note is secured by a lien on the assets of the Acquired Companies, such an upstream transaction gives rise to fraudulent transfer and conveyance risks. A fraudulent transfer or conveyance occurs where an entity makes a transfer (*e.g.,* the granting of a security interest or other lien), without receiving equivalent value, while the entity was insolvent or if it becomes insolvent as a result of the transfer. *See* 11 U.S.C. § 548 and 12 Pa.C.S.A. § 5105. Where the Buyer is a subsidiary, the Sellers may require that the Buyer's parent guaranty the Promissory Note. Fraudulent transfer and conveyance risks may also be relevant in the guarantee situation. If the Promissory Note is secured, the Sellers may seek covenants as to the conduct of the Buyer's or the Acquired Companies' business. For example, if the Buyer has pledged the shares, there may be an agreement to maintain the same line of business, or restrictions on distributions or limitations on the sale of assets other than in the ordinary course of business.

The nature and scope of the Buyer's obligation to the Sellers will often be dictated by factors arising under its credit agreements or debt instruments. For example, such instruments may limit the Buyer's ability to incur debt or grant liens, contain negative or affirmative covenants restricting the type of debt the Buyer may incur and may require that the Buyer's obligation to the Sellers be subordinate to its obligation to senior lenders.

Other terms of the Promissory Note which typically will depend upon the transaction include the interest rate, the amortization schedule, the manner of payment (the Buyer's company check if the Sellers will accept it; possibly wire transfer if the amount warrants it), events of default (note, however, that non-payment as a result of the Buyer's exercise of its set-off rights is specially excluded from the definition of "Event of Default") and remedies. It should be noted that Section 3.5 of the Promissory Note contains limitations on assignment or transfer by the named Sellers. In this regard, assignment and transfer (essentially the transfer of title to an instrument, with the transferee getting no more than the rights of the transferor) should be distinguished from negotiation, which ordinarily involves indorsement and transfer to a holder. In jurisdictions where usury may be an issue, a usury savings provision should be included in the note. Such a provision would provide that in the event the rate of interest provided for in the Promissory Note is determined to exceed the maximum rate of interest permitted by the applicable usury or similar law, the application of such rate will be suspended and there will be charged instead the maximum rate of interest permitted by such law.

Exhibit 2.4(c)

Escrow Agreement

PRELIMINARY NOTE

The Buyer may seek to have a fund available from which it can satisfy claims that it may have against the Sellers following the closing, particularly where the satisfaction involves more than one Seller. One technique is to retain a portion of the purchase price in an escrow account for a specified period following the closing. This provides a source of recovery that is not dependent on the solvency of the Sellers or the Buyer's ability to find them (or their assets) for purposes of commencing litigation or executing any judgment that may be obtained. However, it does have limitations. A Buyer's proposal of an escrow will, if accepted by the Sellers, often lead to a proposal by the Sellers that recourse to the funds held in escrow be the Buyer's exclusive post-closing remedy and that the Sellers' liability therefore be "capped" at the amount held in escrow. In addition, the Buyer must recognize that the existence of an escrow fund does not mean that those funds will be immediately available to the Buyer in the event of a claim. Institutional Escrow Agents are generally unwilling to submit themselves to any risk resulting from the conflicting demands by the Buyer and the Sellers. Accordingly, the typical institutional Escrow Agreement provides that the Escrow Agent may "freeze" and retain the funds at issue until conflicting demands are resolved by agreement of the parties or a non-appealable court order. If the Buyer wishes to be sure that it will have access to funds pending resolution of a disputed claim it should consider retaining a portion of the purchase price or requiring that the Sellers' indemnification and other monetary obligations be secured by a letter of credit that may be drawn in the event of a claim. The Buyer should be aware that, in some circumstances, the Sellers' interests in an escrow fund may constitute securities for purposes of federal and state securities laws. *See Kling &*

Nugent Simon, Negotiated Acquisitions of Companies, Subsidiaries and Divisions, § 1.604 (1992).

The institutional Escrow Agent takes the view that its duties are purely ministerial in nature and that they are not being paid to accept any duty to exercise judgment or liability for anything but the most egregious of their errors. Counsel will normally find that negotiation of the Escrow Agreement is expedited if the Escrow Agent is invited to supply its own preferred version of the exculpatory provisions to be included in the Escrow Agreement. The provisions appearing in Sections 5 and 6 of the Escrow Agreement are based on the exculpatory provisions preferred by one major New York City institution—the substance of these provisions tends to be fairly consistent, although the style varies widely.

The Escrow Agreement contemplates an institutional Escrow Agent. Occasionally a party may propose that its counsel act as Escrow Agent. In most cases, that is a role counsel should avoid.

The reasons that clients often articulate in support of counsel acting as Escrow Agent are avoidance of delay and the institutional Escrow Agent's fees. The party proposing that its counsel act as Escrow Agent may also have an unarticulated reason for doing so (as well as a desire to avoid having the other party's counsel act as Escrow Agent): a belief that its counsel will perform its function as Escrow Agent in a manner that favors its client. In most cases, these benefits are illusory. Negotiation of the Escrow Agreement with an institutional Escrow Agent need not be a lengthy process if counsel is sensitive to the needs of the Escrow Agent to play a purely mechanical role and to be protected from liability. The institutional Escrow Agent's fees may quickly be surpassed by the time charges of a law firm that acts as Escrow Agent. And a party that expects its counsel to favor it while acting as Escrow Agent is likely to be disappointed; a law firm that is willing to act as Escrow Agent will normally seek the same protective provisions in the agreement as an institutional Escrow Agent, including the ability to "freeze" in the face of conflicting demands.

If counsel is to act as Escrow Agent, it will normally wish to add a provision in which the parties acknowledge its dual role and consent to its continuing to act as counsel to its client in matters relating to the acquisition and the escrow (including disputes over the disposition of the funds held in escrow). The expense reimbursement and indemnification provisions could be modified to include as a reimbursable expense the time charges of partners and employees of the Escrow Agent.

Counsel acting as Escrow Agent should also be careful to consider the ethical implications of negotiating the Escrow Agreement with its client. It may be appropriate to suggest that the client be represented by other counsel in that negotiation, an approach that neither the client nor its counsel is likely to desire unless the client has inside counsel who is involved in the transaction.

ESCROW AGREEMENT

This Escrow Agreement, dated as of ___________, 199_ (the "Closing Date"), among _________, a _________ corporation ("Buyer"), __________, an individual resident in __________, ("A"), and __________, an individual resident in __________ ("B" and collectively with A, "Sellers"), and __________, a [national banking association] [bank organized under the laws of __________], as escrow agent ("Escrow Agent").

This is the Escrow Agreement referred to in the Stock Purchase Agreement dated __________ __, 199_ (the "Purchase Agreement") among Buyer and Sellers. Capitalized terms used in this agreement without definition shall have the respective meanings given to them in the Purchase Agreement.

The parties, intending to be legally bound, hereby agree as follows:

1. ESTABLISHMENT OF ESCROW

(a) Buyer is depositing with Escrow Agent an amount equal to $_________ in immediately available funds (as increased by any earnings thereon and as reduced by any disbursements, amounts withdrawn under Section 5(j), or losses on investments, the "Escrow Fund"). Escrow Agent acknowledges receipt thereof.

(b) Escrow Agent hereby agrees to act as escrow agent and to hold, safeguard and disburse the Escrow Fund pursuant to the terms and conditions hereof.

COMMENT

Interest and other earnings on the funds held in escrow are retained by the Escrow Agent and are thus available to satisfy claims. Occasionally, The Sellers will seek to provide that these amounts are to be paid to them currently.

2. INVESTMENT OF FUNDS

Except as Buyer and Sellers may from time to time jointly instruct Escrow Agent in writing, the Escrow Fund shall be invested from time to time, to the extent possible, in United States Treasury bills having a remaining maturity of 90 days or less and repurchase obligations secured by such United States Treasury Bills, with any remainder being deposited and maintained in a money market deposit account with Escrow Agent, until disbursement of the entire Escrow Fund. Escrow Agent is authorized to liquidate in accordance with its customary procedures any portion of the Escrow Fund consisting of investments to provide for payments required to be made under this Agreement.

COMMENT

It is customary for the Escrow Agreement to require that funds held in escrow be invested only in highly liquid, short-term investments. The nature of those investments often depends on the size of the fund. If the amount is modest, a deposit account at the Escrow Agent may be appropriate. If the amounts are larger, investment in short-term U.S. treasury securities may be preferable in order to avoid exposure to the credit risks inherent in uninsured deposits with the Escrow Agent.

3. CLAIMS

(a) If Buyer gives a notice to Sellers and Escrow Agent stating that the Adjustment Amount has been determined in accordance with Section 2.6 of the Purchase Agreement and specifying the dollar amount payable to Buyer pursuant to Section 2.6(b) of the Purchase Agreement as a result of such determination, on the tenth business day following such notice Escrow Agent shall pay to Buyer the dollar amount so specified from (and only to the extent of) the Escrow Fund. Escrow Agent shall not inquire into or consider whether the Adjustment Amount has been determined in accordance with the requirements of the Purchase Agreement.

(b) From time to time on or before ___________, Buyer may give notice (a "Notice") to Sellers and Escrow Agent specifying in reasonable detail the nature and dollar amount of any claim (a "Claim") it may have under Section 10 of the Purchase Agreement; Buyer may make more than one claim with respect to any underlying state of facts. If Sellers give notice to Buyer and Escrow Agent disputing any Claim (a "Counter Notice") within 30 days following receipt by

Escrow Agent of the Notice regarding such Claim, such Claim shall be resolved as provided in Section 3(c). If no Counter Notice is received by Escrow Agent within such 30-day period, then the dollar amount of damages claimed by Buyer as set forth in its Notice shall be deemed established for purposes of this Escrow Agreement and the Purchase Agreement and, at the end of such 30-day period, Escrow Agent shall pay to Buyer the dollar amount claimed in the Notice from (and only to the extent of) the Escrow Fund. Escrow Agent shall not inquire into or consider whether a Claim complies with the requirements of the Purchase Agreement.

(c) If a Counter Notice is given with respect to a claim, Escrow Agent shall make payment with respect thereto only in accordance with (i) joint written instructions of Buyer and Sellers or (ii) a final non-appealable order of a court of competent jurisdiction. Any court order shall be accompanied by a legal opinion by counsel for the presenting party satisfactory to Escrow Agent to the effect that the order is final and non-appealable. Escrow Agent shall act on such court order and legal opinion without further question.

COMMENT

Section 3 provides the procedures for making claims against the escrow fund. Different procedures are provided for claims based on the post-closing adjustment procedures and claims for indemnification. The Model Stock Purchase Agreement provides a procedure for determining the former, so subsection (a) simply provides for payment by the Escrow Agent on the basis of a notice from Buyer that sets forth the amount determined in accordance with that procedure and does not contemplate the possibility of an objection from the Sellers (although a notice from the Sellers disputing the Buyer's notice would normally lead the Escrow Agent to invoke its "freeze" rights under Section 5(i)). If a claim for indemnification is made and not disputed within 30 days, it is treated as admitted and paid by the Escrow Agent. If disputed, the funds are held until ultimate resolution of the claim by the parties or litigation. If the Model Stock Purchase Agreement provides for resolution of claims through arbitration or other forms of alternative dispute resolution, the Escrow Agreement should be modified to provide for release of funds on the basis of the arbitral award.

4. TERMINATION OF ESCROW

On ___________, Escrow Agent shall pay and distribute the then amount of Escrow Fund to Sellers (__% to A and __% to B), unless (i) any Claims are then pending, in which case an amount equal to the aggregate dollar amount of such Claims (as shown in the Notices of such Claims) shall be retained by Escrow Agent in the Escrow Fund (and the balance paid to Sellers in such proportions) or (ii) Buyer has given notice to Sellers and Escrow Agent specifying in reasonable detail the nature of any other claim it may have under Section 10 of the Purchase Agreement with respect to which it is unable to specify the amount of Damages, in which case their entire Escrow Fund shall be retained by Escrow Agent, in either case until it receives joint written instructions of Buyer and Sellers or a final non-appealable order of a court of competent jurisdiction as contemplated by Section 3(b).

COMMENT

Funds held by the Escrow Agent are generally released to the Sellers after a specified period of time, which is often the same as the general time limit provided for the assertion of claims in the acquisition agreement (see Section 10.5 of the Model Stock Purchase Agreement). Funds that are the subject of a disputed claim continue to be held until resolution of the claim; if the amount of the disputed claim is not known, all of the funds will continue to be held until resolution of the claim.

5. DUTIES OF ESCROW AGENT

(a) Escrow Agent shall not be under any duty to give the Escrow Fund held by it hereunder any greater degree of care than it gives its own similar property and shall not be required to invest any funds held hereunder except as directed in this Agreement. Uninvested funds held hereunder shall not earn or accrue interest.

(b) Escrow Agent shall not be liable, except for its own gross negligence or willful misconduct and, except with respect to claims based upon such gross negligence or willful misconduct that are successfully asserted against Escrow Agent, the other parties hereto shall jointly and severally indemnify and hold harmless Escrow Agent (and any successor Escrow Agent) from and against any and all losses, liabilities, claims, actions, damages and expenses, including reasonable attorneys' fees and disbursements, arising out of and in connection with this Agreement. Without limiting the foregoing, Escrow Agent shall in no event be liable in connection with its investment or reinvestment of any cash held by it hereunder in good faith, in accordance with the terms hereof, including, without limitation, any liability for any delays (not resulting from its gross negligence or willful misconduct) in the investment or reinvestment of the Escrow Fund, or any loss of interest incident to any such delays.

(c) Escrow Agent shall be entitled to rely upon any order, judgment, certification, demand, notice, instrument or other writing delivered to it hereunder without being required to determine the authenticity or the correctness of any fact stated therein or the propriety or validity of the service thereof. Escrow Agent may act in reliance upon any instrument or signature believed by it to be genuine and may assume that the person purporting to give receipt or advice or make any statement or execute any document in connection with the provisions hereof has been duly authorized to do so. Escrow Agent may conclusively presume that the undersigned representative of any party hereto which is an entity other than a natural person has full power and authority to instruct Escrow Agent on behalf of that party unless written notice to the contrary is delivered to Escrow Agent.

(d) Escrow Agent may act pursuant to the advice of counsel with respect to any matter relating to this Agreement and shall not be liable for any action taken or omitted by it in good faith in accordance with such advice.

(e) Escrow Agent does not have any interest in the Escrow Fund deposited hereunder but is serving as escrow holder only and having only possession thereof. Any payments of income from this Escrow Fund shall be subject to withholding regulations then in force with respect to United States taxes. The parties hereto will provide Escrow Agent with appropriate Internal Revenue Service Forms W-9 for tax identification number certification, or non-resident alien certifications. This Section 5(e) and Section 5(b) shall survive notwithstanding any termination of this Agreement or the resignation of Escrow Agent.

(f) Escrow Agent makes no representation as to the validity, value, genuineness or the collectability of any security or other document or instrument held by or delivered to it.

(g) Escrow Agent shall not be called upon to advise any party as to the wisdom in selling or retaining or taking or refraining from any action with respect to any securities or other property deposited hereunder.

(h) Escrow Agent (and any successor Escrow Agent) may at any time resign as such by delivering the Escrow Fund to any successor Escrow Agent jointly designated by the other parties hereto in writing, or to any court of competent jurisdiction, whereupon Escrow Agent shall be discharged of and from any and all further obligations arising in connection with this Agreement. The resignation of Escrow Agent will take effect on the earlier of (a) the appointment of a successor (including a court of competent jurisdiction) or (b) the day which is 30 days after the date of delivery of its written notice of resignation to the other parties hereto. If at that time Escrow Agent has not received a designation of a successor Escrow Agent, Escrow Agent's sole responsibility after that time shall be to retain and safeguard the Escrow Fund until receipt of a designation of successor Escrow Agent or a joint written disposition instruction by the other parties hereto or a final non-appealable order of a court of competent jurisdiction.

COMMENT

The parties may wish to include a provision permitting them to replace the Escrow Agent.

(i) In the event of any disagreement between the other parties hereto resulting in adverse claims or demands being made in connection with the Escrow Fund or in the event that Escrow Agent is in doubt as to what action it should take hereunder, Escrow Agent shall be entitled to retain the Escrow Fund until Escrow Agent shall have received (i) a final non-appealable order of a court of competent jurisdiction directing delivery of the Escrow Fund or (ii) a written agreement executed by the other parties hereto directing delivery of the Escrow Fund, in which event Escrow Agent shall disburse the Escrow Fund in accordance with such order or agreement. Any court order shall be accompanied by a legal opinion by counsel for the presenting party satisfactory to Escrow Agent to the effect that the order is final and non-appealable. Escrow Agent shall act on such court order and legal opinion without further question.

(j) Buyer and Sellers shall pay Escrow Agent compensation (as payment in full) for the services to be rendered by Escrow Agent hereunder in the amount of $_________ at the time of execution of this Agreement and $_____________ annually thereafter and agree to reimburse Escrow Agent for all reasonable expenses, disbursements and advances incurred or made by Escrow Agent in performance of its duties hereunder (including reasonable fees, expenses and disbursements of its counsel). Any such compensation and reimbursement to which Escrow Agent is entitled shall be borne [50% by Buyer, __% by A and __% by B]. Any fees or expenses of Escrow Agent or its counsel that are not paid as provided for herein may be taken from any property held by Escrow Agent hereunder.

COMMENT

The allocation of responsibility for the Escrow Agent's fees and expenses is often the subject of negotiation.

(k) No printed or other matter in any language (including, without limitation, prospectuses, notices, reports and promotional material) that mentions Escrow Agent's name or the rights, powers, or duties of Escrow Agent shall be issued by the other parties hereto or on such parties' behalf unless Escrow Agent shall first have given its specific written consent thereto.

(l) The other parties hereto authorize Escrow Agent, for any securities held hereunder, to use the services of any United States central securities depository it reasonably deems appropriate, including, without limitation, the Depositary Trust Company and the Federal Reserve Book Entry System.

6. LIMITED RESPONSIBILITY

This Agreement expressly sets forth all the duties of Escrow Agent with respect to any and all matters pertinent hereto. No implied duties or obligations shall be read into this agreement against Escrow Agent. Escrow Agent shall not be bound by the provisions of any agreement among the other parties hereto except this Agreement.

7. OWNERSHIP FOR TAX PURPOSES

Sellers agree that, for purposes of federal and other taxes based on income, A and B will be treated as the owner of __% and __% of the Escrow Fund, respectively, and that A and B will report all income, if any, that is earned on, or derived from, the Escrow Fund as their income, in such proportions, in the taxable year or years in which such income is properly includible and pay any taxes attributable thereto.

8. NOTICES

All notices, consents, waivers and other communications under this Agreement must be in writing and will be deemed to have been duly given when (a) delivered by hand (with written confirmation of receipt), (b) sent by telecopier (with written confirmation of receipt) provided that a copy is mailed by registered mail, return receipt requested, or (c) when received by the addressee, if sent by a nationally recognized overnight delivery service (receipt requested), in each case to the appropriate addresses and telecopier numbers set forth below (or to such other addresses and telecopier numbers as a party may designate by notice to the other parties):

Sellers: ______________________________
Attention: ______________________________
Facsimile No.: ______________________________

with a copy to: ______________________________
Attention: ______________________________
Facsimile No.: ______________________________

Buyer: ______________________________
Attention: ______________________________
Facsimile No.: ______________________________

with a copy to: ______________________________
Attention: ______________________________
Facsimile No.: ______________________________

Escrow Agent: ______________________________
Attention: ______________________________
Facsimile No.: ______________________________

with a copy to: ______________________________
Attention: ______________________________
Facsimile No.: ______________________________

9. JURISDICTION; SERVICE OF PROCESS

Any action or proceeding seeking to enforce any provision of, or based on any right arising out of, this Agreement may be brought against any of the parties in the courts of the State of __________, County of __________, or, if it has or can acquire jurisdiction, in the

United States District Court for the __________ District of __________, and each of the parties consents to the jurisdiction of such courts (and of the appropriate appellate courts) in any such action or proceeding and waives any objection to venue laid therein. Process in any action or proceeding referred to in the preceding sentence may be served on any party anywhere in the world.

10. COUNTERPARTS

This Agreement may be executed in one or more counterparts, each of which will be deemed to be an original and all of which, when taken together, will be deemed to constitute one and the same.

11. SECTION HEADINGS

The headings of sections in this Agreement are provided for convenience only and will not affect its construction or interpretation.

12. WAIVER

The rights and remedies of the parties to this Agreement are cumulative and not alternative. Neither the failure nor any delay by any party in exercising any right, power, or privilege under this Agreement or the documents referred to in this Agreement will operate as a waiver of such right, power, or privilege, and no single or partial exercise of any such right, power, or privilege will preclude any other or further exercise of such right, power, or privilege or the exercise of any other right, power, or privilege. To the maximum extent permitted by applicable law, (a) no claim or right arising out of this Agreement or the documents referred to in this Agreement can be discharged by one party, in whole or in part, by a waiver or renunciation of the claim or right unless in writing signed by the other party; (b) no waiver that may be given by a party will be applicable except in the specific instance for which it is given; and (c) no notice to or demand on one party will be deemed to be a waiver of any obligation of such party or of the right of the party giving such notice or demand to take further action without notice or demand as provided in this Agreement or the documents referred to in this Agreement.

13. EXCLUSIVE AGREEMENT AND MODIFICATION

This Agreement supersedes all prior agreements among the parties with respect to its subject matter and constitutes (along with the documents referred to in this Agreement) a complete and exclusive statement of the terms of the agreement between the parties with respect to its subject matter. This Agreement may not be amended except by a written agreement executed by the Buyer, the Sellers and the Escrow Agent.

14. GOVERNING LAW

This Agreement shall be governed by the laws of the State of ______, without regard to conflicts of law principles.

COMMENT

The Escrow Agent will often require that the governing law of the state in which its office is located be chosen and that the forum specified in Section 9 be in the same state, even if different from the governing law and forum specified by the Model Stock Purchase Agreement.

IN WITNESS WHEREOF, the parties have executed and delivered this Agreement as of the date first written above.

Buyer:	Sellers:
By: ____________________	____________________ A
Escrow Agent:	
____________________	____________________ B
By: ____________________	

Exhibit 7.4(a)

Opinion of Counsel to Sellers

PRELIMINARY NOTE

Stock purchase agreements customarily call for the delivery at the closing of one or more legal opinions, in which counsel for a party provides assurances to the other party to the transaction concerning its client, the Acquired Companies (in the case of the Sellers' counsel) and the validity of actions taken by its client in connection with the transaction.

Delivery of the required legal opinion by a party's counsel is often a condition to the other party's obligation to close the acquisition, as provided in Section 7.4(a) of the Model Stock Purchase Agreement. This has the effect of making the underlying matters as to which the lawyer is to opine conditions to those obligations as well, typically without the materiality standard that would apply to the same matter if tested under other closing conditions provided in the Model Stock Purchase Agreement. For example, if consummation of the acquisition would result in a default under an agreement to which the Company is party that meets the selection criteria described in paragraph 5 of the opinion, the Sellers' counsel could not deliver the opinion in the form required. Although the default would also constitute an inaccuracy in the representation and warranty in Section 3.2(b) of the Model Stock Purchase Agreement, that inaccuracy would not cause the condition in Section 7.1(a) of the Model Stock Purchase Agreement not to be satisfied unless the inaccuracy were material (which might not be the case if the breach involved only one insignificant agreement).

This result—which may be appropriate as to some elements of the opinion but not as to others—could be avoided by adding appropriate materiality qualifications to the required form of opinion, but this is not likely to be a satisfactory solution. Lawyers are rarely comfortable giving legal opinions that require the opining lawyer to reach a judgment as to the materiality of an adverse matter, for that judgment will typically involve an evaluation of potential business impact that lawyers are often not qualified to make. A better approach is to permit the legal opinion to identify factual exceptions and test those exceptions against the other closing conditions.

It is customary and appropriate in a typical business acquisition to request that the Sellers' counsel provide opinions as to matters that involve legal conclusions based upon matters known to the opining lawyer or capable of verification with reasonable diligence (*e.g.,* due incorporation and good standing of the Acquired Companies, authorized and outstanding capital stock of the Acquired Companies, record ownership of capital stock, validity, binding effect and enforceability of the agreements executed by the Sellers in connection with the acquisition, and effect of the acquisition on an identified list of agreements to which the Acquired Companies are party). It is not appropriate to request opinions as to matters that counsel cannot know or investigate on a reasonable basis (*e.g.,* compliance by the Acquired Companies with all applicable laws), as to factual matters (*e.g.,* accuracy of all of the Sellers' representations and warranties in the acquisition agreement), or that express a certain conclusion as to uncertain legal issues (*e.g.,* compliance with the antitrust laws of an acquisition of a company that is a competitor of the Buyer). It is also not appropriate to request an opinion that has the effect of imposing some of the business risks of the transaction on the opining lawyer.

OPINION OF COUNSEL TO SELLERS

[DATE]

[Name and Address of Buyer]

Gentlemen:

We have acted as counsel to ____________ and ____________ (collectively, "Sellers"), ______________, a ______________ corporation (the "Company") and the Subsidiaries of the Company in connection with the Stock Purchase Agreement dated ____________, 199_ (the "Agreement") between the Sellers and ________________, a ______________ corporation ("Buyer"). This is the opinion contemplated by Section 7.4(a) of the Agreement. All capitalized terms used in this opinion without definition have the respective meanings given to them in the Agreement or the Accord referred to below.

This Opinion Letter is governed by, and shall be interpreted in accordance with, the Legal Opinion Accord (the "Accord") of the ABA Section of Business Law (1991). As a consequence, it is subject to a number of qualifications, exceptions, definitions, limitations on coverage and other limitations, all as more particularly described in the Accord, and this Opinion Letter should be read in conjunction therewith. The law covered by the opinions expressed herein is limited to the Federal Law of the United States and the Law of the State(s) of ____________.

COMMENT

Despite the frequency with which third party legal opinions are delivered, there is relatively little authority governing their interpretation. The principal source of guidance to opining lawyers and opinion recipients is a series of local bar reports, many of which are collected in Fitzgibbon and Glazer on Legal Opinions (Little, Brown & Company, 1992). The proliferation of these reports, and the inconsistent views expressed in the reports issued by different bar groups, demonstrates the degree to which interpretive questions are presented by the typical third party legal opinion.

In 1991, the Section of Business Law of the American Bar Association published the *Third-Party Legal Opinion Report*, which includes the *Legal Opinion Accord* (the "Accord"). 47 Business Lawyer 167. The Accord represents a different approach to establishing the meaning of legal opinions. Instead of attempting to define sound opinion practice and the meaning of opinions, it is designed to be incorporated in, and thus become a part of, those legal opinions that adopt it. The Accord consists of an introduction, a glossary of defined terms and 22 statements of position. These are accompanied by a Commentary and Technical Notes, which although not part of the Accord "provide guidance as to its interpretation and organization." An opining lawyer (referred to as an "Opinion Giver" in the Accord) adopts the Accord by including in the opinion a declaration substantially in the form set forth above.

The Accord specifically addresses four specific types of opinions (remedies, no breach or default, no violation of law and legal proceedings). It also provides a framework applicable to both these specific opinions and other aspects of third party legal opinions: jurisdictions whose law is covered, methods of establishing facts (including rules for defining the knowledge of the Opinion Giver), opinions by implication, a list of legal issues not covered unless expressly addressed, and limitations on use of Accord opinions.

In some states, local bar groups have published supplements to the Accord that should also be incorporated in the opinion.

Based on the foregoing, our opinion is as follows:

1. The Agreement, the Escrow Agreement and the Sellers' Releases are enforceable against the Sellers.

COMMENT

This is the Accord form of remedies opinion; the traditional non-Accord equivalent, which follows, is much longer:

> The Agreement, the Escrow Agreement and the Sellers' Releases have been duly authorized, executed and delivered by the Sellers and constitute legal, valid and binding obligations of the Sellers, enforceable against the Sellers in accordance with their terms, subject to bankruptcy, reorganization, insolvency and other similar laws affecting the enforcement of creditors' rights in general and to general principles of equity (regardless of whether considered in a proceeding in equity or an action at law).

Under Section 10 of the Accord, a remedies opinion includes an opinion that "a remedy will be available with respect to each agreement of the Client in the contract or such agreement will otherwise be given effect." The opinion is based on facts established through assumptions (Accord, Section 4) and information provided by others (Accord, Section 3). It is subject to the General Qualifications (Accord, Section 11), which consist of the Bankruptcy and Insolvency Exception (Accord, Section 12), the Equitable Principles Limitation (Accord, Section 13) and the Other Common Qualifications (Accord, Section 14). It addresses only the law of contracts and such "other laws of [the relevant jurisdiction] as a lawyer in [that jurisdiction] exercising customary professional diligence would recognize to be directly applicable to the Client, the Transaction, or both," but does not address the matters excluded by Section 18 (Opinions by Implication) or Section 19 (Specific Legal Issues).

2. The authorized capital stock of the Company consists of ____ shares of common stock, _____ par value, [of which __________ shares] [all of which] are outstanding. Sellers own all of the outstanding Stock of record and beneficially, free and clear of all adverse claims. As a result of the delivery of certificates to Buyer and the payment to Sellers being made at the Closing, Buyer is acquiring ownership of all of the outstanding Stock, free and clear of all adverse claims.

COMMENT

Assuming the existence of proper stock records, it is normally not difficult for the Sellers' counsel to satisfy himself or herself as to the authorized and outstanding capital stock of the Company or the Sellers' record ownership of the Shares. Establishing beneficial ownership and freedom from adverse claims is more difficult, but the Buyer will generally press to receive some comfort from Sellers' counsel on these matters. The opinion as to the ownership passing to Buyer free and clear of adverse claims is normally given on the basis of Section 8-302 of the Uniform Commercial Code. Sellers' counsel may seek to include an assumption that the Buyer does not have notice of any adverse claim; that is often acceptable to the Buyer, at least if counsel is willing to state in the opinion that the Model Stock Purchase Agreement, the Disclosure Letter and other transaction documents do not constitute such notice.

3. Each Acquired Company is a corporation duly organized, validly existing and in good standing under the laws of its jurisdiction of incorporation as set forth in Part 3.1(a) of the Disclosure Letter, with full corporate power and authority to own its properties and to engage in its business as presently conducted or contemplated, and is duly qualified and in good standing as a foreign corporation under the laws of each other jurisdiction in which it is authorized to do business as set forth in Part 3.1(a) of the Disclosure Letter. All of the outstanding capital stock of each of the Subsidiaries is owned of record [and beneficially] by one or more of the Acquired Companies, free and clear of all adverse claims. All of the outstanding shares of capital stock of each Acquired Company have been duly authorized and validly issued and are fully paid and nonassessable and were not issued in violation of the preemptive rights of any Person.

4. Neither the execution and delivery of the Agreement nor the consummation of any or all of the Contemplated Transactions (a) breaches or constitutes a default (or an event that, with notice or lapse of time or both, would constitute a default) under any agreement or commitment [describe selection criteria] to which either Seller is party or (b) violates any statute, law, regulation or rule, or any judgment, decree or order of any court or other Governmental Body applicable to either Seller.

5. Neither the execution and delivery of the Agreement nor the consummation of any or all of the Contemplated Transactions (a) violates any provision of the certificate of incorporation or bylaws (or other governing instrument) of any Acquired Company, (b) breaches or constitutes a default (or an event that, with notice or lapse of time or both, would constitute a default) under, or results in the termination of, or accelerates the performance required by, or excuses performance by any Person of any of its obligations under, or causes the acceleration of the maturity of any debt or obligation pursuant to, or results in the creation or imposition of any Encumbrance upon any property or assets of any Acquired Company under, any agreement or commitment [describe selection criteria] to which any Acquired Company is a party or by which any of their respective properties or assets are bound, or to which any of the properties or assets of any Acquired Company are subject, or (c) violates any statute, law, regulation, or rule, or any judgment, decree or order of any court or other Governmental Body applicable to any Acquired Company.

COMMENT

The no breach or default opinions given in paragraphs 4 and 5 are discussed in Section 15 of the Accord and the related Commentary.

The most troublesome aspect of these opinions is identification of the agreements and commitments described in paragraphs 4(a) and 5(b). It is not unusual, at least in the case of opinions not covered by the Accord, for the Buyer to request that the opinion cover "any agreement or commitment *known to us* to which any Acquired Company is a party or by which any of their respective property or assets is bound." It is not clear what "known to us" means in this formulation; does it include any agreement or commitment that any present or former attorney or other employee of the law firm acting as counsel to the Sellers ever had reason to believe existed? If it does, in most cases there will be no way in which counsel can identify those agreements and commitments.

The Accord and the model form of opinion take a different approach. The form of opinion specifies criteria to be used in identifying the agreements and commitments to which this opinion is to apply (*e.g.,* all agreements and commitments evidencing or providing for indebtedness for borrowed money, or all agreements and commitments requiring annual payments by or to an Acquired Company in excess of $1,000,000). The opining lawyer receives a certificate of an officer of the Company listing the agreements and commitments that meet these criteria and relies on that certificate absent knowledge (defined as the present awareness of the Primary Lawyer Group—see Accord, Section 6-A) to the contrary. The opining lawyer reviews the agreements and commitments listed on the certificate and gives the opinion.

This approach requires that the parties define the selection criteria in a way that satisfies the Buyer's legitimate interest in having the Sellers' counsel review those agreements and commitments likely to present significant issues while at the same time limiting the scope of that review to one that is feasible and does not involve disproportionate cost in the context of the transaction. It is not appropriate to define the selection criteria in terms of the ultimate conclusion to be reached by the opining lawyer (*e.g.,* all agreements and commitments that prohibit a change of control of the Company); Sellers' counsel could not rely on a certificate expressed in those terms (Accord, Section 3(b)(i)).

6. Except for requirements of the HSR Act, no consent, approval or authorization of, or declaration, filing or registration with, any Governmental Body is required in connection with the execution, delivery and performance of the Agreement or the consummation of the Contemplated Transactions.

We hereby confirm to you that, except as set forth in Part 3.15 of the Disclosure Letter, there is no Proceeding by or before any court or Governmental Body pending or overtly threatened against or involving any Acquired Company or that questions or challenges the validity of the Agreement or any action taken or to be taken by any Acquired Company pursuant to the Agreement or in connection with the Contemplated Transactions, and none of the Acquired Companies is subject to any judgment, order or decree having prospective effect.

COMMENT

This confirmation is discussed in Section 17 of the Accord and the related Commentary.

The Accord is changed for purposes of this Opinion Letter pursuant to § 21 of the Accord as follows:

(a) The Primary Lawyer Group shall include all lawyers presently at our firm who have given substantive attention to the affairs of any of the Sellers or the Acquired Companies since __________.

(b) Accord § 19(e) and § 19(j) are deleted.

COMMENT

Section 10 of the Accord invites modification and private ordering by the parties. The Buyer may seek to expand the Primary Lawyer Group, which defines the lawyers whose knowledge is imputed to the firm rendering the opinion, to include those who, although not involved in the acquisition, are likely to have knowledge that may be relevant to the Buyer (*e.g.,* litigators who may be aware of pending litigation); the expanded definition is based on ¶ 6.3(ii) of the Accord Commentary. The deletion of Accord § 19(e) and § 19(j) is designed to require counsel to consider the environmental laws in effect in some states that require notifications and proceedings in connection with acquisitions in giving the opinion in paragraph 6. There is no standard as to the provisions of the Accord, if any, that the Buyer should seek to have modified; that determination should be made in the context of the specific transaction.

We understand that you are delivering a copy of this opinion to [identify lenders to Buyer] in connection with the financing of the transactions contemplated by the Agreement and agree that [those lenders] may rely on this opinion as if it were addressed to them.

COMMENT

If the acquisition is being financed, the lenders will often seek to have the benefit of the legal opinion delivered by Sellers' counsel. Absent a consent in the opinion (or separately given by Sellers' counsel) Section 20 of the Accord would deny the lenders the right to rely on the opinion.

Very truly yours,

____

Exhibit 8.4

Opinion of Counsel to Buyer

PRELIMINARY NOTE

As is the case with the Buyer's representations in the Model Stock Purchase Agreement, the scope of the opinion required to be delivered to the Sellers by the Buyer's counsel is often limited to matters affecting the validity of the transaction documents. However, where the Buyer is issuing its stock or giving a promissory note for a significant portion of the purchase price, the Sellers may require additional representations from the Buyer and, correspondingly, additional opinions from the Buyer's counsel. See the Commentary to Section 4 of the Model Stock Purchase Agreement.

[DATE]

[Names and Addresses of Sellers]

Gentlemen:

We have acted as counsel to ____________, a ______________ corporation ("Buyer"), in connection with the Stock Purchase Agreement dated ____________, 199_ (the "Agreement") between ______________, ______________, and Buyer. This is the opinion contemplated by Section 8.4(a) of the Agreement. All capitalized terms used in this opinion without definition have the respective meanings given to them in the Agreement or the Accord referred to below.

This Opinion Letter is governed by, and shall be interpreted in accordance with, the Legal Opinion Accord (the "Accord") of the ABA Section of Business Law (1991). As a consequence, it is subject to a number of qualifications, exceptions, definitions, limitations on coverage and other limitations, all as more particularly described in the Accord, and this Opinion Letter should be read in conjunction therewith. The law covered by the opinions expressed herein is limited to the Federal Law of the United States and the Law of the State(s) of ____________.

Based on the foregoing, our opinion is as follows:

1. The Agreement, the Escrow Agreement and the Promissory Notes are enforceable against Buyer.

2. Neither the execution and delivery of the Agreement, the Escrow Agreement and the Promissory Notes nor the performance of Buyer's obligations thereunder (a) violates any provision of the certificate of incorporation or bylaws (or other governing instrument) of Buyer, (b) breaches or constitutes a default (or an event that, with notice or lapse of time or both, would constitute a default) under any agreement or commitment [describe selection criteria] to which Buyer is party or (c) violates any statute, law, regulation or rule, or any judgment, decree or order of any court or Governmental Body applicable to Buyer.

Very truly yours,

____

ANCILLARY DOCUMENTS

Ancillary Document No. 1

Confidentiality Agreement

PRELIMINARY NOTE

Although the Model Stock Purchase Agreement has been drafted from the point of view of the prospective Buyer's first draft, confidentiality agreements are primarily a concern for the Company, and thus the Confidentiality Agreement has been prepared from the standpoint of the Company's first draft. For a more Buyer-oriented treatment, refer to the confidentiality provisions of the Letter of Intent.

The Confidentiality Agreement is usually the first document in the acquisition process, signed by the prospective Buyer before the Company provides any confidential material.

The business people may resist a long, complex document at this point. Depending on the circumstances, a shorter agreement may very well provide the Company with adequate protection. In deciding which provisions to keep and which to delete, careful consideration should be given to the benefits to be gained and the risks posed by a shorter agreement. If the parties anticipate incorporating the Confidentiality Agreement into the Model Stock Purchase Agreement, it would benefit the parties to negotiate a more detailed Confidentiality Agreement initially.

The Confidentiality Agreement is often in letter form from the Company to Buyer, and the Model Confidentiality Agreement takes this approach. However, the Confidentiality Agreement may be structured as an agreement involving the Company's shareholders so that the Sellers individually can benefit from and are subject to the agreement.

If the Letter of Intent and the Confidentiality Agreement are executed at the same time, the parties may want to consolidate them into one document. However, because the Confidentiality Agreement is intended to be enforceable and major portions of the Letter of Intent are intended to be unenforceable, combining these documents could result in one or the other being more or less enforceable than intended. In this case, since the Letter of Intent is a Buyer-oriented document, the confidentiality provisions in the Letter of Intent would need to be revised to protect the Company's disclosure of confidential information.

If a definitive stock purchase agreement is entered into, it will have to deal with the extent to which the Confidentiality Agreement (or portions of it) will be superseded by that agreement, particularly in terms of the typical "integration" provision. See Section 4 of the Model Confidentiality Agreement for one provision that contemplates being superseded by the definitive stock purchase agreement.

For an excellent treatment of issues involved in negotiating a confidentiality agreement, see Lesser, Lederer & Steinberg, *Increasing Pressures for Confidentiality Agreements That Work*, Mergers & Acquisitions: The Dealmakers Journal (March/April, 1992). For a review of confidentiality agreements from a Buyer's perspective, see Mann & Schwartzbaum, *Negotiating Confidentiality Agreements*, Insights, Vol. 6, No. 8 (August 1992).

[Date]

[Name]
[Company]
[Address]

PRIVATE
AND
CONFIDENTIAL

Dear ____________:

In connection with the consideration by ____________________ (the "Buyer") of the possible purchase (the "Acquisition Transaction") of ____________________________________ (together with its subsidiaries, the "Company"), the Buyer has requested access to certain information, properties, and personnel of the Company.

COMMENT

It is important at the outset to define the Buyer's limited use of the confidential information. Moreover, the Confidentiality Agreement describes the transaction as "possible" in order to avoid the implication that any agreement in principle has already been made between the parties or will be created by the Confidentiality Agreement.

In consideration for and as a condition to the Company's furnishing access to such information, properties, and personnel of the Company as the Company, in its sole discretion, agrees to make available to the Buyer, the Buyer agrees as follows:

1. Confidential and Proprietary Nature of the Information

The Buyer acknowledges the confidential and proprietary nature of the Confidential Information (as defined below), agrees to hold and keep the same as provided in this letter agreement, and otherwise agrees to each and every restriction and obligation in this letter agreement.

2. Confidential Information

As used in this letter agreement, the term "Confidential Information" means and includes any and all:

(a) trade secrets concerning the business and affairs of the Company (which includes the materials dated ____________ __, 199_ and provided to the Buyer by ________________), product specifications, data, know-how, formulae, compositions, processes, designs, sketches, photographs, graphs, drawings, samples, inventions and ideas, past, current, and planned research and development, current and planned manufacturing or distribution methods and processes, customer lists, current and anticipated customer requirements, price lists, market studies, business plans, computer software and programs (including object code and source code), computer software and database technologies, systems, structures and architectures (and related processes, formulae, composition, improvements, devices, know-how, inventions, discoveries, concepts, ideas, designs, methods and information), ____________________, and any other information, however documented, that is a trade secret within the meaning of ________ § __-_-___ [applicable state trade secret law]); and

(b) information concerning the business and affairs of the Company (which includes historical financial statements, financial projections and budgets, historical and projected sales, capital spending budgets and plans, the names and backgrounds of key personnel, personnel training techniques and materials, and ______________), however documented, that has been or may hereafter be provided or shown to the Buyer by the Company or by the directors, officers, employees, agents, consultants, advisors, or other representatives including legal counsel, accountants and financial advisors ("Representatives") of the Company (the "Company Representatives") or is otherwise obtained from review of Company documents or property or discussions with Company Representatives by the Buyer or the Buyer's Representatives (including current or prospective financing sources) or Representatives of the Buyer's Representatives irrespective of the form of the communication, and also includes all notes, analyses, compilations, studies, summaries, and other material prepared by the Buyer or the Buyer's Representatives containing or based, in whole or in part, on any information included in the foregoing. Any trade secrets of the Company will also be entitled to all of the protections and benefits under _________ Section ____ [applicable state trade secret law] and any other applicable law. If any information that the Company deems to be a trade secret is found by a court of competent jurisdiction not to be a trade secret for purposes of this letter agreement, then such information will be considered Confidential Information for purposes of this letter agreement. In the case of trade secrets, the Buyer hereby waives any requirement that the Company submit proof of the economic value of any trade secret or post a bond or other security.

COMMENT

The Confidentiality Agreement defines the term "Confidential Information" broadly to include all information concerning the business and affairs of the Company that will be shown to the prospective Buyer. Exceptions are carved out—not from the definition, but rather as exceptions to the obligation of non-use and non-disclosure in Section 6 below (and not, for example, to the obligation to return or destroy if negotiations terminate)—in order to provide for circumstances in which the information is not to be treated as confidential information. Such circumstances include information that becomes generally available to the public (other than by a result of unauthorized disclosure) or information that is otherwise made available to the prospective Buyer without wrongful act on the part of the party providing the information.

In the absence of a confidentiality agreement—and subject to applicable state law—trade secrets, but not confidential information, can be protected from disclosure. *See* Restatement of the Law of Unfair Competition § 41, comment d (1985). Roughly half of the states have adopted a version of the Uniform Trade Secrets Act that defines information as a "trade secret" if it (i) derives economic value from not being generally known to other persons who can obtain economic value from its disclosure or use and (ii) is subject to efforts that are reasonable under the circumstances to maintain its secrecy or confidentiality. *See* Unif. Trade Secrets Act § 1(4), 43 U.L.A. 433 (1988). The Restatement of the Law of Unfair Competition § 39 defines trade secrets slightly differently, but comment b to that section states that the definition is intended to be consistent with the definition in the Uniform Trade Secrets Act. The Uniform Trade Secrets Act and the Confidentiality Agreement complement one another, because protection of information under such trade secret laws provides the Company with another remedy in its arsenal to prevent misappropriation of information. Moreover, the commentary in the Restatement of the Law of Unfair Competition notes that many states have also adopted criminal statutes specifically addressed to the misappropriation of trade secrets. In other states, more general criminal statutes have been interpreted to reach such misappropriations. In some circumstances a misappropriation of trade secrets may also violate federal wire and mail fraud statutes (18 U.S.C. §§ 1341, 1343) and the National Stolen Property Act (18 U.S.C. § 2314).

The Confidentiality Agreement serves three primary purposes: (i) it expands the state law protection of trade secrets to confidential information, (ii) it clarifies and delineates the obligations of the Buyer, particularly with respect to its representatives, and (iii) it helps the Company demonstrate that it used appropriate efforts to protect the information.

The Uniform Trade Secrets Act § 1(4) requires reasonable efforts "under the circumstances" to maintain the secrecy of information constituting trade secrets, and such efforts are at least advisable for confidential information. While executing the Confidentiality Agreement can be important in demonstrating such efforts, it can also be important to stamp materials to be protected "CONFIDENTIAL" to demonstrate such efforts. If the parties decide to require all documents containing confidential information to be stamped, the Company should include a provision that its inadvertent failure to stamp a document is not a waiver of its confidentiality. The Company should, at a minimum, keep a list or copies of all documents disclosed to the Buyer and all persons with whom the Buyer spoke.

It is also important from both the Company's and Buyer's viewpoint to have oral information promptly confirmed by the Company in writing as being confidential and acknowledged by the recipient. In the event of a dispute over the disclosure, the evidentiary problems of proof are lessened when oral communications are reduced to writing. However, because of the discipline required to adhere to such requirement, the Company may be better off not including such a requirement, and thus the Confidentiality Agreement does not. Additionally, there may be oral disclosures made that are so sensitive that neither party wants them reduced to writing (for example, in the context of litigation or environmental issues).

With respect to very important "technical information" of the Company, special issues may arise when the prospective Buyer is a competitor or potential competitor of the Company. In such cases, the prospective Buyer may not wish to review (and the Company may not wish the Buyer to review) certain technical information in order to preclude any future claims of misuse of proprietary information. It is best to list or otherwise describe all such excluded materials in (or on a schedule to) the Confidentiality Agreement. This is a special concern when there is a danger that technical information might be improperly disclosed in the course of the prospective Buyer's interviews with employees of the Company.

Similarly, when the acquisition involves a competitor, special steps need to be taken in connection with the disclosure of pricing or other competitively sensitive information. The potential Buyer's possession of such information could be damaging evidence if the acquisition is not completed and an antitrust claim is subsequently asserted. While the best approach is not to disclose such information unless absolutely necessary for the acquisition, alternatives are to (i) limit disclosure to the Buyer's personnel who are not in a position to use the information in a manner that would violate the antitrust laws or (ii) defer disclosure until as late as possible in the process. Only the Company (and not the Buyer) should reveal such competitively sensitive information, and mutual exchanges of information should be avoided.

Furthermore, it is important, if the acquisition is not consummated, that the Buyer be required to return the competitively sensitive information (together with copies and derivative materials) or, as a less desirable alternative, to certify to the Company that all copies of such information have been destroyed. Section 9 of the Confidentiality Agreement imposes such a requirement.

Note also that in certain circumstances, the Company may be prohibited from disclosing certain information by restrictions under its existing contractual relationships.

The Buyer should consider whether it wants the definition of "Confidential Information" to include any information about the Buyer's business that may be disclosed to the Company or the Sellers in the context of the acquisition negotiations and whether the confidentiality obligations should be reciprocal. This can be especially important to the Buyer if the acquisition does not close.

3. Restricted Use of Confidential Information

The Buyer agrees that the Confidential Information (a) will be kept confidential by the Buyer and the Buyer's Representatives and (b) without limiting the foregoing, will not be disclosed by the Buyer or the Buyer's Representatives to any person (including current or prospective financing sources) except with the specific prior written consent of ____________________ (the "Company Contact") [a designated individual or a designated position, such as chief financial officer] or except as expressly otherwise permitted by the terms of this letter agreement. It is understood that the Buyer may disclose Confidential Information to only those of the Buyer's Representatives who (i) require such material for the purpose of evaluating a possible Acquisition Transaction (but to the extent practicable, only such part that is so required and without revealing the possible Acquisition Transaction), and (ii) are informed by the Buyer of the confidential nature of the Confidential Material and the obligations of this letter agreement. The Buyer further agrees that the Buyer and the Buyer's Representatives will not use any of the Confidential Information either for any reason or purpose other than to evaluate a possible Acquisition Transaction or in any way detrimental to the Company (it being acknowledged that any use other than evaluation of and negotiating the possible Acquisition Transaction will be deemed detrimental). The Buyer also agrees to be responsible for enforcing the terms of this letter agreement as to the Buyer's Representatives and the confidentiality of the Confidential Information and to take such action, legal or otherwise, to the extent necessary to cause them to comply with the terms and conditions of this letter agreement and thereby prevent any disclosure of the Confidential Information by any of the Buyer's Representatives (including all actions that the Buyer would take to protect its own trade secrets and confidential information).

COMMENT

The Confidentiality Agreement defines exactly who will be allowed to use the Confidential Information and the scope and extent of such use.

The Confidentiality Agreement states that the prospective Buyer may not use the evaluation material for any purposes "detrimental" to the Company, but attempts to avoid the result of preventing the Buyer from using adverse information it discovers to negotiate appropriate adjustments in the purchase price. The prospective Buyer may object to such language as overbroad, although the better argument is that any use of the information other than evaluating an Acquisition Transaction is detrimental to the Company.

The foregoing provisions require only that the Buyer inform the persons to whom the Confidential Information is provided of the confidential nature and the obligations under this Agreement. It may be that at least in the early stages of some highly sensitive transactions that the Company will want to add clauses providing that the Confidential Information (1) may not be disclosed except to persons approved in writing by the Company Contact prior to any disclosure and (2) requiring such persons to acknowledge in writing the obligations of the Letter Agreement. If such a clause is included, the Company probably needs to also add language making it clear that such restrictions are intended to apply only during an initial period in which evaluation is limited to basic materials provided to the prospective Buyer and that if the parties decide to proceed further, the Company would waive such restrictions. Such written acknowledgement could be accomplished by having a one sentence cover letter signed by each representative ("I hereby agree to be bound by the attached agreement from X to Y dated Z") or (as a less burdensome alternative) by having the Buyer's representatives sign a statement acknowledging that they are familiar with the confidentiality obligations in the Confidentiality Agreement and agree to be bound by its provisions. Another alternative is to merely provide in the Confidentiality Agreement that the Buyer retains responsibility for any unauthorized disclosures or use of the confidential information and for ensuring compliance with the terms of the Confidentiality Agreement. This approach may be more palatable to the Company if the Buyer's employees have signed secrecy agreements as a condition of employment with the Buyer.

Until the Letter of Intent is signed, the Company may want to limit disclosure of the confidential information to three or four key people. However, compliance with such a limitation may be very difficult for the Buyer and the Buyer should carefully consider the practical implications before signing an agreement that contains such a provision.

4. Nondisclosure of Possible Acquisition Transaction

Except as permitted by the previous paragraph and except as expressly permitted by a definitive acquisition agreement, if any, entered into by the Buyer for the acquisition of the Company, neither the Buyer nor the Buyer's Representatives will disclose to any person (including another prospective purchaser who has been provided Confidential Information) the fact that the Confidential Information has been made available to the Buyer or the Buyer's Representatives or that the Buyer or the Buyer's Representatives have inspected any portion of the Confidential Information. Except with the prior written consent of the other party and except as expressly permitted by a definitive acquisition agreement, if any, entered into by the Buyer for the acquisition of the Company, neither the Buyer nor the Buyer's Representatives will disclose the fact that any discussions or negotiations are taking place concerning a possible Acquisition Transaction, including the status of such discussions or negotiations.

COMMENT

The Confidentiality Agreement prevents the disclosure of information or the fact that negotiations are taking place. This is important if the Company does not want competitors, suppliers, and customers to be aware that the Company is for sale. It is also particularly useful in a competitive bidding situation in which the Company will want to prohibit any information trading between prospective buyers who might be tempted to make a joint bid. In certain circumstances, however, a prospective buyer may seek a reciprocal provision from the Company. Thus, the Company must be prepared to accept such a demand or justify why similar provisions should not apply to its actions.

For practical reasons, the Buyer may object to the provision requiring it not to disclose to someone who has been provided the "book" containing acquisition evaluation materials the fact that discussions are taking place concerning a possible acquisition. However, when such books of evaluation materials are to be given to a broad group of people, the Company may insist on this provision, because the more people aware of the negotiations, the more likely it is that there will be a leak.

5. Company Contact

All requests by the Buyer or the Buyer's Representatives for Confidential Information, meetings with Company personnel or Company Representatives, or inspection of the Company's properties must be made to the Company Contact.

COMMENT

The Confidentiality Agreement imposes a procedural "bottleneck" whereby all communications with employees of the Company must be approved by a designated representative of the Company—the Company Contact—in advance. This procedure ensures that any employees to be interviewed may be properly briefed beforehand by the Company and its counsel, so that no unauthorized disclosures of information will be made.

6. Exceptions

All of the foregoing obligations and restrictions do not apply to that part of the Confidential Information that the Buyer demonstrates (a) was or becomes generally available to the public other than as a result of a disclosure by the Buyer or the Buyer's Representatives or (b) was available, or becomes available, to the Buyer on a non-confidential basis prior to its disclosure to the Buyer by the Company or a Company Representative, but only if (i) the source of such information is not bound by the Confidentiality Agreement with the Company or is not otherwise prohibited from transmitting the information to the Buyer or the Buyer's Representatives by a contractual, legal, fiduciary, or other obligation and (ii) the Buyer provides the Company with written notice of such prior possession either (A) prior to the execution and delivery of this letter agreement or (B) if the Buyer later becomes aware of (through disclosure to the Buyer or otherwise through the Buyer's work on the Acquisition Transaction) any aspect of the Confidential Information of which the Buyer had prior possession, promptly upon the Buyer becoming aware of such aspect.

COMMENT

The frequently seen exception for materials independently developed by the Buyer is not included in the Confidentiality Agreement because of the potential for disputes over what was "independently developed."

The requirement that the Buyer demonstrate prior possession shifts the burden of proof to the person to whom the information is disclosed.

In certain instances, the Company will include a provision prohibiting the prospective Buyer from competing with the Company for a specified period of time. The rationale for this provision is that without the disclosure of confidential information to the prospective Buyer, the prospective Buyer would have difficulty entering into the Company's business. Furthermore, the Company may have difficulty proving that the prospective Buyer did, in fact, use the confidential information in its business. Such a non-competition provision is generally strongly resisted by prospective buyers who are engaged, or have an interest in engaging, in the same business as the Company. However, if the parties do not enter into a definitive agreement, the non-compete provisions may not be enforceable as an unreasonable restraint of competition unless narrowly limited.

7. Legal Proceedings

If the Buyer or any of the Buyer's Representatives are requested or become legally compelled (by oral questions, interrogatories, requests for information or documents, subpoena, civil or criminal investigative demand, or similar process) or is required by a regulatory body to make any disclosure that is prohibited or otherwise constrained by this letter agreement, the Buyer or such Representative, as the case may be, will provide the Company with prompt notice of such request so that it may seek an appropriate protective order or other appropriate remedy. Subject to the foregoing, the Buyer or such Representative may furnish that portion (and only that portion) of the Confidential Information that, in the written opinion of its counsel reasonably acceptable to the Company, the Buyer is legally compelled or is otherwise required to disclose or else stand liable for contempt or suffer other material censure or material penalty; provided, however, that the Buyer and the Buyer's Representatives must use reasonable efforts to obtain reliable assurance that confidential treatment will be accorded any Confidential Information so disclosed.

COMMENT

The Confidentiality Agreement will not protect the Company against disclosures of information required by legal proceedings. However, the Company should ensure that it is in a position to object to the disclosure of any information or, at a minimum, that it is able to limit or control the scope of any court ordered disclosure. The Confidentiality Agreement addresses this concern by requiring the prospective Buyer and its representatives to notify the Company upon their receipt of any such request for information, which enables the Company to seek injunctive relief or other remedies. Moreover, the Confidentiality Agreement provides that if no such relief is available, the Buyer may only disclose information that, in the opinion of legal counsel reasonably acceptable to the Company, it is required to disclose or else stand liable for contempt, censure, or other penalty.

8. Contact with Employees

Without the prior written consent of the Company Contact (a) neither the Buyer nor any of the Buyer's Representatives will initiate or cause to be initiated (other than through the Company Contact) any communication with any employee of the Company concerning the Confidential Information or any possible Acquisition Transaction, and (b) the Buyer and the Buyer's Representatives will not, for a period of two years after the date of this letter agreement, solicit or cause to be solicited the employment of or employ, any person who is now employed by the Company.

COMMENT

Often, a prospective Buyer will seek to interview employees of the Company while in the process of evaluating the acquisition. This is problematic for a number of reasons. First, it may alert the Company's employees to the possibility that an acquisition is under consideration, and the Company may want to keep this information confidential. Second, it raises the concern that the prospective Buyer may solicit these employees for employment rather than continuing with the proposed acquisition.

Thus, the Confidentiality Agreement requires the Buyer to undertake not to solicit any employees of the Company for a period after the date of the Confidentiality Agreement. This provision is crucial with high-tech or other growing companies in which key employees are important to the future success of the Company. The Buyer may argue that this provision should be limited to "key" employees, excluding secretaries, clerks, and those not encountered in connection with (or more broadly, not involved with) the proposed acquisition. A possible resolution is to list the "protected" employees.

9. Return of Confidential Information

If the Buyer determines that it does not wish to proceed with an Acquisition Transaction (the failure to enter into a Letter of Intent on or before ___________________ __, 199_ or a definitive acquisition agreement on or before __________ __, 199__ will be deemed the Buyer's determination that it does not wish to proceed) (and the Buyer will promptly notify the Company Contact of such decision) or if the Company notifies the Buyer that it does not wish the Buyer to consider the Acquisition Transaction any further, then (a) the Buyer (i) will promptly deliver to the Company Contact all documents or other materials furnished by the Company or any Company Representative to the Buyer or the Buyer's Representatives constituting Confidential Information, together with all copies and summaries thereof in the possession or under the control of the Buyer or the Buyer's Representatives, and (ii) will destroy materials generated by the Buyer or the Buyer's Representatives that include or refer to any part of the Confidential Information, without retaining a copy of any such material or (b) alternatively, if the Company Contact requests or gives his prior written consent to the Buyer's request, the Buyer will destroy all documents or other matters constituting Confidential Information in the possession or under the control of the Buyer or the Buyer's Representatives. Any such destruction pursuant to the foregoing must be confirmed by the Buyer in writing to the Company (such confirmation must include a list of the destroyed materials).

COMMENT

The Buyer will generally prefer to destroy materials rather than return them to the Company. In that event, the Company should insist on a list of all such documents. Some buyers insist on the right to retain at least a copy of what was received to protect itself if it is later accused of using disclosed information, but perhaps this is better handled by the buyer's disclosure of prior knowledge (see Section 6(b)(ii) above).

10. No Obligation to Negotiate a Definitive Agreement

The Company and its shareholders reserve the right, in their sole discretion, to reject any and all proposals made by the Buyer or the Buyer's Representatives with regard to an Acquisition Transaction and to terminate discussions and negotiations with the Buyer and the Buyer's Representatives at any time. Without limiting the preceding sentence, nothing in this letter agreement requires either the Buyer or the Company or its shareholders to enter into an Acquisition Transaction or to negotiate such transaction for any specified period of time.

COMMENT

The Buyer will want to add a provision that its confidentiality obligations—but not the obligations of the Company's shareholders—terminate upon the completion of the acquisition.

11. No Representations or Warranties

The Company retains the right to determine, in its sole discretion, what information, properties, and personnel it wishes to make available to the Buyer, and neither the Company nor its Representatives make any representation or warranty (express or implied) concerning the completeness or accuracy of the Confidential Information, except pursuant to representations and warranties that may be made to the Buyer in a definitive acquisition agreement for an Acquisition Transaction if, when, and as executed and subject to such limitations and restrictions as may be specified therein. The Buyer also agrees that if the Buyer determines to engage in an Acquisition Transaction, the Buyer's determination will be based solely on the terms of such definitive acquisition agreement and on the Buyer's own investigation, analysis, and assessment of the business to be acquired. Moreover, unless and until such a definitive written agreement is entered into, neither the Company nor the Buyer will be under any legal obligation of any kind with respect to such an Acquisition Transaction except for the matters specifically agreed to in this letter agreement or in another written agreement.

COMMENT

Because at the time the parties enter into the Confidentiality Agreement, neither the Company nor the Buyer knows either what information might be of particular interest to the Buyer or whether the discussions will lead to a definitive agreement, the Company will in nearly all cases insist upon a disclaimer of any representations or warranties concerning the accuracy or completeness of the Confidential Information. This provision is standard in all confidentiality agreements and should meet with no objections except in the most unusual circumstances.

12. Remedies

The Buyer agrees to indemnify and hold the Company and its shareholders harmless from any damages, loss, cost, or liability (including legal fees and the cost of enforcing this indemnity) arising out of or resulting from any unauthorized use or disclosure by the Buyer or the Buyer's Representatives of the Confidential Information or other violation of this letter agreement. In addition, because an award of money damages (whether pursuant to the foregoing sentence or otherwise) would be inadequate for any breach of this letter agreement by the Buyer or the Buyer's Representatives and any such breach would cause the Company irreparable harm, the Buyer also agrees that, in the event of any breach or threatened breach of this letter agreement, the Company will also be entitled, without the requirement of posting a bond or other security, to equitable relief, including injunctive relief and specific performance. Such remedies will not be the exclusive remedies for any breach of this letter agreement but will be in addition to all other remedies available at law or equity to the Company.

COMMENT

It is important to the Company to have the Buyer acknowledge the right to injunctive relief, to facilitate the Sellers' *promptly* obtaining an injunction because that typically is the Company's best remedy. The Buyer will probably object to the legal fees provision, and perhaps an intermediate position is to provide that the prevailing party gets his legal fees reimbursed.

13. MISCELLANEOUS

(a) *Modification.* The agreements set forth in this letter agreement may be modified or waived only by a separate writing signed by the Company and the Buyer expressly modifying or waiving such agreements.

(b) *Waiver.* The rights and remedies of the parties to this letter agreement are cumulative and not alternative. Neither the failure nor any delay by any party in exercising any right, power, or privilege under this letter agreement will operate as a waiver of such right, power, or privilege, and no single or partial exercise of any such right, power, or privilege will preclude any other or further exercise of such right, power, or privilege or the exercise of any other right, power, or privilege. To the maximum extent permitted by applicable law, (i) no claim or right arising out of this letter agreement can be discharged by one party, in whole or in part, by a waiver or renunciation of the claim or right unless in writing signed by the other party; (ii) no waiver that may be given by a party will be applicable except in the specific instance for which it is given; and (iii) no notice to or demand on one party will be deemed to be a waiver of any obligation of such party or of the right of the party giving such notice or demand to take further action without notice or demand as provided in this letter agreement.

(c) *Person.* The term "person" means any individual, corporation (including any non-profit corporation), general or limited partnership, limited liability company, joint venture, estate, trust, association, organization, labor union, or other entity or governmental body.

(d) *Severability.* The invalidity or unenforceability of any provision of this letter agreement shall not affect the validity or enforceability of any other provisions of this letter agreement, which shall remain in full force and effect. If any of the covenants or provisions of this letter agreement are determined to be unenforceable by reason of its extent, duration, scope or otherwise, then the parties contemplate that the court making such determination shall reduce such extent, duration, scope or other provision and enforce them in their reduced form for all purposes contemplated by this letter agreement.

(e) *Costs.* The Buyer agrees that if it is held by any court of competent jurisdiction to be in violation, breach, or nonperformance of any of the terms of this letter agreement, then it will pay all costs of such action or suit, including reasonable attorneys' fees.

COMMENT

The Buyer will probably object to the legal fees provision, and perhaps an intermediate position is to provide that the prevailing party gets its legal fees reimbursed.

(f) *Assignment.* The Company reserves the right to assign all of its rights under this letter agreement, including the right to enforce all of its terms. In the event of an Acquisition Transaction that involves a sale of assets, the Company currently intends to assign to the buyer rights to enforce the restrictions and other obligations of this letter agreement, including the right to enforce all of its terms.

(g) *Section Headings, Construction.* The headings of Sections in this letter agreement are provided for convenience only and will not affect its construction or interpretation. All references to "Section" or "Sections" refer to the corresponding Section or Sections of this letter agreement unless otherwise specified. All words used in this letter agreement will be construed to be of such gender or number as the circumstances require. Unless otherwise expressly provided, the word "including" does not limit the preceding words or terms.

(h) *Jurisdiction; Service of Process.* Any action or proceeding seeking to enforce any provision of, or based on any right arising out of, this letter agreement may be brought against either of the parties in the courts of the State of ____________, County of ____________, or, if it has or can acquire jurisdiction, in the United States District Court for the ____________ District of __________________, and each of the parties consent to the jurisdiction of such courts (and of the appropriate appellate courts) in any such action or proceeding and waives any objection to venue laid therein. Process in any action or proceeding referred to in the preceding sentence may be served on any party anywhere in the world.

(i) *Governing Law.* This letter agreement will be governed by the laws of the State of ______________ without regard to conflicts of laws principles.

(j) *Counterparts.* This letter agreement may be executed in one or more counterparts, each of which will be deemed to be an original copy of this letter agreement, and all of which, when taken together, shall be deemed to constitute one and the same agreement.

If you are in agreement with the foregoing, please sign and return one copy of this letter agreement, which thereupon will constitute our agreement with respect to its subject matter.

Very truly yours,

[The Company's Name]

____

By: ________________________________
Name: ______________________________
Its: ________________________________

DULY EXECUTED and agreed to on __________ _____, 199_.

[The Buyer's Name]

____

By: ________________________________
Name: ______________________________
Its: ________________________________

Ancillary Document No. 2

Letter of Intent

PRELIMINARY NOTE

A letter of intent is often entered into between a buyer and a seller as a result of the successful completion of the first phase of negotiations of a purchase and sale transaction. The letter generally, but not always, describes the purchase price or a formula to be used to determine the purchase price and certain other key economic and procedural terms that form the basis for further negotiations. A buyer and seller fully expect that the letter of intent will be superseded by a definitive written acquisition agreement.

There are several reasons why letters of intent are used. Both a buyer and seller frequently prefer a letter of intent to test the waters for the prospects of a definitive agreement before incurring the costs of negotiating a definitive agreement and performing, or permitting to be performed, an acquisition review of the target company. The parties may also feel morally, if not legally, obligated to key terms if those terms are set down in writing. Sometimes the purchase price is sufficiently complicated that it is helpful to describe it in writing to ensure that the buyer and the seller have consistent expectations.

Often signing a letter of intent early on, rather than waiting for the definitive agreement, facilitates compliance with regulatory requirements. For example, a premerger notification report can be filed under the Hart-Scott-Rodino Antitrust Improvements Act of 1976 upon entering into a letter of intent, thereby starting the clock on the applicable waiting period. A signed letter of intent may also assist the buyer in convincing some lenders to evaluate the transaction for the purpose of providing financing. The letter of intent often provides a format for the transaction which can be used as the basis for drafting the definitive agreement. Announcements to customers, suppliers and employees about the potential transaction are frequently triggered by the signing of a letter of intent.

Letters of intent are also used to regulate the rights and obligations of the parties while a definitive agreement is being negotiated. For example, a "no-shop" provision is often included preventing a seller from negotiating with another party while negotiations with a buyer are ongoing. A letter of intent generally permits a buyer to inspect the target company's assets and to review its operations, and books and records, while at the same time prohibiting a buyer from disclosing or using in competition with the target company trade secrets and other proprietary information disclosed by the target company to a buyer during the negotiations. A letter of intent often covers how expenses of the acquisition and negotiations, such as brokers' fees and fees and expenses of attorneys and other advisors, will be paid and limits the rights of each party to publicize the acquisition or negotiations without the consent of the other party. Frequently, a letter of intent will establish the time frame for closing the acquisition and, sometimes, certain other milestones prior to the closing.

Many commentators and business lawyers believe that letters of intent generally are more favorable to a buyer than to a seller. Often a signed letter of intent, even if not binding, together with a buyer's inspection of the target company's assets and review of its operations and books and records, will place a seller at a negotiating disadvantage in that there may be an expectation on the part of the target company's employees, vendors, customers, lenders, and investors of a sale to a buyer. A buyer's investigation of the target company may also uncover information that can be used by a buyer to compete with the target company if the sale is not consummated, even if the target company receives protection against the disclosure or use by a buyer of the target company's trade secrets and other proprietary information. A "no-shop" provision in the letter of intent may prevent a seller from introducing other interested parties to the acquisition to enhance its negotiating position with a buyer.

Notwithstanding these considerations, sellers are often as insistent as buyers that a letter of intent be executed before work on a definitive agreement is begun. One reason for a seller's insistence on a letter of intent may be that the negotiation of a letter of intent provides a seller with an excellent opportunity to negotiate certain key acquisition issues at a time when a seller possesses maximum leverage.

While letters of intent are common, no consensus exists among business lawyers regarding their desirability. Many lawyers advise their clients that the great disadvantage of a letter of intent is that provisions intended by the parties to be nonbinding may be later found by a court to be binding. Also, there is often an inherent conflict between the goals of the parties in negotiating a letter of intent. A buyer generally is most interested in securing a "no-shop" commitment and other standstill types of provisions from the seller and seeks to maintain great flexibility regarding the purchase price and other key provisions that may be impacted by the results of a buyer's acquisition review of the target company. A seller, on the other hand, generally will attempt to define more clearly the purchase price, limitations on its exposure with respect to the representations and warranties that will be part of the definitive agreement, and key terms of employment agreements, noncompete covenants and other ancillary arrangements. If possible, a seller will prefer to avoid altogether or to limit the scope of any "no-shop" commitment. Sometimes the negotiation of a letter of intent becomes bogged down in detailed discussions that are generally reserved to the negotiation of the definitive agreement. Because of these twin concerns of the possible, but unintended, binding nature of the letter of intent and the risk that the negotiation of the letter of intent will become bogged down in endless detail, lawyers often advise their clients to forgo a letter of intent and immediately to negotiate a definitive agreement.

Whether or not a letter of intent should be binding can be a matter of great importance and it is important that the lawyer understand the client's desires in this regard. For example, the acquisition may be so economically or strategically attractive that the client is willing, as a business decision, to be bound at this initial stage. The parties might also intend to be bound if the acquisition review has been completed and all economic issues have been settled. Clients must be made aware, however, that a fully binding letter of intent can lead to problems and unexpected results if the parties later are unable to agree to the terms of a definitive agreement. In that event, a court may impose on the parties its interpretation of commercially reasonable terms for any unresolved issues.

The legal principles for when a letter of intent is binding are fairly easy to state:

(1) If the parties intend *not to be bound* to each other prior to the execution of a definitive agreement, the courts will give effect to that intent and the parties will not be bound until the agreement has been executed. This is true even if all issues in the negotiations have been

resolved. *See R. G. Group, Inc. v. Horn & Hardart Co.,* 751 F.2d 69 (2d Cir. 1984); *V'Soske v. Barwick,* 404 F.2d 495 (2D Cir. 1968).

(2) On the other hand, if the parties intend *to be bound* prior to the execution of a definitive agreement, the courts will also give effect to that intent and the parties will be bound even though they contemplate replacing their earlier understanding with the definitive agreement at a later date. *See Texaco, v. Pennzoil Co.,* 729 S.W.2d 768 (Tex. Ct. App. 1987), *cert. denied,* 485 U.S. 994 (1988); *R. G. Group,* 751 F.2d at 74; *V'Soske*, 404 F.2d at 500.

(3) Parties intending to be bound prior to the execution of a definitive agreement will be bound even if there are certain issues that have not been resolved. Depending on the importance of the open items, the courts will either supply commercially reasonable terms for those unresolved issues or impose a contractual duty on the parties to negotiate the resolution of those issues in good faith. *See Itek Corporation v. Chicago Aerial Industries, Inc.*, 248 A.2d 625 (Del. 1968).

When the courts impose a duty to negotiate open terms in good faith, the courts will impose liability if one party acts in bad faith. *See Bruce v. Marcheson Implementos E. Maquinos Agriculas, Tatu, S.A.*, (Civil No. 87-774-A S.D. Iowa 1990) (1990 U.S. Dist. LEXIS 18527); *Fickes v. SunExpert, Inc.* 762 F. Supp. 998 (D. Mass. 1991). On the other hand, if the parties do negotiate in good faith, the fact that a final agreement is not reached will not result in liability. *See Feldman v. Allegheny Int'l, Inc.*, 850 F.2d 1217 (7th Cir. 1988).

In determining whether the parties intend to be bound, the courts generally examine the following factors:

(1) the actual words of the document;
(2) the context of the negotiations;
(3) whether either or both parties have partially performed their obligations;
(4) whether there are any issues left to negotiate; and
(5) whether the subject matter of the discussions concerns complex business matters that customarily involve definitive written agreements.

See Teachers Insurance and Annuity Association v. Tribune Company, 670 F. Supp. 491 (S.D.N.Y. 1987); *Arcadian Phosphates, Inc. v. Arcadian Corp.*, 884 F.2d 69 (2d Cir. 1989); *Texaco*, 729 S.W.2d at 768; *R. G. Group*, 751 F.2d at 75.

Courts have consistently stated that the most important factor in determining whether or which provisions in a letter of intent are binding is the language used by the parties in the document. The language of the letter of intent should, therefore, be definite and precise. The lawyer should advise the client, however, to avoid factual situations that have led some courts to find provisions of a letter of intent to be binding despite language seemingly to the contrary in the document. There are many things that can overcome the words in a letter of intent purporting to make a document or certain provisions in a document nonbinding. Oral communications and other actions are often given great weight by courts in interpreting the intent of the parties. Oral statements such as "Looks like we have a deal!" or handshakes can indicate an intent to be bound. *See American Cyanamid Co. v. Elizabeth Arden Sales Corp.*, 331 F. Supp. 597 (S.D.N.Y. 1971); *Computer Systems of America, Inc. v. IBM Corp.*, 795 F.2d 1086 (1st Cir. 1986). *But see Reprosystem, B. V. v. SCM Corporation*, 727 F.2d 257 (2d Cir. 1984), *cert. denied,* 469 U.S. 828 (1984); *R. G. Group*, 751 F.2d at 75-76; *Seaman's Direct Buying Serv., Inc. v. Standard Oil Co.*, 686 P.2d 1158 (Cal. 1984).

Most letters of intent are intended to be at least partially binding. A buyer may be reluctant to enter into a letter of intent unless it secures a binding promise from a seller that restricts a seller's ability to "shop" the target company for some period of time. Unless a confidentiality agreement is already in place, a seller will want a buyer to be bound to a nondisclosure obligation.

It is important for a client to have its lawyer's advice at the outset if the client contemplates entering into a letter of intent. The issue of whether and what parts of the letter of intent should be binding or nonbinding and the risks of entering into a letter of intent at all are important aspects for a client to understand. The level of detail in the letter of intent and which issues should be confronted or deferred are key strategic questions that should be discussed with the client, and their likely impact on the negotiation of the acquisition should be fully explored. In addition, public companies may have disclosure requirements under the federal securities laws that are triggered at some point in the negotiations, perhaps even before a letter of intent is concluded.

The Letter of Intent contemplates the proposed acquisition by a single corporate buyer of all of the outstanding capital stock of a privately-held company from its two individual stockholders. The purchase price would be payable with a combination of cash and notes. This fact pattern is consistent with the fact pattern that serves as the basis for the Model Stock Purchase Agreement.

The Letter of Intent has been prepared as the Buyer's reasonable first draft, recognizing the custom that a buyer or its counsel will generally prepare the first draft of a letter of intent. There is a broad range of what may be considered reasonable; the Letter of Intent tends toward the buyer-favorable end of that range.

The Letter of Intent is divided into two parts: provisions intended not to be binding and those intended to be binding. The nonbinding provisions consist primarily of the "deal points," such as a description of the proposed transaction, the purchase price, key ancillary agreements, and important conditions. The binding provisions focus on the regulation of the negotiation process, including access for the Buyer to conduct its acquisition review, "no-shop" restrictions and break-up fees, nondisclosure obligations, procedures for making public announcements, payment of the parties' expenses, and termination provisions. The nonbinding and binding portions of the Letter of Intent are clearly delineated to assist a court in determining the intent of the parties, if that becomes necessary. Another, more common practice that also works well is to set out binding and nonbinding provisions without grouping them in separate parts and to include a general statement that the entire letter of intent is nonbinding, except for certain provisions which are then specifically itemized.

Letters of intent that are shorter and more informal than the Letter of Intent can also be effective and many clients prefer a less comprehensive approach. The primary advantages of a comprehensive letter of intent, like the Letter of Intent, are (1) issues that are "deal-breakers" can be identified early in the negotiation process before substantial expenses are incurred in acquisition review and the drafting of a definitive agreement with accompanying disclosure letter or schedules, and (2) resolution of difficult issues at the letter of intent stage can make the negotiation of a definitive agreement considerably easier, permitting the Buyer more time and energy to prepare for the transition to its ownership of the Company. The primary disadvantage of a comprehensive letter of intent is that it may burden the negotiations with too many difficult issues too early in the process and may damage the deal's momentum or even cause a breakdown in the negotiations that may have been able to be avoided if more issues had been deferred until a later time. The lawyer and the client should discuss the strategic impact of a comprehensive letter of intent on the negotiating dynamics of a deal before a letter of intent based on the Letter of Intent is prepared.

In light of the multitude of considerations that are part of negotiating a letter of intent, it cannot be overemphasized that virtually everything in a letter of intent is subject to variation based upon the particular context of the proposed acquisition. There is no such thing as a standard letter of intent applicable to all proposed acquisitions.

__________, 199_

Seller A
[Address]
____

Seller B
[Address]
____

Re: *Proposal to Purchase Stock of the Company*

Dear Sellers:

This letter is intended to summarize the principal terms of a proposal being considered by ________________ (the "Buyer") regarding its possible acquisition of all of the outstanding capital stock of ________________ (the "Company") from ______________("A") and ____________________, who are the Company's sole stockholders (the "Sellers"). In this letter, (i) the Buyer and the Sellers are sometimes called the "Parties," (ii) the Company and its subsidiaries are sometimes called the "Target Companies," and (iii) the Buyer's possible acquisition of the stock of the Company is sometimes called the "Possible Acquisition."

PART ONE

The Parties wish to commence negotiating a definitive written acquisition agreement providing for the Possible Acquisition (a "Definitive Agreement"). To facilitate the negotiation of a Definitive Agreement, the Parties request that the Buyer's counsel prepare an initial draft. The execution of any such Definitive Agreement would be subject to the satisfactory completion of the Buyer's ongoing investigation of the Target Companies' business, and would also be subject to approval by the Buyer's board of directors.

Based on the information currently known to the Buyer, it is proposed that the Definitive Agreement include the following terms:

COMMENT

The Letter of Intent contains a bifurcation between nonbinding and binding provisions. These two parts are clearly delineated by upper case headings. The nonbinding provisions generally include the substantive business terms of the proposed acquisition while the binding provisions focus on the rights, obligations, and behavior of the parties during the negotiation of a definitive agreement or upon the failure of the parties to reach a definitive agreement.

The introductory paragraphs of Part One make explicit the customary practice that the Buyer and its counsel draft the definitive agreement. This allows the Buyer to control the drafting process and the timing of the negotiation process. The Sellers may counter with a request that the Letter of Intent contain specific dates by which drafts will be prepared, comments received, new drafts prepared, and similar deadlines.

The introductory paragraphs also put the Sellers on notice that the form of any definitive agreement will have to be approved by the Buyer's board of directors. In addition, this provision may also provide the Buyer with some protection if the nonbinding provisions are determined to be binding and enforceable. *See A/S Apothekernes Laboratorium v. I.M.C. Chemical Group, Inc.*, 873 F.2d 155 (7th Cir. 1989). The Sellers may object to this provision and instead insist that the Letter of Intent contain a specific confirmation that the Buyer's board has approved the Letter of Intent.

The initial phrase of the last paragraph of this introductory section ("Based on the information currently known to the Buyer") is intended to provide the Buyer with a defensible moral and, if the provisions of Part One are construed to be binding, legal position that its acquisition review of the target company may result in the Buyer offering a lower purchase price or different terms than those contained in the letter of intent.

1. Basic Transaction

The Sellers would sell all of the outstanding capital stock of the Company to the Buyer at the price (the "Purchase Price") set forth in Paragraph 2 below. The closing of this transaction (the "Closing") would occur as soon as possible after the termination of the applicable waiting period under the Hart-Scott-Rodino Antitrust Improvements Act of 1976 (the "HSR Act").

COMMENT

Paragraph 1 and each of the other paragraphs of Part One state the "deal points" of the proposed acquisition. As mentioned in the Preliminary Note, these "deal points" correspond to the assumptions underlying the Model Stock Purchase Agreement, which contains substantial commentary that may also be applicable to the paragraphs of Part One. Consult the Model Stock Purchase Agreement for additional background information and negotiation suggestions.

In Paragraph 1 and throughout Part One, note the use of the word "would." This word is intended to convey the conditional nature of the proposed acquisition and to contrast with the more definite words used in the binding provisions of Part Two, such as "must" and "will." Other conditional terms may also be used, such as "prospective buyer," "prospective seller" and "proposed transaction" to illustrate this point further. While the conditional language of Part One may appear awkward and stilted at times, it provides another indication of the parties' intent that the provisions of Part One not be binding.

It is important to note that, at the stage in the transaction when the Letter of Intent is signed, the transaction itself is still conditional in nature. Most often, many terms have not even been considered, much less discussed and agreed upon. Moreover, the acquisition review process is rarely completed at this stage and quite often not even commenced, and both parties may be oblivious to many potential pitfalls.

Accordingly, the Buyer may want to avoid specifics on many "deal points." This strategy may enhance the Buyer's negotiating position by deferring discussions on these key issues until after the Buyer has completed its acquisition review and the Sellers' negotiating position has been compromised by executing the Letter of Intent as described in the Preliminary Note. The Sellers, on the other hand, in most cases, will want to resolve all important issues at the letter of intent stage when they still possess their greatest negotiating leverage. For example, the Sellers may want to negotiate limitations with respect to their indemnification obligations to the Buyer prior to signing the letter of intent by providing for a "cap," a "basket," an expiration of the indemnification obligations, and reliance on the indemnity provisions as the Buyer's exclusive remedy.

The Buyer may not be prepared to suggest a closing date at this stage of the negotiations, although the Sellers will generally be most interested in trying to establish a time frame for the proposed acquisition. In addition, a variety of factors may affect the selection of a realistic closing date, including the time period required to obtain regulatory approvals if the Company is in a regulated industry.

2. PURCHASE PRICE

The Purchase Price would be $____________ (subject to adjustment as described below) and would be paid in the following manner:

(a) at the Closing, the Buyer would pay the Sellers the sum of $_____ in cash;

(b) at the Closing, the Buyer would deposit with a mutually acceptable escrow agent the sum of $_______, which would be held in escrow for a period of at least _____ years in order to secure the performance of the Sellers' obligations under the Definitive Agreement and related documents; and

(c) at the Closing, the Buyer would execute and deliver to each Seller an unsecured, non-negotiable, subordinated promissory note. The promissory notes to be delivered to the Sellers by the Buyer would have a combined principal amount of $_______, would bear interest at the rate of ___% per annum, would mature on the _____ anniversary of the Closing, and would provide for _____ equal [annual] [quarterly] payments of principal along with [annual] [quarterly] payments of accrued interest.

The Purchase Price assumes that the Target Companies have consolidated stockholders' equity of at least $____________ as of the Closing. The Purchase Price would be adjusted based on changes in the Target Companies' consolidated stockholders' equity as of the Closing, on a dollar-for-dollar basis.

COMMENT

The inclusion of detailed information regarding the purchase price may trigger disclosure obligations under the federal securities laws if either party is a public company and the acquisition is of a material nature. Sometimes a public company will defer detailed pricing discussions until due diligence is complete to delay the need to make earlier public announcements.

If the Buyer expects to require an escrow or other holdback of a portion of the proposed purchase price, it may be important to include a specific provision to that effect in the Letter of Intent. Often, the Buyer is unable at the letter of intent stage to determine accurately, or to defend, the amount proposed to be escrowed. The Buyer will be better able to determine and to explain to the Sellers the risks of the acquisition following the Buyer's acquisition review. Even if the amount of the escrow or holdback is not yet determined, a statement that one will be required will put the Sellers on notice and should make the negotiation of that issue easier when the terms of the definitive agreement are later discussed. It is often difficult to obtain the Sellers' agreement to an escrow or holdback if the issue has not been discussed prior to the signing of the Letter of Intent and the acquisition review fails to reveal any compelling new reasons for one. See discussion of the escrow holdback in the Commentary to Section 2.4 of the Model Stock Purchase Agreement and the Commentary to the Escrow Agreement.

The Buyer may also want to describe in the Letter of Intent known areas of potential liability, such as environmental clean-up and pending litigation, that will affect the purchase price. By putting the Sellers on notice at an early stage that such liabilities will impact the purchase price, escrowed amount, or other amounts held back, the Buyer's position to negotiate these issues in the definitive agreement should be enhanced.

Purchase price adjustment provisions can include a "window"—a range of closing date stockholders' equity values within which neither party pays a purchase price adjustment amount. Other alternative provisions include "caps," "collars," and "floors." See the Commentary to Section 2.5 of the Model Stock Purchase Agreement for additional discussion regarding these alternative provisions. The parties can also place a portion of the purchase price paid, or funds in excess of the purchase price, in escrow to facilitate payment of the adjustment amount.

3. Employment and Noncompetition Agreements

At the Closing:

(a) the Company and A would enter into a _____-year employment agreement under which A would agree to continue to serve as the Company's [Vice President and Chief Operating Officer] and would be entitled to receive a salary of $_____ per year; and

(b) each Seller would execute a _____-year noncompetition agreement in favor of the Buyer and the Company.

COMMENT

The noncompete provisions may be included within the definitive acquisition agreement or, as provided in this Letter of Intent, as a separate agreement. Paragraph 3 does not contemplate separate consideration for the noncompete covenants. Not long ago, when capital gains rates and ordinary income rates were substantially the same and noncompetition payments were currently deductible, the Buyer would have attempted to allocate an aggressive portion of the total consideration to be paid to the noncompete obligation and the Sellers would generally have had little reason to object. Recent federal tax legislation has substantially reduced the advantages of this strategy.

In drafting the Noncompetition Agreement and the noncompete covenants of the Employment Agreement, care should be taken to ensure that the two are consistent and do not cause unnecessary tax risks. See the Commentary to the Employment Agreement and the Noncompetition Agreement for further discussions of these and other issues.

4. Other Terms

The Sellers would make comprehensive representations and warranties to the Buyer, and would provide comprehensive covenants, indemnities and other protections for the benefit of the Buyer. The consummation of the contemplated transactions by the Buyer would be subject to the satisfaction of various conditions, including:

(a) ____

____.

(b) ____

____.

COMMENT

If they have been addressed in early negotiations, specific representations, warranties, and covenants may be added to Paragraph 4, as well as the survival period of representations and warranties, indemnification limits, and related provisions. The

Buyer will generally prefer to defer discussions regarding these provisions to negotiation of the definitive agreement when its acquisition review of the Company is more advanced and the Sellers' negotiating position may be weaker. The absence of specific provisions in the Letter of Intent, however, may encourage the Sellers to request a full discussion of the representations, warranties and covenants that will be required. Moreover, the Sellers may recognize that the negotiation of the letter of intent affords it an excellent opportunity to establish limits on representations, warranties, and indemnities that may become more difficult to obtain after the letter of intent is signed.

While many of the specific conditions to the acquisition may be omitted from the Letter of Intent and included in the definitive agreement, vital, "deal-breaking" terms and conditions should be included at this stage of the negotiations. If the Letter of Intent gives rise to an obligation to negotiate in good faith, the introduction of new terms and conditions not included in the Letter of Intent may constitute bad faith negotiations. In one extreme example, a Buyer's good faith, albeit unsuccessful, attempt to obtain financing was held to be bad faith negotiating because the letter of intent did not make the acquisition contingent on obtaining financing. *See Bruce v. Marcheson Implementos E. Maquinos Agriculas, Tatu, S.A.* (Civil No. 87-774-A S.D. Iowa 1990) (1990 U.S. Dist. LEXIS 18527).

The Buyer may want to list in Paragraph 4 all conditions precedent to the acquisition that will eventually appear in the definitive agreement to ensure that the Sellers are fully aware at an early stage of what will be required. This level of detail in the letter of intent is probably unnecessary, however. A more reasonable and practical strategy is to include only those conditions that differ from the standard conditions precedent that appear in most acquisition agreements.

Any other key terms or assumptions of the proposed acquisition should be added to Paragraph 4 or elsewhere in the non-binding provisions of Part One.

PART TWO

The following paragraphs of this letter (the "Binding Provisions") are the legally binding and enforceable agreements of the Buyer and each Seller.

1. Access

During the period from the date this letter is signed by the Sellers (the "Signing Date") until the date on which either Party provides the other Party with written notice that negotiations toward a Definitive Agreement are terminated (the "Termination Date"), the Sellers will afford the Buyer full and free access to each Target Company, its personnel, properties, contracts, books and records, and all other documents and data.

COMMENT

Paragraph 1 specifies the Sellers' binding obligation to cooperate in the Buyer's acquisition review investigation. The Sellers must not only provide to the Buyer access to the Company's facilities and books and records, but also secure the cooperation of the Company's personnel. The Sellers may want to cross-reference the confidentiality provision in Paragraph 5 or a pre-existing confidentiality agreement between the parties.

The Sellers may be reluctant to disclose certain information about the Company's customers, marketing strategies, new products, and other sensitive areas until after the definitive agreement is executed or even later. Sometimes staged access to such information is negotiated in the Letter of Intent and other times it is deferred to the definitive agreement.

Because a portion of the purchase price is to be paid with promissory notes, the Sellers may request certain information from and due diligence rights with respect to the Buyer. In most cases, the Buyer may seek to limit its disclosure obligations to financial information and developments that may materially and adversely affect the Buyer's business.

See the Commentary to Paragraph 5 and to the Confidentiality Agreement for a more detailed discussion of provisions designed to protect the confidentiality of information provided in the course of an acquisition review.

2. Exclusive Dealing

Until the later of (i) [90] days after the Signing Date or (ii) the Termination Date:

(a) the Sellers will not and will cause the Target Companies not to, directly or indirectly, through any representative or otherwise, solicit or entertain offers from, negotiate with or in any manner encourage, discuss, accept, or consider any proposal of any other person relating to the acquisition of the Shares or the Target Companies, their assets or business, in whole or in part, whether directly or indirectly, through purchase, merger, consolidation, or otherwise (other than sales of inventory in the ordinary course); and

(b) The Sellers will immediately notify the Buyer regarding any contact between the Sellers, any Target Company or their respective representatives and any other person regarding any such offer or proposal or any related inquiry.

COMMENT

Paragraph 2 restricts the Sellers from soliciting or considering other offers to acquire the target company's business until the Letter of Intent is terminated. This provision is commonly known as a "no-shop" provision and is often the primary goal of the Buyer in entering into a letter of intent. If the target company is a public company, the Sellers may insist on a "fiduciary out" with respect to any exclusivity arrangement. See the Preliminary Note and the Commentary to Section 5.7 of the Model Stock Purchase Agreement for a more detailed discussion of "no shop" provisions and the issues they raise.

Paragraph 2 also provides that the Sellers will immediately notify the Buyer of any third party overture. Such notification should better enable the Buyer to react to a competing offer.

3. Break-up Fee

If (a) the Sellers breach Paragraph 2 or the Sellers provide to the Buyer written notice that negotiations toward a Definitive Agreement are terminated, and (b) within [six] months after the date of such breach or the Termination Date, as the case may be, either Seller or one or more of the Target Companies signs a letter of intent or other agreement relating to the acquisition of a material portion of the Shares or of the Target Companies, their assets, or business, in whole or in part, whether directly or indirectly, through purchase, merger, consolidation, or otherwise (other than sales of inventory or immaterial portions of the Target Companies' assets in the ordinary course) and such transaction is ultimately consummated, then, immediately upon the closing of such transaction, the Sellers will pay, or cause the Target Companies to pay, to the Buyer the sum $_______. This fee will not serve as the exclusive remedy to the Buyer under this letter in the event of a breach by the Sellers of Paragraph 2 of this Part Two or any other of the Binding Provisions, and the Buyer will be entitled to all other rights and remedies provided by law or in equity.

COMMENT

The Buyer will often demand reimbursement of its expenses if the Sellers sell to a competing third party, particularly if the Sellers are unwilling to agree to a "no-shop" provision. In lieu of or in addition to such reimbursement of expenses, the Buyer may also require that the Sellers pay a "break-up" fee or "topping" fee as a reward for the Buyer serving as a "stalking horse," which results in the Sellers receiving a more attractive offer for the target company. Paragraph 3 is an example of a "break-up" fee. A "topping" fee is computed by reference to the amount by which a successful third-party offer exceeds the offer made by the Buyer. These types of fees are unusual in private transactions, generally being limited to public company acquisitions and bankruptcy sales, and the Buyer may face considerable resistance from the Sellers with respect to this type of provision. In the case of a public company seller, courts may refuse to enforce such fees if the size of the fees will unduly impede the ability of third parties to make competing bids. *See Revlon, Inc. v. MacAndrews & Forbes Holdings, Inc.,* 506 A.2d 173 (Del. 1986). Otherwise, such fees should be upheld.

4. Conduct of Business

During the period from the Signing Date until the Termination Date, the Sellers shall cause the Target Companies to operate their business in the ordinary course and to refrain from any extraordinary transactions.

COMMENT

The Buyer will want to restrict the Sellers from shifting assets or otherwise affecting the operations of the Company in a way that may reduce the Company's value before specific provisions are put in place through the signing of a definitive agreement. Paragraph 4 could be modified to require the Sellers only to notify the Buyer *in advance* of any extraordinary transactions or conduct outside the ordinary course of business, thereby providing the Buyer with the opportunity both to learn promptly of such activities and to alert the Sellers if the Buyer believes such activities will have a negative impact on their negotiations toward a definitive agreement. The Sellers may object to these levels of restraint on the operation of the Company's business in the absence of any binding agreement on the terms of a sale or earnest money payments by the Buyer.

In any event, the Buyer should take care not to involve itself too directly in the operation of the Company's business prior to the signing of a definitive agreement. Such involvement may be a factor used by the court to determine that the parties intended the letter of intent to bind them to the proposed acquisition. *See Computer Systems of America, Inc. v. IBM Corp.*, 795 F.2d 1086, 1091 (1st. Cir. 1986). *But see Skycom Corp. v. Telstar Corp.*, 813 F.2d 810 (7th Cir. 1987). Moreover, such involvement could also expose the Buyer to environmental liability for the target company's operations even if the acquisition was never completed.

Paragraph 4 may contain more specific prohibitions or exclusions based on the concerns of the parties.

5. Confidentiality

Except as and to the extent required by law, the Buyer will not disclose or use, and will direct its representatives not to disclose or use to the detriment of the Sellers or the Target Companies, any Confidential Information (as defined below) with respect to the Target Companies furnished, or to be furnished, by either Seller, the Target Companies, or their respective representatives to the Buyer or its representatives at any time or in any manner other than in connection with its evaluation of the transaction proposed in this letter. For purposes of this Paragraph, "Confidential Information" means any information about the Target Companies stamped "confidential" or identified in writing as such to the Buyer by the Sellers promptly following its disclosure, unless (i) such information is already known to the Buyer or its representatives or to others not bound by a duty of confidentiality or such information becomes publicly available through no fault of the Buyer or its representatives, (b) the use of such information is necessary or appropriate in making any filing or obtaining any consent or approval required for the consummation of the Possible Acquisition, or (c) the furnishing or use of such information is required by or necessary or appropriate in connection with legal proceedings. Upon the written request of the Sellers, the Buyer will promptly return to the Sellers or the Target Companies or destroy any Confidential Information in its possession and certify in writing to the Sellers that it has done so.

COMMENT

It is common for the parties to have entered into a confidentiality agreement prior to negotiating a letter of intent. If a confidentiality agreement between the parties was previously entered into and continues in effect, Paragraph 5 can be eliminated or modified to reference the prior agreement and affirm its continuing effectiveness. The Confidentiality Agreement has been prepared from the Sellers' standpoint and should be consulted for a more seller-oriented approach to Paragraph 5 of the Letter of Intent.

If the acquisition involves filings under the Hart-Scott-Rodino Antitrust Improvements Act of 1976, the act of filing itself and all information contained in the filing are confidential and may be disclosed only to Congress and in a judicial or administrative proceeding. However, early termination of the applicable waiting period is published in the Federal Register.

6. Disclosure

Except as and to the extent required by law, without the prior written consent of the other Party, neither the Buyer nor either Seller will, and each will direct its representatives not to make, directly or indirectly, any public comment, statement, or communication with respect to, or otherwise to disclose or to permit the disclosure of the existence of discussions regarding, a possible transaction between the Parties or any of the terms, conditions, or other aspects of the transaction proposed in this letter. If a Party is required by law to make any such disclosure, it must first provide to the other Party the content of the proposed disclosure, the reasons that such disclosure is required by law, and the time and place that the disclosure will be made.

COMMENT

The sensitivity of the parties to the public disclosure of the signing of a letter of intent and its terms will vary based on, among other things, the relative sizes and sophistication of the parties, whether a public company is a party, and the strategic value of the public disclosure to either of the parties. Large, sophisticated parties often prepare "canned" press releases that are distributed upon the signing of a letter of intent. Public companies must comply with certain securities law disclosure requirements, as discussed below. This provision is most often hotly contested when one of the parties has a strategic reason for wanting the public to know about the existence of a possible deal. The Sellers may want to attract competitive bidders for the Company. The Buyer may want to gain an advantage in the marketplace with respect to the Company's customers so that the Sellers' negotiating position and ability to back away from a sale to the Buyer are substantially weakened.

Either party may be required to make disclosures regarding the Letter of Intent and related negotiations. An SEC reporting company may be required to disclose the pending acquisition. *Cf. Basic, Inc. v. Levinson,* 485 U.S. 224, 240 n.17 (1988). In addition, disclosure may be compelled in the course of litigation. Paragraph 6 seeks to limit disclosure to situations in which it is compelled. Moreover, Paragraph 6 requires the parties to inform each other in advance if any such disclosures are to be made.

7. Costs

The Buyer and each Seller will be responsible for and bear all of its own costs and expenses (including any broker's or finder's fees and the expenses of its representatives) incurred at any time in connection with pursuing or consummating the Possible Acquisition. Notwithstanding the preceding sentence, the Buyer will pay one-half and the Sellers will pay one-half of the HSR Act filing fee.

COMMENT

Paragraph 7 establishes how the parties will allocate the legal and other fees and expenses in the transaction and the Hart-Scott-Rodino filing fee prior to the execution of a definitive agreement. The definitive agreement, if one is executed, will generally also include a provision dealing with such fees and expenses.

The Buyer may want to require a sharing arrangement, or otherwise address, the cost of a phase one environmental audit if one will be commenced prior to the execution of a definitive agreement.

8. Consents

During the period from the Signing Date until the Termination Date, the Buyer and each Seller will cooperate with each other and proceed, as promptly as is reasonably practical, to prepare and to file the notifications required by the HSR Act.

COMMENT

Paragraph 8 adds a contractual obligation for both parties to pursue jointly appropriate Hart-Scott-Rodino filings. Such filings will start the clock on the applicable waiting period, thereby reducing the time between the execution of the definitive agreement and the closing of the acquisition. It is important to recognize, however, that a Hart-Scott-Rodino filing will likely trigger public disclosure requirements under the federal securities laws for public corporations.

The parties may also agree to obligate each other to pursue, or at least "test-the-waters," with respect to other vital third-party contingencies that must be met and consents that must be obtained. Care should be taken, however, that such a provision requiring cooperation be drafted so that a court will not interpret a global duty of both parties to negotiate all issues in good faith.

9. Entire Agreement

The Binding Provisions constitute the entire agreement between the parties, and supersede all prior oral or written agreements, understandings, representations and warranties, and courses of conduct and dealing between the parties on the subject matter hereof. Except as otherwise provided herein, the Binding Provisions may be amended or modified only by a writing executed by all of the parties.

COMMENT

Paragraph 9 is intended to prevent any prior writings, understandings, discussions, or conduct from being integrated into the Letter of Intent. If a preexisting confidentiality agreement continues in force and is not to be superseded by later confidentiality provisions, a reference to that agreement should be added to this paragraph.

10. Governing Law

The Binding Provisions will be governed by and construed under the laws of the State of ________________ without regard to conflicts of laws principles.

COMMENT

Choice of law and choice of forum clauses should be enforceable in binding portions of a letter of intent at least to the same extent as they would be in other binding contracts. In choosing the law of a certain jurisdiction, lawyers should be aware of that jurisdiction's case law regarding the enforceability of letters of intent and the pitfalls that must be considered.

11. Jurisdiction: Service of Process

Any action or proceeding seeking to enforce any provision of, or based on any right arising out of, this Letter may be brought against any of the parties in the courts of the State of _____________, County of __________________, or, if it has or can acquire jurisdiction, in the United States District Court for the _____________ District of ____________________, and each of the parties consents to the jurisdiction of such courts (and of the appropriate appellate courts) in any such action or proceeding and waives any objection to venue laid therein. Process in any action or proceeding referred to in the preceding sentence may be served on any party anywhere in the world.

12. Termination

The Binding Provisions will automatically terminate on _______, 19___ and may be terminated earlier upon written notice by either party to the other party unilaterally, for any reason or no reason, with or without cause, at any time; provided, however, that the termination of the Binding Provisions will not affect the liability of a party for breach of any of the Binding Provisions prior to the termination. Upon termination of the Binding Provisions, the parties will have no further obligations hereunder, except as stated in Paragraphs 2, 3, 5, 7, 9, 10, 11, 12, 13 and 14 of this Part Two, which will survive any such termination.

COMMENT

The Buyer should be careful to avoid a one-sided termination provision that may lead to a demand by the Sellers that the parties agree to negotiate in good faith toward the execution of a definitive agreement. This type of provision has its dangers. Some commentators have suggested that the inclusion of a good faith requirement in the binding provisions may encourage a court to construe a binding element to the nonbinding provisions as well. *See* Farnsworth, *Precontractual Liability and Preliminary Agreements: Fair Dealing and Failed Negotiations*, 87 Columbia L. Rev. 217 (1987). Accordingly, it may be advisable (as has been done in the Letter of Intent) to avoid the good faith requirement language and rely on a "break-up" or "topping" fee or some other protection for the Buyer against the Sellers' bad faith.

The Buyer may be uncomfortable with the Sellers having the ability to terminate at any time the Letter of Intent and their obligations to negotiate a definitive agreement. Consequently, the Buyer may want to eliminate or greatly restrict the Sellers' ability to terminate unilaterally their obligations under the Letter of Intent even at the risk of the Sellers making reciprocal demands with respect to the Buyer's right to terminate its obligations under the Letter of Intent or of a court imputing, as a result of limited termination rights, an obligation that the parties negotiate in good faith toward a definitive agreement.

13. Counterparts

This Letter may be executed in one or more counterparts, each of which will be deemed to be an original copy of this Letter and all of which, when taken together, will be deemed to constitute one and the same agreement.

14. No Liability

The paragraphs and provisions of Part One of this letter do not constitute and will not give rise to any legally binding obligation on the part of any of the Parties or any of the Target Companies. Moreover, except as expressly provided in the Binding Provisions (or as expressly provided in any binding written agreement that the Parties may enter into in the future), no past or future action, course of conduct, or failure to act relating to the Possible Acquisition, or relating to the negotiation of the terms of the Possible Acquisition or any Definitive Agreement, will give rise to or serve as a basis for any obligation or other liability on the part of the Parties or any of the Target Companies.

COMMENT

Paragraph 15 makes it clear that the parties do not intend to create a legally binding obligation at this time with respect to the provisions of Part One. A clear expression of this intent is desirable and, as noted in the Preliminary Note, courts have on occasion not given less precise words the same effect. For example, some cases have held language that the letter of intent is "subject to" a definitive agreement merely states a condition subsequent rather than the requisite intent not to be bound. *See, e.g., Computer Systems of America, Inc. v. IBM Corp.*, 795 F.2d 1086 (1st Cir. 1986); *Teachers Insurance & Annuity Association v. Tribune Co.*, 670 F. Supp. 491 (S.D.N.Y. 1987); *Texaco, Inc. v. Pennzoil Co.*, 729 S.W.2d 768 (Tex. Ct. App. 1987), *cert. denied*, 485 U.S. 994 (1988). Other cases have found a binding obligation to negotiate in good faith from this "subject to" language. *See Teachers Insurance & Annuity Ass'n.*, 670 F. Supp. at 491. The phrase "no past or future action, course of conduct or failure to act relating to the Possible Acquisition . . . will give rise to or serve as a basis for any obligation or other liability on the part of any of the Parties or any of the Target Companies" is an attempt to remove the possibility that oral communications or other actions can give rise to a binding obligation. The broad exculpatory language to relieve parties of any liability should the other party claim that the nonbinding provisions are binding is intended to allow a party to withdraw from the acquisition at any stage prior to the execution of a definitive acquisition agreement. Notwithstanding this precise language regarding future conduct and lack of liability, a court may give effect to oral communications and other actions in interpreting the intent of the parties. See discussion in the Preliminary Note.

If you are in agreement with the foregoing, please sign and return one copy of this letter agreement, which thereupon will constitute our agreement with respect to its subject matter.

Very truly yours,

BUYER:

By: ______________________________

Name: ________________________

Title: _________________________

Duly executed and agreed as to the Binding Provisions on _________, 199__.

PROSPECTIVE SELLERS:

____

____

COMMENT

The signatures are intended only to indicate agreement to the binding provisions and preserves the argument that the signatories never intended to be bound by the nonbinding provisions of Part One.

APPENDICES

Appendix A

Nine Hypothetical Scenarios

The following hypothetical scenarios illustrate the operation and interaction of:

- the Sellers' representations in Section 3 of the Model Stock Purchase Agreement;
- the Sellers' pre-closing covenant in Section 5.5 of the Model Stock Purchase Agreement (which contemplates the delivery of supplements to the Sellers' disclosure letter);
- the closing condition in Section 7.1(a) of the Model Stock Purchase Agreement (relating to the accuracy of the Sellers' representations); and
- the indemnification provisions in Section 10 of the Model Stock Purchase Agreement.

Each of the hypothetical scenarios is based upon a lawsuit brought by a third party against the Company prior to the scheduled closing date. In scenarios 1 through 4, it is assumed that the lawsuit is brought *before* the acquisition agreement is signed, while in scenarios 5 through 9, it is assumed that the lawsuit is brought *after* the acquisition agreement is signed. Various assumptions are also made about whether the lawsuit is "material" and about when the lawsuit is first disclosed to the Buyer.

In each scenario, it is assumed that:

- the Company received no threat of litigation before the lawsuit was brought;
- the lawsuit does not relate to any product manufactured by the Company or any other matter covered by the express indemnities in Sections 10.2(d), 10.2(e), and 10.2(f) of the Model Stock Purchase Agreement;

- except for inaccuracies resulting from the lawsuit, there are no inaccuracies in the Sellers' representations as of the signing date or as of the scheduled closing date;
- the Sellers have used their best efforts to cause the Company to settle the lawsuit prior to the scheduled closing date and have otherwise complied fully with their pre-closing covenants in the acquisition agreement; and
- all of the conditions to the Buyer's obligation to consummate the acquisition are satisfied in full as of the scheduled closing date, except to the extent that the lawsuit results in a failure to satisfy the closing condition in Section 7.1(a) of the Model Stock Purchase Agreement.

With respect to each scenario, two key questions are posed:

1. ***Can the Buyer refuse to consummate the acquisition without liability to the Sellers (in other words, does the Buyer have a "walk right")?***
2. ***If the Buyer proceeds with the acquisition, will the Sellers be required to indemnify the Buyer and the Company with respect to the lawsuit?***

In addition, in scenarios in which the Buyer has a "walk right" as a result of the lawsuit and elects to exercise that "walk right" (by terminating the acquisition), it is appropriate to pose a further question—*Can the Buyer nonetheless recover damages from the Sellers and the Company by reason of the lawsuit (in other words, can the Buyer "walk and sue")?*

The answers to these questions are of considerable importance to the parties. Accordingly, it is vital that the parties' attorneys fully understand the complex interaction between the various provisions of the Model Stock Purchase Agreement bearing on these questions.

For additional discussions of the issues addressed in this Appendix, see the Commentary to Section 2.4 of the Model Stock Purchase Agreement under the caption "Sellers' Closing Certificate"; the Commentary to Section 5.5 of the Model Stock Purchase Agreement; the Commentary to Section 7.1 of the Model Stock Purchase Agreement under the captions "Time as of Which Accuracy of Representations Is Determined," "Effect of Disclosure Letter Supplements," and "Supplemental 'Bring Down' Representation"; and the Commentary to Sections 10.1 and 10.2 of the Model Stock Purchase Agreement.

SCENARIO #1

(material pre-signing development disclosed in original disclosure letter)

Assumed Facts:

- A few days *before* the signing of the acquisition agreement, a material lawsuit is brought against the Company.
- The Sellers disclose the lawsuit in their disclosure letter (which is furnished to the Buyer at the time the agreement is signed).
- The lawsuit is not settled and remains pending on the scheduled closing date.

1. ***Can the Buyer refuse to consummate the acquisition (i.e., does the Buyer have a "walk right")?***
   NO. Because the lawsuit was disclosed in the disclosure letter at the time of the signing of the agreement, the Sellers' "absence of litigation" representation in Section 3.15(a) was accurate as of the signing date and remains accurate as of the scheduled closing date. Thus, the condition in each of the two clauses in Section 7.1(a) is satisfied and the Buyer does not have a "walk right."
2. ***Will the Sellers be required to indemnify the Buyer and the Company against any damages arising from the lawsuit?***
   NO. Because the lawsuit was disclosed in the disclosure letter, the Sellers' "absence of litigation" representation was accurate as of the signing date, and the representation remains accurate as "brought down" to the closing date. Thus, neither the agreement nor the Sellers' closing certificate contains an inaccurate representation, and the Sellers will have no indemnification obligation under clause (a) or clause (b) of Section 10.2 with respect to the lawsuit.

SCENARIO #2

(material pre-signing development not disclosed in original disclosure letter, but disclosed before closing in supplement to disclosure letter)

Assumed Facts:

- A few days *before* the signing of the acquisition agreement, a material lawsuit is brought against the Company.

- The Sellers neglect to disclose the lawsuit in their original disclosure letter (which is furnished to the Buyer at the time the agreement is signed). The Sellers subsequently disclose the lawsuit in a supplement delivered to the Buyer (pursuant to Section 5.5) a few days after the signing of the agreement.
- The lawsuit is not settled and remains pending on the scheduled closing date.

1. ***Can the Buyer refuse to consummate the acquisition (i.e., does the Buyer have a "walk right")?***

   YES. Because the lawsuit was not disclosed in the Sellers' original disclosure letter, and because the lawsuit is material, the Sellers' "absence of litigation" representation in Section 3.15(a) was materially inaccurate as of the signing date. Thus, the condition in the first clause of Section 7.1(a) is not satisfied, and the Buyer has a "walk right." (Under Section 7.1(a), no effect is given to the supplement to the Sellers' disclosure letter for purposes of determining the accuracy of the Sellers' representations.)

   Note that, if the Buyer elects to exercise its "walk right" in these circumstances, the Buyer may also recover damages from the Sellers for their breach of the "absence of litigation" representation as of the signing date (in other words, the Buyer may "walk and sue").

2. ***If the Buyer proceeds with the acquisition, will the Sellers be required to indemnify the Buyer and the Company against any damages arising from the lawsuit?***

   YES (subject to the "basket" described in Section 10.6). Under clause (a) of Section 10.2, the Sellers are required to indemnify the Buyer and the Company against all damages suffered as a result of any inaccuracy in the Sellers' representations. Because the Sellers' "absence of litigation" representation was inaccurate as of the signing date, the Sellers will be required to indemnify the Buyer and the Company with respect to the lawsuit. (Under Section 10.2(a), no effect is given to the supplement to the Sellers' disclosure letter for purposes of determining the accuracy of the Sellers' representations.)

   Note that, under the terms of clause (a) of Section 10.2, the Buyer retains its post-closing indemnification right even though the Buyer was advised of the lawsuit before the closing and had the right to refuse to proceed with the acquisition. In other words, the Buyer is expressly permitted to "close and sue." It is possible, however, that (notwithstanding the unambiguous language in Section 10.2(a)) the Sellers may attempt to argue that the cases discussed in the Commentary to Section 10.1 effectively override the Buyer's right to "close and sue" in this situation.

SCENARIO #3

(material pre-signing development not disclosed in original disclosure letter, but "cured" before closing)

Assumed Facts:

- A few days *before* the signing of the acquisition agreement, a material lawsuit is brought against the Company.
- The Sellers neglect to disclose the lawsuit in their original disclosure letter (which is furnished to the Buyer at the time the agreement is signed). The Sellers subsequently disclose the lawsuit in a supplement delivered to the Buyer (pursuant to Section 5.5) a few days after the signing of the agreement.
- Before the closing, the Company settles the lawsuit by making a cash payment to the plaintiff. The settlement payment will be taken into account in calculating the purchase price adjustment under Section 2.5.

1. ***Can the Buyer refuse to consummate the acquisition (i.e., does the Buyer have a "walk right")?***
   YES. Because the lawsuit was not disclosed in the Sellers' original disclosure letter, and because the lawsuit is material, the Sellers' "absence of litigation" representation in Section 3.15(a) was materially inaccurate as of the signing date. Thus, the condition in the first clause of Section 7.1(a) is not satisfied, and the Buyer has a "walk right." (Under Section 7.1(a), no effect is given to the supplement to the Sellers' disclosure letter for purposes of determining the accuracy of the Sellers' representation.

   Note that, although the Sellers' "absence of litigation" representation is accurate *as of the closing date* due to the settlement of the lawsuit, the Buyer nonetheless has a "walk right" under the Model Stock Purchase Agreement in this situation.

Note also that, if the Buyer elects to exercise its "walk right" in these circumstances, the Buyer may also seek to recover damages from the Sellers for their breach of the "absence of litigation" representation as of the signing date (in other words, the Buyer may "walk and sue"). However, in light of the settlement of the lawsuit before the closing, there may be some question whether the Buyer has actually suffered any damages as a result of the Sellers' initial failure to disclose the lawsuit (see below).

2. ***If the Buyer proceeds with the acquisition, will the Sellers be required to indemnify the Buyer and the Company with respect to the lawsuit?***

   NO. Under Section 10.2(a), the Sellers are required to indemnify the Buyer and the Company against all damages suffered as a result of any inaccuracy in the Sellers' "absence of litigation" representation. This representation was inaccurate as of the signing date. However, because the lawsuit has been settled, and because under Section 2.5 there will be a reduction in the purchase price to reflect the amount of the settlement payment made by the Company, neither the Buyer nor the Company will suffer any damages as a result of the lawsuit. Thus, the Sellers will not be required to make any indemnification payment under Section 10.2 with respect to the lawsuit.

SCENARIO #4

(immaterial pre-signing development not disclosed in original disclosure letter, but disclosed before closing in supplement to disclosure letter)

Assumed Facts:

- A few days *before* the signing of the acquisition agreement, a lawsuit is brought against the Company. The lawsuit is not "material"—the Company's anticipated liability in the lawsuit is relatively small.
- The Sellers neglect to disclose the lawsuit in their original disclosure letter (which is furnished to the Buyer at the time the agreement is signed). The Sellers subsequently disclose the lawsuit in a supplement delivered to the Buyer (pursuant to Section 5.5) a few days after the signing of the agreement.

- The lawsuit is not settled and remains pending on the scheduled closing date.

1. ***Can the Buyer refuse to consummate the acquisition (i.e., does the Buyer have a "walk right")?***
   NO. Because the lawsuit is not material, the Sellers' "absence of litigation" representation in Section 3.15(a) was accurate as of the signing date in all *material* respects and is likewise accurate as of the closing date in all *material* respects. Thus, the condition in each clause of Section 7.1(a) is satisfied, and the Buyer must proceed with the closing.
2. ***Will the Sellers be required to indemnify the Buyer and the Company after the closing against any damages arising from the lawsuit?***
   YES (subject to the "basket" described in Section 10.6). Under clause (a) of Section 10.2, the Sellers are required to indemnify the Buyer and the Company against all damages suffered as a result of *any* inaccuracy (even an immaterial inaccuracy) in the Sellers' representations. Because the Sellers' "absence of litigation" representation was inaccurate as of the signing date, the Sellers will be obligated under Section 10.2(a) to indemnify the Buyer and the Company with respect to the lawsuit. Under Section 10.2(a), no effect is given to the supplement to the Sellers' disclosure letter for purposes of determining the accuracy of the Sellers' representations.

SCENARIO #5

(material post-signing development disclosed before closing in supplement to disclosure letter)

Assumed Facts:

- A few days *after* the signing of the acquisition agreement, a material lawsuit is brought against the Company.
- The Sellers disclose the lawsuit in a disclosure letter supplement delivered to the Buyer (pursuant to Section 5.5) promptly after the commencement of the lawsuit.
- The lawsuit is not settled and remains pending on the scheduled closing date.
- In the "bring down" certificate delivered by the Sellers to the Buyer on the scheduled closing date (in accordance with Sec-

tion 2.4(a)(v)), the Sellers expressly state that the commencement of the material lawsuit has caused the condition in Section 7.1(a) not to be satisfied.

1. ***Can the Buyer refuse to consummate the acquisition (i.e., does the Buyer have a "walk right")?***
   YES. Because a material lawsuit that was not disclosed in the original disclosure letter is pending against the Company on the scheduled closing date, the Sellers' "absence of litigation" representation in Section 3.15(a) is inaccurate as "brought down" to the closing date. Thus, the "bring down" condition in the second clause of Section 7.1(a) is not satisfied, and the Buyer has a "walk right." (Under Section 7.1(a), no effect is given to the supplement to the Sellers' disclosure letter for purposes of determining the accuracy of the Sellers' representations.) The Sellers have conceded in their "bring down" certificate that the condition in Section 7.1(a) has not been satisfied and thus have effectively eliminated any post-closing indemnification obligations they might otherwise have with respect to the lawsuit (see below).
2. ***If the Buyer proceeds with the acquisition, will the Sellers be required to indemnify the Buyer and the Company against any damages arising from the lawsuit?***
   NO. Under clause (a) of Section 10.2, the Sellers are required to indemnify the Buyer and the Company against any damages resulting from inaccuracies in the Sellers' representations as of the signing date. The Sellers' "absence of litigation" representation in Section 3.15(a) was accurate as of the signing date because the lawsuit was not pending on the signing date. Thus, the Sellers will have no indemnification obligation under Section 10.2(a) with respect to the lawsuit.

   Under clause (b) of Section 10.2, the Sellers are required to indemnify the Buyer and the Company against any damages resulting from inaccuracies in the Sellers' representations as "brought down" to the closing date. However, Section 10.2(b) expressly provides that, for purposes of determining the Sellers' indemnification obligations, any matters disclosed in a disclosure letter supplement *are* to be taken into account if the Sellers' "bring down" certificate (delivered pursuant to Section 2.4(a)(v)) specifically identifies the disclosed matters "as having caused the condition specified in Section 7.1 not to be satisfied." Because the "bring down" certificate expressly states that the lawsuit has caused the condition in Section 7.1(a) not to be satisfied, the disclosure of the lawsuit in the disclosure letter supplement *is* given effect. Therefore, for purposes of clause (b) of Section 10.2, the Sellers' "absence of litigation" representation (as qualified by the disclosure of the lawsuit in the supplement to the disclosure letter) is deemed to be accurate as "brought down" to the closing date, and the Sellers will have no indemnification obligation under that clause with respect to the lawsuit.

SCENARIO #6

(material post-signing development "cured" before closing)

Assumed Facts:

- A few days *after* the signing of the acquisition agreement, a material lawsuit is brought against the Company.
- The Sellers disclose the lawsuit in a disclosure letter supplement delivered to the Buyer (pursuant to Section 5.5) promptly after the commencement of the lawsuit.
- Before the closing, the Company settles the lawsuit by making a cash payment to the plaintiff. The settlement payment will be taken into account in calculating the purchase price adjustment under Section 2.5.

1. ***Can the Buyer refuse to consummate the acquisition (i.e., does the Buyer have a "walk right")?***
   NO. Because the lawsuit was not pending when the agreement was signed, the Sellers' "absence of litigation" representation in Section 3.15(a) was accurate as of the signing date. Thus, the condition in the first clause of Section 7.1(a) is satisfied. Likewise, because the lawsuit is not pending on the closing date, the "absence of litigation" representation is accurate as "brought down" to the closing date. Thus, the "bring down" condition in the second clause of Section 7.1(a) is also satisfied. Therefore, the Buyer has no "walk right" and must proceed with the closing. (If the Sellers had neglected to disclose the lawsuit on a timely basis in a disclosure letter supplement, they would have breached their pre-closing notification covenant in Section 5.5, and the Buyer arguably would have a

"walk right" under Section 7.2(a) as well as a right to recover damages from the Sellers for their breach of the notification covenant.)

2. ***Will the Sellers be required to indemnify the Buyer and the Company after the closing against any damages arising from the lawsuit?***
NO. Because the lawsuit was not pending when the agreement was signed, the Sellers' "absence of litigation" representation was accurate as of the signing date. Likewise, because the lawsuit is not pending on the closing date, the "absence of litigation" representation is accurate as "brought down" to the closing date. Thus, the Sellers will have no indemnification obligation under clause (a) or (b) of Section 10.2 with respect to the lawsuit.

SCENARIO #7

(material post-signing development not disclosed in supplement to disclosure letter)

Assumed Facts:

- A few days *after* the signing of the acquisition agreement, a material lawsuit is brought against the Company.
- The Sellers neglect to disclose the lawsuit in a supplement to their disclosure letter.
- The lawsuit is not settled and remains pending on the scheduled closing date.

1. ***Can the Buyer refuse to consummate the acquisition (i.e., does the Buyer have a "walk right")?***
YES. Because a material lawsuit that was not disclosed in the original disclosure letter is pending on the closing date, the Sellers' "absence of litigation" representation in Section 3.15(a) is materially inaccurate as "brought down" to the closing date. Thus, the "bring down" condition in the second clause of Section 7.1(a) is not satisfied, and the Buyer has a "walk right." By neglecting to disclose the material lawsuit in a disclosure letter supplement, the Sellers have breached their pre-closing notification covenant in Section 5.5; therefore, the Buyer may also have a "walk right" under Section 7.2(a) and

may also be able to recover damages from the Sellers for their breach of the notification covenant.

2. ***If the Buyer proceeds with the acquisition, will the Sellers be required to indemnify the Buyer and the Company against any damages arising from the lawsuit?***
   YES (subject to the "basket" described in Section 10.6). Under clause (b) of Section 10.2, the Sellers are required to indemnify the Buyer and the Company against all damages suffered as a result of any inaccuracy in the Sellers' representations as "brought down" to the closing date. Because the Sellers' "absence of litigation" representation is inaccurate as of the closing date, the Sellers will be required under Section 10.2(b) to indemnify the Buyer and the Company with respect to the lawsuit. However, if the Buyer independently learned of the lawsuit before the closing date, then (notwithstanding the unambiguous language in Section 10.2(b)) the Sellers may attempt to argue that the cases discussed in the Commentary to Section 10.1 effectively override the Buyer's right to "close and sue."

SCENARIO #8

(immaterial post-signing development not disclosed in supplement to disclosure letter)

Assumed Facts:

- A few days *after* the signing of the acquisition agreement, a lawsuit is brought against the Company. The lawsuit is not "material"—the Company's anticipated liability in the lawsuit is relatively small.
- The Sellers neglect to disclose the lawsuit in a supplement to their disclosure letter.
- The lawsuit is not settled and remains pending on the scheduled closing date.

1. ***Can the Buyer refuse to consummate the acquisition (i.e., does the Buyer have a "walk right")?***
   NO. Because the lawsuit was not pending when the agreement was signed, the Sellers' "absence of litigation" representation in Section 3.15(a) was accurate as of the signing date. Thus, the condition in the first clause of Section 7.1(a) is satisfied. Because the lawsuit is not material, the "absence of litigation"

representation is accurate as of the scheduled closing date in all material respects, and the "bring down" condition in the second clause of Section 7.1(a) is also satisfied. Therefore, the Buyer has no "walk right" and must proceed with the closing.

The Sellers' failure to disclose the lawsuit in a disclosure letter supplement is a breach of their pre-closing notification covenant in Section 5.5. However, because the lawsuit is not material, this covenant has been complied with in all material respects. Therefore, the Buyer has no "walk right" under Section 7.2(a).

2. ***Will the Sellers be required to indemnify the Buyer and the Company after the closing against any damages arising from the lawsuit?***

   YES (subject to the "basket" described in Section 10.6). Under clause (b) of Section 10.2, the Sellers are required to indemnify the Buyer and the Company against all damages suffered as a result of *any* inaccuracy (even an immaterial inaccuracy) in the Sellers' representations as "brought down" to the closing date. Because the Sellers' "absence of litigation" representation in the closing certificate is inaccurate as of the closing date, the Sellers will be required under Section 10.2(b) to indemnify the Buyer and the Company with respect to the lawsuit. However, if the Buyer independently learned of the lawsuit before the closing date, then (notwithstanding the unambiguous language in Section 10.2(b)) the Sellers may attempt to argue that the cases discussed in the Commentary to Section 10.1 effectively override the Buyer's right to "close and sue."

SCENARIO #9

(immaterial post-signing development disclosed before closing in supplement to disclosure letter)

Assumed Facts:

- A few days *after* the signing of the acquisition agreement, a lawsuit is brought against the Company. The lawsuit is not "material"—the Company's anticipated liability in the lawsuit is relatively small.
- The Sellers disclose the lawsuit in a disclosure letter supplement delivered to the Buyer (pursuant to Section 5.5) promptly after the commencement of the lawsuit.

- The lawsuit is not settled and remains pending on the scheduled closing date.
- Because the lawsuit is not material, the Sellers do *not* include a statement in their "bring down" certificate to the effect that the condition specified in Section 7.1 has not been satisfied.

1. ***Can the Buyer refuse to consummate the acquisition (i.e., does the Buyer have a "walk right")?***
NO. Because the lawsuit was not pending when the agreement was signed, the Sellers' "absence of litigation" representation in Section 3.15(a) was accurate as of the signing date. Thus, the condition in the first clause of Section 7.1(a) is satisfied. Because the lawsuit is not material, the "absence of litigation" representation is accurate as of the closing date in all material respects, and the "bring down" condition in the second clause of Section 7.1(a) is also satisfied. Therefore, the Buyer has no "walk right" and must proceed with the closing.
2. ***Will the Sellers be required to indemnify the Buyer and the Company after the closing against any damages arising from the lawsuit?***
YES (subject to the "basket" described in Section 10.6). Under clause (b) of Section 10.2, the Sellers are required to indemnify the Buyer and the Company against any damages resulting from *any* inaccuracy (even an immaterial inaccuracy) in the Sellers' representations as "brought down" to the closing date. Clause (b) of Section 10.2 provides that the determination of the accuracy of the Sellers' representations as of the closing date is to be made *without giving effect to any supplement to the disclosure letter*, unless the "bring down" certificate delivered pursuant to Section 2.4(a)(v) expressly states that the matters disclosed in a supplement have caused the condition specified in Section 7.1 not to be satisfied. Because the "bring down" certificate does not state that the lawsuit has caused the condition in Section 7.1 not to be satisfied, the disclosure of the lawsuit in the disclosure letter supplement is not given effect. Therefore, for purposes of Section 10.2(b), the "absence of litigation" representation is deemed to be inaccurate as "brought down" to the closing date and the Sellers will be required to indemnify the Buyer and the Company with respect to the lawsuit.

APPENDIX A
HYPOTHETICAL SCENARIOS ILLUSTRATING THE EFFECT OF A LAWSUIT AGAINST THE COMPANY ON THE BUYER'S "WALK RIGHTS" AND INDEMNIFICATION RIGHTS

	Scenario #1	**Scenario #2**	**Scenario #3**	**Scenario #4**	**Scenario #5**	**Scenario #6**	**Scenario #7**	**Scenario #8**	**Scenario #9**
Was the lawsuit brought before the signing of the stock purchase agreement?	*Yes*—brought *before* signing	*Yes*—brought *before* signing	*Yes*—brought *before* signing	*Yes*—brought *before* signing	*No*—brought *after* signing	*No*—brought *after* signing	No—brought *after* signing	*No*—brought *after* signing	*No*—brought *after* signing
Was the lawsuit disclosed in the original version of the Sellers' disclosure letter?	*Yes*—disclosed in original DL	*No*—not disclosed in original DL	*No*—not disclosed in original DL	*No*—not disclosed in original DL	*Not applicable* (lawsuit not yet brought)	*Not applicable* (lawsuit not yet brought)	*Not applicable* (lawsuit not yet brought)	*Not applicable* (lawsuit not yet brought)	*Not applicable* (lawsuit not yet brought)
Was the lawsuit disclosed in a supplement to the Sellers' disclosure letter?	*Not applicable* (lawsuit already disclosed in original DL)	*Yes*—disclosed in supplement	*Yes*—disclosed in supplement	*Yes*—disclosed in supplement	*Yes*—disclosed in supplement	*Yes*—disclosed in supplement	*No*—not disclosed in supplement	*No*—not disclosed in supplement	*Yes*—disclosed in supplement
Was the lawsuit "material" at the time of the signing of the stock purchase agreement?	*Yes*—material as of signing	*Yes*—material as of signing	*Yes*—material as of signing	*No*—not material as of signing	*Not applicable* (lawsuit not yet brought)	*Not applicable* (lawsuit not yet brought)	*Not applicable* (lawsuit not yet brought)	*Not applicable* (lawsuit not yet brought)	*Not applicable* (lawsuit not yet brought)
Was the lawsuit settled prior to the scheduled closing date?	*No*—not settled	*No*—not settled	*Yes*—settled	*No*—not settled	*No*—not settled	*Yes*—settled	*No*—not settled	*No*—not settled	*No*—not settled
Is the lawsuit "material" as of the scheduled closing date?	*Yes*—material as of closing date	*Yes*—material as of closing date	*No*—not material as of closing date (lawsuit previously settled)	*No*—not material as of closing date	*Yes*—material as of closing date	*No*—not material as of closing date (lawsuit previously settled)	*Yes*—material as of closing date	*No*—not material as of closing date	*No*—not material as of closing date
"WALK RIGHT"—Can the buyer refuse to close because of the lawsuit?	**NO**	**YES**	**YES**	**NO**	**YES**	**NO**	**YES**	**NO**	**NO**
INDEMNIFICATION RIGHT—If the closing occurs, are the buyer and the company entitled to be indemnified by the sellers (subject to any applicable "basket") against any damages arising from the lawsuit?	**NO**	**YES**	**NO** (no indemnifiable damages)	**YES**	**NO**	**NO**	**YES**	**YES**	**YES**

Appendix B

Reporter's Note to the Model Stock Purchase Agreement*

The Model Stock Purchase Agreement distills and expands on the current practice of buyers' lawyers in stock acquisitions of private companies. In the initial negotiating draft of such agreements, able buyers' lawyers craft language that aids in pricing an acquisition and that locks in benefits as priced. A buyer's initial negotiating draft requires disclosure of information that may be material to the price, explicitly allocates the risk of any contingent liabilities, and prescribes remedies for failed conditions and breached representations and warranties. The language of such a document, like the work of a master artisan, is necessarily specialized, self-defining, interwoven, and complex and demands the careful attention of lawyers on both sides of the transaction.

The drafters of a well-crafted agreement generally aim to minimize judicial involvement in the interpretation of the agreement's express language (as opposed to, for example, the necessary involvement of a judge in factual disagreements).[1] Courts will respect the plain meaning of an agreement's language unless the written contract's terms are ambiguous.[2] If a court finds that an identified term is ambiguous, the court will admit contemporaneous extrinsic evidence of the parties'

*By Dale Arthur Oesterle, Monfort Professor of Commercial Law, University of Colorado.

[1]Sometimes, however, a party purposefully chooses ambiguous language over clear language in the belief that the clear language is disadvantageous to that party and the ambiguous language will give it a chance for a more favorable interpretation. For an example of very capable attorneys adopting this approach (and failing), see Mesa Partners v. Phillips Petroleum Co., 488 A.2d 107 (Del. Ch. Ct. 1984) (interpreting a standstill agreement).

[2]Galli v. Metz, 973 F.2d 145, 152-54 (2d Cir. 1992) (applying the plain meaning rule to purchase price adjustment language).

understanding on the meaning of the contested term.[3] If the extrinsic evidence is conflicting, the court may resort to maxims of construction, tempered by the professionalism evident in an acquisition agreement.[4] For example, it is hornbook law that a court choosing between various reasonable meanings of a disputed term may prefer the meaning that operates against the drafting party,[5] but at least one court has refused to apply the anti-drafter maxim in an acquisition agreement because the parties were sophisticated.[6] On the other hand, if the parties show that they attached different meanings to a given term at the time of the contract's execution, courts may accept the interpretation of the party who did not know (or did not have reason to know) of any different meaning attached by the other party if the other party knew (or had reason to know) of the meaning attached by the first.[7]

There are, however, limits to what attorneys can accomplish with even the most thorough and detailed of documents. The most obvious limit is the capacity of general jurisdiction judges to understand and appropriately enforce stock acquisition documents when confronted with subsequent disputes. The now routine complexity of acquisition documents augments the risk that judges may not interpret them in accordance with the understandings of the parties who signed them.[8] If the risk of judicial error becomes substantial, parties may want to investigate alternative dispute resolution mechanisms that guarantee a sophisticated decision maker who understands these transactions.

---

[3]*See id.* at 149, 153 (ambiguity in a "bring down" condition and a price adjustment provision for aged accounts receivables); *see also* Money Point Diamond Corp. v. Jacobson, 1993 U.S. App. Lexis 18845 (4th Cir. July 23, 1993) (extrinsic evidence admitted to interpret an indemnification clause in an asset sale); Armco, Inc. v. Glenfed Fin. Corp. (Armco II), 746 F. Supp. 1249, 1255-56 (D.N.J. 1990) (interpreting an indemnification "basket").

[4]*Cf.* Galli, 973 F.2d at 149 (in a stock acquisition, interpreting ambiguous language so that other clauses are not rendered "superfluous or meaningless").

[5]*See* Restatement, (Second) of Contracts ("Restatement") § 206 (1986).

[6]*See* Nunn v. Chemical Waste Management, Inc., 856 F.2d 1464, 1469 (10th Cir. 1988) (involving a dispute over an environmental warranty).

[7]*See* Restatement § 201(2); *cf.* Armco, Inc. v. Glenfed Fin. Corp. (Armco I), 720 F. Supp. 1129, 1152-53 (D.N.J. 1989) (making a similar argument based on estoppel).

[8]*Cf.* Galli, 973 F.2d at 149 (holding that the failure of a condition to "all obligations of Buyers" that "all representations and warranties . . . shall be true and correct when made and as of the closing" did not suspend the buyer's obligation to pay on promissory notes that were part of the purchase price because the agreement also contained a clause on setoffs); Delta Holdings, Inc. v. National Distillers & Chemical Corp, 945 F.2d 1226 (2d Cir. 1991), *cert. denied,* 112 S. Ct. 1671 (1992) (discounting a representation on overall compliance with GAAP with respect to a line item omitted from the representations covering specific line items).

Another limit to contract detail is the parties' inability to reduce important terms of an agreement to well-defined written obligations because of intricate or uncertain future contingencies. Drafting definitive contractual language may be impractical because of the parties' inability to identify uncertain future conditions or because of their inability to characterize complex adaptions when the contingencies can be identified in advance. In these situations, the parties may create "relational" contracts and rely on broad provisions requiring, for example, "good faith and fair dealing" (which are implied in all contracts even if not expressly included), "best efforts," or "material" performance.[9] Open-ended contract terms rely essentially on the parties' stake in their business reputation and on their underlying sense of business values and ethics.[10] When these restraints fail, such terms give substantial discretion to the sensibilities of enforcing courts.

The Model Stock Purchase Agreement, of necessity, explicitly uses several open-ended concepts, including "materiality," "best efforts," and "ordinary course of business." Moreover, the Model Stock Purchase Agreement contains, as a matter of law, a duty of good faith and fair dealing.[11] In stock acquisitions, the time for performance is extended from the signing of the agreement to the closing (and occasionally thereafter), and the duties owed by both parties in this interim period can be complex and contingent. Parties can cover some future adaptations to contingent events only by general language based essentially on an obligation of bona fides. Particularity in these circumstances may simply not be possible and, if attempted, may be

---

[9]*See, e.g.*, Armco I, 720 F. Supp. at 1138 n.16 (applying an implied duty of good faith to an acquisition agreement). *See generally* Charles J. Goetz & Robert Scott, *Principles of Relational Contracts*, 67 Va. L. Rev. 1089 (1981); Robert Summers, *Good Faith in General Contract Law and the Sales Provisions of the Uniform Commercial Code*, 54 Va. L. Rev. 195 (1968).

Courts are tested when parties execute agreements with general language that pre-date substantial regulatory changes. The cases are hopelessly in conflict on whether standard "as is," indemnity or hold harmless clauses, executed in transactions closed before Congress passed CERCLA in 1980, allocate responsibility between the parties for CERCLA cleanup costs. Some courts answered in the affirmative and others in the negative. *Compare Kerr-McGee Chemical Corp. v. Lefton Iron & Metal Co.*, 14 F.3d 321 (7th Cir. 1994) (yes) *with Southland Corp. v. Ashland Oil Co.*, 696 F. Supp. 994 (D.N.J. 1988) (no). One author described the case law as ranging from the "curious to the bewildering." Douglas A. Henderson, Environmental Liability and the Law of Contracts, 50 Bus. Lawyer 183, 184 (1994).

[10]*See* Drew Fudenberg & Jean Tirole, *Game Theory* 146-65 (1991).

[11]*See* Restatement § 205.

counterproductive.[12] When disputes over the meaning of these open-ended terms arise and the absence of a long-term business relationship does not augment the parties' incentive to settle, such terms may vest substantial discretion and responsibility in general jurisdiction courts.[13]

A last, ubiquitous limit on contracting is a group of common-law doctrines that cannot be nullified by explicit contract terms. The basic principle of contract law is a respect for and facilitation of parties ordering their private affairs.[14] Thus many contract rules of law apply only in the absence of an expression of intention by the parties and may be changed by the parties if they see fit.[15] This basic principle has exceptions, however. A small but powerful body of elite doctrines, embodying notions of essential fairness that have a long pedigree, empowers judges to overlook the express language of even the most detailed contracts to reach results that add to and may even contradict a contract's stipulated terms. The doctrines have always been a part of contract law, although there is some recent concern about their expanding breadth.[16]

Litigators and their clients, burdened with litigation over the meaning of acquisition documents, have often been heard to voice a skeptical, pragmatic view of how judges ultimately decide cases using

---

[12]Consider the cautionary words of Bayless Manning, former Dean of the Stanford Law School and a partner in Paul, Weiss, Rifkind, Wharton & Garrison in New York City:

> We lawyers have an all too familiar propensity to believe that the solution to any problem is more drafting. As a group we continue to believe that particularity conquers ambiguity. That belief is ill-founded. . . . We would do well to adopt as our drafting model the Constitution of the United States rather than the Internal Revenue Code.

Bayless Manning, *Principles of Corporate Governance: One Viewer's Perspective on the ALI Project*, 48 Bus. Law. 1319, 1331 (1993).

[13]*See, e.g.,* Bear Stearns Co. v. Jardine Strategic Holdings, 556 N.Y.S.2d 473 (Sup. Ct. 1990) (to the court's express dismay, interpretation of phrase "material adverse change" required use of extrinsic evidence of the parties' intent); *In re* Chateaugay, 155 B.R. 636, 646-47 (Bankr. Ct. S.D.N.Y. 1993) (the parties used a "reasonable efforts" clause rather than a "best efforts" clause to narrow the obligation, but the court adopted the narrow version but denied summary judgment); *cf.* Bloor v. Falstaff Brewing Corp., 454 F. Supp. 258 (S.D.N.Y. 1978), *aff'd*, 601 F.2d 609 (2d Cir. 1979) (interpreting a best efforts clause in a marketing contract to require Falstaff to treat the plaintiff's brand, Ballantine Beer, differently than its own).

[14]*See* Lon Fuller, *Social Order* 169-87, 211-46 (1981).

[15]*See, e.g.,* Restatement § 252 (conditions) & introductory note to ch. 10 (performance and nonperformance).

[16]*See* John S. Lowe, *Are We Moving Toward a Kinder and Gentler Law of Contracts?*, 42nd Annual Institute on Oil and Gas Law and Taxation, at 1-1.

these wild-card doctrines. There is apparently a "pervasive perception" that acquisition agreements are so "labyrinthine that neither the parties nor the lawyers who drafted them understand them" and that since "the reason for courts to show deference to contracts disappears . . . [i]t appears acceptable for judges and juries to do what they think is fair under the circumstances of the case before them."[17] The effect, they agree, is a spiral of deepening frustration: "Resolution of disputes on equitable principles tends to spur drafters to ever more detailed contractual expositions of their intent in an attempt to recapture the predictive function of the contract, which in turn is likely to result in long and complicated provisions that fuel the predilection of the courts to ignore the literal words."[18]

The spiral description seems overstated in light of the number of recent cases in which judges have respected the explicit language of acquisition agreements.[19] In any event, the spiral can be avoided both by judges who have patience with crafted detail in high-risk, high-stake deals and by lawyers who do not burden stock acquisition agreements with needless and numbing verbiage. The Model Stock Purchase Agreement attempts to contribute on both fronts—its commentary educates those who read such agreements and its provisions synthesize and distill currently popular language. The bedrock of common law that empowers parties to order their private affairs through legally enforceable contracts has safety valves, however, that parties and their lawyers should not ignore.

The best known of the judicial safety valves are the doctrines of unconscionability, duress, and undue influence, but these principles ought not apply to any but the most unusual of stock acquisitions. These doctrines are triggered by severe imbalances in bargaining power or acumen between the parties to an agreement, and in most stock acquisitions the parties are sophisticated, use professional advisers, or are represented by able attorneys (or are all of the above).[20] There are, however, several other common law contract doctrines that may apply to override the express language of stock acquisition agree-

---

[17]*Id.* at 1-46.

[18]*Id.*

[19]*See, e.g.,* Armco I, 720 F. Supp. at 1138 (stating that, when a contract purports to be "a complete expression of entire agreement," courts will not add another item on which the agreement is silent); Armco II, 746 F. Supp. at 1249.

[20]*See* Restatement §§ 174-177, 208.

ments among even discerning parties. An understanding of these doctrines is essential to put the language of the Model Stock Purchase Agreement in context.

The law of fraud and misrepresentation trumps all of contract law. A contract is voidable if one party induces another to agree by way of a material misrepresentation upon which the other party is justified in relying.[21] A false assertion of a material fact supports both a claim in contract (for a breach of a representation or warranty provision in an acquisition agreement) and, in extraordinary circumstances, a claim in tort.[22] In acquisition cases, however, courts have shown a substantial reluctance to allow a contract claim to be "dressed in the garb of a fraud claim."[23] To convert a breach of promise to a claim of fraud, the complaining party must allege and prove that at the time the breached promise was made, the promisor never intended to honor its statement.[24] Moreover, a standard integration clause, such as the one in Section 11.8 of the Model Stock Purchase Agreement, has been held to block all claims of negligent misrepresentation.[25]

A misrepresentation claim can have advantages over a contract claim and vice versa. Liquidated damage limits in the indemnification clauses apply only to contract claims,[26] for example, and contract

---

[21]*See id.* §§ 159-173.

[22]And, perhaps, a claim under the federal securities laws. *Cf.* Landreth Timber Co. v. Landreth, 471 U.S. 681 (1985) (sale of all the stock of a company is a securities transaction subject to the antifraud provisions of the federal securities laws). Rule 10b-5 requires proof of scienter, *see* Ernst & Ernst v. Hochfelder, 425 U.S. 185, 193 (1976), but, in imposing liability for material omissions as well as for material misstatements, is broader than common law fraud doctrine. State securities statutes (the "blue sky laws") may contain provisions that do not require scienter in such cases, however. *See* Richard Climan & Gregg Alton, "Potential Securities Law Liabilities in the Sale of a Privately Held Business," 10 Cal. Bus. Law Pract. 1 (1995). Any contractual waiver or disclaimer of liability under federal or state securities provisions is unlikely to hold. *See, e.g.*, Securities Act of 1933, Section 14, 15 U.S.C. § 77V (1988) (provisions waiving compliance with the '33 Act are "void").

[23]*In re* Chateaugay, 155 B.R. 636, 651 (Bankr. Ct. S.D.N.Y. 1993).

[24]*See, e.g.*, K.M.L. Lab. v. Hopper, 1993 U.S. Dist. LEXIS 11525, at 20-21 (E.D.N.Y. 1993) (stock acquisition).

[25]*See, e.g.*, Profession Serv. Indus. v Kimbrell, 834 F. Supp. 1305 (D. Kan. 1993) (stock purchase agreement); *see also In re* Chateaugay, 155 B.R. at 652 (negligent misrepresentation requires a "special relationship" between plaintiff and defendant absent in most acquisitions).

[26]*See* Restatement § 196. *But see* TBG v. Bendis, 841 F. Supp. 1538, 1565-67 (D. Kan. 1993) (ceiling on indemnification voidable by fraudulent inducement even when suit is for breach of express warranty in stock acquisition agreement).

language cannot limit or otherwise waive rescission as relief for a proven misrepresentation. On the other hand, a Buyer's discovery during a due diligence investigation of facts that contradict a Sellers' representation may affect the scope of a potential misrepresentation claim but not a claim for breach of contract.[27] The discovery is evidence for a defense to an action for deceit based on a lack of justified reliance.[28] Moreover, an agreement's tight language defining materiality may have less influence over a court's determination of materiality in a misrepresentation count than a breach of contract count.

A close cousin of misrepresentation is mistake. In an intricate stock acquisition agreement, one party may misunderstand the effect of the language or may understand the language but be mistaken on underlying material facts.[29] Unilateral mistake that has a material effect on the agreed exchange and that is adverse to the mistaken party does not allow that party to void a contract *unless* either enforcement of the contract would be unconscionable or the other party had reason to know of the mistake or caused the mistake. Even so, a court may refuse to void a transaction on the grounds that it is reasonable in the circumstances to allocate the risk of mistake to the mistaken party.[30]

Parties can, by express language, explicitly allocate the risk of anticipated, potential mistakes.[31] As is evident from the Model Stock Purchase Agreement, in stock acquisitions parties routinely allocate the effect of mistakes on underlying facts pertinent to the acquisition (actionable environment damage, for example) but rarely, if ever, allocate the effect of mistaken understandings of the language of the agreement. The absence of any argument on excusable, unilateral mistake in the published cases on disputed acquisition agreements supports the common view that courts will rarely release a party from an

---

[27]*See, e.g.*, TBG, 841 F. Supp. at 1562 (justifiable reliance is an essential element of common law fraud in a stock acquisition).

[28]*See CBS v. Ziff-Davis Publ.*, 553 N.E.2d 997 (N.Y. 1990) (distinguishing the tort and contract actions); *see also Atari Corp. v. Ernst & Whinney*, 981 F.2d 1025, 1030-31 (9th Cir. 1992) (affirming summary judgment of the buyer's misrepresentation claims for lack of justifiable reliance when the buyer knew at the closing of the inaccuracy of the financial statements, but reserving the issue of contract damages). *But see Hendricks v. Callahan*, 972 F.2d 190, 194 (8th Cir. 1992) (refusing to follow *Ziff-Davis*).

[29]*See, e.g.*, Armco I, 720 F. Supp. at 1155-56. In rare cases, an aggrieved party to an acquisition may argue for rescission based on mutual mistake. *See, e.g., Reliance Finance Corp. v. Miller*, 557 F.2d 674, 678 (9th Cir. 1977) (mistake in financial statements not material).

[30]*See* Restatement §§ 153-154.

[31]*See id.* § 154.

acquisition agreement based on that party's failure to appreciate the effect of explicit language. Perhaps lawyers in most cases find it too difficult a task to prove that an opposing party to an intricate agreement had *culpable* knowledge of a mistaken party's misunderstanding at the time of signing.

Contract law also gives common law judges some quantum of residual power to excuse the nonoccurrence of express conditions and require performance. Central to the Model Stock Purchase Agreement is a careful definition of "walk rights": the parties' performance is made subject to several explicit conditions. Performance is not due if an express condition does not occur, but it is also not due if the non-occurrence of a condition is legally excused.[32] Several grounds for excuse of the non-occurrence of a condition exist.

In the absence of explicit language stating which representations and covenants are conditions and which conditions are material, a party may have the right to withhold performance if the other party has breached a covenant or a representation, but a court must construe the breach to be material and the breached covenant or representation to be a condition precedent to performance.[33] Explicit language can eliminate any doubt about which representations and obligations are conditions precedent, but *cannot* completely foreclose a court's investigation into a condition's materiality. Courts rarely excuse as trifles express conditions that parties stipulate to be material, but judges reserve the power to do it.[34]

---

[32]*See id.* § 225.

[33]In garden variety contracts, courts hold that the obligation of one party to perform is subject to a "constructive" condition—the absence of an "uncured material failure" by the other party to render performance that is due. *See id.* §§ 237-238. The definition of "material" in this context is "necessarily imprecise and flexible" and includes factors that do not depend on the express language of an agreement. *Id.* The forfeiture suffered by the failing party, the likelihood of cure, and standards of good faith and fair dealing are significant, in addition to the expectations of the injured party based on the terms of the agreement. *See id.* § 241, comment a. Language in the Model Agreement transforms this constructive condition into an express condition in an attempt to use the narrower concept of materiality that attaches to express conditions.

[34]*See id.* §§ 226, 229. Section 1-102(3) of the Uniform Commercial Code provides:

> The effect of provisions of this Act may be varied by agreement, except as otherwise provided in this Act and except that the obligations of good faith, diligence, *reasonableness* and care prescribed by this Act may not be disclaimed by agreement but the parties may by agreement determine the standards by which the performance of such obligations is to be measured if such standards are not manifestly *unreasonable*.

U.C.C. § 1-102(3) (emphasis added).

The likelihood of a judge excusing an expressly "material" condition is increased (for a given level of triviality) if the enforcement of the condition would create disproportionate forfeiture. It is black letter law that a court may excuse the non-occurrence of a condition if otherwise there would be a disproportionate forfeiture *and* the occurrence of the condition is not a "material part of the agreed exchange."[35] At issue is the effectiveness of an agreement's declaration that a specified condition is material or an agreement's tight, internal definition of materiality (with quantifications of value, for example) in a judicial application of the second part of the test.

The reluctance of courts to permit forfeitures is evident from the case law; in a few cases, judges have exercised their residual power to hold a non-occurrence of a condition to be a nonmaterial, trifling departure despite ostensibly express language to the contrary. An alternative method of reaching the same result, which perhaps does less violence to the language of the agreement, is finding that a party's insistence on compliance with technical conditions, even if defined expressly to be material, can violate an implied, non-waivable duty of good faith and fair dealing.

A judge also has in her quiver a bevy of other judicial doctrines to excuse the non-occurrence of conditions, most of which aim at the prevention of hardship. They are, in their order of likely use, findings of waiver (an intentional relinquishment of a known right by, for example, a subsequent promise, without consideration, to perform a duty despite the non-occurrence of a condition); findings of an inadequate statement of reasons for rejection of performance; findings of involvement by an opposing party in the non-occurrence of a condition; and findings of impracticability.[36]

The doctrine of waiver and the related doctrines of substituted performance, substituted contract, and accord and satisfaction deserve special mention.[37] Under the common law, the parties, regardless of the language in an acquisition agreement, hold the inherent power,

---

[35]Restatement § 229.

[36]*See id.* §§ 84, 246-248, 255, 271; *see also* Clayton R. Gillette, *Commercial Rationality and the Duty to Adjust Long-Term Contracts*, 69 Minn. L. Rev. 521 (1985) (applauding common law courts' tendency to construe narrowly the doctrine of impracticability and its cousins, frustration of purpose and impossibility).

[37]*See* Restatement §§ 279-282.

through mutual assent, to renegotiate the acquisition and replace the terms of the original agreement with substituted performance or a substituted contract.[38] Some states modify by statute the basic common law principle and recognize contract provisions to the effect that a contract cannot be changed or modified orally.[39] However, because courts apply the statutory language to bar only executory waivers or modifications, parties even in these states can waive a "no oral waiver" provision (or otherwise be estopped from relying on it) by fully or partially executed oral waivers or modifications.[40]

The doctrine of substituted performance can come into play when both parties recognize before the closing that one party cannot fully perform its obligations. If the breaching party offers to perform, albeit imperfectly, can the other party accept without waiving its right to sue on the original breach? The common law has long been that if a breaching party *expressly conditions* its substitute performance on such a waiver, the non-breaching party may not accept the substitute performance, even with an express reservation of rights, and also retain its right to sue under the original contract.[41] A seller who refuses to close without the buyer's waiver of the seller's breach puts to the

---

[38] *See, e.g., J.A. Moore Constr. v. Sussex*, 688 F. Supp. 982, 988 (D. Del. 1988); *Beatty v. Guggenheim Exploration*, 122 N.E. 378, 387-88 (N.Y. 1919) (Cardozo, J.) (holding that terms that flatly prohibit modification and terms that impose formal requirements for modification such as writings are unenforceable: "The clause which forbids a change, may be changed like any other"). *But see* Christine M. Jollis, *Contracts as Bilateral Commitments: A New Concern About Contract Modification*, Dis. Paper No. 128, Harvard Law School (July 1993) (arguing that parties should be able to limit by contract their ability to enter into contract modifications).

[39] *See, e.g.*, N.Y. Gen. Oblig. Law § 15-301 (McKinney's 1989); *see also* UCC § 2-209(1).

[40] *See, e.g.*, Latham Four Partnership v. SSI Medical Servs., 581 N.Y.S.2d 891 (Sup. Ct. 1992) (holding that a landlord was estopped from relying on a "no oral modification" provision); *see also* Wisconsin Knife Works v. National Metal Crafters, 781 F.2d 1280 (7th Cir. 1986) (discussing the waiver language in UCC §§ 2-209(4) and (5)).

[41] *See* United States *ex rel.* Int'l Contracting Co. v. Lamont, 155 U.S. 303, 309-10 (1884); Restatement § 278, comment a. The UCC may be to the contrary. *See* UCC § 1-207. There are three related cases, each assuming a buyer with knowledge of a seller's breach at or before the time of closing and a seller unwilling to agree to a buyer's reservation of right to sue on the breach after closing ("close and waive or sue"). In case one, a seller believes it is offering full performance and a buyer, unbeknownst to the seller, believes that a seller has not met all its obligations. Can the buyer close, without notifying the seller of the belief, and sue for damages? In case two, a seller believes it is offering full performance but knows of a buyer's claim that the seller's offer of performance is defective. Can the buyer close and sue by unilaterally reserving its rights? In case three, a buyer and a seller agree at the time

buyer an election to sue or close. If the buyer closes, it waives its claim for damages due to the breach. At issue is whether courts will respect express language, such as that in Section 10.1 of the Model Stock Purchase Agreement, that defeats the seller's power under the common law to force an election and that allows the buyer to "close and sue."[42]

---

of closing that the seller has not offered full performance in accordance with an agreement. Can the buyer close, accepting a substitute performance, and then sue for damages?

The traditional common law doctrines of substituted performance and accord and satisfaction give negative answers in all three cases. *See id.* There is some authority to the contrary in cases involving acquisitions. The Court of Appeals of New York, disagreeing with the Eighth and Tenth Circuits, has held for the buyer in case two. *Compare* CBS, Inc. v. Ziff-Davis Publishing Co., 553 N.E.2d 997 (N.Y. 1990), *with* Hendricks v. Callahan, 972 F.2d 190 (8th Cir. 1992) (applying Minnesota law); Land v. Roper Corp., 531 F.2d 445 (10th Cir. 1976) (applying Kansas law); Professional Service Indus. v. Kimbrell, 834 F. Supp. 1305 (D. Kan. 1993) (applying Kansas law). The Second Circuit has, in dicta, suggested that in case three an express reservation of rights may preserve a buyer's right to sue for damages. *See* Galli, 973 F.2d. at 150-51 (a buyer, closing in the face of an acknowledged breach by the seller, cannot have relied on the non-occurrence of the breach and waives any claim to damages). In dicta, the *Galli* court suggested that a buyer could preserve its rights with a unilateral, ex post reservation of rights at the closing. *See id.*; *see also* U.C.C. § 1-207 (on accepting performance under reservation of right).

[42]None of the cases cited in note 41 dealt with an acquisition agreement that included a provision similar to Section 10.1. Section 10.1 is intended to allow a buyer more control over the form of its remedy for a seller's breach. Under the language of Section 10.1 a buyer can walk and sue for expectation damages or can choose instead to accept a lesser performance and sue for the difference between the accepted performance and the promised performance. The latter choice is unavailable under common law contract doctrines unless the seller explicitly agrees to the buyer's reservation of a right to sue at the closing. Section 10.1 attempts to make this ex post agreement (executed after the discovery of the alleged breach) on the reservation of the buyer's rights into an ex ante agreement (executed before the discovery of the alleged breach). The courts in the cases cited in note 41 use reliance as the deciding issue, and all but *Ziff-Davis* hold that a buyer, knowing of defective performance and closing anyway, suffers no damages because it could not rely on the non-occurrence of the breach when it closed. The language in Section 2010.1 attempts to stand the reliance analysis on its head by stipulating that a buyer upon closing is in fact relying on its right to sue for defective performance later.

Although Section 10.1 is a useful provision from a buyer's perspective, it might not afford the buyer with the intended protection in all circumstances. For example, can a buyer sue for specific performance under the language of Section 10.1, forcing a seller to close with defective performance and preserving the buyer's rights to sue? This is an unusual decree ("I order you to do what you can do"); judges may also balk at the double lawsuit nature of the relief ("Buyer wins an injunction; we'll see you again after the closing"). If courts refuse to grant such relief, knowledgeable sellers in cases two and three in note 41 can always force a buyer to an election, "execute a signed waiver of your right to sue or I will not close," and the language of Section 10.1 is of little consequence. Only in case one, when the seller does not know of the alleged breach, does Section 10.1 have teeth.

Some case law on remedies may also empower judges to depart from the explicit language of an acquisition agreement.[43] The contract principle of avoidable consequences, which precludes an injured party from recovering damages for losses that reasonably could have been avoided, cannot be waived or limited by express contract provision.[44] In typical contracts, the doctrine translates into a requirement that an injured party seek "cover," a substitute transaction. In complex acquisitions, however, the availability of suitable substitute acquisition partners is inherently problematic. However, some academics, with support from a rather sparse case law, claim that the duty to mitigate includes a duty to accept alternative offers of performance from *a breaching party* in selected cases.[45] At issue is whether a breached stock acquisition agreement presents such a case.

Although the balance of the case law imposes no duty on a victim to renegotiate with a breaching party,[46] courts seem to be developing an exception requiring a victim to deal with a breaching party if, as is often true in acquisitions, there are no alternative, substitute transactions available in the market because of the specialized nature of the broken contract.[47] Even in such a case, however, a breaching party can unwittingly nullify the victim's obligation to accept if the breaching party insists on a waiver of rights under the original contract as a condition to its performance.

In addition to the common law doctrines noted above, an acquisition lawyer must be alert to statutory provisions that change basic contract law principles. The best example is, of course, Section 107(a) of the Comprehensive Environmental Response, Compensation and Liability Act of 1980 (CERCLA).[48] While a majority of courts and commentators agree that private parties in an acquisition can allocate the risk of CERCLA cleanup costs by contract, neither can escape by

---

[43]For remedial doctrine on liquidated damage clauses and clauses extending the statute of limitations, see the comment to Section 10.6.

[44]*See* Restatement § 349. *See generally* Charles Goetz & Robert Scott, *The Mitigation Principle: Toward a General Theory of Contractual Relations,* 69 Va. L. Rev. 967 (1983).

[45]*See, e.g.*, Goetz & Scott, *supra* note 44, at 1004-09; Robert Hillman, *Keeping the Deal Together After Material Breach—Common Law Mitigation Rules, the UCC, and the Restatement (Second) of Contracts,* 47 U. Colo. L. Rev. 553 (1976).

[46]*See* Goetz & Scott, *supra* note 44, at 975 n.26 & 992-93 nn.55-59.

[47]*See id.* at 1004-09.

[48]42 U.S.C. § 9607 (a) (1988 & Supp. V 1993).

contract their underlying liability to the government.[49] A few courts, however, prohibit private parties from contracting to distribute the risks of environmental liability under all circumstances.[50]

CONCLUSION

The Model Stock Purchase Agreement attempts to assist lawyers in their pursuit of the three goals of acquisition contract drafting. A drafter aims to craft language first that embodies the understanding between the parties, second that conveys that understanding accurately to judges asked to enforce the agreement, and third that eliminates the discretion of judges to ignore an understanding accurately conveyed. The third goal, while it can be approached, is in the end inherently unreachable. Courts retain a residuum of power through a variety of common law doctrines to add, modify, or even refuse to accept the parties' express contract terms.

Stock acquisitions of the type assumed in the Model Stock Purchase Agreement generally call for frugality in the courts' use of this residual power. The parties are typically sophisticated and have professional advice from specialized accountants and lawyers (and, often, investment bankers). The agreements embody an explicit allocation of risks and responsibilities that courts ought to be wary of adjusting in response to potentially opportunistic claims for relief after risks have materialized. Moreover, judicial readjustment of any given bargain, even under the mantle of fairness, will have an impact on future negotiations. The potential for excessive judicial intervention will add volatility risk to the payout calculations of both sides in any given transaction. The added risk must be priced. The added variance in potential outcomes will lead a knowledgeable buyer to offer less and knowledgeable sellers to demand more. In an extreme case, the added volatility risk could, by itself, eliminate any possible bid-offer overlap and prevent the acquisition from occurring, to the detriment of both sides.

---

[49]*See* Douglas A. Henderson, *Environmental Liability and the Law of Contracts,* 50 Bus. Law. 183, 184 (1994).

> The bizarre range of decisions issued to date on contractual transfers of hazardous waste liability suggests . . . that the beauty of the common law [of contract] may have crashed and burned at the intersection of environmental law and the law of contracts. Despite almost fifty decisions on contracts under [CERCLA], it remains unclear when parties can and cannot contractually shift environmental responsibilities under CERCLA.

[50]*See, e.g.,* Harley-Davidson, Inc. v. Minstar, Inc., 837 F. Supp. 978 (E.D. Wis. 1993); AM International, Inc. v. International Forging Equipment, 743 F.Supp. 525 (N.D. Ohio 1990), *rev'd in part*, 982 F.2d 989 (6th Cir. 1993).

Committee on Negotiated Acquisitions

MEMBERS	*CITY/STATE*	*MEMBERS*	*CITY/STATE*
Nelea A. Absher*	New Orleans, LA	John H. Grayson, Jr.*	Memphis, TN
Thomas L. Ambro	Wilmington, DE	Joel I. Greenberg*	New York, NY
Jack M. Arnold	New Orleans, LA	Harvey Greenfield	New York, NY
Cameron Baker*	San Francisco, CA	James B. Griswold	Cleveland, OH
Robert J. Banta	Dallas, TX	Alan S. Gutterman	San Francisco, CA
Joseph W. Bartlett	New York, NY	James J. Hanks, Jr.*	Baltimore, MD
Howard J. Barnhorst II*	San Diego, CA	Randall Hanson	Winston-Salem, NC
Frank B. Bennett*	Minneapolis, MN	Robert T. Harper*	Pittsburgh, PA
George W. Bermant	Snowmass Village, CO	H. Clark Harvey, Jr.*	Cleveland, OH
		Kimon C. Hatza	Philadelphia, PA
Stephanie Bess	Philadelphia, PA	Andrew D. Hendry	New York, NY
James Biehl	Princeton, NJ	Rebecca H. Hilborne	Tulsa, OK
Marc D. Bishop	Greensboro, NC	Robert J. Hill	Washington, D.C.
Arthur M. Borden	New York, NY	Stephen A. Hochman	New York, NY
Catherine L. Bridge	Indianapolis, IN	Henry W. Hope	Houston, TX
Neal H. Brockmeyer*	Los Angeles, CA	Thomas B. Hyman*	Atlanta, GA
Donald W. Brodsky	Houston, TX	Mary Ann Hynes	Riverwoods, IL
David A. Bronner*	Chicago, IL	Carl B. Israel	Boston, MA
Eric V. Brown, Jr.*	Kalamazoo, MI	Richard P. Jaffee	Philadelphia, PA
Charles H. Brownman*	Houston, TX	W. Alan Kailer	Dallas, TX
Dave Bruscino	Cleveland, OH	Robert J. Kalupa	Milwaukee, WI
Timothy R. M. Bryant	Chicago, IL	Christopher Kaufman*	San Francisco, CA
Paul G. Bursiek	Boulder, CO	David D. Keen	Milwaukee, WI
Richard E. Climan*	Palo Alto, CA	Mark A. Kimball	Minneapolis, MN
Jon S. Cohen*	Phoenix, AZ	Stephen H. Knee*	Newark, NJ
Joseph J. Connolly*	Philadelphia, PA	Peter L. Koerber*	New Orleans, LA
Gordon E. Cooper	Toronto, Ontario, Canada	Timothy W. Kuck	Minneapolis, MN
		Ellen B. Kulka	Washington, D.C.
Robert G. Copeland*	San Diego, CA	William D. Lambert	St. Louis, MO
Lawrence J. Corneck	New York, NY	Guy P. Lander	New York, NY
Elizabeth A. Dellinger*	Cleveland, OH	Tracy T. Larsen	Grand Rapids, MI
Deidra D. Dixon	Cleveland, OH	Roger E. Lautzenhiser	Columbus, OH
Nora J. Dobin	Houston, TX	Theodore W. Lenz*	Nashville, TN
Nathaniel J. Doliner*	Tampa, FL	John W. Leopold*	Montreal, Canada
James C. Doub*	Baltimore, MD	David A. Lipkin	Seattle, WA
Byron F. Egan*	Dallas, TX	Julius L. Loeser	Los Angeles, CA
Karl J. Ege*	Tacoma, WA	John R. MacKay II	Roseland, NJ
Theodore M. Elam	Oklahoma City, OK	Bertram K. Massing	Beverly Hills, CA
Reid Feldman	Paris, France	Brian J. McCarthy	Los Angeles, CA
Marc H. Folladori	Houston, TX	Paul McCarthy	Chicago, IL
Lloyd Frank*	New York, NY	Karen W. McDonie*	Philadelphia, PA
Diane H. Frankle*	Palo Alto, CA	Thomas R. McGuigan*	Miami, FL
Layne Bryan French	Houston, TX	Mark M. McGuire*	Purchase, NY
J. Pat Garrett*	Houston, TX	Don I.N. McKenzie*	Nashville, TN
Vincent F. Garrity, Jr.*	Philadelphia, PA	William McKenzie, Jr.	San Diego, CA
Daniel J. Godar	St. Louis, MO	L.R. McMillan II*	New Orleans, LA
Edwin H. Goldberger*	Chicago, IL	Francis J. Mellen, Jr.	Louisville, KY
Michael L. Gravelle*	Little Rock, AK	Jeffrey Meyer	Columbus, OH

*Frequent attendee of last $2^1/_2$ years

MEMBERS	*CITY/STATE*	*MEMBERS*	*CITY/STATE*
Arthur H. Miller*	Philadelphia, PA	Kathryn Smyser	Houston, TX
Dale A. Oesterle*	Boulder, CO	Alan R. Spier*	Hartford, CT
Martin C. Oetting*	Detroit, MI	Brooks Stough	Palo Alto, CA
Samuel W. Oliver, Jr.*	Birmingham, AL	Steven R. Suleski*	Madison, WI
Gordon A. Park*	Toronto, Ontario, Canada	Nancy Strauss Sundheim	Blue Bell, PA
		H. William Swanstrom	Houston, TX
George W. Patrick	Philadelphia, PA	Lawrence J. Swire	New York, NY
John G. Petrovich	Los Angeles, CA	H. Lawrence Tafe*	Boston, MA
Eric M. Reifschneider*	Chicago, IL	George M. Taylor III*	Birmingham, AL
Frank B. Reilly, Jr.*	Newark, NJ	Bruce V. Thomas	Richmond, VA
Vernon E. Rew, Jr.	Fort Worth, TX	Samuel C. Thompson, Jr.	Coral Gables, FL
John F. Rhem, Jr.	Houston, TX	J. Robert Tyler III*	Richmond, VA
Darrel A. Rice	Dallas, TX	Thomas W. Van Dyke*	Overland Park, KS
Steven T. Sager	Cambridge, MA	Ariel Vannier	Baltimore, MD
J. Alexander Salisbury*	Charlotte, NC	Gregg Vignos	San Francisco, CA
Margo S. Scholin	Houston, TX	Michael K.L. Wager*	Columbus, OH
James H. Schwab	New York, NY	Barbara Wagner	Cincinnati, OH
W. Scott Seeley*	East Cleveland, OH	Robert Walmsley, Jr.*	New Orleans, LA
Theodore Segal	Baltimore, MD	Leigh Walton	Nashville, TN
John Sefton*	Jacksonville, FL	Stephanie G. Watson	Washington, D.C.
Andrew H. Seiden	San Francisco, CA	Arnold F. Williams*	Los Angeles, CA
Robert E. Shields*	Philadelphia, PA	Norman A. Zilber*	San Francisco, CA
Stuart Sinai	Troy, MI	Paul E. Zimmer	Dayton, OH
Richard G. Small*	Providence, RI	James B. Zimpritch	Portland, ME

*Frequent attendee of last $2^1/_2$ years